FLASH 4 WEB ANIMATION
f/x & Design

Ken Milburn and John Croteau

CORIOLIS

The Coriolis Group, LLC
14455 N. Hayden Road, Suite 220
Scottsdale, Arizona 85260

480/483-0192
FAX 480/483-0193
http://www.coriolis.com

Library of Congress Cataloging-In-Publication Data
Milburn, Ken, 1935-
    Flash 4 Web animation f/x and design / by Ken Milburn and John Croteau.
        p. cm
    Includes index.
    ISBN 1-57610-555-5
    1. Computer animation.   2. Flash (Computer file).
3. Multimedia systems.   4. Web sites—design.   I. Croteau, John.   II. Title.
TR897.7.M57   2000
006.6'96--dc21   99-049093
                                           CIP

Printed in the United States of America
10 9 8 7 6 5 4 3 2

President, CEO
Keith Weiskamp

Publisher
Steve Sayre

Acquisitions Editor
Mariann Hansen Barsolo

Marketing Specialist
Beth Kohler

Project Editor
Michelle Stroup

Technical Reviewers
John Croteau
Dorian Nisinson

Production Coordinator
Meg E. Turecek

Cover Design
Jody Winkler
additional art provided by Brandon Riza

Layout Design
April Nielsen

CD-ROM Developer
Robert Clarfield

OTHER TITLES FOR THE CREATIVE PROFESSIONAL

I'd like to dedicate this book to all my good friends, especially Bob Cowart, Janine Warner, Sundeep Doshi, and Bill and Beverly Niffeneger. Without all of their help, this book could never have happened. I'd also like to thank Margot Maley at Waterside Productions for being my friend as well as being a great agent.
—Ken Milburn

I dedicate this book to my late father, John A. Croteau, whose encouragement inspired me in my quest for knowledge.
—John A. Croteau III

ABOUT THE AUTHORS

Ken Milburn is a freelance writer, photographer, and illustrator. He specializes in writing computer books and magazine articles related to graphics and Web design. More than 250 of his articles have appeared in such national publications as *InfoWorld, PC World, MacWeek, MacUser, Popular Computing, PC Computing, Computer Graphics World, Publish Magazine, Windows Magazine,* and *DV* magazine.

Ken is the author of two previous books from Coriolis on Flash and Photoshop 4. He is currently at work on *Master Photoshop 5.5 Visually* and *The Digital Photography Bible* for IDG Books.

Ken's illustration work has been featured on three separate occasions by *Design Graphics Magazine.* He has also appeared in *Computer Graphics World* and on the cover of *Media* magazine. He is a member of Artisan's Gallery in Mill Valley, California.

John Croteau is a recognized expert in Macromedia Flash. He is the founder and principal architect for Flash Central (**www.FlashCentral.com**), a Web site dedicated to providing help for Flash developers; the Flash Bible (**www.FlashBible.com**), a site that provides the latest in tutorials training designers in the newest techniques for Flash; and the Flash Tech Resource (**www.FlashTechResource.com**), one of the oldest technical resources for Flash designers and developers with more than a thousand links to specific technical notes, tutorials, and articles on Flash.

At UCON 99, John appeared on stage as a guest speaker and, together with Jon Gay, provided technical support for Ralph Mittman at the "Optimizing Flash" conference.

John can often be found on various lists that provide help to Flashers (Flash developers) especially the Flasher List (**www.FlashCentral.com/Tech/Resources/FlasherL.htm**) and the Macromedia newsgroup (**news://forums.macromedia.com/macromedia.flash**). John's personal Web site is **www.FlashTek.com**.

ACKNOWLEDGMENTS

The first person I have to thank is my current co-author, John Croteau. There are many who would tell you than John is the leading authority on Macromedia Flash. His Web sites, mentioned in various places in this book, answer thousands of user questions about Flash technical matters. It's a rare Flash developer who doesn't know John and hasn't depended on him for his ability to solve Flash problems. Because John acted as the technical editor for all my chapters, I expect that this is a significantly more accurate and informative book than the last edition. The chapters that John has written himself deal with the more highly technical aspects of Flash.

Special mention and thanks need to go to Carole Omalyev for her help in creating the example drawings for the Tool & Garden site that are scattered throughout this book.

I'd also like to thank the editorial staff at Coriolis for giving me the chance to continue with new Flash editions. I'd especially like to thank Michelle Stroup, my brilliant project editor and Catherine E. Oliver, the equally brilliant copyeditor and easily one of the best in this business. Thanks also go to Meg Turecek, the production coordinator, and April Nielsen, the designer of the color section and of the series itself.

Any technical book is better when it has the support of the publishers of the product it is written about. Macromedia has certainly been Johnny-on-the-spot whenever their assistance was called on. I especially want to thank Jane Chuey and Leona Lapez of Macromedia's thoroughly professional PR department.

Finally, there are several coffee houses who deserve credit for keeping me awake during some very long writing hours—especially the Fairfix Café in Fairfax; Brewed Awakening; Café Roma; and The Wall in Berkeley.

—Ken Milburn

I want to start by thanking Jonathan Gay for creating Flash. When I first saw FutureSplash, I considered it a nice tool with some potential. But it was not until Macromedia purchased the program and the Flash 2 public beta was released did I see Flash as the future—and this is when I began using and learning about Flash. I haven't stopped since.

Next, I want to thank everyone on the Macromedia Flash team who probably make up one of the best groups of people I have ever met. It is very unusual to get help and support from top management such as I have received from David Mendels, Eric Wittman, and Jon Gay. This spirit of cooperation has continued despite my being a harsh critic of Macromedia at times. This spirit is further evinced in all of the Flash team with the amount of help they have provided me and others in the Flash community when, quite obviously, much of this time is on their own time. I'd like to thank each and every one of them individually (like Erica Norton), but I'll just have to refer you to the About Flash link in the Flash program for a complete list of them.

With the help of my friend and collaborator Dorian Nisinson, I have developed Flash Central and the Flash Bible as two of the premier places of learning Flash on the Web. I also want to thank my family and friends for having patience and tolerance for my obsession with Flash. A final word of thanks goes out to all Flashers—especially those on the Flasher List who have helped me in my quest to learn about Flash and create new and innovative things on the Web.

—*John Croteau*

CONTENTS AT A GLANCE

TABLE OF CONTENTS

Chapter 9
Automating Flash With ActionScript   241

Chapter 10
Using Flash With Other Macromedia Software   271

Chapter 11
Using Text In Flash   299

INTRODUCTION

Flash 4 continues to grow in both power and popularity. The user interface has been redesigned to make it more familiar to users of other graphics programs—especially to users of other Macromedia graphics programs.

Once again, Flash has added significant new features since the last version of the product. There's a much higher level of integration between Flash and other Macromedia products. Virtually all of the major players in Web browsers (Microsoft, Netscape, AOL, WebTV, and many more) have the Flash 4 player built into their latest versions. It's much easier to produce a Flash file that can recognize and adapt to the browser that is reading it.

Nothing on the planet has ever been able to produce a high-performance, full-screen, animated, interactive Web page as well as or as easily as Flash can. Flash 4 simply makes that fact more true than ever.

There has been a redesign of Flash 4's interface aimed at making it more "standard" to what graphics professional expect to find in a mainstream graphics program. We've included an entire appendix (Appendix A) devoted to these new features. Because there are many more of them than there is room to list here, you may want to take a look at that appendix before you decide if you need to upgrade your knowledge of Flash.

If you're just curious about Flash in general and want to know more about whether it's worth learning more about, glance over Chapter 1 of this book.

Introducing A New Co-Author

Those of you who bought the last version of this book wishing that there were more detail on such Flash features as Tell Target, Generator, Scripting, and dynamic data interchange will be excited to know that my new co-author, John Croteau, is one of the leading experts on Flash. John has written three chapters, full of information, that cover those subjects.

This is John's first book on the subject, but he has long been the Flash guru's guru. He is one of the independent advisers to Macromedia for Flash and some of their other products. John is best known as the father of several of the industry's most valuable Web repositories of Flash information:

- *FlashTek (Advanced Web sites with Flash)*—**www.FlashTek.com/**

- *Flash Bible (Fast track to good Flash)*—**www.FlashBible.com/**

- *Flash Central(The Universe Starts Here)*—**www.FlashCentral.com/**

- *The Flash Tech Resource (Tech Notes)*—**www.FlashCentral.com/tech/**

What This Book Covers

This book teaches you how to use Flash 4's new features. It has also been expanded to provide much more detailed technical information, especially about ActionScripting, form entry, and interactive dynamic data. If you are just becoming familiar with Flash, you'll be glad to know that the basics are also thoroughly covered.

Who This Book Is For

If you are already spending your days and nights consumed by Flash 4, there's a good chance you'll find work similar to yours in the Color Studio section of this book. However, there's still a very real possibility that this book has more to teach you about Flash. Having said that, it's fair to say that this book will take you much farther along the path to true expertise than did its predecessor. That's our goal for future editions of this book, too.

Conventions Used In This Book

We deferred to the conventions used in Macromedia's documentation when deciding what terminology to use to describe Flash's features.

Though the terms sound synonymous, we make a distinction between telling you to *choose* something and telling you to *select* something. The word *choose* is always associated with a tool or a menu command; in other words, you are choosing to make a specific thing happen. The word *select* is always associated with designating the object of your choice. So, for instance, you select a line, shape, layer, or frame.

Flash 4 is full of menus—only some of which are found on the menu bar. Others are located on Layer Name bars, attached to frames, or found in a dialog box or palette. For that reason, for all commands that are *not* attached to the menu bar, we preface them with their locations—for instance, "From the Frames menu, choose Insert Keyframe." Commands that are on cascading or hierarchical menus are given in the sequence in which they are encountered, and they are separated by pipe characters (vertical bars)—for example, "Choose Modify|Style|Plain."

All keyboard shortcuts are given with the Mac key name first, followed by the Windows key name. The two are separated by a slash (/). The equivalent keys are Cmd/Ctrl, Opt/Alt, Delete/Backspace, and Return/Enter. The Macintosh has one modifier key, Control, that is named the same as a Windows modifier key. However, the Control key on the Macintosh is used primarily to substitute for the right mouse button in Windows. So if you want to display an in-context menu, you Control-click on the Mac and right-click in Windows. Keys that are identical to both systems (such as Shift, Space, or any of the alphanumeric or function keys) are given only once in a key sequence.

PART I

HONING FLASH ESSENTIALS

A FLASH SNAPSHOT

1

KEN MILBURN

If you loved Flash before, you're gonna love 4 more. As you'll see further on in this chapter, the program is loaded with powerful new features. The result of these additions is an even more versatile authoring tool.

Macromedia has integrated Flash even more tightly with other products in its line. The Flash player code has been integrated into the major Web browsers. New publishing features in Flash make it possible to create content that can recognize and adapt to the browser that is reading it. (Note that the new features in Flash 4 are comprehensively mapped out for you in Appendix A at the end of this book.)

Now it's truer than ever that no other product can produce a high-performance, full-screen, animated, interactive Web page as well or as easily as Flash can. Flash 4's interface has been redesigned to make it feel more comfortable to graphics designers and Web professionals. Its feature set has been enhanced to the point where most of these professionals are doing cartwheels. Still, you'll find that the program hasn't forgotten its roots. It still offers a great deal of help to beginners.

This chapter describes what Flash 4 offers to various levels of users. For those who are already familiar with earlier versions of the program, this chapter also describes new features and tracks the development of features in various versions of the program.

Figure 1.1

This Flash site has an animated background, an interactive text menu, and rollover mouse events—an impossible combination for unaided HTML.

If you're already familiar with Flash and want to dig right in and start learning the program, you can skip most or all of this chapter. If you wonder what all the excitement is about, look at Figure 1.1 to see a Web page

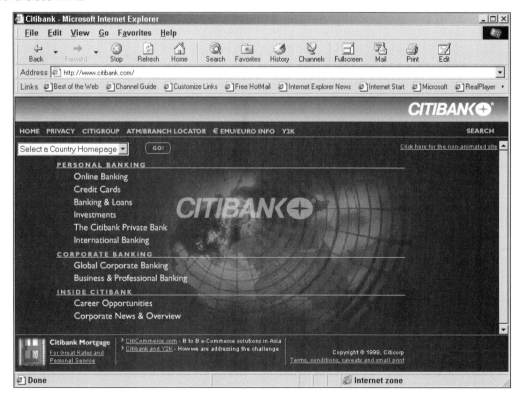

that just wouldn't be practical to design using traditional HTML. Then imagine that this Web page always fits the browser window in the same way, regardless of how you size the screen.

What Flash Does Better Than HTML

If you're a Web author and you also design graphics or illustrations for print, Flash is easily the best bargain in computer graphics. The characteristics that make Flash such a bargain include the following:

- Flash is equally useful for presenting interactive content on or off the Web.

- Flash animations are way faster than the alternative type of Web animation, animated GIFs.

- Size doesn't matter.

- Image and text quality.

- Flash is still easy to use.

- Evaporating plug-in barrier.

Equally Useful For Presenting Interactive Content On Or Off The Web

Flash's Web publication qualities are so outstanding that they tend to mask the fact that Flash is equally useful for producing offline interactive content.

You don't have to use a browser in order to see Flash content. The program comes with an offline player that can be freely distributed. It's small enough that you can put it and a Flash presentation on a floppy disk, so you can have a demo that doesn't need to be installed. Of course, you can also put longer or more complex demos on a CD-ROM.

Flash is also invaluable as a digital artist's sketch pad and for helping art-klutzy business people to create visual conceptualizations. Because Flash can output files that can be read by higher-end illustration programs, those concepts can be fleshed out by a professional. There's no need for the pro to re-create the original.

Flash has several advantages that contribute to its versatility:

- Flash is the best tool available for sketching ideas for Web pages, presentations, graphic designs, and illustrations. Many commercial illustrators conceptualize or prepare graphics in Flash and then export their sketches to FreeHand or Illustrator for fine-tuning.

- Flash is a powerful illustration and presentation program that can be put to good use (with great results) even if you don't know how to draw.

- Flash allows you to create animations without prior training or experience as an animator.

- Flash can prepare content for virtually all Web, multimedia, presentation, and graphics programs running on Macintosh and Windows computers.

In all the Web hoopla, you might have missed the fact that Flash is every bit as capable of creating content for conventional multimedia and print. In this book, I will tell you everything that I think you'll want to know about using Flash to prepare Web content. I intend to be equally zealous in talking about its considerable abilities in preparing content for the other media as well.

Just to tease you a bit more, did you know that Flash will let you import a scanned image and instantly turn it into a fully scalable drawing that uses a fraction of the file space required by the original? Or that Flash's powerful animation tools can be used to create animated Graphics Interchange Format (GIF) files that can be used on any Web page? Or that you can import graphics into Flash from just about any source and modify them to your heart's content without having an iota of drawing talent?

These are only some of all the wonders that this easy-to-use and inexpensive program has to offer.

Way Faster Than Bitmapped Graphics

A full-screen Flash animation consisting of several scenes can load into a viewer's browser and begin playing in less than 10 seconds. It would typically take more than a minute (and potentially many minutes) to load and play a traditional Web movie of comparable size and complexity. This enormous performance gain occurs because Flash describes images by using vector graphics, rather than the bitmaps used in more traditional Web animation techniques.

Those who aren't familiar with the terms *vector* and *bitmap* might appreciate a description: The content of a Flash Web page consists of mathematical formulas (vectors) that describe the geometry of shapes and the characteristics of colors. Because these instructions are stored as plain text, very little data is needed to describe an entire screen of moving graphics. Such image geometry is known in the trade as *vector graphics*.

Traditional Web animation techniques, on the other hand, describe images as a matrix (raster) of colored pixels. The size of individual pixels is fixed, as is their total number in a given image. In addition, it takes several bits of data to describe each pixel. So, a small image of 360×240 pixels typically requires 74,000 bytes of data. Remember, this is for a single frame, and Web animations typically need to run at several frames *per second* (8 to 15 is typical). As a result, you could have several frames of a Flash movie stored in a file that is only one-third the size of the single bitmapped frame.

The image sizes used in the preceding examples are typical, but you should be aware that many variables can affect the size of a given image. Some of these variables are the number of colors (in bitmaps) or geometrical shapes (in vector drawings), the file format, and the method of compression used to store the file. Even so, a Flash file will almost always load and play at several times the speed of a bitmapped animation.

Size Doesn't Matter

In traditional Web publishing, graphics are generally kept as physically small as possible in order to minimize the amount of data that needs to be transmitted. Full-screen graphics are practically unheard of. They would take so long to load that you'd lose all of the site's visitors before they could see the rest of the content. The problem is, it can be hard to hold the viewer's attention with static pages.

Flash graphics, however, perform consistently regardless of their size. This occurs because the information that produces the graphic is exactly the same except for one tiny instruction—what size to scale the graphic.

Scalability has benefits that go beyond performance. For instance, you can zoom in and out dynamically. This makes scalability a major boon for displaying road maps (say, for giving directions to your business) and detailed technical drawings (such as those you might want to include on an instructional site).

Do you ever wish you could make a browser window smaller without cutting off part of the site's content? Do you ever wish you could zoom in to see details in a map or a technical drawing you've found on the Web? Well, with Flash you can. Flash can be instructed to automatically adjust the size of a window's content whenever the viewer changes the size of the window. Figure 1.2 shows the same Web page with the browser window scaled to two different sizes.

Image And Text Quality

Another major benefit of using vector graphics is that the quality of drawings and text is always as high as it can be on a given computer. Because vector graphics *tell* the viewer's computer how to draw the image, the image always looks as good as it possibly can on that computer. In contrast, bitmapped animations are often made by resizing and distorting a matrix of pixels of a fixed size. In this process, some needed pixels are lost or exaggerated, and image quality suffers significantly.

The elements of a Flash page are so clean and professional that viewing a Flash page for the first time can be startling (especially if it contains lots of

Figure 1.2

Despite the fact that the browser windows are different sizes, all the content is proportionately scaled by Flash.

hard-edged graphics such as buttons, text, and logos). Another Flash benefit is that you'll never see any stray or mushy pixels in areas of solid color or gradients. (We geeks call those stray pixels *artifacts*.)

Flash also gives authors the option of displaying graphics as fully anti-aliased. *Anti-aliasing* is a process that smoothes hard edges by blending the edge pixels with pixels of the background color, thus softening the edge. Because no pixels are contained in the file itself, Flash accomplishes this anti-aliasing by using the pixels on the viewer's screen.

Still Easy After All These Years

Anyone can create attractive and business-like Web content in Flash. The program comes with a great set of tutorials, and they've only gotten better in version 4. The tutorials are written and performed in Flash, so you get an immediate feel for what the program is capable of. More important, you quickly gain confidence that you can produce content on that same level.

The program even helps you draw by recognizing basic geometric shapes as you draw and by straightening out your lines (see Figure 1.3). So even if Flash doesn't automatically turn you into a great artist, at least your work will look neat and competent.

Figure 1.3

On the left is a typical jittery hand-drawn line. On the right, the line has been smoothed automatically by Flash.

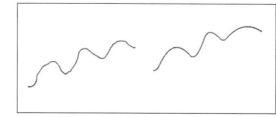

In a sense, version 4 of Flash is more difficult than earlier versions. Everything you could do before is just as easy in version 4. It's just that you can do so much more that the additional features make the program seem a bit more complicated.

Flash 4 is also much more capable when it comes to programming for interactivity and for use with dynamic content. Of course, those features also make the program more complex, but not so complex that you'll never learn to use it. You can pick most of the new scripting commands from lists, and their meanings are pretty clear.

That is not to say that you'll learn and make immediate use of all of the program's potential with no effort. As is the case with any other powerful and versatile tool, practice makes perfect (or at least it brings you *closer* to perfection and makes it harder for the competition).

The Evaporating Plug-in Barrier

When the last version of this book was published, I swore that Flash was about to become as universally viewable as HTML. In the meantime, according to Macromedia, the number of viewers who can see Flash content without exerting any effort has increased from around 40 percent of all those with access to the Web to around 78 percent. In other words, the percentage has doubled in a year's time.

One of the reasons for this huge upsurge in Flash accessibility is the fact that all modern, graphically capable browsers currently made have built-in Flash support. This even includes such esoteric browsers as the latest for the Palm Pilot and for Web TV.

Add to this the fact that the other plug-ins that are most popular for viewing multimedia Web content—QuickTime 4 and Real Audio—also incorporate Flash. (Macromedia's Shockwave is another super-popular plug-in that supports Flash. No surprise there, huh?)

Then there's the fact that Macromedia has made the source code for creating Flash content available to anyone who wants it. As a result, you can expect to see Flash technology built into many new Web-authoring products, including Netscape Communicator.

As of summer 1998, the Flash plug-in was built into the two browsers that command more than 90 percent of the current browser market: Netscape Navigator and Microsoft Internet Explorer. Of course, Flash will be built into future versions of browsers from Netscape and Microsoft.

What if a viewer with an older browser doesn't have a plug-in? Flash 4's new Publishing features include the ability to automatically write HTML code that can "read" a visiting browser and configure the Flash presentation accordingly. If there's no plug-in in a browser that requires one, Flash will automatically provide a link that will download the plug-in and provide instructions for installation.

The Flash 4 plug-in can be downloaded and installed in less than five minutes—at no cost. The entire code is under 200K. More than 40 million of these plug-ins for legacy browsers have been downloaded from the Macromedia site.

So, you can now create a site in Flash, and set it up so that no viewer gets shut out. Furthermore, in the not-too-distant future, almost every Web viewer will have the plug-in anyway.

Flash And The Web

All the raving you may have heard about the prowess of Flash on the Web is well warranted. If you don't believe that and have ready access to the Web, check out the sites for any of the case studies in this book. If you're just thinking about using Flash, have an ancient browser, and don't have the program and, therefore, don't have the plug-in, don't worry. Any of these sites will give you the option of installing the plug-in. It uses less than 150K of your system's memory, won't cause any conflicts that I've been able to find, and downloads and installs in less than five minutes. If you have Netscape Navigator 4 or Microsoft Internet Explorer 3 (or later), the plug-in will even load automatically.

Although Flash can create Web content that doesn't require any plug-ins, a complete Flash site is a revelation as to how a Web site should look and work. It's far superior to ordinary HTML pages. The reasons for this are detailed in the following sections, but here's the short list:

- You can use much smaller—and therefore faster and more efficient—page and graphics files.

- Graphics and animations can be of any dimension without speed penalties.

- Page contents can be made to scale automatically to fit the user's window.

- Any object or any area on the screen can be a button.

- Buttons can change to static images when the mouse pointer is over them, and can link to animations, new scenes, or URLs when clicked on.

- Graphics and text can be anti-aliased, which makes edges smooth, clean, and professional-looking.

- You can mix Flash and HTML on a page.

- The plug-in automatically downloads for the most recent versions of the most popular browsers.

Automatic Anti-Aliasing Of Animations And Graphics

Flash's Web output is automatically anti-aliased (unless you elect to turn off that feature). Therefore, the edges of graphic elements are never jagged or pixelated, as they often are with the bitmapped graphics commonly found on the Internet.

Animations And Graphics Of Any Dimension

Because vector graphics are drawn according to coded instructions rather than by using a fixed-size pixel mosaic, the resolution speed and definition of graphics do not depend on file size. It is nothing short of astonishing to see a full-screen animation load and play *instantly* over a 14.4Kbps connection. Remember, however, that the secret to speed and performance is still the size of the files. If you make drawings that consist of hundreds of elements, but you use few symbols in those drawings, you can expect much poorer performance than for drawings and animations consisting of fewer shapes, simpler shapes, and symbols.

Fast Animations, Even Over 14.4Kbps Connections

Besides the vector-graphics advantage, animations download quickly because of a technology called *data streaming*. This means that the information in the file is organized *top down*, so that what's needed first arrives first on your computer. Thus, the animation can start playing the moment anything gets to your computer; you don't have to wait for an entire file to load before it can play.

If you are using a browser with the Flash plug-in installed and you visit a Flash site, any delay in viewing the Flash graphics will be caused by factors beyond the control of Flash, such as heavy Web traffic or the presence of many non-Flash graphic elements on the same page as the Flash elements.

Automatically Scales To Fit The Window

You can specify that the content of a Flash *movie* (which can be a static collection of graphics or an animation) is either displayed at a fixed size or scaled to fit the window in which it is being viewed. This capability is a great advantage in designing Web pages that will look the same on anyone's browser.

Automatic Anti-Aliasing Of Shape Edges And Type

Above-average anti-aliasing creates uniquely smooth edges and readable type. Flash allows you to specify whether you want your Flash movies viewed in Rough mode or High Quality mode (the default). If High Quality mode is turned off, anti-aliasing is turned off. Normally, however, anti-aliasing is calculated by the player each time the screen or the graphic is rescaled. The result is that the content of your screens always look sharp and professional.

Flash And HTML

Entire Web sites can be designed using nothing but Flash and a rudimentary knowledge of a few HTML tags. Actually, as of Flash 4, it is no longer a requirement that you know HTML. The new Publish command creates all the HTML tags that you're likely to need.

You can also use most of the WYSIWYG (What You See Is What You Get) Web-authoring programs to place Flash 2 or Flash 3 content into Web pages, but you will want to edit the HTML code to include the **<EMBED>** and **<OB-JECT>** tags. Macromedia's Dreamweaver 2 does an especially good job of preparing the right tags.

You can place JavaScripts in your HTML documents to detect the presence of a Flash plug-in in a visitor's browser and then play either a Flash version or a non-Flash version of the site, accordingly. You will find out how to do this in a later chapter. This book's companion CD-ROM includes a JavaScript-detection script that you can cut, paste, and modify.

Zoom-In Increases Detail

On a Flash page, you can put highly detailed graphics and text that otherwise would be too small to see, and viewers can zoom in to see the detail up close. This is a real boon when you want to present additional detail that would be appreciated by just a few viewers; for example, such a feature might be used on a page featuring a city map or a hidden clue in an interactive training demo or adventure game.

Flash As A Visualization Tool

Flash is, in my opinion, the best sketch pad for visualizing graphic designs, presentations, Web pages, and animations. Why? First, it makes the process of dashing out and putting your ideas in sequence as easy and intuitive as doodling on a napkin over a business lunch. It's even intelligent enough to straighten your squiggles into straighter lines and geometric shapes.

The ease with which you can sketch is, by no means, the end of the story. Flash is rich with graphics and animation tools that let you turn your sketches into *comprehensives* (highly polished previews) for client approval and into finished work. Even if Flash doesn't have all the tools you might want from Illustrator or Photoshop, you can export your work to those programs and use their tools. You can also use all the fancy font techniques that Illustrator or FreeHand can produce and just drop them into Flash. Not enough? You can use virtually all the clip art on the planet—even bitmapped clip art. Just import the file and choose Modify|Trace Bitmap to quickly manufacture an editable vector drawing of the image.

Note: In this book, an instruction that reads "choose Command|Subcommand| Subcommand" means that those commands can be found on the menu bar unless otherwise noted.

Flash is also a great tool for quickly drawing storyboards. You can sketch a different scene in each frame of the movie. You can use the Onion-Skinning feature, which lets you see through one or more frames as though they were sheets of celluloid lying atop one another. (This feature is covered in the chapter on animation.) So you can even register the elements on one page over any elements to be repeated on the next page, making it easy to keep layouts consistent from page to page.

If you want to distribute hand-printed, comic-strip storyboards to colleagues and clients for approval, it's no problem. You can set the Page Setup options to print storyboards with any number of frames across the page (in either landscape or portrait orientation). You can have these thumbnails framed in a box, squared off in a grid, or simply printed side by side on a blank page.

After your storyboard has been approved, you can polish the frames into finished Web content, offline presentations, animations (it's no problem to insert frames), or illustrations—whatever the job calls for.

Flash As A Graphics And Animation Utility

Flash is so useful for creating Flash movies that people tend to forget that it's also a great tool for creating graphics and animations to be used in other forms and formats. Flash can export animations as GIFs, as QuickTime or AVI movies, and even as frames to be inserted in Director or Authorware (to be viewed with an ActiveX control). All you have to do is choose File|Publish and then check the desired destination format in the resultant dialog box. File types to which you can export motion sequences from Flash are:

- Flash Player or Generator Template (.SWF)

- Future Splash Player (.SPL)

- Windows AVI (.AVI)

- QuickTime (.MOV)

- Animated GIF (.GIF)

- WAV Audio (.WAV) (exports the soundtrack of the movie)

- EMF Sequence (.EMF)

- WMF (Windows Metafile) sequence (.WMF)

- EPS (Encapsulated PostScript) sequence (.EPS)

- Adobe Illustrator sequence (.AI)

- AutoCAD DXF sequence (.DXF)

- Windows bitmap sequence (.BMP)

- JPEG sequence (.JPG)

- GIF sequence (.GIF)

- PNG sequence (.PNG)

Sequences are still images that have been saved with sequential numbers automatically added to their file names. This allows some other multimedia programs to import the sequence as a movie.

Of course, if you export to a non-Flash movie format other than QuickTime 4, you will lose sound and interactivity.

Flash also can import and export static images to many common file formats. Choose File|Export Image from the menu bar, and choose the desired format.

You can use Flash to convert digitized photos and scans (bitmaps) into drawings (vectors). Use File|Import to place the bitmap in the active layer and frame; then choose Modify|Trace Bitmap from the menu bar.

There's another facet of using Flash as a graphics utility. To minimize the file size of bitmapped illustrations to be used as elements in HTML Web pages, use Flash to autotrace them. If you export a file as a GIF bitmap, the resultant file is usually even smaller than a JPEG of the same dimensions. For instance, if the JPEG version of an image is 50K, the GIF image exported from the drawing might be only 17K. This file-size reduction occurs because autotracing averages the color within any of the traced subshapes to a single color. The result is that the file contains more information that can be repeated with a single instruction. For information about how to export a drawing as a GIF file, see the "Exporting To GIF" section later in this chapter.

Flash As An Illustration And Presentation Program

Flash is useful both as an illustration program and as a program for making offline presentations. As an illustration program, it is especially useful for business people whose primary job isn't illustration. This is true because of Flash's easy interface, its built-in lessons and help, its ability to automate the straightening and smoothing of lines, and its recognition of primitive shapes. In addition, editing shapes is much easier in Flash than in traditional drawing programs. The series of figures that follows will illustrate some of these differences.

Flash is a reasonably capable, all-purpose illustration program for several reasons. First, it uses the same type of Bezier-curve vector graphics as the high-end illustration and presentation programs. Second, Flash can import and export files to vector formats that can be exchanged with other programs. Third, the graphics produced in Flash—as in its illustration-program colleagues—are resolution-independent. Finally, Flash offers a wealth of drawing, animation, and interactivity features that can't be found in its competitors.

Flash doesn't do everything that illustration programs do. (For instance, there are no blends, plug-ins, or visible control points.) However, even if you're enough of a pro to use the more sophisticated features of FreeHand, Illustrator, or CorelDRAW, Flash provides a faster and more intuitive starting point. If you really need more features, you can simply export your work to Illustrator format and import it into any of the previously mentioned programs.

Drawing procedures are essentially the same whether you're making drawings for a static illustration or for an animated Flash movie. These procedures are explained thoroughly in Chapter 4. However, to give you a quick look at the difference between drawing in Flash and drawing in an illustration program (FreeHand, in this instance), take a look at Figures 1.4 and 1.5.

Here's another thing to consider: If you're new at illustration but need to create flyers or brochures with images, simply import vector clip art from any of dozens of CD-ROM or Internet libraries available. Then it's easy to modify and enhance with text, gradient backgrounds, and additional shapes. To import or export graphics into Flash, choose File|Import or File|Export from the menu bar.

Another way to draw graphics without knowing how is to simply trace photographs. Flash will autotrace them for you, though this isn't ideal if you want to control the smoothness and the exact shape of curves or the order in which groups of colors overlay one another. The alternative is to place the photograph in a frame, create a new frame, and use the Onion-Skinning feature to hand-trace the original image.

If you are going to use Flash to create Web-page graphics, be sure to set up the work area to match the dimensions and proportions of your desired output page. Otherwise, you'll get the default Web-screen work area of 550×400 pixels. To change this, choose Modify|Movie from the menu bar. The only settings you need to change are the width and height dimensions.

Figure 1.4

In Flash, you reshape lines by dragging their edges (top).

Figure 1.5

In FreeHand, you reshape lines by placing Bezier control points and dragging their handles (bottom).

Teaming Flash With Other Multimedia Web Tools

You can use Flash as a sketch pad and animation utility in conjunction with other multimedia and Web tools. It's an easy way to combine smooth anti-aliased drawings, text, and bitmapped graphics into a GIF or JPEG file, which you can then place in any standard Web page. There's no big trick to doing this: Simply export the current frame as an image (choose File|Export|Image), and then choose either GIF or JPEG as the file format. Flash 4 does a much better job of exporting bitmapped graphics than its predecessors did because it gives you control over compression.

Which file format should you choose? Here are some guidelines:

- If you want the graphic to have a transparent background (so it floats on a Web page), or if the image is composed of relatively flat colors, hard-edged (but anti-aliased) graphics, and text, you'll get the smallest file and therefore the highest performance from exporting to GIF format.

- If the image is a photograph significantly larger than 72×108 pixels, save it as JPEG.

- If your image contains some photographic material and lots of text, or if the image is a small photograph, export it to GIF, but be sure to check the Smooth box and the Dither Solid Colors box.

Exporting To GIF

Figure 1.6 shows the options in the Export GIF dialog box. The following sections explain the settings available in this dialog box.

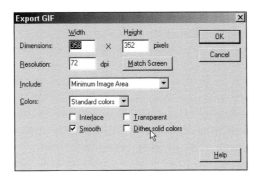

Figure 1.6
Flash 4's Export GIF dialog box.

Height And Width

These settings default to the actual size of the current image or to full document size in pixels, depending on your choice in the Include box.

Resolution

You can enter any dpi (dots per inch) setting. If you click on the Match Screen button, the resolution is set to 72 dpi.

Include

This is a drop-down list box. The choices are Full Document Size (which saves a file as large as the entire workspace specified for the current movie) and Minimum Image Area (which crops the image to include only that rectangular portion of the workspace that actually includes a picture).

Colors

Your options are Black and White or 4, 8, 16, 32, 64, 128, and 256 colors. There's also an option for Standard Colors, a cryptic name for the 216-color palette used by Netscape Navigator and Microsoft Internet Explorer. Pick the smallest number that will give you an acceptable representation of your image while maintaining the smallest possible file size.

Interlace

When checked, this option saves the file to a format that will load quickly on a Web page, first at low resolution, then graduating to full resolution. Use this option for larger GIFs that may take some time to load.

Smooth

When checked, this option enables Flash's anti-aliasing feature, thus dithering abrupt transitions between colors. Dithering produces smoother text edges and minimizes banding in gradient colors.

Transparent

When checked, this option makes the background color of your movie the transparent color for your GIF file. In other words, any portion of the workspace that is not actually covered by a drawing will be transparent.

Dither Solid Colors

When checked, this option dithers all colors that don't exactly match the colors in the palette with which you are working. Dithering places the palette's colors side by side in the pixel mosaic so that, if viewed from a distance, they appear to create colors more closely matching those in the original.

Exporting To JPEG

Flash also gives you sophisticated options for exporting to JPEG format. By looking at the dialog box in Figure 1.7, you'll see that there aren't as many options as for GIF, and the first three (Dimensions, Resolution, and Include) are the same. In addition, however, the Export JPEG dialog box contains a Quality field (enter a number between 0 and 100) and a Progressive Display checkbox. If you plan to export a Flash file for editing in applications such as Photoshop, be sure to save the file at the highest setting (or save in an uncompressed PNG format).

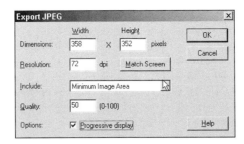

Figure 1.7
Flash 4's Export JPEG dialog box.

Exporting Bitmaps To Lossless Formats

When you want to save an image for use in other titles or for editing in an image-processing program (such as Fireworks or Photoshop), it's best to save it in a format that preserves all of the original picture information. If you want to export a true-color graphic in a lossless format, you can use either the BMP (Windows only) or PNG formats.

When you export as BMP, choose 24-bit Color from the Color Depth pull-down menu. If you have a transparency mask that you want to keep with the image, choose either 24-bit Color or 24-bit Color With Alpha Channel.

Using Flash With Director And Authorware

Macromedia, as you're probably aware, also makes other highly regarded multimedia authoring programs, namely, Director and Authorware. Flash's Shockwave Flash files (an export format) can be viewed directly in both of these programs.

You can place the content you create in Flash into Director or Authorware by exporting either images or movies as still motion sequences and then importing them into the target application. Depending on which platform you're working on, you can save images and motion sequences as BMP (Windows 95/NT) or PICT (Macintosh) files or file sequences. You can also export Flash animation sequences (movies) as either AVI (Windows 95/NT) or QuickTime files that can be imported directly into Director's Cast or Authorware's Timeline.

Using Flash With Video Editing Programs

Any of the graphics file types listed in the export list above can be used in Adobe Premiere, and at least some of them can be read into other video editing and effects programs. You've probably already caught on to this by now, but all you have to do to export a Flash movie as an animation sequence is choose File|Export|Movie and then select your chosen format.

New Features In Flash 4

There are dozens of enhancements in Flash 4—so many, in fact, that giving a detailed description of each change would prove tedious. It's easier to get a handle on what the new features mean if you think of them in functional categories. The functional categories are:

- QuickTime 4 support
- Action scripting
- Color sets
- Interface redesign
- Auto-filled shapes
- Changes in color-chip modifiers
- Changes in tools
- Image support
- Interactivity
- Forms
- Actions
- Editable text
- Flash Player interactivity
- Library changes
- Sound and MP3 support
- Timeline redesign
- Windows and Inspectors
- New Publish command

Interface Redesign

When you open Flash 4 for the first time, you're immediately aware that you've entered a different world. If you're familiar with earlier versions of Flash, one look at Figure 1.8 will convince you. And the changes are more than cosmetic. The principle behind the new interface design is to make the interface more compliant with the Macromedia corporate interface standards. Macromedia plans to make its applications more Web-centric and more integrated with one another. Macromedia has also made it a point to recommend two monitor display systems so that all the Inspectors and Options menus can be moved away from the workspace.

Some tools in the Toolbox have been repositioned, and the Toolbox has some new modifiers, including the ability to make rounded rectangles and the ability to create viewer-editable text fields. The Toolbox icons are smaller and their colors are more subtle.

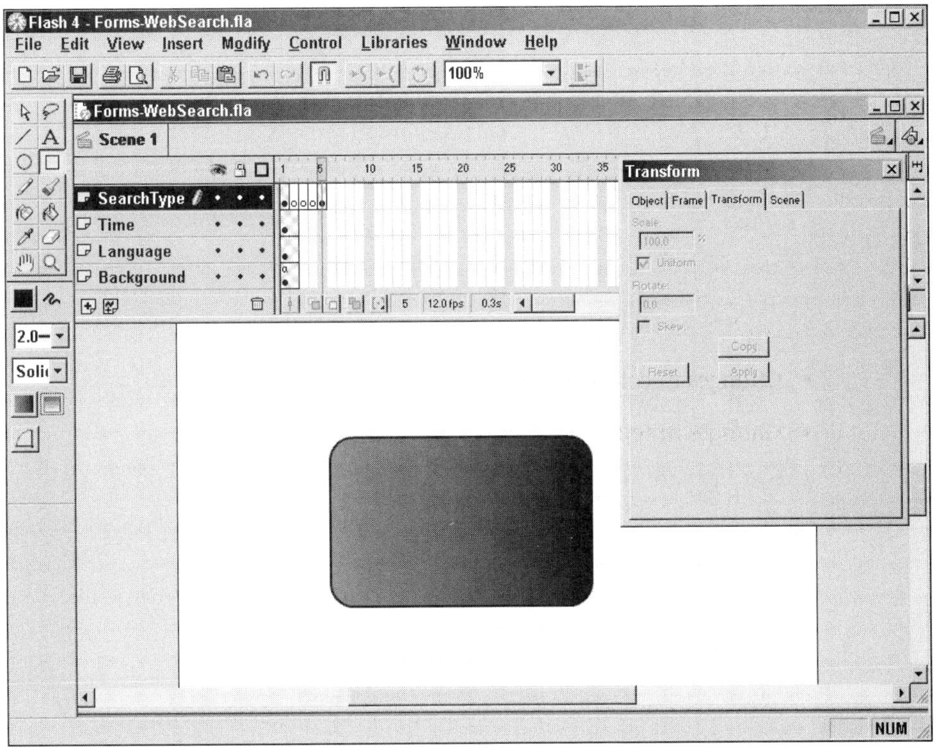

Figure 1.8
The redesigned Flash 4 interface.

The Timeline has undergone more changes than any other single interface element. It now floats, meaning that you can drag it anywhere on screen. If you have a two monitor system, you can even drag it over to the second monitor.

You will find more interface-design changes listed elsewhere in this section as new features.

New Publish Command

In the "olden days," you could devote a career to redesigning a site for all the different browser and media publishing applications it might be intended for. Flash 4's new Publish command opens a dialog box with tabs and checkboxes that list all the media types that Flash can automatically publish to:

- Flash movie
- Generator template
- HTML page
- GIF image
- JPEG image
- PNG image

- Windows Flash projector

- Macintosh Flash projector

- QuickTime movie

If you check multiple options, Flash will publish to all of them. Each of these publishing formats also has a tab that lets you set specific properties for that format.

QuickTime 4 Support

Flash 4 is now built into QuickTime 4. You have to own Flash 4 to do the authoring, however. Here's how it works: You import a QuickTime production on its own layer. You can then create any sort of Flash production on another layer. For example, you might use Flash to create interactive buttons with JavaScript-like events. You can then use Flash's action scripting to control the playback of the QuickTime movies. Other potential uses of Flash include creating animated title graphics and logos. When you've finished creating the QuickTime/Flash "production," you export it as a QuickTime 4 movie. When the movie is played, it can utilize all the features of any Flash elements that were incorporated.

The really nice surprise is the speed at which all of this plays. The Flash content doesn't slow down the playback of the movie at all.

Actions And Action Scripting

Actions have been given the muscle of Schwarzenegger and the agility of Baryshnikov. Actions are now so powerful that you can design highly customizable user interfaces in Flash 4. Because the Web is cross-platform by nature, these interfaces are equally at home on any platform. That flexibility has implications for offline interactive title design as well. Some of the most important potential characteristics of these interfaces are:

- Viewers can reposition features by dragging

- Hierarchical menus that can be cloned

- Buttons that maintain their state even if your viewer leaves the site and returns

The Actions commands in Flash 4 have been expanded in many respects (see Figure 1.9). The chief change is the addition of a scripting language called Action Script. Action Script makes it possible to create dynamic content—that is, content that appears depending on viewer response. ActionScript can have variables, and these can be named dynamically. Expressions can have either numeric or string values. You can make subroutine calls. What all this means will, naturally, seem obscure to a non-programmer. Chapter 9 is devoted entirely to the subject.

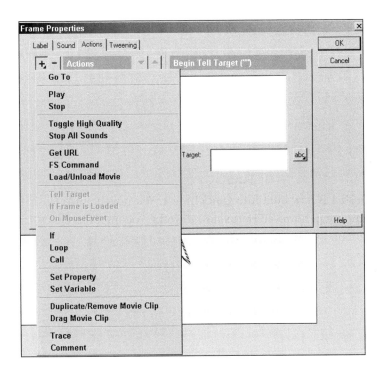

Figure 1.9
The greatly extended Flash 4
Actions menu.

Scripting is far from the only new feature that's been added to Actions. The user interface has been redesigned to give it expanded capabilities. The Go To, Get URL, FS Command, Load Movie, Unload Movie, Tell Target, If Frame is Loaded, On MouseEvent, If, Loop, Call, Set Property, Set Variable, Duplicate Movie Clip, and Drag Movie Clip commands are all either new or expanded.

Color Sets

One of the truly nagging aspects of producing Web animations is maintaining color consistency from object to object when objects have been created and imported from hordes of alien sources. Flash 4's new Color Sets feature lets you control the palette across the entire production.

In Flash 4, you can now import and output flat (no gradients) RGB color from Photoshop and Fireworks ACT palettes. You can also import color sets from GIF files. This means that you can match the colors you see in the originating program with those in the Flash file that you import them into.

You can add, replace, and save colors in any given set. You can save any set as the default for future Flash productions. If you change a palette, you can also choose a Load Default command from the Color menu. The same menu allows you to turn the graphics into monochrome with a Clear Colors command, sort the palette by color luminosity, or auto-convert all the current colors to their nearest Web-safe equivalents.

The color sets now reside with the specific Flash document file, rather than in a system file.

Inspector Windows

Flash 4 provides Inspector Windows that show all the properties associated with a particular:

• Object

• Frame

• Transformation

• Scene

• Generator

Inspectors tell you everything you could want to know about the characteristics of the working category they are attached to. You can change many of these properties directly by entering data in fields or by clicking buttons. These properties inspectors' tabbed content windows can be dragged anywhere on screen (or to a second monitor) so that they can be accessed in a way that is most convenient for you. You can see the new Object Inspector in Figure 1.10.

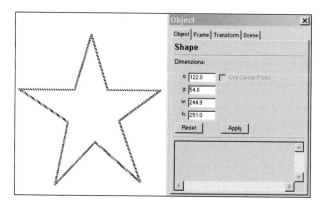

Figure 1.10
The new tabbed Inspector window.

Changes In Color-Chip Modifiers

There have been some changes in the color-chip modifiers. Color chips have been reduced in size. Partly, this goes along with the more subtle and professional-looking interface design. What is more important, it makes room for some other modifiers.

Immediately to the right of the color chip is a color-type indicator. It indicates whether the color will be applied to a stroke, to a fill, or to text.

The Oval and Rectangle tools have two color chips: one for stroke, the other for fill. In each case, the type-indicator icons are highlighted when that chip is active.

Changes In Tools

The Toolbox has been redesigned to feel more familiar to users of other graphics programs. These changes aren't major, but they are nice. The Line, Circle, and Rectangle tools now appear as instantly accessible, rather than appearing as Pencil modifiers. (For those of you who are new to Flash, a *modifier* is a button that appears at the bottom of the Toolbox when one of the tools is selected. Modifiers change the behavior of the tool.) The Hand tool is now present in the Toolbox. As in Photoshop, double-clicking the Hand tool zooms the entire image to fit in the frame.

All of the tools now have hot keys, so you can activate a tool by pressing a single key. If you are already familiar with the hot keys in Flash 3, you'll have to relearn a few because they've been changed to conform more closely to those used in other Macromedia programs.

Several new commands have been added to the Modify Curves menu:

- *Lines to Fills*—Converts any selected shape's line strokes to a filled shape. This command allows you to fill a line with an effect or to soften its edges. This is especially great when zooming an image out because no matter how small an image is, lines display a minimum of 1 pixel in thickness, so objects become blacker (if outlines are black) as they shrink. Fills do not have this property.

- *Expand Shape*—Allows you to either expand or shrink the selected shape by a specified amount. This command can be useful for resizing broken-apart text.

- *Soften Edges*—Oooh! This one is lovely because it lets you make shapes that "fade" into the background. The edges fade into translucency by the author-specified distance. You can control the number of steps for softening, too.

There's a new Polygon Lasso tool, which appears in the form of a modifier button for the Freeform Lasso tool. Most graphics programs already have this tool, so it's going to be a welcome addition. It allows you to make perfectly straight-edged polygon selections. You can also mix polygon and freehand selection by pressing the Opt/Alt key while using either the Freehand Lasso tool or the Polygon Lasso tool.

You can now have *automatic fills* for basic shapes. When you choose a Rectangle or Oval tool, a color-chip modifier now appears. It lets you select the fill for that shape. The brush and bucket also use the fill color specified by this modifier (unless you change it when you use the brush or bucket). You can also select a *non-color modifier,* which causes shapes to be drawn without strokes or fills.

Bitmap Image Support

The important change in Flash 4's support of imported bitmap (photo) images is that they now look on export as they did when you imported them. That is because Flash can use the imported JPEG compression instead of its own. So if you've carefully tweaked a JPEG file for maximum quality and minimum file size by using some fancy third-party utility designed for that purpose, you won't have your efforts canceled. It's a much bigger deal than Macromedia would have you believe.

If you use Flash's JPEG compression you can choose the level of compression when you export JPEGs. In addition, GIFs are always saved to lossless compression, and PNG files are always saved using high-quality JPEG compression. In addition, Flash has a lossless format similar to PNG, which is often ideal for exporting GIFs and PNG images.

Editable Text Fields

You can now integrate information-gathering forms into a Flash 4 Web site. Creating user-editable text-entry fields is as easy as clicking a modifier button when you choose the Text tool from the toolbox. The form you see in Figure 1.11 is made of these new editable text fields.

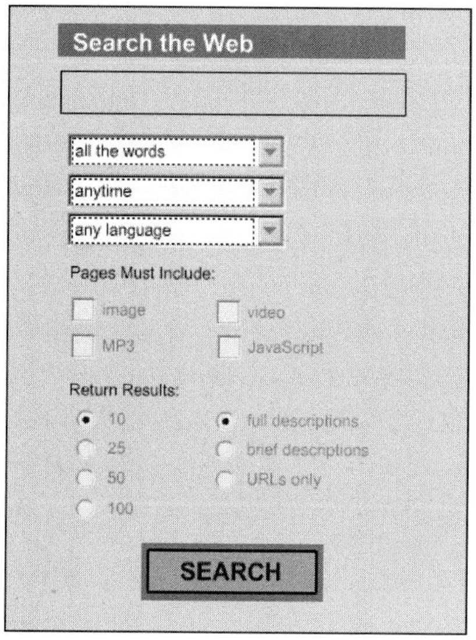

Figure 1.11
Flash 4's editable text feature allows you to create interactive forms for collecting data from viewers.

These new text-entry fields can be used to:

• Allow a viewer to enter text that would cause specific dynamic content to appear if the field were connected to a Generator database.

• Create Web-application front-ends by using new Actions commands called Get and Post. These commands allow you to paste the entered data into any CGI script to generate dynamic content.

- Allow a user to enter content for an email or for a comment on a Web page.

- Allow content to be loaded from text files using Load Variables.

- Enter a password in order to proceed to an otherwise locked portion of the Flash movie.

You can attach a variable name to a text field, and you can make the variable name read-only. You can also specify that the field use the same font you used to design the field or the browser's closest approximation of that font. Other options include whether the field can have multiple lines of text, whether text can word-wrap, and whether an entry will be masked by asterisks (for password entry). Flash 4 also has built-in fonts—sans, serif, and typewriter—that use system fonts on the users computer to display text. This saves having to have specific fonts on a user's computer or saving shapes as is standard with standard Flash text.

When the text field is viewed, it appears as normal text until a mouse-over event occurs. At that time, the cursor changes to a carat (^) and you can enter text. You can also highlight text to copy it to the Clipboard or to replace it with newly typed text. The cursor can be used to scroll text up and down if more text has been entered than will fit in the allocated space.

Redesigned Symbols Library

For those new to Flash, a *symbol* is any entity that you can create or import in Flash. Because symbols are stored as separate entities, they can be made to appear in many forms and places in a Flash movie without significantly increasing that movie's file size. Symbols are stored in libraries. You can see the redesigned Library window in Figure 1.12.

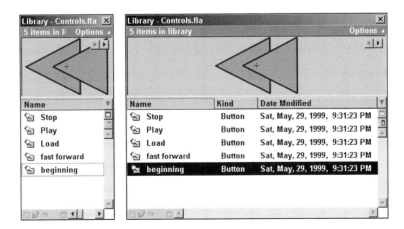

Figure 1.12

Narrow (left) and Wide views of the Flash 4 Library.

In Flash 4, the Library doesn't exhibit the problems Flash 3 had with dealing with large numbers of symbols. List View displays five columns of information about each symbol: name, usage, kind (of symbol), exported size, and exported format.

At the bottom of the Library window are Asset Management buttons. These are reminiscent of the palette buttons in Photoshop. You can also use these buttons to see and edit a symbol's properties and to delete a symbol. There's no need to first make a menu selection.

Press Ctrl and right-click on a symbol item to display a shortcut menu that changes in context with the type (graphic, movie clip, button) of symbol.

It is no longer necessary to issue the Insert Symbol command if you want to start creating a new symbol on its own stage. Just click the New Symbol button at the bottom of the Library window.

Sound And MP3 Support

Alas! Flash *still* doesn't support MIDI files. It's a puzzlement because MIDI files are to sound what vector files are to graphics. Unfortunately, adding MIDI support would substantially increase the plug-in size so it hasn't been added. All the same, great strides in sound have been made in Flash 4. One of the great weaknesses of earlier versions of Flash was the lack of support for importing advanced technology for highly compressed analog audio. The most advanced of these technologies, MP3, is now integrated into the program. At last, you can make long-running animations that are accompanied by mood music and voice-over narration. The MP3-compressed files will upload to the viewer's computer before he gets bored and leaves.

You can apply the MP3 sound to either animations or button events, and you can call sounds from Action Scripts. You can import audio that you've recorded or that's on a CD, then compress it to MP3 audio inside the program. You have total control over the quality and degree of compression.

Timeline Redesign

The infamous Flash Timeline has been completely redesigned and its functionality augmented. Macromedia's goal is to provide "faster learning and a more efficient workflow." The redesign makes the tweening process easier to understand and more powerful. (Tweening is the process of drawing the frames between the start of a motion and its peak. In other words, drawing the in-between frames. The job used to be handled by assistant animators. In Flash, it's done by the program.) It's now more difficult to inadvertently add items to the Timeline or move symbols off the motion guide. Drag-and-drop editing capabilities make it easier to do such things as moving or changing the start and stop points of a span of frames. You can see the new Timeline design in Figure 1.13.

The new Timeline design makes it easier to see the number of the current frame, improves the support for layers, makes it easier to dissect the struc-

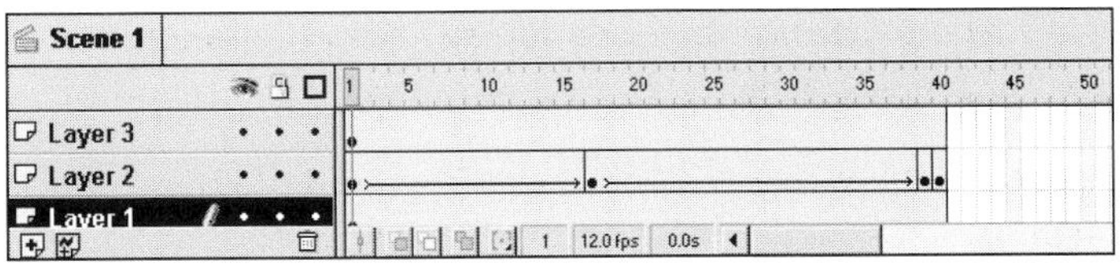

Figure 1.13
The Flash 4 Timeline has been redesigned to make it easier to read.

ture of a movie, and supports "widgets" and object behaviors. Widgets are premade animations that allow a user to modify its graphics without having to redo complicated scripting inside.

There's also a new Timeline command for motion tweening. You can highlight a number of frames, insert frames, move the object in the first frame to the position you want it to assume in the last frame, and ask for a motion tween.

Other, non-Timeline changes make it easier to create and edit animations. You can work on multiple layers by using an *outline colors mode* that shows the outlines on each layer in a different color. This makes it easy to see which objects overlap. There are also *Motion Guide Layers* that make it easier to do motion-tweening along a predetermined path.

New Tutorials

The Flash 4 tutorials have been completely redesigned. You now see the tutorial on one side of the stage and the Work Area on the other. This arrangement gives you an immediate comparison of your work to the tutorial's. Check out Figure 1.14.

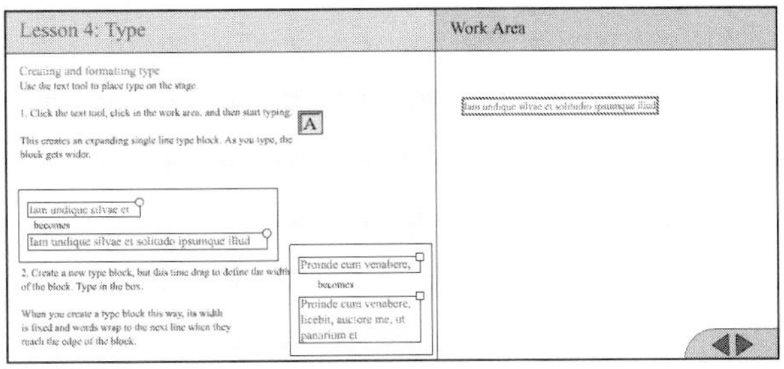

Figure 1.14
The lesson is on the left, your workspace is on the right. It's easy to compare your efforts with the instruction samples.

If you're buying this book because you're new to Flash or haven't updated since purchasing an early version, you may want to know a little more about the features that were introduced in Flash 3. Appendix B covers these features.

Moving On

I hope this chapter has given you an overview of the many ways in which you might find Flash useful, whether the content you create is intended for the Web or for more traditional, offline media.

In the next chapter, you'll learn more specifics regarding what makes Flash so useful in designing Web sites and interactive offline titles, such as in training materials and on floppy portfolios. The adventure begins now!

MACROMEDIA SYNERGY

2

This chapter introduces you to the synergy that exists between Flash and other Macromedia products, especially Dreamweaver, Fireworks, FreeHand, and Generator. Most of the techniques discussed here are covered in greater depth in later chapters. They are introduced here to help you plan ahead as you design your projects.

KEN MILBURN

Flash isn't an HTML editor, so it doesn't fit the usual category of a what-you-see-is-what-you-get (WYSIWYG) Web authoring tool. However, give or take a few HTML tags, you can use Flash to author entire Web sites. Why would you want to? Because the results look better and reduce the viewer's waiting time. Also, those characteristics of HTML that make precision placement of design elements such a pain are not a factor when you're designing in Flash. Furthermore, when you want to add animation or event-triggered actions, you don't have to use another type of software (such as a GIF animator, Java, or JavaScript). Even if your Web sites contain elements that you can't author in Flash (such as Cascading Style Sheets), you can design everything else in Flash and then use another authoring tool to create the few pages needed to contain those elements.

Another huge advantage of Flash is that you can design once and then deliver either online or offline (and either with or without a browser). This chapter will help you decide whether you want to plan carefully—so that your creations will be optimized for the Web—or simply design without restrictions for offline playback from CD-ROM, floppy disk, hard drive, or a local area network (LAN). Figure 2.1 shows a Flash movie playing in a browser; Figure 2.2 shows the same movie playing offline as a Projector.

To play a Flash movie without a browser, first choose File|Export Movie from the main menu, and then export to the SWF Flash file format. Now, as long as you have Flash installed, you can double-click on the movie's file name in your computer's directory (an open folder on the Macintosh or in the

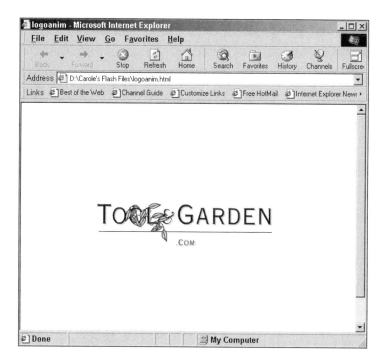

Figure 2.1

A Flash movie playing online in a browser.

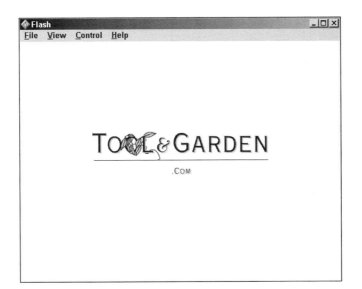

Figure 2.2
A Flash movie playing offline in the Player.

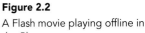

Figure 2.3
Creating a Projector movie. Choose File|Publish Settings and check the boxes as shown.

Explorer in Windows). The movie will appear in the standalone player window. (See Figure 2.3.)

If you want to distribute your Flash 4 file as an offline presentation, simply ship the SWF file along with the appropriate player for the destination platform. Better yet, distribute it as a standalone (no external player required) presentation. A standalone Flash movie is called a Flash Projector. From the menu bar, choose File|Publish Settings. (See Figure 2.3.) In the Publish Settings dialog box, check the boxes for the standalone-player platform versions you'd like to use. The standalone player automatically makes the file an executable application and, in the case of Windows, adds the necessary .exe extension.

Choosing Whether To Design For Browsers Or For Offline Viewing

Because anything you create in Flash 4 can be distributed either on or off the Web, it's tempting to think that you can create your projects once and that they will automatically fit either method of distribution. That's a good idea most of the time, but there is a catch: If you're designing for the Web, you must constantly compromise your design in the interest of minimizing file size in order to maximize online performance. Remember, it will still be some time before the world at large will have connections—such as DSL or cable modems—that are faster than 56K.

On the other hand, as long as a project is designed for efficiency, there's nothing to keep you from using it for both online and offline delivery.

You should design a movie specifically for offline media if the presentation or interactive title would benefit significantly from:

- Gradient morphs

- Higher frame rates

- Detailed drawings (such as maps and scientific illustrations)

- Many animated layers

- Heavy use of imported bitmapped graphics

- High-fidelity stereo sound or extensive voice narration

A Precision Placement Tool

You can place drawing elements and text in a Flash movie with the same precision and just as intuitively as in traditional programs for page design (Quark and PageMaker) or illustration (FreeHand, Illustrator, and CorelDRAW).

Flash lets you choose ruler units (pixels, inches, decimal inches, centimeters, millimeters, and points). If you are designing for the screen, you will want to choose pixels as your unit of measurement. If you are designing for the printed page, you will want to use one of the other units. Flash does not let you choose picas for setting ruler or grid spacing. However, if you have an illustration program, you can export to Adobe Illustrator format, open the file in your illustration program, and tweak your placement there, then export the result in the same illustration format and import it back into Flash.

Flash 4 also doesn't directly support guidelines such as those found in most illustration programs. You can, however, use a guide layer. (A *guide layer* is a layer that doesn't show up on playback.) You can use any of the Flash drawing tools on a guide layer to make guidelines, motion paths, and text annotations or to hold any sort of visually helpful hint (such as a starburst or exclamation point to attract attention).

Perfect Type And User Text-Entry Fields

The placement and appearance of text in Flash are even better in Flash 4 than in Flash 3. The ability to adjust leading and kerning of text makes it nearly as accurate as in any page-makeup or illustration program. (See Figure 2.4.)

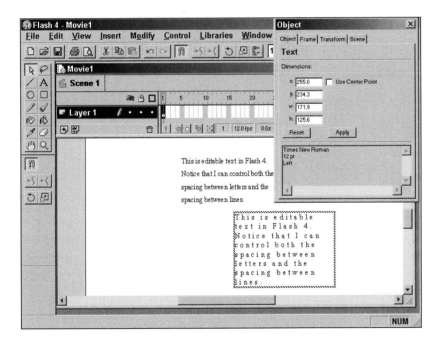

Figure 2.4
The top block of text shows an example of leading; the bottom block shows kerning.

One advantage is that Flash doesn't force you to limit your Web pages and interactive titles to only those fonts supported by the majority of browsers. Furthermore, Flash doesn't require you to use HTML nested tables in order to force type to be positioned where you would like it.

Flash provides you with a way to design interactive Web content that features fully anti-aliased (edge-smoothed) type in any outline font that's installed on your computer. The result will appear correctly in any Web browser or on any offline viewer's computer, regardless of whether the fonts you used are installed on that computer.

Flash 4 provides text modifiers for font, type size (in points), text color, bold, italic, paragraph alignment, and paragraph properties. See Figure 2.5.

You can modify text at any time by reselecting it and then dragging the text cursor over any range of letters to change their properties. The only restriction to changing the text properties is that the paragraph properties always apply to an entire paragraph.

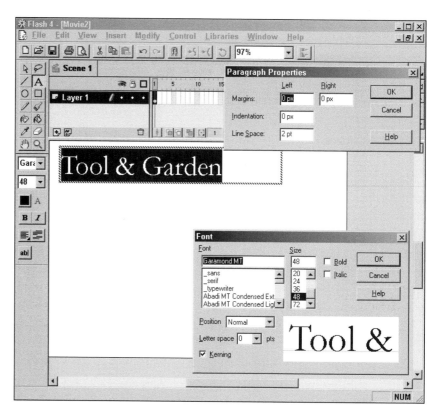

Figure 2.5
The Paragraph Properties and Font dialog boxes over text on the screen.

Paragraph properties allow you to control the left and right margins, paragraph indentation, and line spacing. The new Font Properties dialog provides the ability to control kerning (spacing between individual letters) and letter spacing (equidistant spacing between all letters).

CREATING TEXT EFFECTS

Although there are no type styles for underlines, outlines, or shadows, Flash lets you create these effects with ease.

To create underlines, use the Pencil tool with the Line modifier.

To create outlines, select the text and choose Modify|Break Apart from the menu bar. Then use the Ink Bottle tool to make the outlines in any color and thickness.

To create drop shadows, select the text and press Cmd/Ctrl+D to duplicate it. Change the text color to the appropriate gray, make both groups of text into symbols, move the shadow into position, and then (if necessary) choose Modify|Arrange|Bring To Front to place the main set of letters over the shadow.

You cannot create rounded or beveled edges or surface-lighting effects automatically, as you may be used to doing in Photoshop. However, you can create some similar effects by hand (see the tutorial in Chapter 11).

New User-Editable Text Fields And Aliased Text Options

Flash 4 becomes even more powerful when used with the host of new Action Scripting capabilities and with Macromedia Generator. Generator makes it possible to create a Web site whose dynamic content is contained in a database. It's easy to create a text-entry field in Flash because you enter text the way you normally do. The difference is that you first click the Text Field button (modifier) at the bottom of the Toolbox as shown in Figure 2.6.

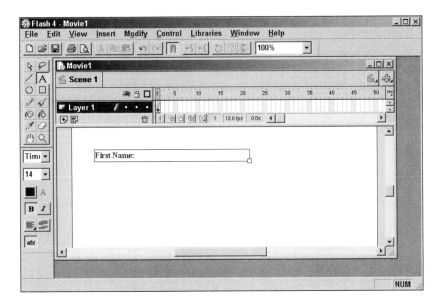

Figure 2.6
Notice that the small square is at the lower-right corner of a text-entry field, signifying that this is an editable text field.

In the Flash 4 authoring environment, you can anti-alias text separately from anti-aliasing shapes. Turning off anti-aliasing results in faster performance while playing back in the authoring environment.

Easy Shapes

It seems like every art director I run into lately admits to doing his or her concept sketches in Flash and then exporting the result to an illustration program for tweaking. The principal reason for doing this is that Flash provides a way to let you draw as naturally as if you were sketching on paper. At the same time, it produces precision geometry that can be easily read and tweaked by even the most sophisticated illustration software, which is the software usually used to specify graphic design for single-page print projects. Examples of single-page projects include book and album covers, all sorts of advertisements, and package design.

You can sketch intuitively in Flash by using the Pencil tool and the shape-recognition modifiers. These ensure that you'll have smoother lines and fewer control points than you would if you used only the Freehand tool in your illustration program. Making rough shape adjustments is also faster and easier in Flash because you can do so by simply dragging the outlines. See Figure 2.7.

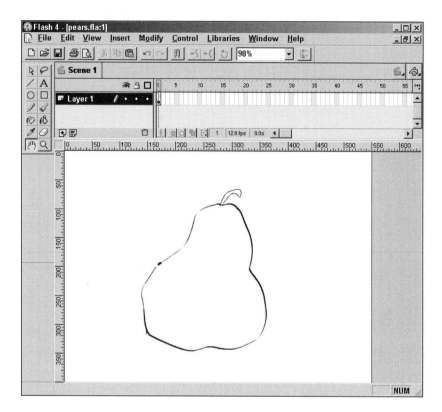

Figure 2.7
Hand-drawn sketch of a pear as it would appear in Flash 4.

You can export your work to the Adobe Illustrator file format by choosing File|Export and then Adobe Illustrator (the .ai file extension) in the resulting Save As dialog box. Import the Illustrator file into your illustration program, and use all the power of that program to precisely control Bezier-curve control points and to make radical drawing commands, such as blends. See Figure 2.8.

Flash 4 is also a great tool for simplifying drawings made in more complex illustration programs. If you export the file from the originating illustration program and then import it into Flash, all the layers will be shown as groups. See Figure 2.9.

If you import a drawing made of overlapping shapes, there will be many grouped objects. You can see these groups if you press Cmd/Ctrl+A or choose Edit|Select All from the main menu. The objects that are grouped will be enclosed in selection rectangles, as in Figure 2.10.

If you ungroup all the subgroups, each of the shapes will be dropped onto the canvas and will, at that point, auto-edit one another so that each line and color becomes its own independent shape. Because there are no longer

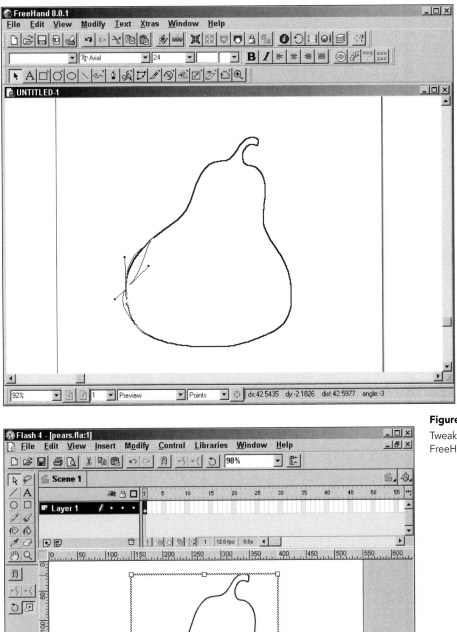

Figure 2.8
Tweaking control points in
FreeHand.

Figure 2.9
A FreeHand drawing imported
into Flash.

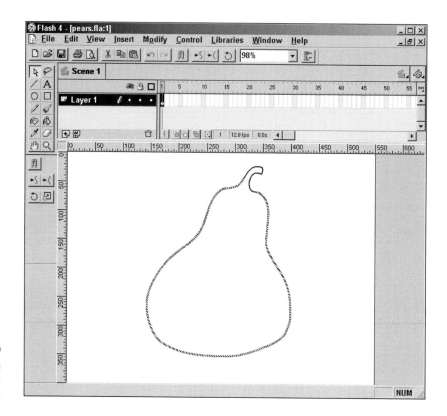

Figure 2.10

The imported FreeHand drawing after it has been broken apart in Flash 4.

any underlying shapes, the file size will often be a fraction of the original, and you'll still retain all the visible information in the file.

This is a terrific way to store clip art or art for your own library that you may want to use later. It's also a terrific way to simplify a drawing so that you can add even more layers and details in your illustration program. If you group everything after reimporting from FreeHand after using the technique described previously, all the new elements will remain independent, making them much easier to select and adjust.

Finally, if you plan to use an illustration-program drawing inside a Flash movie destined for the Web, the kind of optimization described previously is a must.

Exporting To Bitmapped File Formats

The really big news in Flash 4 is that you can now export your work to QuickTime movies. QuickTime movies that you export can contain all the mouse events and other features of Flash. This means that you can view a QuickTime 4 movie that has Flash-created interactivity built into it.

As in earlier versions of Flash, you can use Flash 4 to create graphics and animations for conventional Web content. You can also use the same features to create bitmapped (pixel-based) images from individual frames for use in photo-editing programs such as Photoshop and MetaCreation's Painter.

There are many reasons why you might want to use Flash 4 for creating content for conventional Web media. Animated GIFs have become the ubiquitous form of animation used on the Web, and they can be a simple and efficient element for inclusion in complex interactive projects (such as Director movies or PowerPoint presentations). You can export any or all of a Flash 4 movie as an animated GIF, as Windows AVI (the Windows movie file format), or as a sequence of still images in all of the still-image formats supported by Flash 4. (This last option may be a good way to import animations into programs that can't import animated GIF or AVI movies.)

To export a movie, choose File|Export Movie. In the Export Movie dialog box, do the following: Choose a file format from the Save As Type drop-down list box, type a file name, and click on OK. See Figure 2.11.

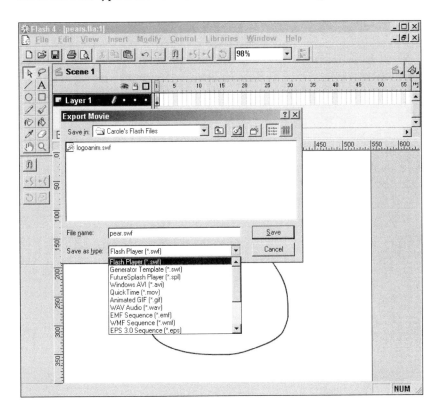

Figure 2.11

The Export Movie dialog box with the Save As Type list box dropped down.

You can also export any individual frame to GIF, JPEG, or PNG format. The result can then be either enhanced in another program or used on a standard HTML Web page.

Following is information you'll find helpful when you are choosing which file format is best suited for your needs.

GIF Format

GIF files are used for very small (thumbnail) photos or for flat-colored, hard-edged text and graphics. GIF is the most commonly used format for Web graphics. Compression is lossless (no changes are made to the pixel structure of the image) and is most efficient when the subject is composed of defined edges and solid colors.

JPEG Format

The JPEG format is often used on the Web for photographs and other images that feature continuous-tone colors and soft edges. Because browsers must decompress the image before it can be viewed, larger images are more appropriate and more efficient than smaller ones. Smaller images contain fewer pixels and are therefore less likely to contain more than 216 colors (the maximum number in a Web-safe palette).

JPEG compression is highly efficient, but it can cause the loss of detail or the introduction of image artifacts (minute blotches), especially at higher compression ratios.

PNG Format

PNG is a new cross-platform file format invented for the Web. It is the only Web format that can contain alpha channel masks. (Alpha channel masks make it possible to have graduated or partial transparency in an image.) However, only Netscape and Microsoft browsers that are version 4 or later will recognize PNG files without having a special plug-in installed.

Use the PNG format when higher-fidelity to the original image or graduated transparency is a must. Use this format also when you want to export the highest-quality bitmap for further editing in an image editor such as Photoshop 5, Fireworks, Image Ready, or Photo-Paint.

Using The New Publish Feature

Bye, bye, Aftershock. Placing your files into an HTML page and converting your multimedia elements for incorporating them into a Web page is now much smoother and easier.

Actually, perhaps I bid it adieu a little too soon. Aftershock is still around, but for the most part, the new Publish feature is much easier to use.

The use of the Publish feature will be covered extensively in Chapter 13. For the time being, suffice it to say that you can simultaneously publish your Flash documents to a great many formats simply by checking the boxes in

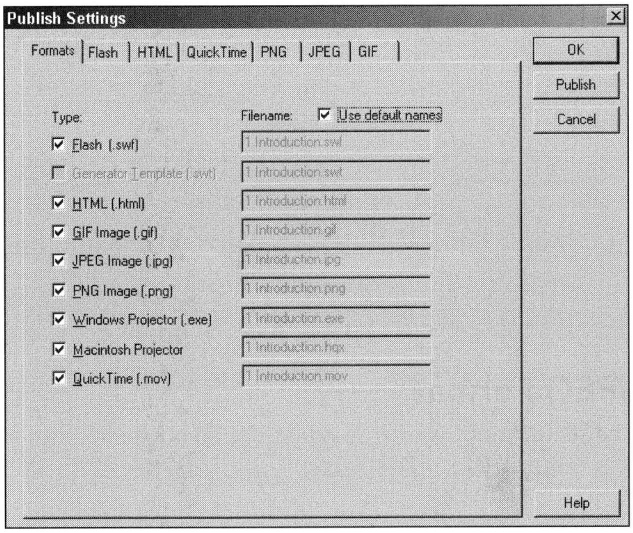

Figure 2.12
The new Publish settings dialog box in Flash 4 automatically qualifies your current Flash 4 movie for all of the formats shown.

the dialog box shown in Figure 2.12. The Publish feature even automatically puts the proper HTML tags around your Flash movie when you publish to HTML.

Integration With Other Macromedia Products

Macromedia has been working on integrating its applications so that they not only serve their intended purpose, but serve one another as well. At this writing, Macromedia was in the process of releasing FreeHand 9, which promises to be much more Flash-friendly than FreeHand 8 is. The other two products that should be of interest to you are Dreamweaver (Macromedia's WYSIWYG Web-authoring tool) and Director (Macromedia's hyper-powerful, industry-standard multimedia authoring tool).

Dreamweaver 2 lets you insert a Flash movie precisely where you want it in any existing HTML document. All you have to do is open your target document in Dreamweaver 2, choose Insert|Flash Movie, and navigate to the movie you want to insert. (See Figure 2.13.) Furthermore, you can then simply drag the corner of a bounding box to scale the movie to the exact size that you want it to appear. Dreamweaver 2 also provides several professionally designed table pages so that you can quickly insert Flash components exactly where you want them in a layout.

Director, as of version 6.5, allows you to import Flash movies as sprites. Director (or your Director-enriched Shockwave Web pages) can then play Flash's vector-based movies alongside the conventional animated bitmapped content. As of this writing, only Flash 2 movies are supported in this manner. You can use Flash 4, of course, but you have to save the files in Flash 2

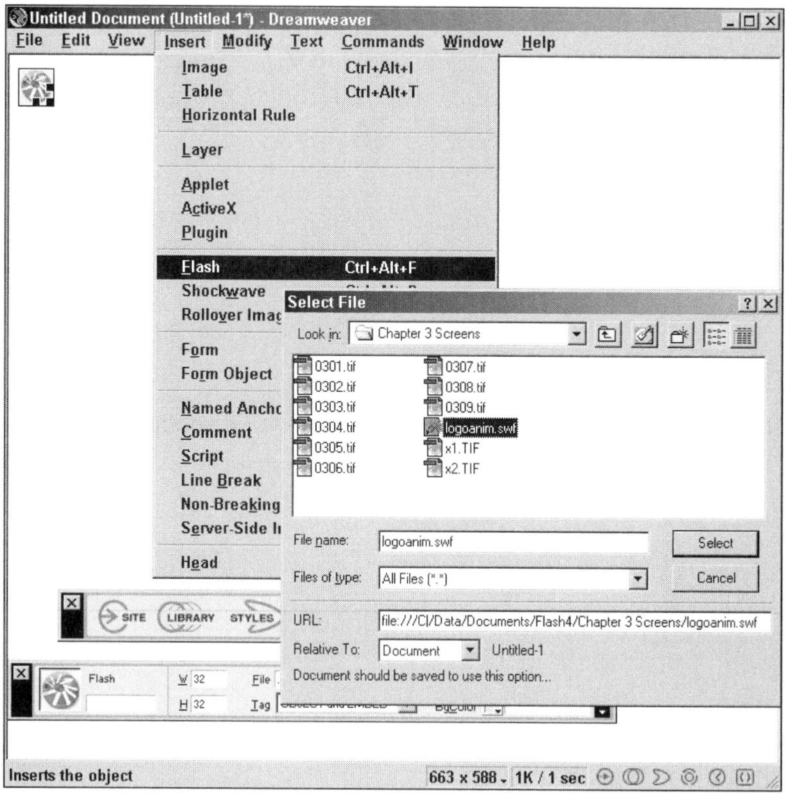

Figure 2.13
Placing a Flash movie into an HTML document in Dreamweaver 2.

format. As a result, you won't be able to take advantage of Flash 4's new graphics features such as morphing and transparency. Director 7.02 allows import of Flash 4 movies as well as using Flash 4 as sprites. Director 7.0 only supports Flash 3 but the upgrade to 7.02 is free.

Creating Templates For Flash Generator

Flash Generator is yet another Macromedia application. (It does not ship with Flash 4 or with the Design in Motion suite; it's sold independently.) Generator is a Web server tool that automates the creation of both Flash and standard GIF graphics according to input from users or viewers. For example, a Generator-based site might show one graphic if you answer "Yes" to a question, another if you answer "Maybe," and yet another if you answer "No." Generator 1 does not support Flash 4, but Generator 2 does support Flash 4, and adds many new features.

You can't create a Generator site in Flash, but you can create a Generator template. You do this in two ways:

• Adding text variables to a movie

• Installing Generator extensions to Flash 4

The second option requires that you own Generator; the first doesn't. All you need to do is use the Flash Text tool to place the required code inside curly braces, {}. When that movie is subsequently processed in Generator, the text in the braces will be replaced by the appropriate text from an associated text file or from the command line.

You will learn more about creating text templates for Flash Generator in Chapter 11. Operations that require you to own a copy of Generator are outside the scope of this book.

Moving On

Well, so much for the theory and overviews. Now that you have an idea of what you can accomplish with Flash 4, it's time to get down to the specifics of creation. Chapter 3 will teach you the fundamentals of drawing in Flash 4.

DRAWING
REFERENCE 3

This chapter provides you with a quick reference
to all the tools, icons, and commands used for
drawing in Flash 4. Use this chapter to find the
right tools, modifiers, and editing capabilities
when you are in the midst of a job or when
your learning piques your curiosity.

KEN MILBURN

Figure 3.1

The Toolbox with the Arrow tool chosen.

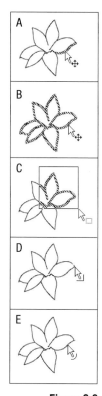

Figure 3.2

The various ways to select an image in Flash.

In addition to a quick reference for all the drawing tools and modifiers, there's a healthy discussion of Flash's drawing aids, methods for refining and customizing drawings, how to assemble and break apart groups and symbols (collectively known as overlays), and a section on how to insert objects from other applications. Finally, there's a section that covers what you shouldn't expect from Flash as a drawing program.

The Drawing Tools And Their Modifiers

Flash 4's new Toolbox has added a few tools, but it still looks deceptively simple. It now has 14 tools, but most of these existed previously as modifiers. If you have any experience with graphics programs, you are already familiar with the basic functions of the drawing tools: Arrow, Lasso, Line, Text, Oval, Rectangle, Pencil, Brush, Ink Bottle, Paint Bucket, Dropper, Eraser, Hand, and Magnifier. Further on in this chapter, you'll find these tools described in more depth. Chapter 5 will give you some tips and tricks for using them.

The Toolbox is divided into two parts: tools and tool modifiers. All the Flash tools, with the exception of the Dropper, have modifiers. Modifiers dictate the behavior of the chosen tool. Their icons automatically appear in the lower half of the Toolbox when you choose their parent tool. Figure 3.1 shows the Toolbox.

Arrow Tool

To choose the Arrow tool, click on its icon in the Toolbox or press the "A" key. When the Arrow is the chosen tool, the cursor changes to an arrow. You use the Arrow tool to make and change selections. Selected entities are always identified by a checkered pattern imposed upon them. In order to modify a shape by using any of Flash's commands or modifiers, you must first select it (this includes turning entities into groups or symbols), in one of the ways shown in Figure 3.2 and described here:

A. To select a single entity, click the arrow cursor directly on an entity (line, fill, group, symbol, or text). You can select multiple entities by pressing Shift+click for each additional one. (This is a change from earlier versions of Flash. If you wish to return to the old method of adding to the selection with each click, choose File|Preferences from the main menu and uncheck the Shift Select box, which is now checked by default.)

B. To select all connected entities, double-click the arrow cursor on any entity (except overlays).

C. To select only a section of an entity, drag a marquee around a section of the drawing. If you cover only a part of the drawing, that part will be separated from the rest of the drawing, cutting all lines and fills that intersect the marquee path. This is useful for isolating a section of an entity that is to be smoothed, straightened, or optimized.

D. To locate and move a corner point, move the arrow until it is accompanied by a corner symbol. If you then drag, you will move the corner and the lines attached to it.

E. To locate or move a curved line or fill edge, move the arrow until it is accompanied by a curve symbol. If you then drag, you will reshape the curve.

Arrow Tool Modifiers

When you select the Arrow tool, its modifiers appear in the lower section of the Toolbox. Figure 3.3 shows the Arrow tool modifiers. Here are the functions of the Arrow tool modifiers:

- *Snap*—Causes the arrow's drag point to jump precisely to a grid intersection or to a particular spot on an entity, whichever is closer. You can snap an entity to another entity's center, midpoint, or endpoint. You can also make one object abut another. When Snap is on, the Snap icon is ghosted and the arrow cursor has a circle adjoining it. See Figure 3.4.

Figure 3.3
The Arrow tool modifiers.

Note: Press Ctrl+Option to drag on a line to create a new corner point.

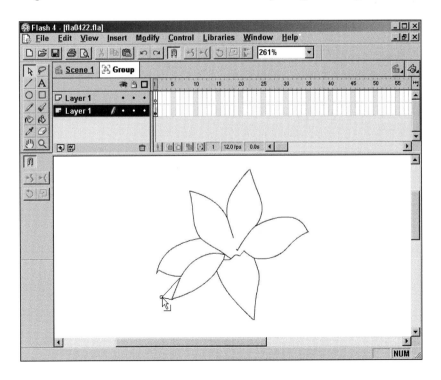

Figure 3.4
Moving a corner point with Snap turned on.

• *Smooth*—Causes the selection to have a smoother curve. Repeatedly choosing this modifier continues to make the curve smoother. Experiment by using this modifier with the multilevel Undo and Redo commands. See Figure 3.5.

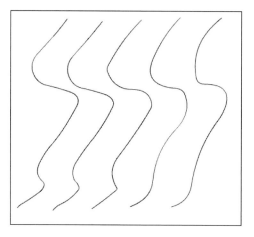

Figure 3.5
The same smoothed pencil line copied four times. Each successive line was smoothed by one more click than its predecessor.

• *Straighten*—Causes the selection to have a straighter line. Repeatedly choosing this modifier continues to make the curve straighter (or smoother). Experiment by using this modifier with the multilevel Undo and Redo commands. See Figure 3.6.

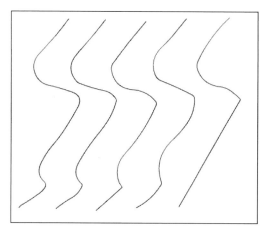

Figure 3.6
The same smoothed pencil line copied four times. Each successive line was straightened by one more click than its predecessor. Notice that straightening causes complex curves to become simpler curves before they are converted to straight lines.

• *Rotate*—Performs two kinds of transformations: rotating and skewing. Dragging a corner handle with the arrow cursor rotates the selection freely. If you do this with Snap turned on, it's easy to rotate in 90-degree (and smaller) increments. Dragging a center handle with the arrow cursor slants the selection. See Figure 3.7.

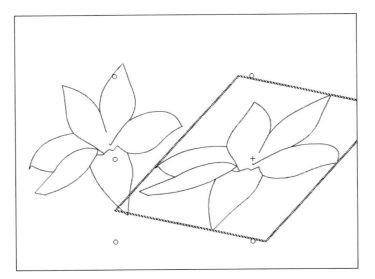

Figure 3.7
Slanting and rotating with the Rotate modifier.

- *Scale*—Corner handles resize the selection in all dimensions simultaneously. Press Shift while scaling with the corner handle to preserve the proportions of the original. Dragging the center handle shrinks or stretches in a single dimension. See Figure 3.8.

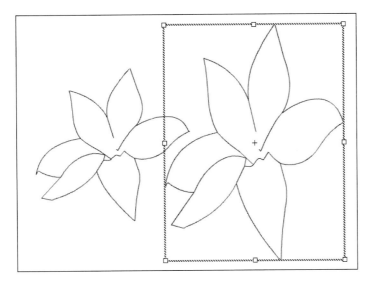

Figure 3.8
Scaling and stretching with the Scale modifier.

Lasso Tool

To choose the Lasso tool, click on its icon in the Toolbox or press the "L" key. The cursor changes to a lasso. The Lasso tool lets you shape freehand selections; in other words, they can be any shape. If you don't end the selection marquee where you started it, it will close automatically. The shape you select will autoedit any shapes you encircle on the canvas, but without affecting overlays (groups and symbols).

Starting a new selection with the Lasso tool, unlike the Arrow tool, drops the current selection and starts a new one. If you need to select multiple areas, press Shift before making subsequent selections. You can deselect all by clicking anywhere in the frame with the lasso cursor.

The Lasso tool has two options that seem to have nothing whatever to do with the Lasso tool or with making selections. These are the Magic Wand modifiers, and they work only on imported bitmapped (GIF, JPEG, or PNG) images.

Lasso Tool Modifiers

When you select the Lasso tool, its modifiers appear in the lower section of the Toolbox. See Figure 3.9. Here are the functions of the Lasso tool modifiers:

Figure 3.9

The Lasso tool modifiers are the Magic Wand (left), the Magic Wand options, and the Polygon Lasso mode.

- *Magic Wand*—Modifies color areas of a bitmap. You must first select the bitmap and break it apart (choose Modify|Break Apart).

- *Magic Wand options*—Opens a dialog box. Threshold sets the range of colors that will be chosen for recoloring. Smoothing lets you select the level of smoothing.

- *Polygon Mode*—Lets you select an area by clicking to draw straight lines between points. Making a selection can be much faster when you don't need to follow the precise curves of an edge when making a selection.

Line Tool

The Line tool now appears as a separate tool rather than as a modifier for the Pencil tool. The Line tool is used to draw straight lines by clicking to place the start point and dragging to place the end point.

If you draw lines with the Snap modifier turned on, a large snap circle will appear by the cursor when lines are drawn at right angles. If the Snap modifier in the Toolbar is pressed, Snap is active. To turn it off, click it. Turning off Snap allows you to draw straight lines at any freeform angle from the preceding line. Figure 3.10 shows two polygons. At left is a polygon drawn with the Line tool when Snap is turned on. At right is a polygon drawn with Snap turned off.

Figure 3.10

Two polygons. The one at left was drawn with Snap turned on. The one at right was drawn with Snap turned off.

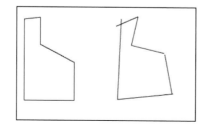

Line Tool Modifiers

When you select the Line tool, its modifiers appear in the lower section of the Toolbox. See Figure 3.11. Here are the functions of the Line tool modifiers:

- *Color*—Displays a palette of 216 Web-safe colors. (Works the same as the Text tool's Color modifier. See the section on Text-tool modifiers.)

- *Line Thickness*—Lets you draw a line of any thickness between hairline (H) and 10 points. You can choose any preset size from the menu or enter any whole number or decimal-point size up to the 10-point limit.

- *Line Style*—Lets you choose from a number of styles, including solid, dots, dashes, and "natural media" styles. You also can create custom line styles. However, you should be aware that the non-solid line styles are complex shapes that will geometrically increase the size of your data file and, therefore, are best avoided especially when designing for the Web.

Figure 3.11
The Line tool modifiers.

Text Tool

To choose the Text tool, click on its icon in the Toolbox or press the "T" key. The cursor changes to an A with a crosshair at the upper left. The Text tool is used to enter text.

Text is always entered as an overlay so it won't dissect graphics on the underlying canvas (unless you break the text apart). Another advantage of text being entered as an overlay is that you can edit it any time.

To edit text, select it with the Text tool and drag across the portion that you want to edit. You can now enter new text, replace text, or use any of the Text tool modifiers to change the selected text.

In Figure 3.12, the text was entered, the brush strokes were painted on top and partially highlighted, and then the font size and style were changed. The brush strokes immediately appeared behind the letters because the brush strokes were painted on the canvas, and the text is always an overlay unless it's broken apart.

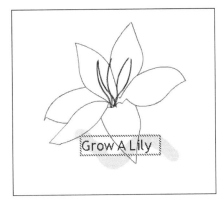

Figure 3.12
Text is automatically grouped when entered.

You can scale text to any proportionate size by dragging the handle. See Figure 3.12.

You can also edit text as shapes. To do this, choose Modify|Break Apart from the menu bar. The text will become checkered to indicate that it is selected, as in Figure 3.13.

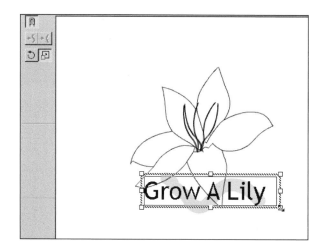

Figure 3.13
Text immediately after it has been broken apart.

Immediately after text or an object has been broken apart or ungrouped—while it is still checkered as in Figure 3.13—the shapes are still temporarily "floating" above the canvas. To avoid auto-editing the underlying shapes on the canvas, press Cmd/Ctrl+G or choose Modify|Group. You can then continue to edit the group independently by selecting it and choosing Edit|Selected from the menu bar.

When you've selected an ungrouped or broken-apart underlay, it immediately becomes part of the image on the canvas. Letters have to be selected individually because dragging a marquee or using a Lasso would result in selecting other, contiguous shapes as well. See Figure 3.14.

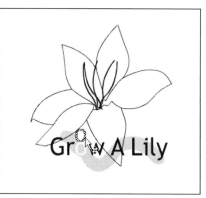
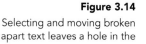

Figure 3.14
Selecting and moving broken apart text leaves a hole in the underlying shape.

Even if you select text individually and move it, you will leave holes in the shapes that were touching it. See Figure 3.15, and notice that the Arrow tool has been used to reshape an edge of the *y* in the word *Lily*. After text has been broken apart, it can be edited just like any other shapes in Flash.

Figure 3.15
Editing the edges of broken-apart text after individually selecting letters.

The Text tool in Flash 4 creates three kinds of text: label, block, and editable text fields. Label text expands from the cursor to accommodate as much text as you type. (Its name comes from the fact that it's a very useful way to enter callout labels on a drawing.) (See Figure 3.16.) To enter label text, choose the Text tool from the Toolbox or press the "T" key; then click where you want the label to appear.

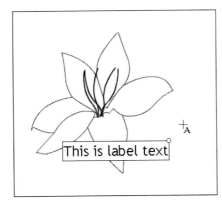

Figure 3.16
Entering label text.

To enter block text, choose the Text tool, and drag the cursor to indicate an area large enough to accommodate the paragraph you want to enter. Block text looks like Figure 3.17, and is the mode you will usually use for creating headlines, banners, and blocks of copy.

You can change block text to label text, and vice versa, by double-clicking on the small handle at the upper-right corner of the text-edit frame. If the handle is round, you are in label mode; if it's square, you are in block mode.

The new text-entry mode in Flash 4 is called *editable text*: text fields that can be accessed by a Web-site visitor. These fields are used to enter data or to

Figure 3.17
Entering block text.

display Flash variables that will be fed to database collection software located on your organization's server or be sent to be used externally with CGI, Cold Fusion, ASP or other server-side languages. Combined with the new internal scripting of Flash 4, these text entry fields provide a new level of interactivity completely in Flash. These fields can be used to collect information from visitors. They can also be used to designate positioning for dynamic text that will be fed from Macromedia Generator. Such dynamic text can, for example, quote current prices for a catalog item (such as one of the tools in the Tool & Garden catalog), traffic conditions on Highway 880, or the date-ability quotient of the visitor.

To enter editable text, click on the Text tool's Text Field modifier, and then click at the point where you'd like the text to start (see Figure 3.18). For user-editable text to be recognized as a text-entry field by a Web browser, you will need to set and identify variables, as explained by John in Chapter 11. To display text properties: select the text, right-click (Windows) or Control-click (Mac) to open the in-context menu, and choose Properties. The Text Field Properties dialog box appears (see Figure 3.19).

You can turn a regular text field into an editable text field at any time. Use the Arrow tool to select the text field that you want to change. Then choose the Text tool and select the Text Field modifier.

Flash's text can be displayed in the authoring environment as anti-aliased at any time. Actually, Flash graphics can be displayed in the authoring environment in three ways: Fast, Smooth, and Text Smooth. Only the latter

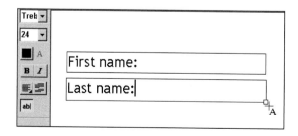

Figure 3.18
Entering user-editable text fields.

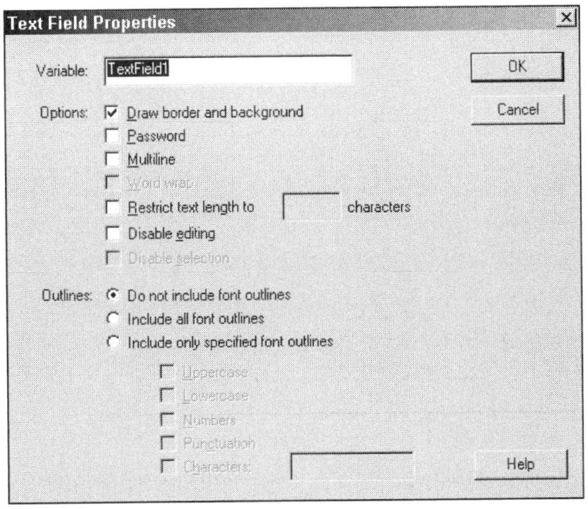

Text Field Properties
Variable: TextField1
OK
Cancel
Options: Draw border and background
Password
Multiline
Word wrap
Restrict text length to characters
Disable editing
Disable selection
Outlines: Do not include font outlines
Include all font outlines
Include only specified font outlines
Uppercase
Lowercase
Numbers
Punctuation
Characters:
Help

Figure 3.19
The Text Field Properties dialog box.

displays text as anti-aliased. Figure 3.20 shows the same text as in Figure 3.19, but with Text Smooth turned on. To turn on anti-aliasing for text, choose View|Antialias Text from the menu bar.

Grow A Lily
You can do it in your sleep
Grow A Lily
You can do it in your sleep
Grow A Lily
You can do it in your sleep

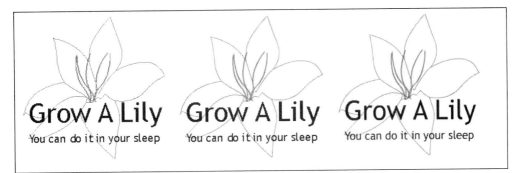

Figure 3.20
The image at left is displayed in Fast mode; at center, it is displayed in Smooth mode; at right, it is displayed in Text Smooth mode.

You can change the size and proportion of text without breaking it apart. To do this, do one of the following:

- Choose Modify|Transform|Scale.
- Choose Modify|Transform|Scale and Rotate.
- Choose the Arrow tool and use its Scale modifier.

Figure 3.21 shows text that has been stretched in a single dimension. Using this method to scale text does not remove its overlay status.

Text Tool Modifiers

When you select the Text tool, its modifiers appear in the lower section of the Toolbox. See Figure 3.22. Here are the functions of the Text tool modifiers:

- *Font*—Opens a Font menu so you can choose any font installed on your system. You can change fonts within a block or label by highlighting the text and choosing a new font. You can also change fonts with the Modify|Font command.

Figure 3.21
Text stretched in a single dimension with the Scale command.

Figure 3.22
The Text tool modifiers.

- *Font Size*—Opens a menu so you can change the font size. If you don't find the size you want on the menu, you can enter any number you like in the Font Size field.

- *Color*—Displays a default palette of 216 Web-safe colors. These are the best colors to use when you're designing for any 256-color display because this palette avoids colors that are used by the system or browser. You aren't limited to this palette, however. You can create your own colors by clicking on the Palette icon at the top of the color palette. The Flash Color Chooser will appear, and you can pick from as many colors as your display will allow. You can use this Color dialog box to change the standard palette by choosing a color and then clicking on the New or Change buttons. Clicking on New adds a color, and clicking on Change changes the color of any selected swatch in the palette. If you want a specific RGB value, you can enter numbers directly in the R, G, or B boxes. Both of these Color dialog boxes are shown in Figure 3.23.

- *Bold*—Toggles Bold on and off. If you click on this button before you enter any text, all the text you enter will be bold. You can also highlight any amount of text after you've entered it and then click on the Bold button to change it to bold and vice versa. Only the highlighted text will be changed.

- *Italic*—Toggles Italic on and off. Works just like the Bold toggle.

- *Alignment*—Opens a menu with four alignment options: left-aligned, centered, right-aligned, or justified.

- *Paragraph Properties*—Opens a dialog box (shown in Figure 3.24) that lets you set margins, indentation, and line spacing by any of the acceptable units of measurement. (The default is pixels.) Acceptable abbreviations for unit types are px for pixels, pt for points, cm for centimeters, mm for millimeters, and " for inches.

- *Text Field*—Allows you to create a user-editable text field.

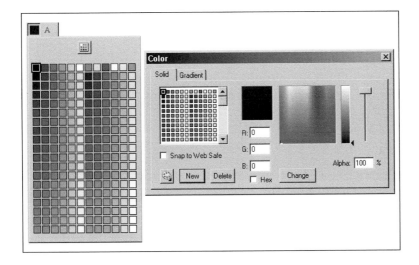

Figure 3.23
The Color dialog box.

Figure 3.24
The Paragraph Properties
dialog box.

Pencil Tool

To choose the Pencil tool, click on its icon in the Toolbox or press the "P"
key. The cursor changes to a miniature pencil (unless Line is the chosen
pencil mode, in which case the cursor changes to a small crosshair).

The function of the Pencil tool is drawing lines. One of the differences between the Pencil tool and the Brush tool is that the pencil line is always
down the center of the stroke, whereas the brush stroke actually fills, outlined by an invisible pencil. When you change the shape of a line, no matter
how thick, you are moving its centerline.

Pencil lines are always drawn on the canvas unless you first enter Group
Edit mode (press Cmd/Ctrl+G) while nothing is selected. When you draw on
the canvas, as soon as you draw one line across another, all lines are cut at
the intersection. Also, any sharp changes in the direction of your stroke will
cause Flash to create a corner point (terminate one line and start another).
In Figure 3.25, each line was made with a single stroke. I have selected
alternate lines to show how Flash terminates and starts lines.

When you use the Pencil tool to draw lines, the lines will take certain shapes,
which depend on several factors (discussed in more detail in other sections
of this chapter):

• The settings you have chosen in the Drawing Assistant

• The Pencil mode you have chosen

• The rough shape you indicate as you draw the line

Figure 3.25
Single-stroke lines made with the Pencil tool.

Figure 3.26
The Pencil tool modifiers.

Figure 3.27
The menu for the Pencil Mode modifier.

Practice drawing lines in different modes until you get a feel for how Flash interprets strokes at various settings. A few minutes of practice will give you a pretty good (and invaluable) knowledge of what to expect.

As is true of all shapes created in Flash, you can change the course and curvature of lines at any time after drawing them. You can also change the style of existing lines at any time with the Ink Bottle tool.

Pencil Tool Modifiers

When you select the Pencil tool, its modifiers appear in the lower section of the Toolbox. See Figure 3.26. Here are the functions of the Pencil tool modifiers:

* *Pencil Mode*—Opens a menu with three options (see Figure 3.27).

  * *Straighten*—The most versatile mode. It recognizes shapes, straightens lines that are nearly straight, smoothes curves, and joins any short wavy lines. Straighten mode recognizes the following shapes: rectangles, ovals, semicircles, and ninety-degree curves.

  * *Smooth*—Softens curves and reduces the number of wiggles in unsteadily drawn lines. Smoothing also reduces the number of line segments.

  * *Ink*—Leaves lines pretty much as you drew them but with some slight smoothing.

* *Color*—Works the same way as the Text tool's Color modifier. For details, see the section on Text tool modifiers.

* *Line Thickness*—Lets you draw a line of any thickness between hairline (H) and 10 points. You can choose any preset size from the menu or enter any whole number or decimal-point size up to the 10-point limit.

* *Line Style*—Lets you choose from a number of styles, including solid, dots, dashes, and "natural media" styles. You can also create custom line styles.

The Power Of Custom Line Styles

The Line Style dialog box (Figure 3.28) is a powerful tool for giving personality to your drawing strokes. To see what I mean by that, look at Figure 3.29.

Each line in Figure 3.29 has a custom line style applied to it. To open the Line Style dialog box, pull down the Line Styles modifier menu and choose Custom. In Table 3.1, I describe each of the custom line styles.

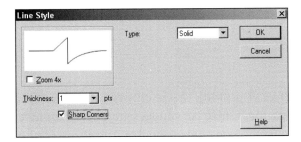

Figure 3.28
The Line Style dialog box.

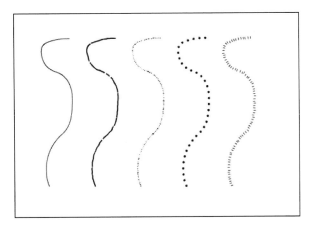

Figure 3.29
Several customizations (solid, dashed, dotted, ragged, and stippled) applied to the same line.

Table 3.1 Custom line styles.

Style	Variables	Description
Solid	Thickness and Sharp Corners only. These two variants are available for all line types.	The default line type. Creates a solid line. Specifying Sharp Corners breaks the line any time the curve reverses direction.
Dashed	Length of dash. Space between dashes.	A steady line of uniform thickness with regular intervals between dashes of a specified length. Be sure there's enough space between dashes to accommodate line thickness.
Dotted	Dot spacing.	Evenly spaced dots of the specified thickness.
Ragged	Pattern (7 variations), Wave Height (4), Wave Length (4).	Gives an "unsteady hand" or arty look to your strokes. Variations are numerous enough to keep Van Gogh happy.
Stippled	Dot Size (4), Dot Density (4), Variation (4).	Also gives an arty look that can resemble anything from charcoal to a mezzotint to etching.
Hatched	Thickness (4), Space (4), Jiggle (4), Rotate (4), Curve (4), Length (4).	Drawn with spaced vertical line segments that can vary from regular to a random freehand look.

Brush Tool

The Brush tool "paints" fills with either a solid color or a gradient. (See Figure 3.30.) The area that is painted in overlapping strokes becomes one single shape whose edges you can edit as if they were lines. To choose the Brush tool, click on its icon in the Toolbox or press the "B" key. The cursor changes to a brush.

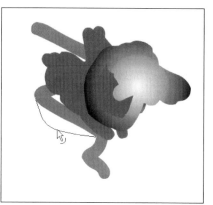

Figure 3.30
Strokes made with the Brush tool.

Each of the nine brush shapes can be set to 10 different sizes. Flash doesn't, however, provide any means for you to make custom brush shapes or to use brushes that are larger than 10 pixels in diameter.

Use the Brush tool when it's more natural and intuitive for you to paint a shape or colors than it is for you to outline and fill them. Better yet, draw the silhouette of your subject with the Pencil tool, fill it with the Bucket tool, and then add interior details with the Brush tool.

Remember that brush strokes can be reshaped, smoothed, straightened, and transformed with the Arrow tool.

The moment you paint a brush stroke atop another shape, you have altered (cut a hole in) the underlying shape. To avoid this, press Cmd/Ctrl+G or choose Modify|Group when there is nothing selected. Then your strokes will be overlaid. Using this method, you can overlay strokes within overlaid strokes.

Brush Tool Modifiers

When you select the Brush tool, its modifiers appear in the lower section of the Toolbox. See Figure 3.31. Here are the functions of the Brush tool modifiers:

Figure 3.31
The Brush tool modifiers.

- *Brush Mode*—Opens a menu with several options (see Figure 3.32).

  - *Paint Normal*—Paints on top of and auto-edits any other shapes on the same canvas or in the same group.

- *Paint Fills*—Paints on the canvas and on any fills (including brush strokes) but won't paint or otherwise affect any pencil lines.

- *Paint Behind*—Paints only those parts of the canvas that aren't covered by other shapes.

- *Paint Selection*—Paints only those portions of active selections covered by a brush stroke.

- *Paint Inside*—Paints only inside the selected shape.

- *Pressure*—Activates variable brush sizes for pressure-sensitive pads.

- *Color*—The same Color modifier used for the Text, Pencil, Ink Bottle, and Bucket tools.

- *Brush Size*—Opens a menu with 10 brush sizes, from 1 to 10 pixels in diameter.

- *Brush Style*—Opens a menu with nine options for brush shape and angle.

- *Fill Lock*—A toggle. Lets each gradient fill act as if it were a hole that looked through to a layer in which the full frame had been filled with the gradient.

Figure 3.32
The menu for the Brush Mode modifier.

Ink Bottle Tool

To choose the Ink Bottle tool, click on its icon in the Toolbox or press the "I" key. The cursor changes to a miniature ink bottle. You use the Ink Bottle to change the style of existing lines. Choose the Ink Bottle, use its modifiers to pick or to customize the line style (see the preceding section, "The Power Of Custom Line Styles"), and click on the line or lines whose style you want to change.

Ink Bottle Tool Modifiers

When you select the Ink Bottle tool, its modifiers appear in the lower section of the Toolbox. See Figure 3.33. Here are the functions of the Ink Bottle tool modifiers:

- *Color*—Works the same as the Color modifier for the Text tool.

- *Line Thickness*—Lets you draw a line of any thickness between hairline (H) and 10 points. You can choose any preset thickness from the menu or enter any whole number or decimal-point size up to the 10-point limit.

- *Line Style*—Lets you choose from a number of styles, including solid, dots, dashes, and "natural media" styles. You can also create custom line styles.

Figure 3.33
The Ink Bottle tool modifiers.

Figure 3.34
The Paint Bucket tool modifiers.

Figure 3.35
The Gap Size menu.

Figure 3.36
The Dropper cursor changes to show whether it is ready to pick up a line style or a fill. Note the Pencil and Bucket sub-icons.

Paint Bucket Tool

The Paint Bucket tool is used to fill any area enclosed (or partially enclosed) by a pencil line or to refill selected strokes and fills with a different color, gradient, or bitmap. To choose the Paint Bucket tool, click on its icon in the Toolbox or press the "U" key. The cursor changes to a paintbucket icon.

You can fill several filled objects with a single new fill in a single click. First, select all the fills (or filled objects) that you want to change. Then choose the Paint Bucket tool, use the modifiers to choose the fill you want to use, and click in any one of the selected fills. The other selected fills will change simultaneously.

Paint Bucket Tool Modifiers

When you select the Paint Bucket tool, its modifiers appear in the lower section of the Toolbox. See Figure 3.34. Here are the functions of the Paint Bucket tool modifiers:

- *Color*—Yep, it's the same old Color modifier.

- *Gap Size*—Opens a menu with several options (see Figure 3.35).

  - *Don't Close Gaps*—Choose this when you want to make sure that the fill doesn't accidentally fill areas that were meant to be blank. This isn't always obvious in complex drawings.

  - *Close Small Gaps*—Similar to the previous choice, but a bit more forgiving when you meant to enclose an area but didn't quite make ends meet. Gaps must be extremely small for the fill to take effect.

  - *Close Medium Gaps*—Good for when you've been a little sloppy about enclosures or when you want some artistic license in choosing whether or not all your fills need to be completely outlined. Medium gaps are still pretty tiny.

  - *Close Large Gaps*—Gaps that you can actually see without your glasses. This option still won't fill objects with gaping gaps, though.

- *Gradient Lock*—Locks the gradient to the size of the movie frame.

- *Gradient Transformation*—Lets you scale and rotate the gradient.

Dropper Tool

To choose the Dropper tool, click on its icon in the Toolbox or press the "D" key. The cursor changes to an eyedropper.

Use the Dropper to copy the properties of one entity to another. The Dropper picks up either the line style or the fill, depending on the location of the cursor. The Dropper cursor changes sub-icons to show you whether it is ready to pick up a line style (Pencil sub-icon) or a fill (Brush sub-icon). See Figure 3.36.

Once you've picked up a line style or a fill, the cursor changes to either the Paint Bucket or the Ink Bottle to show you what types of entities you can change. There are no modifiers for the Dropper tool.

Eraser Tool

Erasing auto-edits the erased shapes, subdividing them into new shapes, as shown in Figure 3.37. To choose the Eraser tool, click on its icon in the Toolbox or press the "E" key. The cursor changes to an eraser.

Figure 3.37
These flower parts were part of the same shape before an eraser stroke passed through.

The Eraser tool erases lines and fills. It can be customized to erase just lines, just fills, just the selected fills, or just the fill on which you start erasing. Use the Eraser modifiers to select one of five sizes and to set the eraser shape.

Eraser Tool Modifiers

When you select the Eraser tool, its modifiers appear in the lower section of the Toolbox. See Figure 3.38. Here are the functions of the Eraser tool modifiers:

- *Eraser Mode*—Opens a menu with several options (see Figure 3.39).

  - *Erase Normal*—Erases any line or fill that you brush over.

  - *Erase Fills*—Erases only fills, and leaves lines intact.

  - *Erase Lines*—Erases only lines, and leaves fills intact.

  - *Erase Selected Fills*—Erases only fills that have been selected, but won't erase selected lines. If you want to erase particular lines, select the previous option and be careful.

  - *Erase Inside*—Erases only fills inside the enclosed area from the point where you start erasing.

- *Faucet*—A toggle. Acts like a "reverse bucket fill" by eliminating any line, fill, or selection on which you click. Multiple selections will all be erased if you click on any one of them.

- *Shape/Size*—Opens a menu with five sizes of circles and rectangles.

Note: The Eraser can erase only lines and fills on the canvas; it cannot erase overlays. If you need to erase part of an overlay, select the overlay and either choose Edit|Edit Selected to edit the overlay, or choose Modify|Break Apart to return the overlay to the canvas.

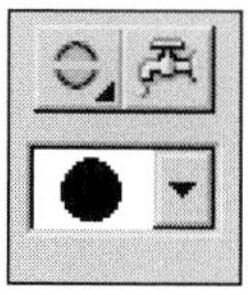

Figure 3.38
The Eraser tool modifiers.

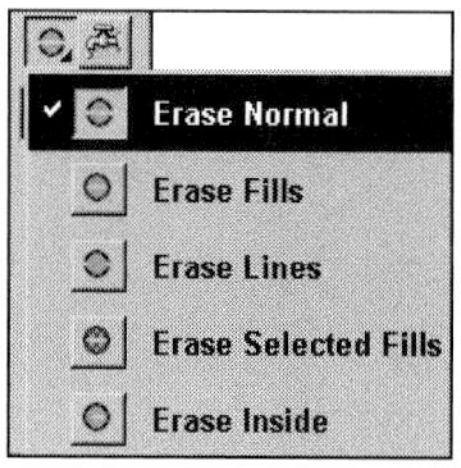

Figure 3.39
The menu for the Eraser Mode modifier.

Figure 3.40
The Magnifier tool modifiers are Zoom In (+) and Zoom Out (-).

Hand Tool

The Hand tool is used to move (pan and scroll) the canvas within the Flash window. To choose the Hand tool, click on its icon in the Toolbox or press the "I" key. The cursor changes to a hand.

When you press the Spacebar, the Hand tool becomes active regardless of which tool has already been chosen. When you release the Spacebar, the already chosen tool re-activates. When you double-click on the Hand tool, the entire canvas is made to fit within the window.

There are no modifiers for the Hand tool.

Magnifier Tool

To choose the Magnifier tool, click on its icon in the Toolbox or press the "M" key. The cursor changes to a magnifying glass.

When you select the Magnifier tool, its modifiers appear in the lower section of the Toolbox. See Figure 3.40.

The Magnifier tool works pretty much like similar tools in other programs. In Flash 4, you can activate the Hand tool while you're zooming in. When the Magnifier is in Zoom In mode, you can zoom out by pressing Opt/Alt before clicking with the Magnifier.

To zoom in, press the "M" key and click to zoom in at 100 percent magnification increments, centered at the spot where you clicked. You also can drag a rectangle to indicate the area of the movie you would like to make as large as possible. As soon as you release the mouse button, the image magnifies to the degree you have indicated.

To zoom out with the Magnifier tool, you click on the Zoom Out modifier. Dragging a rectangle with the zoom-out cursor actually zooms *in*—even in Flash 4.

You also can change magnification by choosing View|100% (which scales the drawing to actual size), View|Show Frame (which shows the entire movie frame), or View|Show All (which zooms the drawing to its limits, without regard to frame size).

Flash's Drawing Aids

To help you visualize the spacing and measurement of your drawing elements, Flash provides several drawing aids: grids, guide layers, Snap, and alignment. The following sections highlight Flash's drawing aids.

Grids

Flash's grids lie beneath anything you draw. They don't print, and they aren't visible in exported movies (that is, anything your audience might see). Figure 3.41 shows a drawing in which the grid is visible.

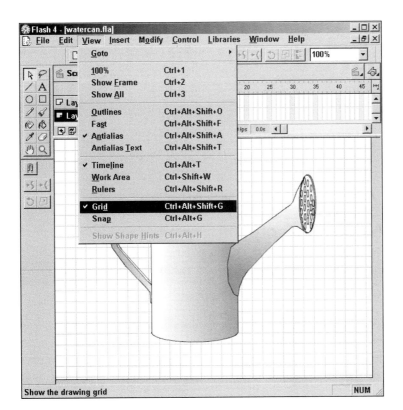

Figure 3.41
Drawing with the grid visible.

You can turn the grid off and on in two ways:

• Choose View|Grid from the menu bar to check or uncheck it.

• In the Movie Properties dialog box, check or uncheck the Show Grid box.

There is no longer a Show Grid icon in the Toolbar, nor can you press Cmd/Ctrl+Opt/Alt+G.

Flash's grids are always square and spaced according to the settings you choose in the Movie Properties dialog box. (To open the Movie Properties dialog box, choose Modify|Movie from the menu bar.) You may want to change the color of the grid to contrast more with the content of your movie. Grids are shown in light gray by default, but in the Movie Properties dialog box you can make them any color. (See Figure 3.42.) The Movie Properties dialog box also lets you choose the units of measurement.

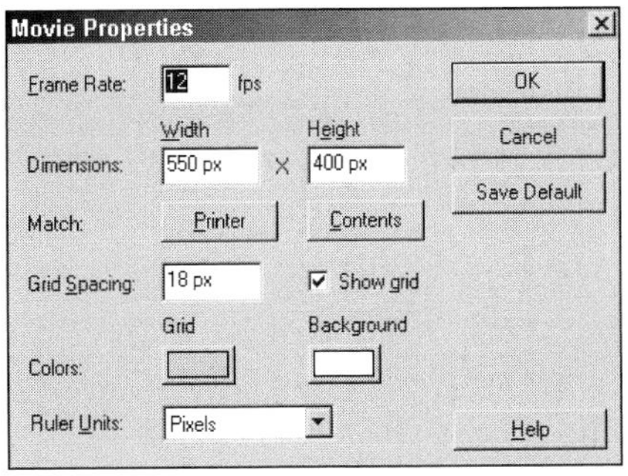

Figure 3.42
The Movie Properties dialog box.

Guide Layers

A guide layer is a special kind of layer that doesn't print, export, publish, or interfere with anything you draw on other layers. On the other hand, you can draw anything on a guide layer, such as motion paths, asymmetrical grids, guide lines, or positioning Xs.

To create a guide layer, place the cursor on an existing layer name bar and right-click (Windows) or Ctrl+click (Mac). A Layers menu will pop up. Choose Insert Layer. This creates a new layer. Draw any kind of guides you want on it. Then, to designate this layer as a guide layer, choose Guide from the Layer menu.

You also can make a guide layer into a regular layer. To convert a guide layer to a regular layer, choose Guide again from the Layer pop-up menu. The checkmark next to Guide will disappear.

Snap

Snap causes tools to jump to the nearest grid point, end point, or midpoint of another line or to the edge of another entity—whichever is closer. You know when Snap is turned on because a small circle appears at the tip of the selection tool's arrowhead. An easier way to know that Snap is on is to look at the magnet icon (either in the Toolbar or in the Arrow modifiers). You toggle Snap on and off by clicking on the Snap modifier in either location or by choosing Snap from the View menu.

To adjust the Snap distance, choose File|Assistant. In the Assistant dialog box, select a snap-distance option from the Snap To Grid drop-down list box. Options range from Off to Normal to Always Snap (see Figure 3.43).

Figure 3.43
Choose a snap distance from the Assistant dialog box.

Alignment

Flash's Align dialog box (choose Modify|Align) lets you align selections (a shape or any part of it) with one another. You can specify that they be aligned horizontally or vertically, and you can specify for each direction that they be aligned by their centers or by their sides. You can also specify that all objects be made the same size and that they be spaced evenly. Figure 3.44 shows drawings before and after they have been aligned horizontally by their centers, sized equally, and spaced evenly.

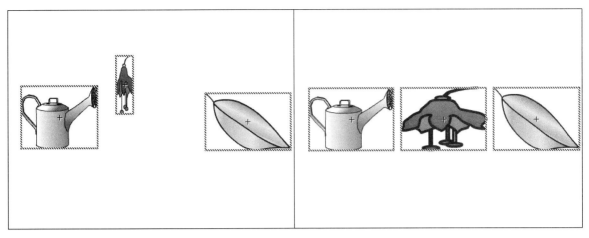

Figure 3.44
Before and after the objects are aligned, sized, and spaced with the Align command.

To align several objects, first select them. You can use any of the selection tools, and you can even use the Lasso to select parts of objects. From the menu bar, choose Modify|Align. In the dialog box (Figure 3.45), set the parameters you want by clicking on the appropriate diagram icons and then clicking on OK.

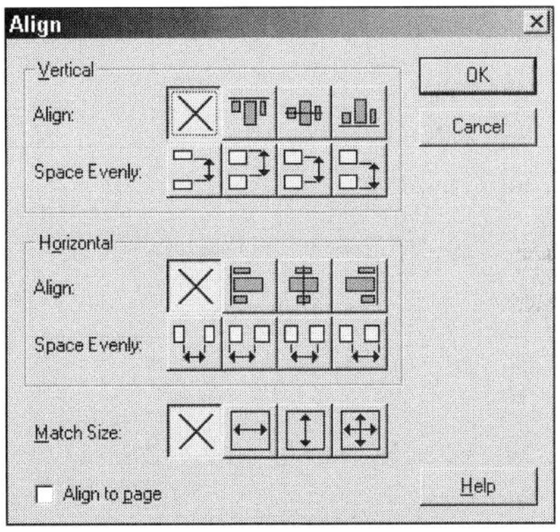

Figure 3.45
The Align dialog box.

Commands And Tools For Refining Drawing Elements

Flash has several ways of helping you to fine-tune the way your lines and strokes appear. These commands and tools are found in several places in the Flash interface, and many of them duplicate functions that can be found in the tool modifiers. The next sections focus on commands and tools that will help you refine your drawing elements.

Assistant

You can activate the Assistant and change its settings at any time. To do so, choose File|Assistant to open the Assistant dialog box.

Note: When you size all objects to the same size, they are sized to match the largest object selected. Also, the objects will all be placed inside the movie frame, regardless of how you set alignment and spacing. This can mean that all the objects end up stacked on top of one another. If this happens, press Cmd/Ctrl+Z.

Use the Assistant dialog box to set preferences for drawing and shape-recognition tolerances. The options are Snap To Grid, Connect Line, Smooth Curves, Recognize Lines, Recognize Shapes, and Click Accuracy. All of these options can be set to on, off, or one of several tolerance settings (see Figure 3.46). Each tolerance setting doubles the value of its predecessor. Normal is the default for all tolerance settings.

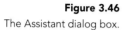

Figure 3.46
The Assistant dialog box.

The degree to which a tolerance setting works depends entirely on screen resolution. In other words, the settings function on the basis of the number of screen—not file resolution—pixels. So, one way to instantly get tighter control without resetting the Assistant is to zoom in. If you want a freehand line to be less smooth, zoom in; if you want the line smoother, zoom out.

Transformations

The Transform command on the Modify menu lets you reshape or re-orient any active selections, including overlays. Though you can do the same thing with the Scale and Rotate modifiers as with the Scale and Rotate commands on the Transform sub-menu, other commands on this menu are unique. (See Figure 3.47.) Here are the commands on the Transform sub-menu:

- *Scale*—Works exactly like using the Scale modifier for the Arrow Tool. A bounding box appears around the selection. Drag the corner handles to size both horizontally and vertically. Center handles squeeze or stretch.

- *Rotate*—Works exactly like using the Rotate modifier for the Arrow Tool. A bounding box appears around the selection. Drag the corner handles to spin the selection. Center handles slant the selection.

- *Scale and Rotate*—(Cmd+Opt+S/ Ctrl+Alt+S) Opens a dialog box that lets you enter an exact percentage to scale and/or a precise degree of rotation. (Precede the number with a hyphen [-] to indicate counter-clockwise rotation.)

- *Rotate Left*—Turns the selection counterclockwise by 90 degrees.

- *Rotate Right*—Turns the selection clockwise by 90 degrees.

- *Flip Vertical*—Turns the selection upside down but doesn't reverse it from left to right (as rotating it would).

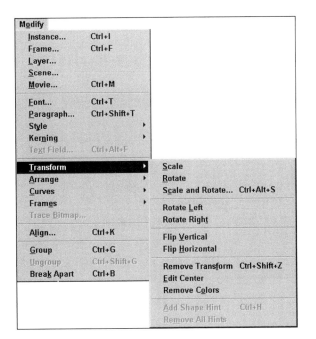

Figure 3.47

The Transform sub-menu.

- *Flip Horizontal*—Swaps left to right.

- *Remove Transform*—Returns the selection to its original state, regardless of how many transformations (uninterrupted by other commands) you have made since the current selection.

- *Edit Center*—Lets you move the center of an overlay. Pay attention: This means any overlay—a group, a symbol, text, or (of course) a selection. This command is dimmed unless you've moved or transformed the current selection. Selections that have been moved can be considered a kind of overlay because they temporarily float above the drawing until they are deselected, at which point they drop back down onto the canvas and auto-edit any other object they intersect. The purpose of the Edit Center command is to give you more control over transformations by changing the center around which they are calculated. As soon as you choose the Edit Center command, a cross appears at the current center of the selection. Drag this cross to move the center.

- *Remove Colors*—Changes the color of fills to white and the color of lines to black. However, the fill is still there, you just won't be able to see it if it's against a white background with no outline surrounding it.

- *Add Shape Hint*—Active only when you are tweening between two selected symbols. Shape hints are placed at the corresponding locations of shape features in the start and stop frames to help in tweening.

- *Remove All Hints*—Removes all shape hints.

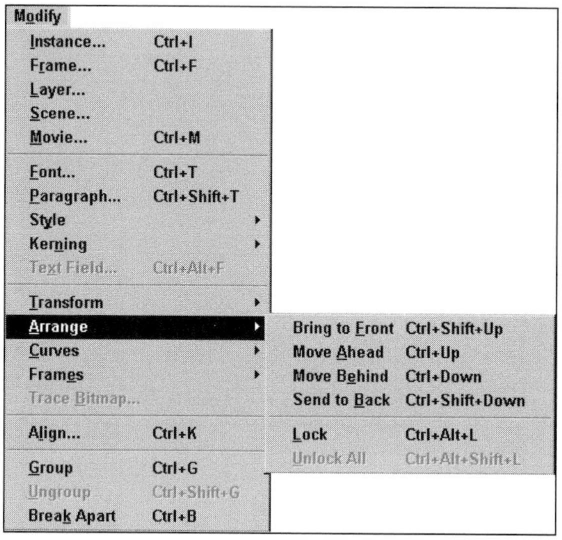

Figure 3.48
The Arrange sub-menu.

Arrange

The Arrange command lets you control the stacking order of overlays within a given layer. If you want to stack shapes without letting them auto-edit one another, you must first make them into either groups or symbols (both are overlays).

To change the stacking order of an overlay, choose Modify|Arrange, and then choose whether you want the overlay to move to the top of the stack (Bring to Front), to the bottom of the stack (Send to Back), up one layer (Move Ahead), or down one layer (Move Behind). As you can see in Figure 3.48, each of these commands has a hot key.

Curves

Also on the Modify menu is a command called Curves that brings up a sub-menu. In Flash 4, this sub-menu has three new commands: Lines to Fills, Expand Shape, and Soften Edges. Here are the commands in the Curves sub-menu:

- *Smooth*—Works the same way as the Smooth modifier in the Toolbar.

- *Straighten*—Works the same way as the Straighten modifier in the Toolbar.

- *Optimize*—Cmd+Opt+Shift+C or Ctrl+Alt+Shift+C. Reduces the number of curves used to define the shape of an item. Optimized curves result in small file sizes, which result in better animation performance. Optimization can be applied multiple times. See Figure 3.49.

- *Lines to Fills*—Changes lines to brush strokes. You can then use the Ink Bottle to place outlines around the original lines. Also allows you to fill lines with gradients or to reshape the edges of lines. See Figure 3.50.

- *Expand Shape*—Increases or decreases the overall size of a shape by a specified amount. Doesn't always produce predictable results.

- *Soften Edges*—Radiates "rings" from the outline of a shape, with each ring filled with a lighter color. Rings can be made to radiate in or out. You can also specify the number of rings (steps) for the softening effect. See Figures 3.51 and 3.52.

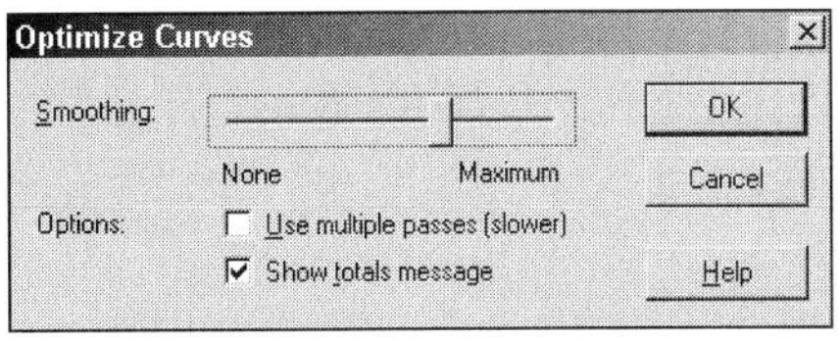

Figure 3.49
The Optimize Curves dialog box.

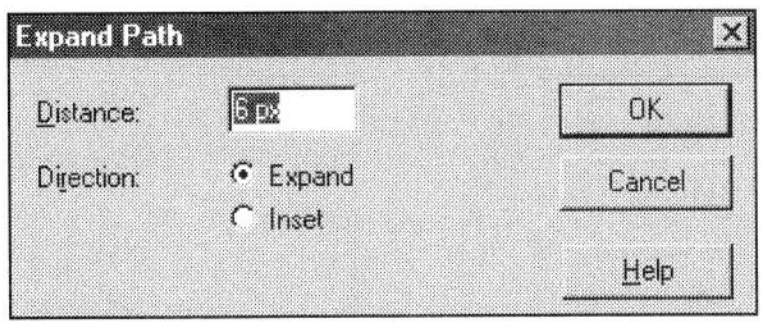

Figure 3.50
The Expand Path dialog box that appears when you choose the Expand Shape command.

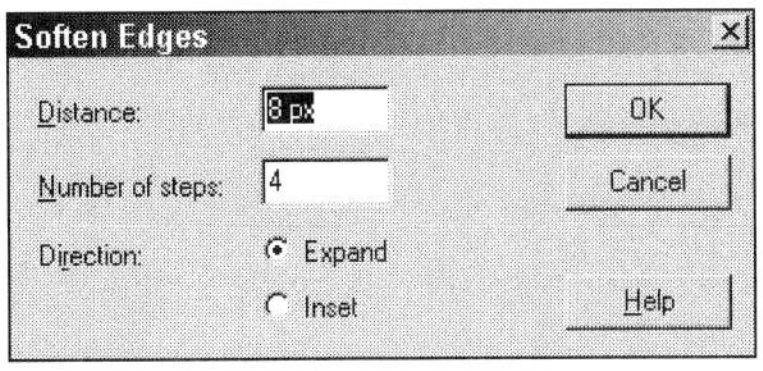

Figure 3.51
The Soften Edges dialog box.

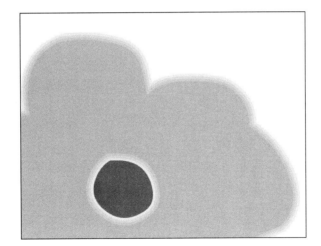

Figure 3.52
The edges of this flower have been softened.

Assembling And Disassembling Groups And Symbols

It is very easy to turn selections into overlays—either groups or symbols. Both have the advantage of being editable in a space of their own, where the edit won't affect any other part of the movie.

It is possible to have groups within groups. Following are instructions for working with groups:

- To create a group, make your selection and press Cmd/Ctrl+G (or choose Modify|Group).

- To edit a group, select the group you want to edit and choose Edit|Edit Selected, or double-click on the group after it has been selected.

- To quit editing a group, choose Edit|Edit All, or double-click in an empty space within the frame.

- To disassemble a group, press Cmd/Ctrl+Shift+G, or choose Modify|Ungroup.

To create a symbol, make your selection and choose Insert|Create Symbol. A Symbol Properties dialog box opens to allow you to name the symbol and to check whether this symbol should behave like a graphic, a button, or a movie clip. Symbols can include multiple groups, other symbols, and even multiple frames. (Animated symbols are discussed in Chapter 5.) If you check the Button Behavior box, the symbol will automatically inherit four frames, the first being the current selection and the other three blank. The symbol also will know how to behave like a button when you pass the mouse over it or click on it. You are then free to add any content you like to the other three frames. Chapter 6 provides more detail on this procedure.

Inserting Objects Created In Other Applications

You can place components—such as images, charts, or spreadsheets—from other applications directly into a Flash movie. To do this, choose Insert|Object from the menu bar, and choose the application type that you want to include.

What You Shouldn't Expect From Flash As A Drawing Program

Flash is such a strong and easy-to-use drawing program that you may come to think that there's nothing you can't do with it. That might actually be true, if you put enough effort into it, but for certain types of drawings, or for drawings incorporating certain types of elements, you can work faster and more efficiently in a more specialized, vector-based drawing program.

Flash doesn't have unlimited drawing sizes or the precision needed for architectural and engineering drawings. It has no 3D modeling capabilities, either.

More expensive illustration programs—such as CorelDRAW, Adobe Illustrator, and Macromedia FreeHand—accept a variety of third-party special-effects plug-ins, do morphs or blends from one shape to another, and allow you to control cyan, magenta, yellow, and black (CMYK) output to printers, color separators, and printing presses. Also, drawing in an illustration program allows you to manually control curved lines with great precision because you can use the visible control points and handles that Flash (in the interest of more intuitive sketching) eschews.

Moving On

In Chapter 4, I'll give newcomers to Flash, as well as those who feel they can't even draw a straight line, a few tutorials that should start to make you feel comfortable with at least doing the workaday drawing chores. You'll even learn how to trace photos and how to use pre-drawn art. Even if you're experienced with illustration software, you'll benefit from these tutorials as a means of becoming comfortable with Flash's unique approach to drawing.

PART II

PROFESSIONAL FLASH TECHNIQUES

BASIC DRAWING TECHNIQUES 4

KEN MILBURN

*This chapter teaches you how to draw in Flash—
even if you've never been able to draw any other
way. If you're already experienced with creating
graphics in Flash, you'll probably want to skip ahead
to the advanced drawing techniques covered in
Chapter 5. But if you're a Web programmer who
wants to become more fluid at drawing, you may
want to practice with these tutorials several times.*

Drawing in Flash is more like drawing on paper than is any other drawing program, such as Illustrator or FreeHand. Instead of drawing by carefully placing points and then dragging control handles to shape curves, you simply sketch freehand. But drawing in Flash is also very different from drawing on paper: Flash recognizes your attempts at drawing basic geometric shapes, such as circles and squares, and it straightens or smoothes your freehand lines.

This chapter shows you how easy it is to draw with Flash. It also gives you lots of tips for controlling and refining your drawings, as well as ways of making them look more professional.

You Don't Need Drawing Talent

Even though Flash is a very useful drawing program, you don't have to be a practiced artist to produce worthwhile results. You have several options for including artwork in your Flash creations.

- You can use clip art. Plenty of professional-looking artwork is available at reasonable prices on CD-ROM. Hundreds of similar libraries are also available from other companies, such as SoftKey and Corel.

- You can hire someone else to draw your art, which can then be scanned. You can buy a decent scanner for less than $100 these days. If you don't have a scanner and don't want to buy one, you can go to your local quick-print shop (such as Kinko's or PIP). The shop can scan the work for you, or you can rent time on the scanner and computer and save the work to a disk. The scanned image should be saved as a 24-bit Portable Network Graphics (PNG) file so that if you import it into Flash and then decide to publish it as is, you won't be losing data due to the fact that Flash recompresses and resamples imported bitmaps. Once you have the image in your computer, you can use the Trace Bitmap command to convert the scanned image into a Flash drawing.

- You can hand-trace imported bitmaps. This is a technique that many animators and technical illustrators use. Later, I'll show you how to turn a sketch into a Flash drawing.

- You can use libraries of symbols that were created by other artists. These symbols are already Flash drawings, so you'll have less editing to do. You'll find a whole library of Carole Omalyev's "Tool & Garden" drawings on the CD-ROM that accompanies this book.

- You can simply modify text in a graphical way. Remember that text can be any size or color in Flash, and text can be moved or turned into a button.

You may not have to draw in Flash, but you'll want to learn to edit in Flash—especially if you don't draw very well. The exercises that follow will show you how to adapt your drawings to your needs by tracing and editing existing art.

Limbering Up Before The Exercises

In the next few sections, you will get some hands-on practice with Flash's drawing tools and commands. In order to save space and to teach you the quickest way to do things, I have used shortcut keys in lieu of menu commands. Flash has a shortcut key for each tool in the Toolbox, and all of these shortcuts are listed in Appendix A. (Remember that the tool shortcut keys are not case sensitive.)

Also, I may not take the time to explain all the reasons for everything I'll ask you to do. My fear is that if I did, the exercises would appear to be ponderous, and you would be afraid to do them. So you'll have to take it on faith that I'm teaching you productive habits that will serve you well in a variety of situations, and not just the one at hand. As you complete each exercise, the reasons for a procedure will usually reveal themselves.

Flash 4 has some good news for those of you who are used to working in other graphics programs, such as Illustrator, CorelDRAW, FreeHand, and Photoshop. By default, you now make cumulative selections by pressing the Shift key before you add to the selection. If you still prefer the old method of adding to selections automatically, you can make that choice in the Preferences dialog box.

Flash also has some "gotchas" when you're making selections. If you accidentally click on the canvas (any part of the frame that's not covered with a graphic line or fill), all selections will be dropped. If you're asked to do something with a selected item and nothing happens, double-check to make sure that you haven't accidentally dropped the last selection you clicked on. The simple way to check is to choose Edit|Undo (Cmd/Ctrl+Z) a few times to see if a selection marquee reappears. It's also the easy way to regain a selection if you should accidentally drop it.

The other selection quirk is that if you make a selection with the marquee tools (Arrow or Lasso), all other selections will be dropped. So how do you add to a selection you've made with a marquee tool? You press and hold Shift while you surround another area.

You will have a much easier time completing these exercises if you've read Appendix A to familiarize yourself with the program's various functions. Pay special attention to the Timeline components: layers, frames, keyframes, pop-up menus, Onion Skin buttons, and the frame pointer.

A NOTE ABOUT FILE EXTENSIONS

All of the graphics files that were created for you to use in these exercises are referred to by their file names and extensions (needed by Windows versions of graphics programs). However, Windows Explorer won't show you those extensions unless you have File Extensions turned on. Please turn on File Extensions if you are a Windows user, and leave them that way while you're using this book. To turn on File Extensions, open Windows Explorer and choose View|Options. In the Options dialog box, make sure that "Hide MS-DOS File Extensions" is *not* checked. (See, you're already learning good habits.) Now you'll know which graphics file has been saved in FLA (Flash movie) or JPEG format and why there seem to be two files with the same name. You'll also learn to name files so that they can be read with equal ease on both Macs and PCs. (Name everything according to the MS-DOS 8.3 convention—eight characters for the file name, a period, and a three-character extension describing the file type.)

Another thing you should know about file extensions—even if you're a Mac user—is that HTML requires the use of extensions in order to recognize legitimate file formats for Web graphics. So, for instance, if you have a link to a JPEG file that doesn't have a .jpg extension, the browser will not recognize it.

Tracing A Scanned Sketch

One of the easiest ways to learn to draw is to trace an existing drawing. The original drawing gives you a sense of where you've been and where you need to go. You don't have to guess at shapes and proportions; you just move your pencil over what's already there. If you're not very good at drawing, your erased lines and excess scribbling won't show up in the final Flash 4 tracing, either.

Tracing has advantages for many professional artists, too. They can sketch on paper much faster and more expressively than they've learned to draw on the computer.

Finally, paper is a universal and highly transportable medium. If a client sketches an idea on a napkin, it's easy to digitize it into a file that can be read by any computer in the world. By the way, virtually any scanner— even hand-held scanners and fax machines—can scan images with enough fidelity that you can easily trace them. It's possible, these days, to buy a workable monochrome scanner for less than $50, and a more than adequate color scanner for under $100.

In the first exercise, you will trace my sketch and then use Flash's "artificial-intelligence" features to make it look as though a real pro had done the job. Follow these steps:

1. Choose File|Import. In the Import dialog box, find bugsketch.png on the CD-ROM.

2. If you import a sketch that's too large for the current movie, it's best to rescale it in an image editor such as Fireworks or Photoshop. If your movie is set to the default size (550×400 pixels), the sketch will be way too big. Choose the Arrow tool and then the Scale modifier. Press the Shift key and drag one of the corner handles to reduce the

size of the sketch. If necessary, you can drag the bug to the position you want it to occupy on the canvas. See Figure 4.1.

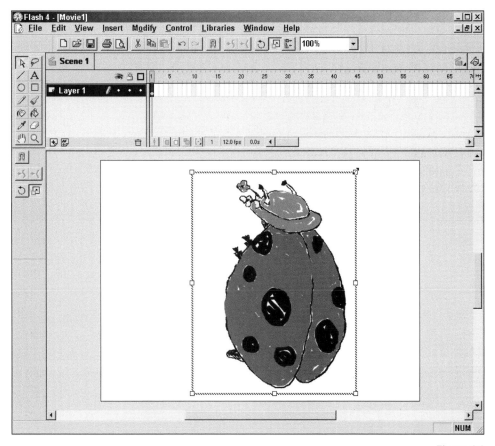

Figure 4.1

The imported scan, scaled to fit the canvas.

3. When you've finished scaling the sketch, click outside it to de-select it.

   Now we are going to use one of the several techniques that Flash provides for tracing an image without touching the original. First, you can trace anything that you first turn into a symbol or a group because such overlays become independent entities. However, it's hard to turn a symbol off when you want to see the original drawing. A better idea is to turn the sketch into a regular symbol, use the Alpha command to lighten it so that your tracing will stand out, and then put it on a separate layer. Then you can turn the layer on and off. We'll use that technique later in this chapter. The easiest technique is onion-skinning, as described in the next few steps.

4. Choose the Arrow tool, and place the cursor in the Timeline in the second frame. Ctrl+click (Mac) or right-click (Windows) to pop up the Frames menu (see Figure 4.2). Choose Insert Blank Keyframe.

Properties...	
Create Motion Tween	
Insert Frame	F5
Delete Frame	Shift+F5
Insert Keyframe	F6
Insert Blank Keyframe	**F7**
Clear Keyframe	Shift+F6
Select All	
Copy Frames	Ctrl+Alt+C
Paste Frames	Ctrl+Alt+V
Reverse Frames	
Synchronize Symbols	

Figure 4.2

The Frames menu.

Figure 4.3

The Convert To Symbol command and the Symbol Properties dialog box.

5. Notice the icons in the Timeline Status Bar at the bottom of the Timeline. The leftmost one—a tiny red person—is the Center Frame icon. Immediately to its right is the Onion Skin icon. Click on it. You'll see a grayed image of the ladybug sketch. Now you can trace in this second frame, and the ladybug will act as a perfect template. If you want to see your drawing without the template, just click on the Onion Skin icon, and the image of the scanned sketch in Frame 1 will disappear.

6. Now you can start tracing. Trace the outlines of the important parts of the ladybug first. Don't color them in yet. Choose the Pencil tool and the Smooth modifier. The other modifiers should be set as follows: Color = black, Line Width = H(airline), Line Style = Solid.

7. Trace the hat. Get the silhouette shape, and draw the division between the crown and the brim. (Don't include the antennae or the flowers. Don't color inside.)

8. Save the hat outline as a symbol by choosing Insert|Convert To Symbol (shown in Figure 4.3). In the Properties dialog box, type "Hat" in the Name field and click on OK. You can now re-use this hat in as many different places in the movie as you like.

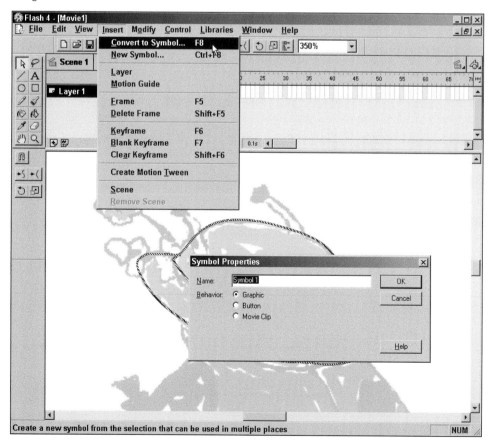

9. Repeat Steps 7 and 8 to trace each part of the ladybug. You should trace and save as a symbol only one instance of each element that is repeated: a spot on the back, an antenna, a foot, a flower, and so on. In Figure 4.4, you can see each of the objects that has been traced and saved as a symbol.

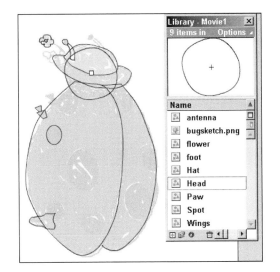

Figure 4.4
The portions of the body that have been traced appear as dark lines. Each portion has been saved as a separate symbol.

10. Save the file as ladybug1.fla. On some other occasion, you will be able to open this file as a Library (symbols only), place any of the symbols in the active movie, and then edit the symbols for line style and fill. Keep the movie open after you've saved it—we still have more to do.

    Now we're going to edit the symbols in the current Library so that they're filled with the colors we want and so that they're repeated in the drawing as many times as needed.

11. Click on the outline with the Arrow tool to select the head. Because it's a symbol, a square marquee appears around it. We want to fill the head with black, so we need to edit it. Press Cmd/Ctrl+E. Whoa! The rest of the picture disappears! That's okay. Now we can change the symbol without affecting the rest of the picture.

12. Choose the Paint Bucket tool. In the modifiers, the Color Swatch should be black. If it's not, click in the Color Swatch. The Swatches appear. Click on black.

13. Place the Paint Bucket cursor inside the head outline and click. The head fills with black. At the same time, the symbol in the Library changes color. See Figure 4.5.

14. Go back to editing the entire movie so that you can see the other symbols. To do that, press Cmd/Ctrl+E again. When you do that when a symbol is selected, you go into Edit Symbol mode. When you do it in Edit Symbol mode, you go into Edit Movie mode.

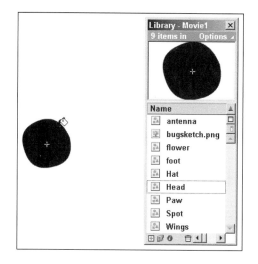

Figure 4.5
The black-filled ladybug head. Notice that it's simultaneously filled with black in the Library.

15. Use the same technique to select the flower. We need to duplicate this symbol before we fill it because we need two colors of flowers. (There is a more efficient technique for coloring instances of symbols, but it has limitations. We'll discuss that technique in Chapter 7.)

16. With the flower selected, press Cmd/Ctrl+D (Edit|Duplicate). A copy of the flower symbol appears, and it is now the selected overlay. Press F8 to execute Modify|Convert To Symbol. In the Symbol Properties dialog box, enter "flower2" as the symbol name. Now we can fill this flower with yellow.

17. You probably jumped ahead and tried to fill the flower, but it didn't work. That's because the center of the flower and its petals were automatically grouped when we saved the symbol. Before you can fill them, you have to break them apart. Click on one of the lines to select the group, and press Cmd/Ctrl+B. Now you see that the lines themselves are selected. Press Cmd/Ctrl+Shift+A to deselect all.

18. You may want to reshape these petals slightly because this flower is a different symbol. Reshaping the petals will make the symbol duplication less obvious. To do this, choose the Arrow tool. Move the pointer close to the lines until you see a curve symbol appear alongside the Arrow icon. This indicates that you can drag the shape of the line. Continue doing this until you've changed the shape of the flower slightly.

19. Now it's time to color the flower. Choose the Paint Bucket tool. Pick a deep yellow from the Swatches. In the modifiers, choose Fill Large Gaps. Click inside the petals, and all but the center of the flower fills with yellow.

20. With the Paint Bucket still the active tool, choose a dark brown color for the center of the flower. Click inside the center of the flower to fill it. If you like, you can choose the Brush and, from the Brush modifiers' Brush Size menu, choose a fairly small brush. Paint a few pistils protruding from the center of the flower.

21. When you've finished editing the flower, press Cmd/Ctrl+E. You're back to editing the movie. Notice that your flower is now yellow in the Library as well. Drag the flower's name from the Library list onto the canvas. Another yellow flower appears. Drag both flowers to their rightful positions on the brim of the hat. See Figure 4.6.

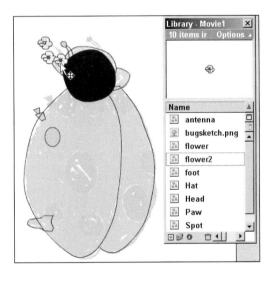

Figure 4.6
The ladybug with two yellow flowers on her hat.

22. Apply what you've learned in Steps 15 through 21 to the rest of the symbols. Save the body for last so that its filled shape doesn't hide the other symbols or keep you from seeing where to place them. Also save the spot for next to last so I can show you how to change instances of a symbol—and so they'll all end up on top of the stack of symbols. A little further on, I'll show you how to arrange the rest of the symbols so that they appear in the right stacking order.

23. Edit the spot so that it's filled with black. From the Library list, drag one spot for each spot in the sketch. Position each spot so that it rests atop a corresponding spot on the sketch.

24. From the Arrow tool modifiers, choose the Scale modifier, and click on one of the spots. Drag the handles until you've shaped that spot to match the underlying spot in the sketch. You can scale each of the spots in turn without ever having to deselect.

25. You'll need to rotate some of the spots. Choose the Arrow tool's Rotate modifiers, click to select a spot, and drag the corner handles to rotate until the spot is at the angle you want. You can also skew the spot by dragging the center handles. Play with these modifiers until you feel comfortable with them.

26. The last symbol you need to work with is the body. Select it and press Cmd/Ctrl+E to edit the symbol. You want to fill the two separate sides of the body (they're really wings) with a gradient in order to give them some shape and depth. (You may be tempted to use the gradient in more places, but keep them at a minimum to boost Web animation performance.)

27. Choose the Paint Bucket tool. Click on the Swatch to display the Swatches palette. Unless you've changed it, you'll see a red circular gradient at the bottom of the palette. Click on it to select it. Fill each wing with the same gradient, as shown in Figure 4.7. (You'll learn how to edit gradients in Chapter 6.)

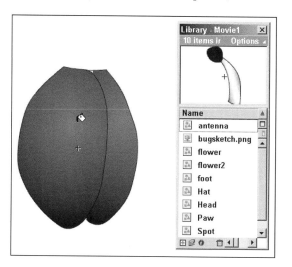

Figure 4.7
Filling the wings with a circular gradient.

28. Press Cmd/Ctrl+E to return to Edit Movie mode.

29. Uh, oh. What a mess. Some symbols are sitting atop symbols that should be partially hiding them. The head is a big sinner in this respect, but it's an easy problem to fix. Select the head. To move it lower in the stacking order (behind other symbols), press Cmd/Ctrl+Down

Arrow. To move it higher, press Cmd/Ctrl+Up Arrow. If you want to move a symbol (or any other selected entity) all the way to the top or bottom of the stack, press Cmd/Ctrl+Shift+Up Arrow or Down Arrow.

30. When you've finished arranging everything, click on the Onion Skin icon so that you can see the drawing on its own. Select Frame 1. Ctrl+click/right-click to pop up the Frames menu, and choose Delete Frame. This makes the movie much smaller by getting rid of the no longer needed bitmap sketch.

31. You also need to get rid of the bitmap stored in the Library. Go to the Library and select bugsketch.png. At the top right of the Library window, you'll see a small arrow just to the right of the word "Options." Click on the arrow to pull down the Library menu, and choose Delete (see Figure 4.8). This makes the FLA working file smaller. (I've kept it in the file on the CD-ROM in case you need it for reference).

32. Now save the movie under a new name so that you still have the empty symbols that you created before you filled them. See the finished drawing in Figure 4.9.

Figure 4.8
The Library Options menu.

Figure 4.9
This ladybug is the Tool & Garden site's mascot.

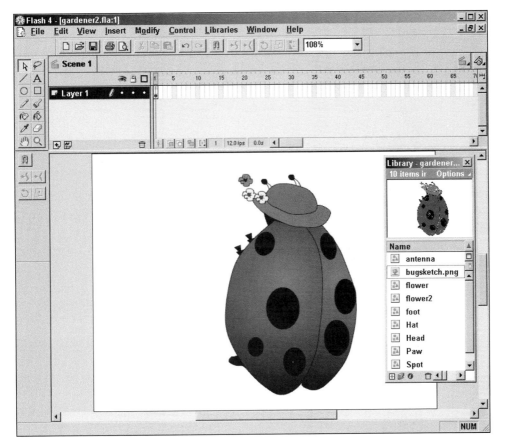

SAVING DRAWINGS AS SYMBOLS

If this is just one of the many drawings you'll use in your movie, you should save the drawing as a symbol. To do so, choose Insert|Symbol. A dialog box will appear that allows you to name and categorize the symbol.

Modifying Clip Art

Almost all of the vector clip art in the universe can find its way into Flash. The most direct route is for the clip art to be already available on CD-ROM or on the Web in Adobe Illustrator (AI) or Encapsulated PostScript (EPS) format. Otherwise, load the clip art into the program it was designed for, export it as an AI or EPS file, and then import it into Flash. Users of CorelDRAW should especially take advantage of this route because CorelDRAW comes with thousands of useful clip art images. If you don't have the originating program, use a graphics-file-translation program, such as HiJaak Pro for Windows NT/95. Macintosh users will have a tougher time finding vector file translation software; however, all of the illustration programs can translate between all of the most popular formats. The granddaddy of all graphics file translators, DeBabelizer, translates only between bitmapped image formats.

Another option is to auto-trace bitmapped clip art. You can do this in Flash with the Modify|Trace Bitmap command, but you can also use the auto-tracing capabilities built into most illustration programs (notably FreeHand or CorelDRAW). You can also use Adobe's dedicated auto-tracing program, Streamline. All of these options are attractive if you want more editing control over the traced image than Flash allows with the Trace Bitmap command.

The problem with commercial vector clip art, especially if it is free or inexpensive, is that it tends to be produced as quickly as possible. So curves are made of many straight lines, and grouped objects overlap in ways that make them hard to edit because it's difficult to see how they're constructed. Again, Flash comes to the rescue!

The following exercise will show you a procedure in Flash that makes it easier to edit clip art than if you had first imported it into a more advanced illustration program such as Illustrator, CorelDRAW, or FreeHand.

JUST SAY NO

If you are opening files from a commercial CD, the files may often have names such as SYMB0001.EPS. This file name indicates that this is a symbol and that it's file number 1. Flash, on the other hand, will think that the numbers indicate sequential frames and will ask if you want to select them all at once. If that happens, just say no.

1. Choose File|Import. From this book's companion CD-ROM, import the file fish.eps. Carole Omalyev drew this fish in Macromedia FreeHand 8 and exported it in Adobe Illustrator 7 format. Freehand 8 has added Flash .swf file export, which even makes exporting gradients from Flash easy. If you have Freehand 8, be sure to get the 8.02 update to benefit from the latest improvements in Flash export. You can download the update free from Macromedia's site.

2. The fish file opens as many grouped objects. You'll know this because when you press Cmd/Ctrl+A to Select All, you'll see several overlapping selection frames. See Figure 4.10.

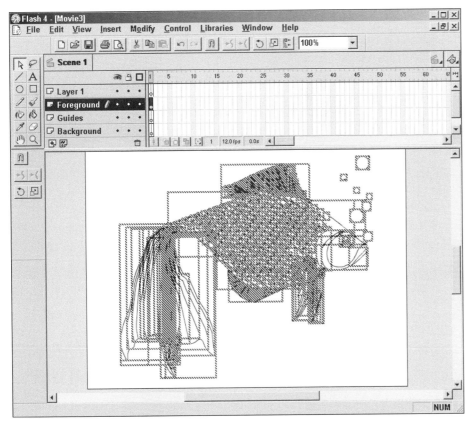

Figure 4.10

The imported clip art, showing the selected groups.

3. While the groups are still selected, press Cmd/Ctrl+G to group all of them into one main group. Because grouping objects puts them on a separate overlay above the canvas, any editing you do to a group will not affect anything on the canvas or in other overlays (such as text and symbols).

4. If you want the object to be a different size, this is a good time to rescale it. Choose the Arrow tool and click on the Scale modifier. Press the Shift key and drag the corner handle of the group until the fish is the size that you're going to need most often in your movie.

5. Next, we're going to simplify the drawing by getting rid of all or most of the fish's scales. (Each of these is a separate object and can be replaced by separate instances of the same symbol, which would have to load into a browser only once in an entire movie.) To re-move scales, you could start by ungrouping the fish, but that would mean that any of its shapes would be automatically merged with any of the shapes already on the canvas of your movie. We don't want that to happen, so we'll do this another way.

EDIT FIRST, DRAG LATER

In illustration programs other than Freehand 8, you can drag and drop vector art into Flash, but many characteristics won't translate properly. If you want to drag and drop vector art into Flash from an illustration program, first edit out all the blends, gradients, and fills. The vector art will be faster to edit in Flash if you have only out-lines to contend with.

Using Flash To Pre-Edit Clip Art

If you own any of those CDs with titles like "800,000 Clip Art Images," chances are great that they'll be very difficult to edit in an illustration program. You can fix these easily in Flash and then do all sorts of editing in your illustration program. Just import an image into an empty Flash 4 movie, and press Cmd/Ctrl+A to Select All. Now press Cmd/Ctrl+B repeatedly until all the groups flatten into one. You'll know when that happens because you won't see any rectangles surrounding portions of the drawing. Press Cmd/Ctrl+Shift+A to deselect everything. All the shapes will drop to the canvas and auto-edit one another. Now press Cmd/Ctrl+A to Select All, and choose Modify|Curves|Optimize. When the Optimize dialog box appears, move the slider to indicate the degree of optimization you want to exert, and click on OK. Most, if not all, of those itty-bitty straight lines that made up the original are now single-vector smooth curves. Now export the movie as an .AI file, and you'll have a much easier time editing it in your illustration program.

Click on the fish. Because the fish is a group, a rectangular marquee surrounds the entire fish to show that it's grouped into a single object. Choose Edit|Edit Selected. Any shapes on the canvas that aren't part of the selected group will be ghosted.

6. Press Shift+click to select a number of fish scales; then press Delete/Backspace to remove them. See Figure 4.11. (Another way to get rid of lots of scales without having to individually select them is to use the Arrow tool or the Lasso tool to drag a marquee around them.) Be careful not to select anything other than scales.

Figure 4.11
Multiple objects are selected. Pressing Delete/Backspace clears the objects from the Workspace.

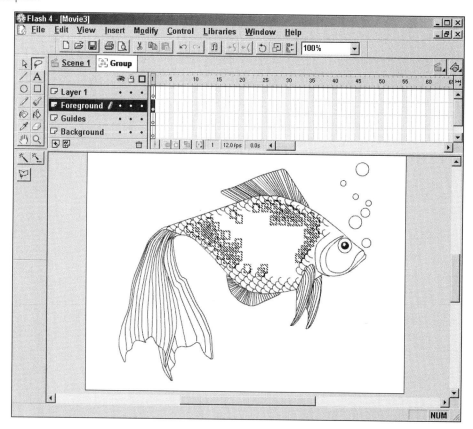

7. You want to keep one scale as a symbol. Select it, press F8, and name it "scale" when the Symbol Properties dialog box opens.

8. After you've eliminated as many scales as you would like, it's easier to continue to simplify the drawing. This drawing contains many fine lines that define the fins. If we get rid of half of these lines, we'll double the performance of this illustration when it's used on the Web. Again, hold the Shift key while you use the Arrow tool to select every other line; then press Delete/Backspace to kill them.

9. Next, look for objects (besides the scales, of course) that can be made from repeated symbol instances. The bubbles and the outer rim of the eye qualify. Select one of the bubbles, press F8, and name the symbol "bubble." Now your fish should look like the one in Figure 4.12.

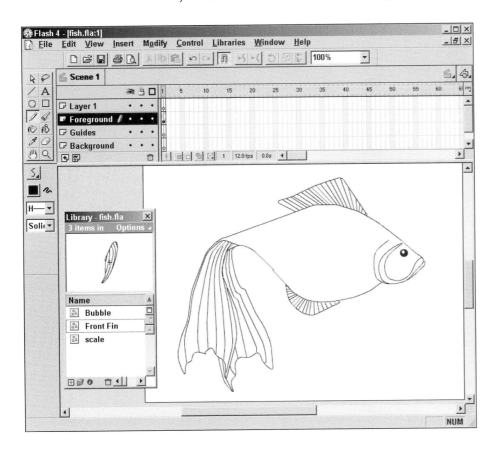

Figure 4.12
The initial stage of the simplified fish, before the symbol instances are put back in.

> ## BEWARE OF THE FANCY STUFF
>
> One of the problems with clip art is that it's likely to be unnecessarily complicated. For instance, a line that could be a single geometric curve may be made of many single segments. This greatly increases file size because there must be a separate data instruction for each line segment. Or, there may be a decorative pattern (such as the scales on the fish) that just isn't needed. Remember, superfluous detail produces a larger file, which results in slower performance.

10. Turn the right front fin into a symbol, and delete the other fin. There will then be a gap in the body of the fish. Choose the Pencil tool, choose H from the Line Width modifier menu, and select Smooth from the Pencil Mode modifier menu. Draw in the gap.

11. Press Cmd/Ctrl+A to Select All. If any fills have been selected, press Cmd/Ctrl+Shift+A to deselect everything; then click inside the areas

that have been filled to delete them. We are doing this because we will insert our own fills after we have smoothed the lines. Also, we don't want to have to smooth the fills at the same time we smooth the lines because overlapping could cause some unwanted detail and increase file size. In Flash, if the fill matches the outline perfectly, there is no cost for the fill. So a very good optimizing technique is once you are done drawing and editing an object, remove either the fill or the outline and reapply them. This ensures that your fill and outline match and do not add to the file size.

12. There's one more very important thing you should do to minimize the number of vectors in the fish drawing. Most imported vector art (especially packaged clip art) contains thousands of straight lines. You can simplify these with the Optimize command, as we did in the exercise above.

    Another technique involves combining these straight lines into longer curved lines by selecting a series of end-to-end lines and then using the Smooth modifier to join them. This technique works only when the angle between lines is less than the amount specified in the Drawing Assistant. (See Figure 4.13.) Open the Drawing Assistant by choosing File|Assistant.

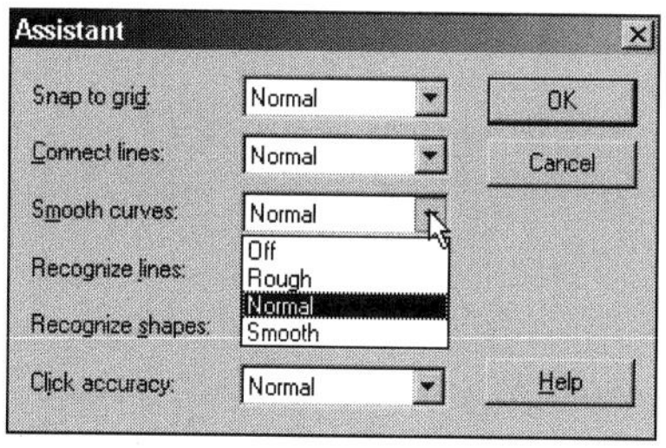

Figure 4.13

The Flash Drawing Assistant. Each item has a list of options from which you can choose stricter or looser control over the various aspects of shape recognition.

13. Now we can optimize the curves in the fish. Press Cmd/Ctrl+A to Select All. Click repeatedly on the Smooth icon in the Toolbar. You will be able to see the fish change shape on screen. At some point, the fish either will become too altered to suit your tastes or will cease to become simplified. Immediately press Cmd/Ctrl+Z to move back a step.

14. Save your file.

15. Now we want to fill the body of the fish and the fins. Click on the Paint Bucket tool, and then click in the Color Swatch box to display the Swatches palette. We want to fill with a custom gradient, so now is a good time to learn how to do that. At the top of the Swatches palette is a small button with an icon of color swatches. This is the Swatches Edit box. Click on it to open the Color dialog box (see Figure 4.14).

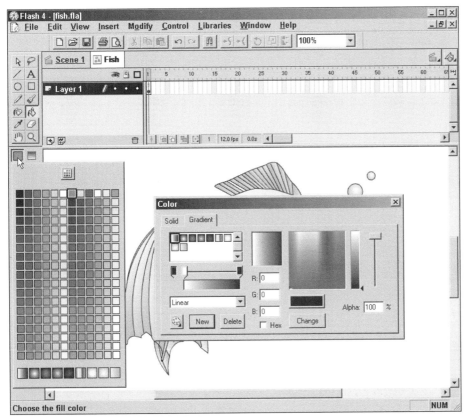

Figure 4.14
The Swatches Edit box and the Color dialog box.

16. Click on the Gradient tab, then click on the small circular red gradient. Below the gradient swatches you'll see some color sliders. Click in the left slider so that you can change its color. Click and drag in the color picker until the color swatch above the Change button is a medium orange. Repeat this step for the other slider color, but make the color a light yellow.

17. You now have a circular gradient that graduates from orange in the center to light yellow on the outside. We want it to be the opposite, so drag the sliders until they have exchanged positions.

18. Click the New button and close the Color dialog box.

19. Because the fish is grouped, you need to edit the group. Choose the Arrow tool and double-click on one of the lines in the fish. There is an open gap under the dorsal fin. Use the Pencil tool to close the gap.

20. Choose the Paint Bucket tool, and click on the Lock Fill modifier (the padlock icon at the bottom of the modifiers). Before you click to fill, be sure to place the arrow in the center of the widest part of the fish's body. Fill each part of the fish's body. Notice that the fill matches in contiguous parts. That's because you chose the Lock Fill modifier.

Note: If you accidentally double-click on a fish scale (or any other editable object), you will have executed the Edit|Edit Selected command for that object. Everything else on the screen will fade by 50 percent, indicating that you can edit only the one small object. To resume editing the scales, choose Edit|Edit All or double-click on a portion of blank canvas that's outside the area of the group. When you're in Edit All mode, all lines and colors are shown at their normal intensity.

21. You need to edit some of your symbols so that you can fill them. Fill them any way you like. If you have trouble making the Paint Bucket tool work, be sure to break the symbol apart before you fill it. If you've forgotten how to do that, just click to select the item and press Cmd/Ctrl+B until only the lines are selected.

22. Put one of the fins and the bubbles back into the picture. To do so, just drag their names out of the Library list onto the canvas and continue dragging until the pieces are in their proper places.

23. Now you can turn the fish into a symbol so that you can put the other front fin behind it. Press Cmd/Ctrl+A, then press F8. Name the fish "fish".

24. Drag the "Front Fin" name from the Library onto the canvas and into position on the fish's body. Then press Cmd/Ctrl+Shift+Down Arrow to send it to the bottom (back) of the overlays stack.

Learning To Draw Freehand With Flash

If you completed the previous exercises, you already have a pretty good idea of what you can accomplish with Flash's drawing tools. This section will show you more tools and familiarize you with their uses.

If you haven't had much drawing practice, you'll have an easier time in Flash than you will either on paper or in other programs. That's because Flash employs several means to make your drawing strokes more steady and professional. It's also because, when it comes to creating art from scratch, Flash has some of the most desirable qualities of both painting and drawing programs.

Paint programs seem a bit more intuitive because you draw in them simply by changing the color of the medium, just as you create an image on paper or canvas. The only difference is that in a paint program, you change the color of individual pixels on a screen, and in traditional media you change the color by applying color (paint, ink, chalk, or whatever) to the surface.

Drawing in Flash is like drawing on paper in that each new line or stroke alters shapes in the image that you put on the canvas. It's also unlike drawing on paper or in a paint program in that you can scale the drawing to any size without losing a speck of resolution. Also, you can easily reshape any existing shape.

To illustrate the differences among drawing programs—and to show how much easier sketching is in Flash (especially for novice artists)—I've drawn a flower in three programs: Photoshop, the classic bitmap editing program (Figure 4.15); FreeHand 8 (Figure 4.16); and Flash (Figure 4.17).

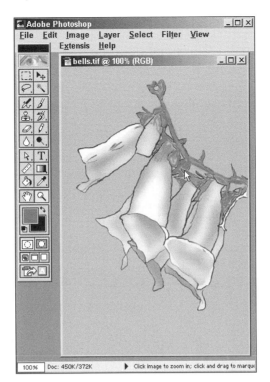

Figure 4.15
A sketch drawn in Photoshop.

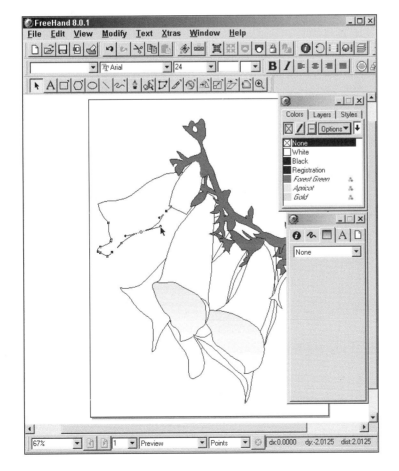

Figure 4.16
The same sketch drawn in
FreeHand.

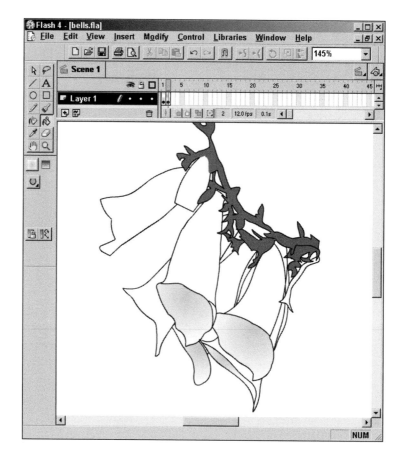

Figure 4.17
The same sketch drawn in Flash.

Photoshop is a paint or bitmapped graphics program. When you paint with an unsteady hand, you get unsteady lines. Also, just as on paper, the only way to edit your sketch is to erase what was already there or to paint over it. There's no way to reshape lines or outlines or to erase part of the graphic without leaving gaps in the picture. If you make this image bigger, the pixels that compose the image get bigger, too.

In the FreeHand drawing in Figure 4.16, you will notice that the curved lines are perfectly smooth. The shape and direction of the lines are controlled by the location of the control points (the small squares that intersect the curves) and by the length and direction of the handles. This isn't a very intuitive method for making a shape, but it offers extremely precise control. It's harder to delete unwanted lines in FreeHand than it is in Flash. (You have to cut the line with the Knife tool, then select the unwanted portion of the line and delete it.)

In the Flash sketch shown in Figure 4.17, it was never necessary to painstakingly edit control points to get the desired curves. The flowers were sketched freehand with the Pencil tool while the Smooth modifier was active. The sketch in Figures 4.15 through 4.17 was drawn the same way, then scaled to give it the right perspective and copied to make the thick edge. Because shapes are automatically divided where they intersect one another, all you have to do to delete unwanted lines is to select them and press the Delete/Backspace key.

The following exercise will show you how to draw a flower pot from scratch. In the process, you'll learn how to draw quickly and effectively in Flash. First, take heed of the hints in the next section.

Hints For Drawing Efficiently

Here are some hints concerning good habits to form when you're drawing in Flash:

- Keep your fingers on the Cmd/Ctrl+Z (Undo) and Cmd/Ctrl+Y (Redo) keys. Flash can misinterpret the shape you're trying to draw and sometimes oversmooth or overstraighten lines. Also, it's easy to accidentally let a line touch another line, thereby joining it or dissecting it. The easiest cure is to undo and then start over by drawing a new shape.

- To draw symmetrical shapes, draw half the unit, copy and paste it, and then flip the copy. To keep it from inadvertently editing any existing shapes, be sure to group the pasted unit before it's deselected.

- Group pasted shapes before you deselect them. Then you can move, adjust, and edit them before you drop them onto the canvas.

- Always draw all the simple shapes independently on a blank canvas. You will find that you'll never have to draw those shapes from scratch again. You will build a library of subjects, drawn in your own style, that you can use over and over again.

Making A Basic Freehand Drawing

In this exercise, you'll draw a flower pot. The exercise contains just enough shapes to let you get used to the Flash drawing tools and their modifiers and to show you how to practice the good habits you are forming. After you've learned to draw simple subjects like this one, you can draw complex scenes by adding new simple shapes.

By the way, this exercise uses simple oval shapes to let you experience the power of Flash's shape recognition. Ordinarily, it would be faster to draw these ovals with the Pencil tool's Oval modifier. Follow these steps to draw the flower pot:

1. Open Flash and choose File|New to create a new movie. You will automatically get a blank frame set to the default settings for a movie. You are now going to draw a rough geometric shape, an oval. If you're as bad at this as I am, there will be a brief moment when your oval looks something like Figure 4.18. Before you draw the oval, read the next step.

Note: It would be easier to draw an oval with the Oval tool, but I want you to get an idea of how Flash's shape recognition works, so please bear with me for the moment. Then you can go back to using the Oval tool. OK?

2. To draw the oval, choose the Pencil tool from the Toolbox. Notice that the bottom of the Toolbox changes to show the modifiers for the Pencil tool. At the top of the Pencil modifiers is a button for a drop-down menu called the Pencil Mode menu. Drop down the menu and choose Straighten. (For some odd reason, Straighten is the mode that Flash uses for shape recognition—whether the shape is oval or rectangular.)

On the frame canvas, draw an oval approximately like the one shown in Figure 4.18. When you complete the loop, the line will automatically transform into a perfect oval. Well, maybe. If you've been really sloppy, press Cmd/Ctrl+Z to Undo, and try again. Flash has multiple Undo and Redo capabilities (with a default of 20 levels), so you can quickly recover from an error.

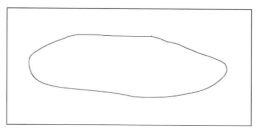

Figure 4.18
The oval before smoothing.

3. Let's assume that your oval is (oops) vertical instead of horizontal and that it's a bit on the chubby side. (This is going to be the profile of the top rim of the flower pot, viewed from an angle slightly above.) No problem.

Choose the Arrow tool (press the "A" key), and click on the oval. The entire oval becomes highlighted with a checkered pattern. Press Cmd/Ctrl+G to group the oval. (Grouping turns the shape into an overlay that floats above the main canvas.) You know this has happened when you see a single checkered selection frame around the entire group (which in this instance is only the oval but could be a drawing with any number of parts, including other overlays).

Make sure that the Snap icon in the Arrow modifiers is enabled. From the Arrow modifiers, choose the Rotate icon. A bounding box with circular handles appears around the oval. Slowly drag the upper-right corner handle in a clockwise direction. The oval rotates in small increments. It is snapping to the grid intersections, even though you don't have the grid displayed. Stop when the oval has a perfectly horizontal orientation.

4. Now, you want to squeeze the oval a bit so that it looks as though you're seeing the pot from a slightly elevated viewpoint. From the Arrow modifiers, choose the Scale icon. The group frame now appears with eight square handles. You can scale the shape in all directions by dragging the corners. Right now, you want to squeeze the shape. Use the arrow to drag either the top or the bottom center handle inward.

5. If you want to scale while preserving the proportions of the original shape, press Shift while dragging. Hold down the Shift key while using the corner handles to scale the oval to the overall size you want.

6. You want to make a rim for the pot. The easy way is to press Cmd/Ctrl+D to duplicate the oval. This pastes the grouped oval so that it won't auto-edit the other oval if you accidentally deselect it.

7. Turn off Snap. (Make sure the Snap icon is not enabled—if it is, click on it.) Drag the oval up so that it is just below the top oval. You can use the arrow keys on your keyboard to move a selection (including a selected group) in one-pixel increments.

8. Now you are going to draw the foot of the pot. Select one of the ovals and press Cmd/Ctrl+D to place another oval group above the canvas. Use the same procedures as in Step 5 to scale this new oval to about two-thirds its original size.

   Then place the new oval so that it is centered below the top oval. You can do this with absolute precision in seconds by using Flash's Align command. Make sure the Arrow tool is still active, and drag a rectangle around the top set of ovals. When they are selected, click on the newest oval to select it. Choose Modify|Align. In the dialog box, click on the icon that indicates that selections will be aligned vertically at their centers. Make sure that no other icons are selected, and click on OK.

9. Copy, paste, group, and align another foot oval, and drag it to just below the original. (See Figure 4.19.)

10. After all the ovals are properly scaled and in position, either select each group individually (click on the shape with the Arrow tool) or press Cmd/Ctrl+A to Select All; then press Cmd/Ctrl+U to ungroup. Doing this drops all the shapes onto the canvas, where any overlapping shapes will auto-edit one another.

OPTIMIZING DRAWINGS

If you want to make your drawings even more Web-efficient, save any repeated geometric shapes (such as the oval in the flower pot drawing) as a symbol, and rescale it for each of the oval sections of the following drawing.

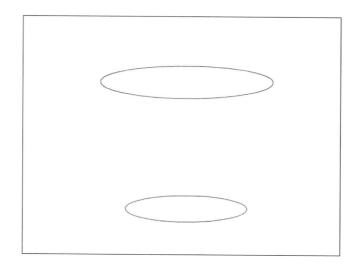

Figure 4.19
The ovals for the foot and lip of
the flower pot.

All you have to do to remove any superfluous lines is to select them
with the Arrow tool and press Backspace/Delete. There's no need to
cut lines or add control points—that happens as soon as one shape
(line, paint stroke, or fill) is laid atop another. This is what is meant
by *auto-editing*.

11. To make it easier to draw the two symmetrical sides of the pot, turn
on the grid. Choose View|Grid, or press Cmd+Opt+Shift+G (Mac) or
Ctrl+Alt+Shift+G (Windows). Count grid spaces to find the center of
the pot. You want to draw a temporary guideline here.

12. Choose the Pencil tool and the Line modifier. Click to start the vertical line that will divide the pot, and Shift+Drag to turn Snap on so
that you can draw an absolutely vertical line. See Figure 4.20.

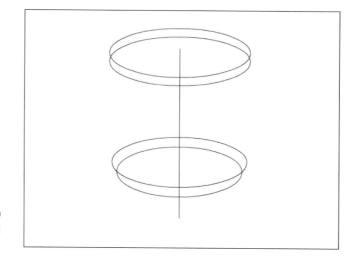

Figure 4.20
The pot with your vertical
guideline in place.

13. Now it becomes easier to draw the sides of the pot. Choose the Pencil tool and make sure that Smooth is chosen from the Pencil Mode menu. With nothing selected, press Cmd/Ctrl+G. The lines you have drawn so far dim to indicate that you have created a new, blank group.

    Draw a curved line from near the lip of the pot to the foot of the pot. If smoothing doesn't give you the profile you want, press Cmd/Ctrl+Z to undo and try again. (It's faster than erasing pencil lines.)

14. One of the pleasant experiences of drawing with Flash is that it's so easy to edit what you draw. When you place the Arrow tool cursor near the end of a line or a corner, a corner symbol appears next to the arrow. When you place the arrow anywhere else along a line, the arrow cursor displays a curve symbol next to it. When you place the arrow inside a selection, a four-way arrow symbol appears, indicating that dragging will move the selection.

    Now that you know all this, shape the line just the way you want it. If you make the line too wiggly or bumpy, select it and repeatedly click on the Smooth modifier button in the Arrow modifier box.

15. When you get the line shaped exactly the way you want it, use the Arrow tool to drag it exactly into place. (See Figure 4.21.)

16. Choose Edit|Edit All. All the shapes return to their normal color.

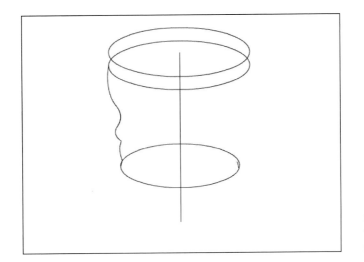

Figure 4.21
The flower pot with the side curve in place.

17. Click on the new edge curve to select it. The group frame appears.

18. The easy way to make sure that the pot is symmetrical is to copy the left side, and then paste and horizontally flip the pasted copy. Then join the copy precisely to the original. Flash makes this child's play.

Press Cmd/Ctrl+C (or choose Edit|Copy), then press Cmd/Ctrl+V (or choose Edit|Paste). A copy of the curved left edge appears, bounded by a selection rectangle indicating that it is a group.

19. Choose Modify|Transform|Flip Horizontal. Click on the Snap modifier. While the lines are still selected, place the cursor at the left end of the topmost line, and drag it until it snaps to the topmost line in the left-hand side of the pot. What you see should look like Figure 4.22. Click anywhere outside the selection to drop it onto the canvas.

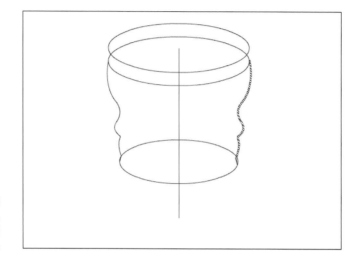

Figure 4.22

The copied and flipped left side of the flower pot, still selected and snapped to the original.

20. Now you can turn off the grid and get rid of the center line. Choose View|Grid. The checkmark next to the grid option disappears, and so does the grid.

    Choose the Arrow tool and select each section of the center line. (Use Shift+click if you've set your preferences this way.) When all the sections have been selected, press Delete.

21. Now you want to fill the pot with soil. Choose the Arrow tool and select the topmost curve of the pot. Press Cmd/Ctrl+C, then Cmd/Ctrl+V. A selected copy of the curve appears near the center of the canvas. Use the Arrow tool to drag the selection into place.

22. Next, you will outline the inside of the pot. You'll use the same techniques that you used to make the edges of the pot:

    • Press Cmd/Ctrl+G to start a new, empty group.

    • Choose the Pencil tool with the Smooth modifier.

    • Draw one side of the inside of the pot.

Choose the Arrow tool and select the line you just drew. Be sure to use the Smooth modifier as many times as necessary. Then copy and paste the line.

When the copy of the left side of the line appears, choose Modify|Transform|Flip Horizontal. Finally, drag the flipped copy into place.

Choose Edit|Edit All. The drawing should now look like Figure 4.23.

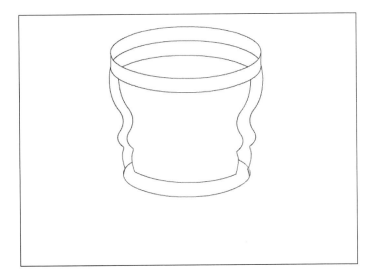

Figure 4.23
The flower pot with the finished lines.

23. Now you will ungroup everything so that any overlapping lines will auto-edit one another. (This procedure makes it very easy to clean up any overlapping or unwanted lines.) Select everything in the image. Either choose Edit|Ungroup or press Cmd/Ctrl+Shift+G.

24. Click in an empty space to deselect everything. To clean up the unwanted lines, choose the Zoom tool and drag a rectangle around any areas that have the small lines you want to remove. When you find a line that you want to eliminate, choose the Arrow tool, select the line segment you want to erase, and press Delete/Backspace. The selected line disappears.

    Keep selecting and deleting line segments until the picture looks like Figure 4.24.

25. The drawing is almost done. Now it's time to add the color that represents the soil. You can do this in two ways: with the Brush or with the Paint Bucket. You'll learn more by using the Brush, so choose the Brush tool. Click on the Brush Mode icon to open the Brush Mode menu, and choose the Paint Inside mode.

26. Click on the color swatch in the Brush modifiers. Drag across the pop-up palette and choose an appropriate color for soil, such as burgundy. Now, just paint to fill. As long as you start your stroke inside the lines you wish to fill, no color will accidentally overlap the lines. Don't you wish your mom had given you such a coloring book?

27. OK, next you'll try filling the pot with the Paint Bucket. But first you have to get rid of the fill you just painted. Press Cmd/Ctrl+Z repeatedly until the pot is empty. Be sure not to undo any of the lines.

28. Choose the Paint Bucket tool. Choose the Close Small Gaps modifier (and you can choose to close larger gaps if you have them). This will permit a fill even if you have gaps between lines that are too small to notice.

29. Click and drag in the color swatch, and choose a burgundy color.

30. Click inside the lines that enclose each area you want to fill. You can see the finished flower pot in Figure 4.24.

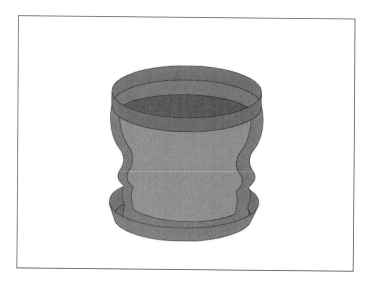

Figure 4.24
The finished, filled flower pot.

31. Drag a marquee around the entire drawing (or press Cmd/Ctrl+A). Then group and scale it to the size you would like.

32. Now, you want to save it to the Library for future use. While the group is selected, press F8 or choose Insert|Convert to Symbol. In the dialog box, type a name for the symbol. Since this isn't a button (not yet, anyway), leave the Button Behavior box unchecked.

33. When you want to use the flower-pot symbol again, do the following: Choose Window|Library. You'll see the flower pot. To copy the

flower pot into this or any other frame, simply drag it onto the canvas. (You can do this as many times as you like without using one speck more RAM for your movie. Furthermore, you'll never have to redraw this flower pot.)

To open the Library from another movie, all you have to do is choose File|Open As Library. When you open the chosen movie, all that opens is its Library, and you can use any of its symbols, sounds, or bitmaps in the current movie. When you do, these items will be added automatically to your current movie's Library.

Drawing With Animation In Mind

In the following exercise, you'll use a pair of very useful techniques to make drawings that you intend to animate. One of these techniques is tracing a photo, which is useful because photos (including movie or video frame captures) can arrest movement so accurately. Also, if you need a drawing of some everyday thing, you can always find one and snap a picture of it (digital cameras are great for this). The other technique is to create overlays for each component of the drawing so that you can move them from frame to frame.

In this exercise, you will trace a photo of a human figure. Drawing people is one of the hardest challenges for non-artists, but you're going to find out how easy it can be. Pretend you shot this photo of one of your co-workers. Actually, I photographed my neighbor, Isabel Reichardt. All the figure's limbs will eventually be converted to individual symbols so that they can be animated later. We start with the photo seen in Figure 4.25.

To trace and animate the figure in the photo, follow these steps:

1. Open a new movie.

2. To import a file contained in a non-Flash (but Flash-compatible) format, choose File|Import or press Cmd/Ctrl+R, and use the Import dialog box to find the desired file. You will need to choose PNG Image from the Files Of Type drop-down list box. Import the file gardner1.png from this book's companion CD-ROM. It will appear centered.

3. If you've ever worked with an illustration program, you're probably familiar with drawing in a tracing mode. We're going to trick Flash into emulating such a tracing mode. In tracing mode, the image you're tracing is on a separate, locked layer that's been dimmed so that your tracing lines will stand out. So the first thing we want to do is dim the image.

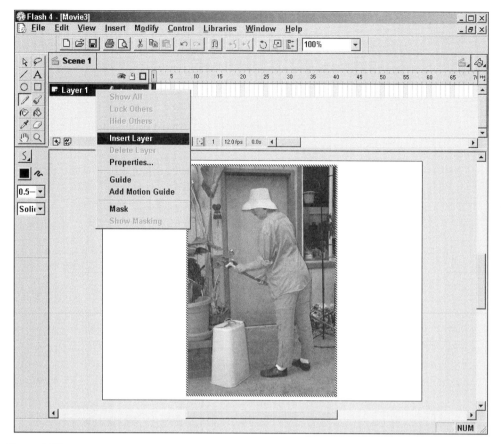

Figure 4.25

The imported photo of Isabel pretending to be a gardener.

4. Choose Window|Library. The Library window opens. You will see gardner1.png listed as a symbol, but that's because Flash puts bitmaps in the Library automatically. In order to dim the image, we have to make it into a real symbol. Press Cmd/Ctrl+A to Select All (there should be nothing else in the movie at this point).

5. Choose Insert|Convert To Symbol. When the Symbol Properties dialog box opens, the default Behavior will be Graphic. Leave it that way and click on OK. A new symbol, named Symbol 1, appears in the Library.

6. Choose Modify|Instance. The Instance Properties dialog box opens. Click on the Color Effect tab, and then choose Alpha from the Color Effect drop-down list box. Drag the Alpha % slider until the amount is approximately 50%. The exact figure isn't critical. The photo now looks as though a piece of tissue was dropped over it.

7. Now that we have the dimmed image that we want to trace, we want to make sure that our tracing will be a separate entity. There are several ways to do this. One of the easiest is to draw on a new layer.

   Place the pointer on the Layer Name bar, and Ctrl+click (Mac) or right-click (Windows). An in-context menu called the Layer menu pops up (see Figure 4.26). Choose Insert Layer. A new layer, labeled Layer 2, appears in the Timeline.

8. You will be working on Layer 2. You want to lock Layer 1 (the one with the photo) so that you don't accidentally draw on it. Click on its Layer Name bar to activate it (it will turn black with white lettering). Click on the dot under the column that shows the padlock at its head. A padlock takes the place of the dot. The layer is now locked.

9. Click to activate Layer 2. This is where you will now do all your drawing for this exercise.

10. Choose the Pencil tool (press the "P" key). In the Pencil modifiers, choose Hairline for line thickness, Solid for line style, Ink for Pencil mode, and black for the color. (If you really need to contrast your outlines, you can temporarily make them contrast outrageously with the photo, then use the Ink Bottle later to change them to something more "normal.") Plan to keep these settings for the Pencil tool for all of your outline tracing.

Choose the Magnifier (press the "M" key), and drag a marquee tight around the face and neck. Press the "P" key (to choose the Pencil tool), and trace an outline for the figure's hat. The result should look like Figure 4.27.

Figure 4.26
The Layer menu.

Figure 4.27
Tracing the hat.

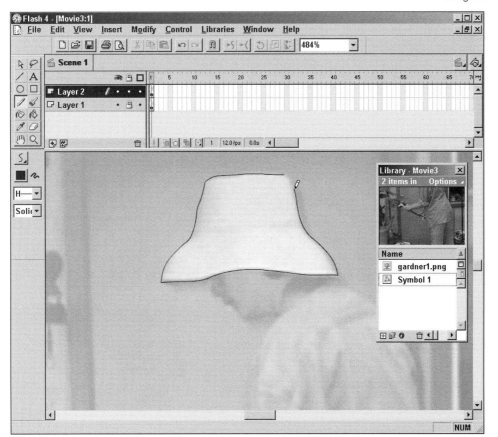

11. Choose the Arrow tool, drag a marquee around the hat you've traced, and press F8 to save what you've done so far as a symbol. In the Symbol Properties dialog box, choose Graphic as the Behavior and type "Hat" in the Name field. (If you need to edit the hat later, simply click with the Arrow tool to select the hat and choose Edit|Edit Symbol.)

12. Trace the outlines of the other parts of the figure in the same manner as above. Each time you complete a portion of the body that you may want to use in a different position in a later frame, save it as a symbol.

13. When tracing, start by tracing the silhouette of the shape you want to draw. Then zoom in and use the Arrow tool to reshape the lines so they fit the outlines of the shape as closely as possible. You probably will want to keep either the Smooth or the Straighten modifier active as you draw, but sometimes the line will correct itself too much. Don't let that bother you until you're through.

    Zoom in tighter, and use the Pencil tool to draw new lines that are tighter, making sure that the ends overlap the original lines.

    When you're done, use the Arrow tool to select the extra lines, and press the Delete key to erase them.

14. After you've outlined all the shapes and saved each as a symbol, you'll want to fill or paint inside the shapes. One at a time, select the target symbol with the Arrow tool and then choose Edit|Edit Symbol (or press Cmd/Ctrl+E). Everything but the symbol disappears from the screen.

15. From time to (most of the) time, when you insert a selection as a symbol, it will pop to the top of the overlay stack. A lot of the symbols in this drawing are partially hidden behind other symbols in the finished drawing (for instance, the hands are behind the shirt, as are the legs).

    To place the symbol in the desired stacking order, select it (it will have a rectangular marquee surrounding it when selected); then press Cmd/Ctrl+Up Arrow or Cmd/Ctrl+Down Arrow until you see the symbol in the right place.

16. To fill the larger areas with color, use the Paint Bucket tool. In the Paint Bucket tool modifiers, click on the color swatch to see the color swatches. Pick the color or gradient that you want to use, and click

inside the outline that you want to fill. (If the fill doesn't happen immediately, choose a different Gap Size from the Gap Size modifier menu and try again.)

17. Next, use the Brush to paint shaded areas of color (in the shirt, for instance). If you have a pressure-sensitive pad, you'll want to choose the pressure toggle in the Brush modifiers. Also in the Brush modifiers, choose Paint Inside from the Brush Mode menu. Choose appropriate brush sizes (larger brushes generally make smoother shapes).

18. Now you are finished with the drawing. The head, hands, and feet have been saved as symbols, so you no longer need the photo. Click to activate Layer 1, and then click on the Lock icon in the Layer Name bar for Layer 1. This unlocks the layer. See Figure 4.28.

Figure 4.28

The shaded gardener with Layer 1 turned off.

19. While Layer 1 is still active, click on the trash (Delete Layer) icon that's at the bottom of the Layer Names.

20. Save your movie at this point. You don't want to add more frames to it because you will want to use this figure as an animated symbol in

another movie. To do so you'll want to open this movie as a Library from within the movie in which you want to use the figure as a symbol. At that point, you will convert the symbol to a movie clip and edit the symbol to animate its arms, legs, and head so that the lady appears to be watering something.

Moving On

I hope that this chapter has made you feel comfortable with drawing in Flash and with using Flash's unique drawing tools.

In Chapter 5, I'll give you some advanced drawing tips and tricks and will introduce you to some drawing techniques that weren't possible (or were not as easy) until Flash 4 came along.

ADVANCED DRAWING TECHNIQUES

5

KEN MILBURN

Now that you've learned how to draw in Flash, you can start learning about some of the developments in Flash 4 that can take your drawings to new levels of sophistication.

This chapter covers new hot keys in Flash 4, new Color Sets, techniques for using the Freeform and Polygon Lasso tools, and new curve effects. Not all of the chapter is devoted to new Flash 4 developments, however. You'll also learn tricks for making your drawings more efficient, and for making soft-edged shapes.

Finally, you'll learn about what you might be able to do in your illustration program that's just too much trouble or too difficult to do in Flash, how best to import drawings from Macromedia FreeHand, and how to put objects created in other applications into a Flash file.

The New Hot Keys For Drawing Tools

In Flash 4, you can access any tool in the Toolbox with a single keystroke. Look, Ma—no mouse! Actually, what this means when it comes to using the mouse (or your digitizing pad) is that you can switch tools without interrupting your drawing. All you need to do is tap a key with your other hand.

Now it's as easy to get to a Toolbox tool in Flash 4 as it is in Photoshop. In fact, not only has the Toolbox been redesigned to make both Photoshop and FreeHand users more at home with Flash, but the newly assigned hot keys will feel very familiar as well.

So, without further ado, Table 5.1 shows the up-to-date set of drawing-tool hot keys.

Because most of these keys are simply the initial of the tool itself, you should be able to memorize all of these in about 2.5 seconds. Doing so should cut your drawing time dramatically.

Table 5.1 Drawing-tool hot keys.

Tool	Hot Key
Arrow	a
Lasso	l
Line	n
Text	t
Oval	o
Rectangle	r
Pencil	p
Brush	b
Ink Bottle	i
Paint Bucket	u
Dropper	d
Eraser	e
Hand	Spacebar (temporarily switches to the Hand tool until Spacebar is released)
Magnifier	m

Understanding And Using The New Color Sets

Color Sets are predefined indexed color palettes. Flash 4 simply includes a few more than did Flash 3, including those that are standard for Web browsers, the Macintosh Operating System (Mac OS), and Windows. You can create, modify, or import the color palettes and save them for future use. When your present palette is getting overcrowded, open the palette, select the palette modification button at the top center of the palette, then select the icon in the lower-left corner to save your current palette and open a new one.

Tracing Bitmaps

There is nothing new about being able to automatically convert bitmapped images into drawings in Flash. This section simply covers the operation more thoroughly than the previous chapter did. This section also includes an exercise that lets you experience auto-tracing step-by-step.

When Flash imports a bitmap, it is automatically saved into the movie's Library as a symbol. When you auto-trace the instance of the bitmap that's on the canvas, the tracing will replace that instance of the symbol. However, if you won't be needing the bitmap in any other part of the movie after tracing it, you should highlight the bitmap's symbol name and choose Delete from the Library menu.

Okay, now that you have all the background information, let's go to work tracing the symbol. It should take all of a couple of minutes:

1. Choose File|Import to open the Import dialog box. Navigate to the folder where the file you want to load resides, and load the file. (The file used in the example is fuchsia2.jpg on the CD-ROM.)

2. The bitmap will appear on the stage as a symbol instance, as indicated by the checkerboard marquee surrounding it.

3. Choose Modify|Trace Bitmap to open the Trace Bitmap dialog box. (See Figure 5.1.)

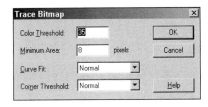

Figure 5.1
The Trace Bitmap dialog box.

IMPORTING BITMAPS

Before you can trace a bitmap, you have to import it into Flash. The biggest problem with doing that is that the bitmap image has to be in a format that Flash will accept: GIF, JPEG, or PNG (for Mac and Windows); PICT (Mac only); or BMP (Windows only). If the file isn't already in one of those formats, you'll want to convert it in your image-editing program. Better yet, convert it and optimize it in a program made for prepping Web images, such as Macromedia's Fireworks or Adobe's ImageReady (now a part of Photoshop 5.5). Flash 4 will automatically accept the optimization settings for GIF and JPEG images when they are imported, so optimizing them in a program that is especially well attuned to the job will ensure maximum performance and predictable appearance in Flash 4.

CREATING LINE DRAWINGS IN FLASH

Tracing a drawing in Flash actually produces nothing but fills. There are no outlines. If you want to create a line drawing, pick up the color of any of the fills with the Eye Dropper. Then choose the Ink Bottle, and click inside the fills that are the same color. The fill will now have an outline. If you choose the Arrow and click in the fill after it's been outlined, you can delete it with the Delete/Backspace key. Now you have an outlined drawing. There's an easier way, but you have to own another program. Export the traced drawing as a bitmap and then open it in Adobe Streamline and auto-trace it using outlines. Also, several illustration programs can create an outlined, auto-traced drawing. You can then save that drawing as an EPS or (in the case of FreeHand) SWF file and import it into Flash.

4. In the Color Threshold field, enter a number between 1 and 256.

   The Color Threshold field indicates the number of colors you'd like to use to trace the image. The lower the number of colors, the simpler the resulting drawing. The simpler the drawing, the faster the performance. If you use too few colors, however, you might end up with something unrecognizable or unattractive. As with all these commands, experimentation is the key. If you don't like the results, press Cmd/Ctrl+Z to undo and start over.

5. In the Minimum Area field, enter a number that indicates the smallest area in the image that should be traced. This is another control for simplifying the image.

6. Choose a Curve Fit setting. The choices are Pixel, Very Tight, Tight, Normal, Smooth, and Very Smooth. These choices will determine the number of curves in the drawing. The more curves, the larger the resulting file.

7. Choose a Corner Threshold setting. The choices are Many Corners, Normal, and Few Corners. These choices will determine the number of corner points in the drawing. The more corner points, the larger the resulting file.

8. When you've made your best guess as to the proper settings, click on OK. A drawing will appear. Click outside the drawing to deselect it so that you can see what it looks like. See Figure 5.2.

9. If you don't look too closely, you might even be fooled into thinking that the result above is still a photograph. You can see more clearly how the drawing was made if you just view the outline. Choose View|Outline. What you see will look like Figure 5.3.

Optimizing Your Drawings

The word "optimizing," when referring to the preparation of graphics meant to be published on the Web, simply means doing whatever it takes to make an acceptable version of that image upload as quickly as possible. That

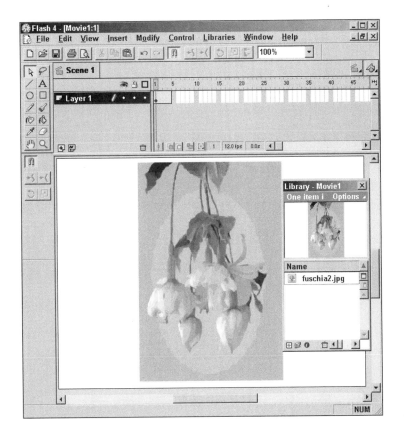

Figure 5.2
A traced bitmap.

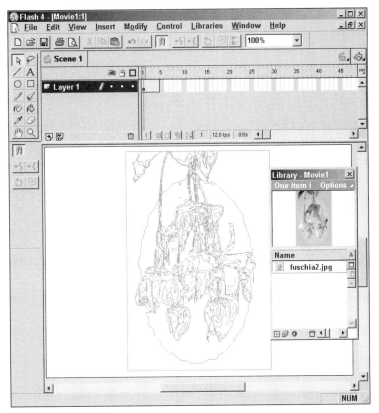

Figure 5.3
The outlines of the traced bitmap.

involves making the best compromise between fidelity to the original art-work and minimum file size. We've learned the hard way that making viewers wait is the surest way to encourage them to browse elsewhere.

This book has raved about Flash's performance compared to that of typical bitmapped Web animations and illustrations. That's because a Flash draw-ing of only a few bytes can take up an entire screen. There's a gotcha, though. Put hundreds of wiggles and minuscule shapes into that drawing, and its file might get bigger than a comparable bitmapped graphic. So it's just as important to optimize Flash's vector graphics as it is to optimize a GIF or JPEG file. The way you optimize a Flash graphic is to cut the number of curves (lines) and corners (the points where lines meet) to a minimum. Fewer shapes equals fewer geometric instructions, which equals smaller files.

There are essentially three ways to optimize your drawings in Flash:

- Automatically (with the Optimize command)

- Semi-automatically (with the Smooth modifier)

- Manually (with the Arrow tool)

It isn't generally possible to make the very best optimization (except through sheer dumb luck) without using all three of these techniques. I have put them in the order above because it is usually the best sequence for optimiz-ing complex drawings. Let's use our auto-tracing of the fuchsias as an example. Figure 5.4 shows a detail of the outline of the fuchsia drawing. You can see that it's very complex.

Figure 5.4
Detail of the unoptimized outline of the fuchsia drawing.

Automatic Optimization

Here's how to make this complex drawing much simpler. Notice that even at maximum settings, the appearance of a very complex drawing like this one doesn't change all that much, but the outlines certainly do. For this exercise, we'll optimize the whole drawing so you can see what the command can do.

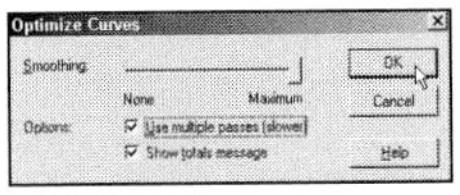

Figure 5.5
The Optimize Curves dialog box.

1. Choose View|Outlines. You will see the drawing in outline mode (you can use your drawing or ours).

2. Press Cmd/Ctrl+A to Select All. All the outlines will be highlighted.

3. Choose Modify|Curves|Optimize to open the Optimize Curves dialog box. (See Figure 5.5.)

4. The control that has the most influence is the Smoothing slider. Drag it to as high a setting as you think you can tolerate (one that doesn't make your drawing so efficient that it becomes unrecognizable). The ideal setting will be different for every image—indeed for every size of the same image—so don't be afraid to experiment.

5. Check the Use Multiple Passes box if you want to get the maximum optimization. Be aware, though, that multiple passes could "over-optimize" your drawing. If it does, just press Cmd/Ctrl+Z to Undo and run the Optimize command again with different settings.

6. Check the Show Totals Message box. The Totals message—shown in Figure 5.6—will tell you exactly how many curves you've eliminated with this one simple command.

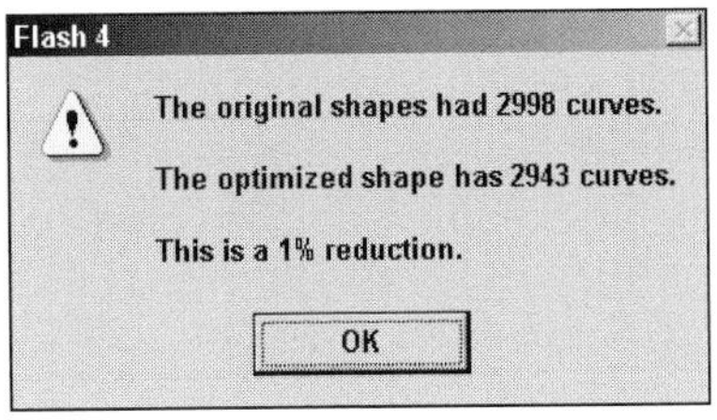

Figure 5.6
The Totals message.

As you can see, this isn't a greatly optimized file. We've eliminated only about 50 curves out of 3,000. You can do a lot better by isolating smaller sections of complex images.

7. Zoom in on the drawing. You can be in either Outline or Antialiased mode. Choose the Lasso tool, and select a small section of the drawing that has particularly jagged edges (see Figure 5.7). Repeat Steps 3 through 6. Repeat these steps on as many areas of the image as seems to make sense. Then move on to semi-automatic smoothing.

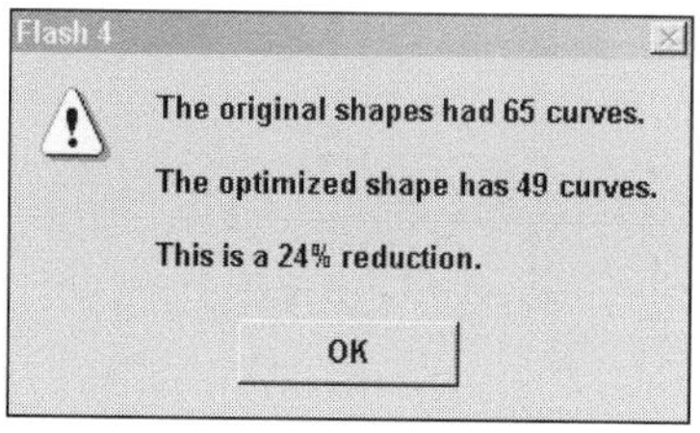

Figure 5.7

Automatic optimization works more efficiently on small areas.

Semi-Automatic Optimization

Semi-automatic optimization involves using the Smooth modifier, which you can pick as an Arrow tool modifier or from the Toolbar. Use the Arrow tool to select a shape that has needlessly irregular edges. When the shape is selected, click on the Smooth modifier. The more times you click on the Smooth modifier, the smoother the shape will become. Keep clicking until you see that you've gone one step too far; then press Cmd/Ctrl+Z to Undo the last step.

Manual Optimization

Manual optimization is simply using the Arrow tool to edit shapes (see the previous chapter) and using the Brush tool to paint smoother shapes. For instance, you can look for lines with lots of corners and pull the corners out into straight lines. Then select the shape and use the Smooth modifier until the separate lines are joined into a single curve.

Another trick is to use the Brush and the Eye Dropper. If you see a jagged line, pick up the color of the shape with the Eye Dropper, and then use the Brush to paint a smoother line. As long as all the shapes are on the canvas, they will be automatically joined into a much smoother shape.

Using The Lasso Tools

If you've ever used a photo editing program (such as Photoshop), you probably know that a Lasso tool is used to make freeform selections. Most drawing programs, however, don't have a Lasso because you simply click objects to select them. In Flash, though, you can select parts of objects, and the result is much the same as selecting a freeform part of an object in Photoshop. That is, you isolate the selected area from its surroundings. The selected area can then be moved, scaled, filled, and so forth. In Figure 5.8, you see two identical shapes, but part of one of the shapes has been freeform-selected with the Lasso tool and moved away from what was once another part.

Using the Lasso tool is an excellent way to select crowded shapes that would be partly selected by dragging a rectangular marquee with the arrow tool. The Lasso tool also lets you smooth (optimize) small sections of a curve or shape or re-color sections of a line. You'll find this feature very powerful when you use it with the new Curve Effects that are now possible in Flash 4 (see the next section).

BECOME AN OPTIMIZATION CONVERT

You won't really appreciate the value of optimization until you preview the results. Do yourself a favor and spend 20 minutes optimizing a copy of a drawing in all the ways suggested above. Then load both the original and the optimized drawing onto a Web site and look at them over a modem connection. What you see will probably make you want to turn optimization into a religion.

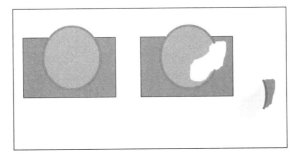

Figure 5.8
A freeform selection made with the Lasso tool has been moved, rotated, and recolored.

The Lasso Tool Modifiers

The Lasso tool is actually three selection tools in one: Freeform, Polygon, and Magic Wand. The Magic Wand works only on broken-apart bitmap images. All of these are available in the modifiers section of the Toolbox when the Lasso tool is selected (see Figure 5.9).

The Freeform Lasso

If you don't select any of the modifiers, you can drag the Lasso to make any freeform selection.

The Polygon Lasso

The Polygon Lasso makes a straight line between clicks. It is a very fast way to make rough selections and a very accurate way to select areas that require a perfectly straight border.

Figure 5.9
The Lasso tool has been selected.

The Magic Wand

The Magic Wand doesn't do anything unless you first import a bitmap, select it, and then choose Modify|Break Apart or press Cmd/Ctrl+B. This breaks the bitmap into discrete areas of color that are part of the canvas. You can then select one area of colors that fall within a given range of shades. You can also automatically optimize small variations in color by choosing a smoothing range.

To pick the range of shades, click on the Magic Wand modifier button. The Magic Wand Settings dialog box will open (see Figure 5.10).

Figure 5.10
The Magic Wand Settings dialog box. In the Magic Wand Settings dialog box, enter a number between 1 and 256 in the Threshold field to indicate the range of shades that the Magic Wand should include in its selection. Then select a Smoothing option: Pixels, Rough, Normal, Smooth.

Magic Wand Settings		
Threshold:	10	OK
Smoothing:	Normal ▼	Cancel
		Help

Painting With A Bitmap (The Bitmap Fill)

This is a very underused feature in Flash. Using either the Paint Bucket tool or the Brush tool, you can actually paint a bitmap into a part of the canvas. The way you go about this is counter-intuitive, but it works.

Keep in mind what you just learned about the Magic Wand. Let's suppose that you want to paint a part of the fuchsia into an oval:

1. Import a bitmap. For this exercise, we'll use fuchsia.jpeg. You could just as well choose your own file. While the bitmap is still selected, press Backspace/Delete to remove it from the canvas. Don't worry—you still have the file stored as a symbol in the Library.

2. Draw the shape in which you want to paint the fuchsia. For this exercise, we'll just make an oval. Choose the Oval tool. In the Oval Tool modifiers, choose green for a line color, a 4-pixel line, a Solid line style, and no fill.

3. Drag to draw your oval in the center of the screen.

4. Press Cmd/Ctrl+A to Select All, and then press F8 to convert the oval to a symbol. When the Symbol dialog box appears, type a name ("Oval" will do) and make sure that Graphic is the chosen symbol type; then click on OK.

5. Press Delete/Backspace to temporarily delete the symbol from the canvas.

6. Choose File|Import. When the Import dialog box appears, navigate to the file you want to import (fuchsia.jpg is on the CD) and double-click on its name.

7. Press Cmd/Ctrl+B to Break Apart the bitmap. Don't deselect it. If you (oops!) do, press Cmd/Ctrl+A to Select All again.

8. Choose the Eye Dropper tool and click inside the selection. You will see that the fill color resembles a part of the bitmap.

9. Press Backspace/Delete to get rid of the bitmap.

10. Choose Window|Library, and drag the Oval symbol onto the canvas.

11. While the Oval symbol is still selected, press Cmd/Ctrl+E to Edit Symbols. You can now edit the symbol separately from the movie.

12. Choose the Brush tool. In the modifiers, choose Paint Inside. Make brushstrokes inside the oval. When you release the mouse button, the paint will become the bitmap (see Figure 5.11).

You may be wondering how you could do all of the above steps if you had already started working on a file. There are two ways:

*   Open another file, then follow the steps above. When you're done, drag the painted oval symbol into your current movie.

*   Place the cursor on the current layer, and Ctrl/Right-click to display the Layers menu. Choose Insert Layer. If necessary, click on the new layer

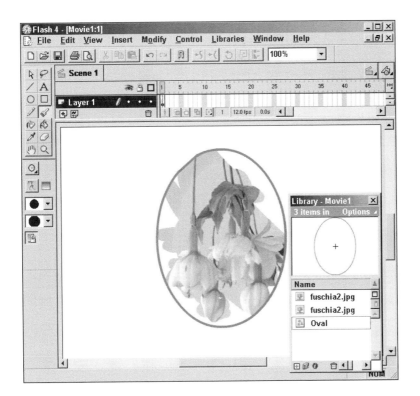

Figure 5.11
The fuchsia painted inside the oval.

to make it the active layer. Then use the steps above to create the painted oval symbol. When you've finished, you can delete the layer and you'll still be able to drag the symbol from the Library onto any layer you're working on.

You can do much more with painting bitmaps than this simple exercise implies, but you've got the basics. There are a few fundamentals you need to keep in mind:

• The chosen bitmap will remain the selected paint or fill color until you choose a different color from the palette. After you've done that, you will need to Break Apart and Eye Dropper another bitmap in order to paint with a bitmap.

• The bitmap is placed on the canvas where the bitmap was broken apart, and it will tile (repeat) the image when you paint into areas outside the space occupied by the original bitmap. All of your painting will appear in the same position that the original bitmap occupied on the canvas. So be sure to place your bitmap in the same location as the area you want to paint into. This is one of the main reasons why it is best to do this process in a separate editing space by working on another layer or editing a symbol. After you create your bitmap fill, you can make a symbol out of it. The fill will remain exactly as you drew it and will no longer be tied to the canvas spot from which you pulled the bitmap's fill.

- Any of the tools that use the current fill color will be able to paint with the same bitmap. So if you had wanted to simply fill the oval with the fuchsia, you could have used the Paint Bucket tool. If you wanted to paint the oval with the bitmap, rather than fill it, you could have used the Ink Bottle tool.

Tricks With Curve Effects

Flash 4 adds a new level of sophistication to your ability to control the appearance of curves (in Flash terminology, a curve and a straight line are the same animal). Now you can fill a curve with a blend or a bitmap, make its edges fade away or intensify, or expand and contract the dimensions of a fill. Of course, expanding and contracting the dimensions of a fill wouldn't seem to have much to do with curve effects. Nevertheless, that's where Macromedia has placed the command. You just have to use the Lines To Fills command before using either the Expand Shape command or the Soft Edges command. Figure 5.12 shows all three of the curve effects applied to the same shape.

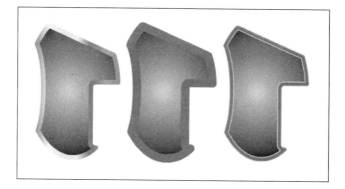

Figure 5.12

Left to right: Lines To Fills, Expand Shape, Soften Edges.

All three of these commands are found under Modify|Curves. If you want to practice with the next three exercises and don't want to draw your own shapes first, choose File|Open As Library to open the curves.fla movie on your CD-ROM.

Converting Lines To Fills

You can convert any line to a fill. This enables you to edit the fill's shape (by using the Arrow tool) and to change the fill (by using any of the capabilities of the Paint Bucket tool). You must also use the Lines To Fills command on any curve or line that you wish to affect with the Soften Edges or Expand Shape commands.

To apply the Lines To Fills command:

1. Select the line that you want to fill. If the line has several segments, double-click to select the entire outline.

2. Choose Modify|Curves|Lines To Fills. The curve is now a fill.

3. To change the current fill to something else, choose the Paint Bucket tool. Select a different fill color or gradient by clicking on the swatch in the Paint Bucket modifiers panel (just below the Toolbox). Now click on what was formerly a line.

That's all there is to it.

Making Vignettes With The Soften Edges Command

You can use the Soften Edges command on any fill. The command places a series of fill outlines around the selected shape. The number of outlines is determined by you. To soften the edges of a shape:

1. Select the shape.

2. Choose Modify|Curves|Lines To Fills. The curve is now a fill.

3. Choose Modify|Curves|Soften Edges. The Soften Edges dialog box opens (see Figure 5.13).

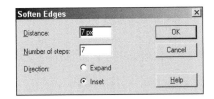

Figure 5.13
The Soften Edges dialog box.

4. In the Distance field, type the distance, in pixels, across which you want the fade to occur.

5. In the Number Of Steps field, type the number of steps between the current color of the fill and white.

6. Click on the radio button that indicates whether you want the fade to move inward (Inset) or outward (Expand) from the present fill border.

7. Click on OK. The edge-softening will occur.

There's quite a bit that you can do with the Soften Edges command. Zoom in close to the softened edge so that you can see the graduated fills that now surround the original shape. Choose the Arrow tool, and select one or more of the fills. You can now do anything to that fill that you can do with any other fill, such as filling it with a bitmap.

Expanding And Contracting Shapes

After you have converted the line to a fill (shape), you can enlarge or reduce the shape in much the same way as you just softened its edges. This

> **Note:** One caution: Use the Soften Edges command sparingly. You have increased the amount of data needed to describe this shape by the number of steps over which the fade will occur.

> **THINK ABOUT SOFTEN EDGES AND FILE SIZE**
>
> Although some of the things that you can do with the Soften Edges feature might make the resultant illustration a bit data-heavy for Web use, keep in mind that there are lots of uses for Flash offline. You can export anything to a drawing program as an EPS file, and you can import any Flash movie into Director. Of course, you can also place a Flash movie on a CD-ROM and distribute it. In that case, bandwidth problems all but disappear.

SOFTEN EDGES MAKES CONCENTRIC SHAPES AND BEVELED BUTTONS

You can very quickly draw concentric shapes by using the Soften Edges command, provided you stick with simple shapes such as circles, ovals, rectangles, and rounded rectangles. Draw any of these as a filled shape, then delete the outline. Select the fill and choose Modify|Curves|Soften Edges. In the Soften Edges dialog box, the distance of the expansion is divided by the number of steps to get the distance between each concentric shape. When you click on OK, you will get concentric fills. Use the Ink Bottle to place an outline around them and then delete the fills. Then you have your concentric shapes (see Figure 5.14).

It's also easy to make a beveled-edged button in Flash, with this command. Use the concentric shapes tip to put a concentric shape outline around your button shape. You only need one Soften Edges step and it should be the width of the "bevel." Fill the outside shape with a darker color than the inside shape. Choose the Brush and the Paint Inside modifier and make sure the brush width is wide enough to cover the outside border. Now just paint a highlight into the top and left borders of the button (see Figure 5.15).

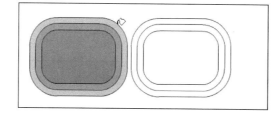

Figure 5.14

The Soften Edges shape is on the left, with the Paint Bucket used to make the outlines. At right, the fills have been deleted, so you see the perfectly concentric shapes.

Figure 5.15

A beveled-edge button drawing in Flash.

can be very useful if you want to create a series of the same shape in different sizes or just want to thicken a line. Be careful, though. Some shapes will do weird things if you try to expand or contract them too much.

Here's how to contract a shape. This time, we'll contract the fill that's already inside the line. Except for one click of a radio button, the procedure for expanding a shape is the same.

1. Choose the Arrow tool, and click on the shape to select it.

2. Choose Modify|Curves|Expand Shape. The Expand Shape dialog box opens (see Figure 5.16).

3. Type a number of pixels in the Distance field.

4. Click on the Inset radio button.

5. Click on OK. The shape will shrink.

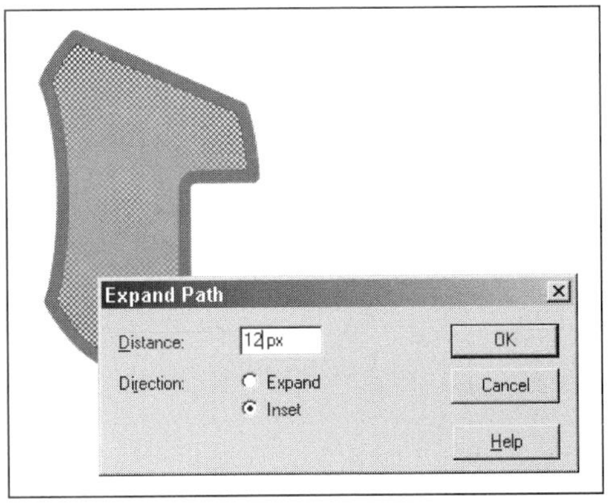

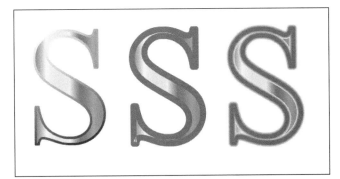

Figure 5.16
The Expand Path dialog box.

One way to change a shape radically is to keep shrinking it until some of its parts start to disappear or invert. You can then select the shape and scale or rotate it. Experiment with the command, and you'll discover that it can do some surprising (and sometimes unpredictable) things.

Applying Curve Effects To Text

You can apply all of these effects to text, too. Just select the text, break it apart, use the Ink Bottle to put a curve around it (be sure it's a different color than the text so that you can select it all), and then use any of the three commands in this section. Figure 5.17 shows all three of the curve effects applied to the letter S.

Figure 5.17
The letter S, broken apart and outlined, has had all three curve effects applied to the outline.

When To Use Another Drawing Program

There are a good many things that illustration programs, computer-aided-design programs, and three-dimensional modeling programs can do much faster and more effectively than Flash can.

Illustration Programs

Illustration programs are very good at doing blends. *Blends* are gradients that follow the form of a shape. The originating program does this by copying and reducing the original shape several times and placing each succeeding copy inside its predecessor. At the same time, each copy is shaded a different color. When you look at the finished result, there appears to be a smooth gradient from the interior to the exterior of the object. Figure 5.18 is an example of a smooth blend.

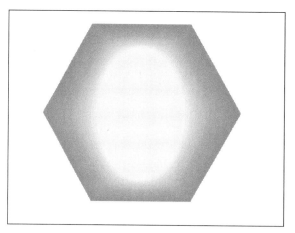

Figure 5.18
A smooth blend, created in FreeHand 8.

Blends can be beautiful, but they don't translate to Flash as very efficient drawings because they might be made of dozens of copies of the same drawing. Of course, this means that the shape needs several times as much data. That doesn't mean that you should never use blends, however. For one thing, you could cut the data size in half by deleting every other shape. Another option would be to use the blend as a bitmap. The bitmap's data file might be larger than a drawing file, but that would depend on the physical size of the bitmap and on how you compressed the bitmap.

Another problem with using blends created in drawing programs is that they are hard to import directly as EPS or AI files. The best scenario is to first import the drawing into FreeHand, then export it as a Flash movie (SWF). The movie will then be imported with each part of the blend on a separate layer—making it much easier to edit.

Illustration programs can also streamline a great many drawing procedures—too many to list them all here. Besides, individual talents vary from one program to another. Illustration program features that you'd probably want to use most often are:

Figure 5.19
Text that has been placed along a path and given a drop shadow in FreeHand 8.

- Regular geometric shapes, such as the hexagon shown in Figure 5.18

- Geometric shapes with rounded corners

- Special effects, such as beveled edges and drop shadows

- Auto-tracing that's more versatile than Flash's

- The ability to place text along a path (see Figure 5.19)

FreeHand 8 also lets you create drawings that incorporate full and partial transparencies and that use the same alpha transparency as Flash 4.

Finally, in all illustration programs, you draw Bezier curves by placing control points and then editing the direction handles of the control points. This method gives you more precise control over the shape and direction of your lines.

Computer-aided-design programs are used to create engineering and architectural drawings. Because they operate with a precision that usually exceeds one-thousandth of an inch and because they offer many controls for pattern, line thickness, grids, and the joining of lines, these programs are suited to many types of engineering and scientific drawings. The types of drawings that you'd probably want to create in one of these programs—floor plans and simple maps—can be created in almost any inexpensive CAD program. On the other hand, if your business centers around engineering, you'll probably be importing drawings from such professional packages as Autodesk's AutoCAD.

Virtually all CAD programs are capable of exporting their files to DXF format. To be on the safe side, if possible, simplify the drawing in the CAD program before exporting it. Leave out fancy patterns, bitmaps, and elements that are created by advanced or unique features in the program.

3D Programs

3D programs are close relatives to CAD programs. Many of them are capable of exporting their files in DXF format, but this often means exporting only one two-dimensional view. Note that the DXF format handles both 2D and 3D images. Flash can import only 2D images.

What many folks want to do is create a 3D animation, such as a spinning logo design, in a 3D program and be able to import that directly as a Flash movie. To do that, you must find a 3D program that will export an animation as a sequence of frames in one of the formats that Flash can accept—ideally, EPS, AI, WMF, or 2D versions of DXF. This process usually works best if you export the animation without fills. Then you can add your own fills and gradient fills in Flash. If you import the fills, they may be re-interpreted in the process, and that can be a mess.

If you're an advanced modeler and use 3D Studio Max, you can create very complex animations and export them directly into Flash by using a third-party plug-in program made by Digimation and called, confusingly enough, Illustrate! Illustrate! is a "toon renderer," meaning that instead of the usual photo-realistic shading that high-end 3D models are rendered to, it renders flat-colored, outlined-edge, cartoon-like illustrations. These can be excellent for use in Flash because the flatter colors and simpler lines mean higher Web performance. If you want to know more, you can read about Illustrate! on the Web at **www.davidgould.com**.

Note: Previous versions of Flash would recognize a color as being the transparent color in a GIF file only if that color were indexed to 0. Flash 4 recognizes as transparent any color that the originating program designated as transparent.

QUICK TRANSFER OF SIMPLE DRAWINGS TO FLASH FROM OTHER CAD PROGRAMS

The quickest way to move a drawing from a non-Macromedia illustration program to Flash is to have both programs open and running. In the illustration program, select the drawing (or as much of it as you want to transfer). Then drag the selection into the Flash window. When the drawing is in Flash, break the drawing's groups apart and optimize the curves to simplify the drawing. Delete all the fills and replace them with Flash fills and gradients as needed.

There is another 3D Studio Max plug-in called Vecta3D. If you already own Flash 4, you'll find a sample of the program on the Macromedia CD. You'll need to own a copy of 3D Studio Max in order to see it work, though. The Vecta3D program is published by Ideaworks, and you may be able to find more information on the Web at **www.ideaworks3d.com**.

If all else fails, you can probably hand-trace a movie made in the 3D animation program you own. Here's how:

1. In your animation program, complete the animation. Then use the program's File Export command to save the animation as a series of still bitmapped images. Your choices will have to be JPEG, PICT (Mac), BMP (Windows), or PNG—others won't import into Flash. The animation program will add a series of sequential numbers to each frame. Flash will automatically recognize the sequential numbers as frames and will import them in the proper order.

2. In Flash, insert a new layer. Then drag the layer containing the frames you just imported so that it's beneath the new layer.

3. Highlight all the frames in the new layer that correspond with frames in the import layer. Ctrl/Right-click and choose Insert Blank Keyframe from the Frames menu.

4. Choose a bright color for your outlines so that they will contrast with the photos in the underlying layer. Trace your shapes.

5. When you've finished tracing, delete the layer containing the imported frames.

6. Frame by frame, use the Ink Bottle to change the color of your outlines to something more acceptable. Then use the Paint Bucket and the Brush to fill in colors as desired. In order to maintain consistent color, it's a good idea to fill only a couple of different-colored areas in each frame. Then go back to the first frame and add a couple more colors. Keep repeating the process until you're done.

I know, I know...it sounds like a lot of trouble. Well, it does take time. On the other hand, unless you're a practiced animator, it will take a lot less time than trying to figure out how to animate spinning text—or even a revolving cube—one frame at a time.

Transferring Files From Other Types Of Drawing Programs

Thank heaven, there's always a way to get material from one of these programs into Flash. There's one compelling reason to use a drawing in Flash that was created in another program: Someone else created it, and you can't or don't want to ask the artist to re-create it in Flash. Because most of

Note: The imported frames will be entered in the current layer, starting at the currently selected frame. You may want to press Cmd/Ctrl+F8 (Insert|New Symbol) to create a new Movie Symbol before importing the frames. You can then position the imported movie anywhere you like.

EXPORTING VECTOR FILES FROM FREEHAND 8 AS FLASH MOVIES

If you own FreeHand 8, the most accurate route to getting non-Macromedia vector files into Flash will often be to first import them into FreeHand 8. Then, export the drawing as a Flash movie (a procedure described in Chapter 10) and you'll have a perfect—or near perfect—translation.

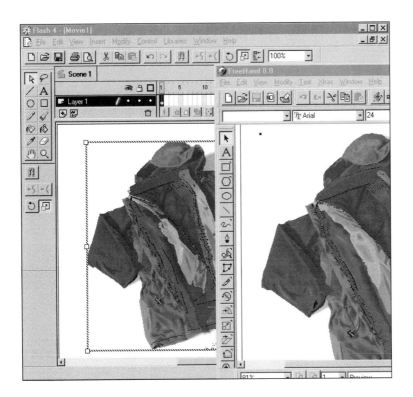

Figure 5.20
This parka is one of FreeHand 8's samples. You can see that the parka is a near-perfect copy when it's dragged into Flash, although the text has been dropped.

our productions collect images from a variety of sources, it's good to know that you can collect vector images from most of them—with one caveat. Vector file formats come in different "flavors," meaning that not all images in a given format have data that can be imported directly into Flash. The reason is that the programs that spawned these formats added features as they evolved. Often, that means that the specifications for their file formats changed over time. Two of the most popular formats for storing vector graphics are AI (Adobe Illustrator) for illustrations and DXF (AutoCAD's Data Exchange Format) for CAD and 3D drawings.

The best way to import a drawing from another program is to open the other program, open the drawing, and drag it into Flash 4 (see Figure 5.20). Of course, the other program must support drag and drop, but if it's a popular late-generation program, the chances are pretty good that it does.

You can also import files in the Adobe Illustrator 7 format. Some colors might change, however, and you might have trouble breaking apart very complex drawings (those with dozens of groups).

Inserting Objects Created In Other Applications

Flash can import a limited number of vector formats. Even within those formats, special features have been added to some programs after Flash 4 was developed, so Flash will not be able to support them. In addition, some programs add many small specialized features to their variations of the formats, and Flash does not recognize them.

Some versions of formats create color in the CMYK color space, whereas Flash uses RGB colors. Unfortunately, there is no single standard way to translate CMYK colors to RGB colors, so some colors will be incorrect in most cross-program translations.

Because of these variations in file formats, there is no one best way to import vector images into Flash. Usually the Flash SWF format will import best into Flash, but other times, using Copy and Paste or using a different format such as AI will work better. If one method does not work, try another, and take note of variations and features that will not import with the particular combination of programs you use.

Moving On

In this chapter, you learned how to use some of the more advanced drawing tools, including those that are new in Flash 4. You also learned about what other drawing programs might be able to contribute to your productivity and how to place elements from other programs into a Flash file.

In the next chapter, you will learn how to use the basic tools for making animations.

FLASH
ANIMATION
6

This chapter introduces you to the fundamentals of Flash 4 animation, including working with some of the new features. Also, brief tutorials show you how to create the simplest and most effective types of animation.

KEN MILBURN

Flash's animation capabilities are what attracted all the attention in the first place. Because Flash's animations are vector drawings rather than bitmap paintings, the animator has a great speed advantage in creating as well as displaying animations (especially on the Web).

The relatively small file size of a Flash animation is also a benefit in offline uses. You can store an entire animated and interactive presentation on a single floppy disk. Because both Windows and Mac users can read DOS-formatted floppy disks, you can distribute a near-universal, low-cost presentation. Because you save the file as a self-running "projector," the destination computer doesn't even need to have a browser.

So that you can get a feel for the basics of animation and for how easy it can be, this chapter will start with an exercise that lets you create a very simple animation. The most effective Web animations are often the simplest. Furthermore, the simplest also load and play the fastest.

Next, I'll discuss the kinds of animation techniques that are equally easy and especially effective as attention-getters. You'll get a good idea of how you might make those animations. I'll progress to a brief discussion of the different types of animation procedures (frame by frame, tweened, and still frame) and the purpose of each. Then a reference section will follow a discussion of the tools, commands, Timeline, and hidden Timeline menus that give Flash all its animation power.

The Basics Of Animation

Think of an animation as nothing more than a stack of still images shown to the viewer in rapid succession. The old-fashioned flip book is probably the best visual metaphor. You get the illusion of movement because the drawings change slightly from page to page and because the pages are flipped quickly enough to create the illusion of motion. With the advent of the motion picture camera, these still pages became known as *frames*, and the frames are shown rapidly by sliding them past a light, a lens, and a shutter at high speed. Well, video and computer animations are just electronic adaptations of the same idea.

To create animations, you start with Flash's powerful but easy-to-use set of drawing tools, using them to create the pictures in your frames. You can then use frames, overlays, symbols, layers, and scenes to assemble your drawings into a whole "production," which Flash calls a *movie*. The length of a Flash movie and the number of scenes it can contain are limited only by your computer and your distribution requirements. You can use Flash to produce anything from an animated Graphics Interchange Format (GIF) animation for use on a Web page to a series of numbered stills for incorporation into other animation or video-editing programs such as Macromedia Director or Adobe Premiere. Because Flash movies can even contain *actions* (instructions to do such things as play a specific scene or sound) and *buttons,* you can use Flash to produce a multimedia application for distribution on a CD-ROM. Flash has even been used in creating film and TV productions but more likely, you'll use these interactive capabilities to drive the navigation of a Web site.

Now that I've said all that, you have to start with a good idea of what it takes to put together an animation. Remember, making small changes in each frame creates the illusion of motion. You have to make these changes in careful increments from one frame to the next, and it's important that objects move a planned distance in a planned direction from the original. Otherwise, your movie will be amateurish and jerky. (Okay, so that can be an effect, but it's probably not the one you'll want to use most of the time.)

Movies are created in this logical order: frame by frame, layer by layer, scene by scene. Movies can be made to play continuously from scene to scene or to stop at the end of a scene while waiting for viewer interaction, such as clicking on a button or scene tab.

Making A Basic Animation

This exercise will make you realize how easy it is to grasp the basics of animation. You're going to change the form and size of a flower over time. At the end of the exercise, you'll save your work as a symbol so that you can use it as an element in a presentation or on a Web site. Follow these steps:

1. Start a brand new movie. Choose the Pencil tool, and then choose the Straighten modifier from the Pencil Mode menu. Draw an oval. It can be pretty rough—Flash probably will whip it into perfect shape as soon as you close the loop. If not, just press Cmd/Ctrl+Z and try again.

2. Choose the Smooth modifier from the Pencil Mode menu, and draw looping arcs all around the circle. See Figure 6.1.

3. You can edit the curvature of the arcs by choosing the Arrow tool and dragging their edges. Remember, whenever an arc intersects the oval, it divides (auto-edits) the line that makes up the oval.

4. Choose File|Preferences and click on Shift Select to check its box. (It's a good idea to leave this setting enabled so you can make multiple selections in the same way as in your other graphics programs.)

   When you have the basic shape the way you want it, erase the superfluous lines. Shift-click all the lines that make up the oval. (See Figure 6.2.) When you are done, press Delete/Backspace or choose Edit|Clear.

5. Choose the Text tool. Click inside the flower and enter the word "New!" in large type. To set the type size, either click and drag the Type Size modifier menu, or simply highlight the existing point size and enter the size you like. (I chose 72 points.)

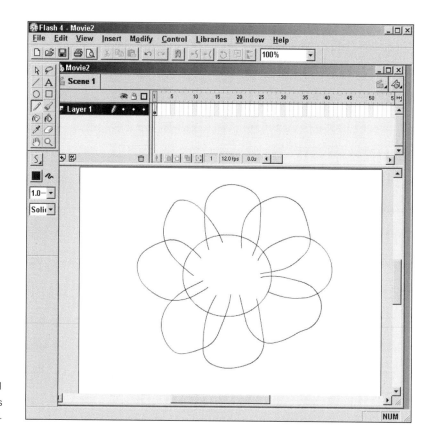

Figure 6.1
Drawing the flower with ovals
and arcs.

6. To choose from any of the fonts installed on your system, pull down the Font modifier menu and drag to highlight the font you want. I used a free Microsoft font called Comic Sans, made especially for screen display (as on the Web), but you should feel free to pick your own favorite.

7. Because type is an overlay, it won't cut into the flower. This makes it easy to edit and replace the type, so you can use the same flower (or starburst, or what have you) for many attention-grabbing notices or instructions.

8. When you have finished entering the type, choose the Arrow tool and click on the Scale modifier. Drag the handles until the type fills the center of the flower. See Figure 6.3.

9. You may also want to thicken the lines that form the edges of the petals. Double-click on the flower to select all the lines at once, then choose the Ink Bottle tool. Choose a four-pixel line thickness from the Line Thickness menu in the modifiers. Click on any of the selected lines, and all their line styles change at the same time.

10. Next, choose the Paint Bucket and a bright, light-orange color. Click inside the flower to fill it. Pick a darker color for the center of the flower, and fill it as well.

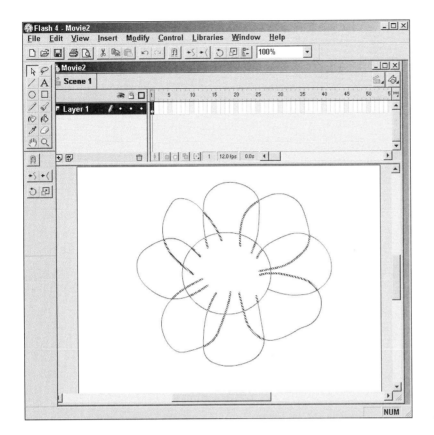

Figure 6.2
Shift-click to select the superfluous lines.

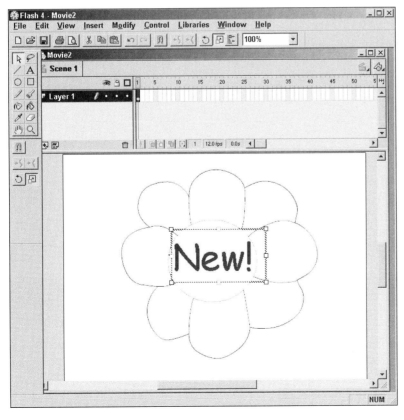

Figure 6.3
The flower with type.

11. Now, you want to group the flower. Choose the Arrow tool. Select all the outlines and the color fills in the flower (but not the text). Press Cmd/Ctrl+G to group the flower and its fill. The text seems to disappear because each new group is automatically moved to the top of the stack. See Figure 6.4.

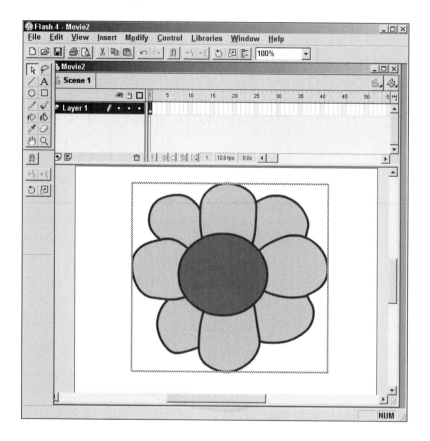

Figure 6.4
The grouped flower, automatically moved to the top of the stack.

12. Press Cmd/Ctrl+Down Arrow key—or choose Modify|Arrange|Send To Back—to place the flower overlay beneath the text overlay.

13. Select both overlays then press Cmd/Ctrl+K to select the Align tool. This will select the Align tool window. In the Vertical Align row, select the third item, which aligns an item to vertical centers. Also, in the Horizontal Align row, select the third icon, which aligns on horizontal centers. Make sure Match Size has the X selected and Align to page is deselected. Now click on OK. Notice that both items will have their centers matched, but they will both move to a common center. There is no way in Flash to align one to the fixed position of the other, they will both move.

14. Press Cmd/Ctrl+A again to select all, and check the location of the centers. (See Figure 6.5.) If you see more than one crosshair, you

need to repeat the step above to position one of the overlays so that its crosshair registers on top of the other one. (There's a little guess-work involved here because the fills in the shapes tend to hide the grid intersections. One way to help solve this problem is to go into the Preferences dialog box and change the grid intersections so that there are very few of them.)

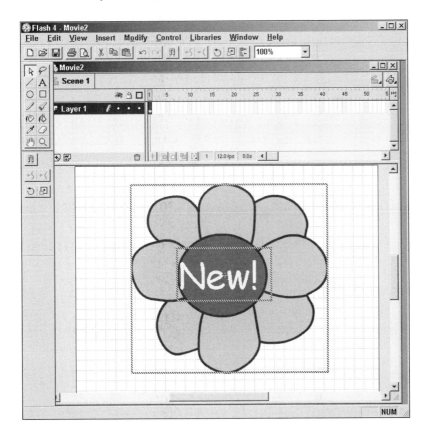

Figure 6.5
With both overlays selected, the centers are perfectly aligned.

15. Now that you have all the basic parts in place, you can start animating. Take a look at the Timeline (shown in Figure 6.6). Place the cursor in the space for the second frame and drag to frame 4. When you release the mouse button, you'll see a black band. These black high-lights appear any time you click on a frame position in the Timeline.

    To display the Frame menu, point to the Timeline and right-click (Windows) or click and hold (Mac). (This menu is also shown in Figure 6.6.)

16. When the Frame menu appears, choose Insert Frame. New frames will be inserted for frames 2 through 5. If you move the current frame pointer across all four frames, you will see four exact copies of the flower as we have drawn it.

Properties...	
Create Motion Tween	
Insert Frame	F5
Delete Frame	Shift+F5
Insert Keyframe	F6
Insert Blank Keyframe	F7
Clear Keyframe	Shift+F6
Select All	
Copy Frames	Ctrl+Alt+C
Paste Frames	Ctrl+Alt+V
Reverse Frames	
Synchronize Symbols	

Figure 6.6

The Frame menu.

17. You want each of these frames to be slightly different from all the others. In order to do that, you must make each frame a *keyframe*, a frame in which something changes from the previous frame. Highlight frames 2 through 4. Then display the Frame pull-down menu—place the cursor on the frame, and right-click (Windows) or click and hold (Mac)—and choose Insert Keyframe.

(You could have inserted the keyframes without first inserting frames, but this way you can see the difference between repeated static frames and keyframes.)

18. Press Esc. The highlight disappears, and a solid black dot appears in each of the frames.

19. Click on the leftmost Onion Skin button. Onion-skin markers appear on either side of the current frame pointer. You can drag these markers to change the number of onion-skin layers that are visible before and after the current frame.

20. Let's make the flower vibrate in and out while the letters grow and spin. First, it will help to turn on the grid so that you can maintain the relative position of the two elements as they move. Choose View|Grid (unless, of course, you still have it on). Also, look at the View menu again and make sure there is no checkmark alongside Snap. If there is, choose View|Snap to toggle Snap off.

21. You are going to animate changes in one element and then the other, starting with frame 1. Make sure the frame pointer is at frame 1. Select the text overlay, and choose Modify|Transform|Scale And Rotate. The Scale And Rotate dialog box opens (see Figure 6.7).

    This dialog box is very handy in animation because it lets you scale, rotate, or do both at the same time, in perfectly precise increments—thus ensuring smooth movement from frame to frame. Type "25" in the Scale field and "180" in the Rotate field. Click on OK. The text will be one-fourth its original size and upside down.

Scale and Rotate

Scale: 25 % OK

Rotate: 180 degrees Cancel

Help

Figure 6.7

The Scale And Rotate dialog box.

22. Drag the current frame pointer to frame 2. The text overlay is still visible, but at its original size and orientation. Select the text overlay. Press Cmd+Opt+S (Mac) or Ctrl+Alt+S (Windows) to open the Scale

And Rotate dialog box. Type "50" in the Scale field and "120" in the Rotate field. Click on OK.

Repeat this step for frame 3, typing "75" in the Scale field and "60" in the Rotate field. In the fourth frame, the text is already upright and full sized, so you don't need to do anything.

23. Now comes the fun part. Press Cmd/Ctrl+Shift+A to Deselect All. Press Enter/Return and watch the movie—that is, if you don't blink. The text starts small and simultaneously spins and zooms out.

    Next, you want to animate the flower so that it moves at the same time that the text is rotating and zooming.

24. Drag the current frame pointer to frame 1 and select the flower. Press Cmd+Opt+S or Ctrl+Alt+S to open the Scale And Rotate dialog box. Type "90" in the Scale field and "0" in the Rotate field. Click on OK. The flower shrinks slightly.

25. Drag the current frame pointer to frame 3. Make sure that only the flower is selected. Open the Scale And Rotate dialog box and click on OK. (The figures you entered last time are still in effect.)

    Press Return/Enter to play your movie. You can see the frames in sequence in Figure 6.8.

Figure 6.8
The four frames of the animation.

26. If the movie plays too fast, it is because Flash's default frame rate is 12 frames per second (fps). You will see that figure in the Frame Rate Setting box (the center box just below the layer names—it contains a number followed by "fps"). Double-click in the Frame Rate Setting box to open the Movie Properties dialog box. This is a valuable shortcut because you can change any of the movie properties this way. (See Figure 6.9.)

    All you have to do to change the frame rate is enter a different number (in a range from 0.1 to 120) in the Frame Rate field. Yes, you can change many other properties for this movie at the same time, but remember that changing a movie's properties affects the entire movie and not just one frame or scene.

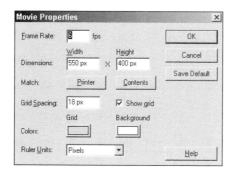

Figure 6.9
The Movie Properties dialog box.

Figure 6.10
Inserting frames to freeze
a frame.

27. When this movie ends, you want the frame to pause long enough for the viewer to read it. Flash doesn't let you control the playing time of a single frame (as animated GIFs do). This isn't a problem, really. Just insert duplicate frames after the frame you want to freeze—as many as it takes to have the frame pause for as long as you want, given the current frame rate. In this instance, we want the animation to pause for several seconds before it starts playing again. Place the cursor in the frame Timeline and drag for an additional 24 frames. From the Frame menu, choose Insert Frame. See Figure 6.10. In Chapter 9, we will show you how to add a timed pause using a plug and play routine we have created for you using Flash 4's built in scripting language, ActionScript, but for short delays it is often easier just to add a few frames.

28. Press Esc to evaporate the I-beam and the highlighted frames. You will see a vertical bar at frame 28 to indicate the end of the movie. If you move the current frame pointer through these frames (or press the > key), Flash will propagate the same image as the one in the last frame through all the other frames. Remember, if you make any change in any of these frames, it will be reflected in all the others because these are not keyframes.

29. Okay, let's wrap this up by making the animation loop and then saving it as a symbol so that you can use it as a part of any other movie. Choose Control|Loop Playback. Now, press Return/Enter and watch what happens: The animation plays and then keeps repeating. Press Enter again to stop playing the animation.

Saving Movies As Symbols

So, you've done your first animation. It may not seem like much, but all the other animation trickery just embellishes on these basic steps. You can make much more powerful movies by making small movies like this and saving them as symbols. Later on, you will find any number of ways that you can insert the symbols into a movie in such a way that you can have several movies play simultaneously. You can even use a symbol to make a movie play when a mouse event, such as a click, occurs. Here are the steps for saving your movie as a symbol:

1. To save the movie as a symbol, highlight all the frames of the animation. Click in the first frame in the top layer, then Shift-click in the last frame of the lowest layer. This will highlight all the frames. Right-click (Windows) or click and hold (Mac) on the selected frames; then choose Copy frames.

2. Deselect all, then choose Insert|Create Symbol. In the dialog box that opens, enter a name and select Movie Clip. Click on OK. A new, clean symbol editing space will open. Select the new blank frame then right-click (Windows) or click and hold (Mac) onto the frame. Choose Paste Frames and all the frames and their contents from the timeline will be moved into the new symbol.

3. The new movie clip symbol is in the Library and the old animation is on the stage. Delete the old frames and drag the new symbol from the Library onto the stage. Choose File|Save As, and name the movie "MySymbols" (or whatever you wish).

Well, that was quick and easy! Now, you have a really good idea of what it takes to produce animation in Flash. From this point on, you just ice the cake.

Easy Animation Techniques

Many animation tricks are so easy that you could put a nearly endless variety of materials on a Web site or in a presentation without ever doing anything more elaborate. After working through the previous exercise and reading this list (and the few helpful hints that follow each technique), most of you will be able to employ all of these tricks. If not, the tools and command references in the Animation Reference section of this chapter surely will show you the way. Try to think of different types of subjects and situations to which you could apply these.

Concentric Shapes

This technique draws attention to a static subject by having a series of concentric shapes (such as circles) radiate outward from it. This technique is very easy. Place your shape in the center of the frame, and then draw a series of shapes around the subject. Copy the frame over as many keyframes as there are concentric shapes; then select and erase the shapes in subsequent frames.

The following example animates concentric circles. This time, we are sending out radial waves from a sunburst above a mountain. I'm assuming that you can draw the mountain with the Pencil, the Smooth modifier, the Paint Bucket, and the Rectangle tool. The mountain should look something like Figure 6.11. Then go through the following steps to create light waves.

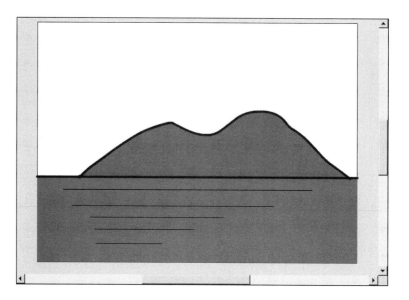

Figure 6.11
The mountain drawing.

1. Start by turning on the grid so that you can snap to grid intersections. Choose View|Grid.

2. Select all the elements that make up the mountain. Press Cmd/Ctrl+G to group them.

3. Choose the Oval tool, pick a yellow fill from the modifiers, and draw a circle to represent the sun. Select the sun. Press Cmd/Ctrl+G to make it a group.

4. Move the sun group to the top of the stack. Select the sun group and then choose Modify|Arrange|Bring To Front.

5. You are now going to make the concentric circles. You want them in a group so that you can change the position of all of them at once and so that they don't auto-edit the other shapes in the movie. Make sure that nothing is selected and then press Cmd/Ctrl+G. You have made an empty group. The mountain and the sun fade to lighter shades.

6. Choose the Oval tool. In an area of the canvas well away from the mountain, press Shift and drag to draw a small circle. Use a hairline outline and no fill color so that you can see where the circle registers over the sun. See Figure 6.12.

Choose the Arrow tool, double-click on the circle to choose it, and then drag it so that it surrounds the sun perfectly. Use the Paint Bucket to fill the circle with a slightly lighter shade of yellow. Then delete the outline, and group the fill.

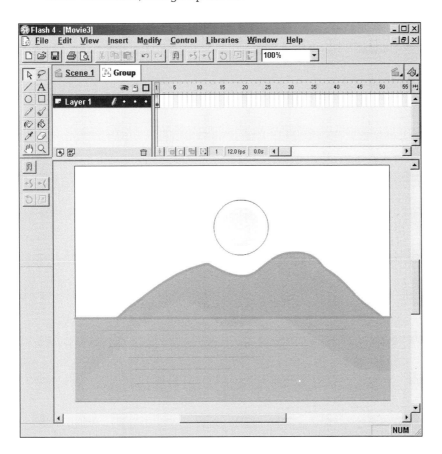

Figure 6.12
Drawing a perfect circle.

7. While you're still in Symbol Edit mode, repeat Step 6 to draw another concentric circle. Fill and group each circle in turn; then press Cmd/Ctrl+Down Arrow to move it behind the original. The result should look like Figure 6.13.

8. Now, you want to go back to editing the movie. When you do this, the circles will automatically become one group. Either choose Edit|Edit All or double-click outside the group. All the elements of the movie will be seen in their regular colors.

9. Move the group of concentric circles behind the mountain. Choose the Arrow tool and click on one of the circles. The group will be selected. Drag them into position behind the mountain. If necessary, choose Modify|Arrange|Send To Back to place the circles behind the mountain. Then drag the sun group so that it is partially hidden behind the mountain. The frame should now look like Figure 6.14.

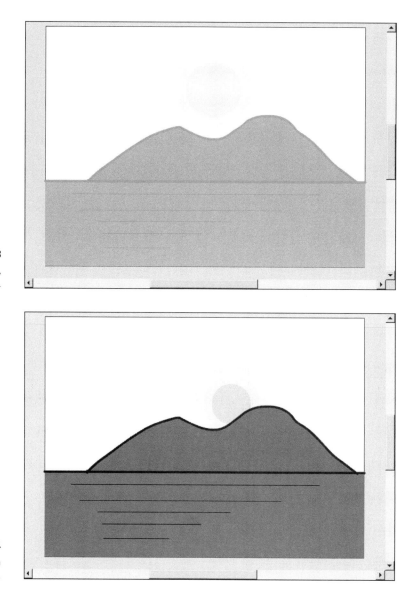

Figure 6.13
Perfectly concentric circles, drawn in their own groups.

Figure 6.14
The finished mountain and sun drawing, using concentric circles.

10. Now, you start the animation. Choose the Arrow tool. In the Timeline, drag across frames 2 through 5. Each frame turns black to indicate that it has been selected.

11. Now, insert keyframes for each of the selected frames. Place the cursor on the black bar that makes up the selected frames, and right-click (Windows) or click and hold (Macintosh). The Frame menu appears. Choose Insert Keyframes (or just press F6).

12. Drag the Frame pointer to frame 1. Select the concentric-circles group. This group should *not* include the sun, which should be just in front of the concentric circles. Select the circles group and press Delete/Backspace.

13. Move the pointer to the next frame. Select the circles group. Choose Edit|Edit Selected, and erase all but the smallest circle. Double-click outside the group to return this frame to Edit All mode.

14. Move the pointer to the next frame, double-click in the circles group, and erase the two outermost circles. Double-click outside the group to return this frame to Edit All mode.

15. Move the pointer to the next frame, and erase the outermost circle.

16. The last frame shows all the circles. (You don't want to erase any.) Select this frame and drag across the next two or three frames. Right-click (Windows) or click and hold (Mac) on the selected frames; then choose Insert Frames from the Frame menu. This will cause the last frame to stay still (showing all the circles) for a moment. Choose Control|Loop Playback to cause the movie to loop. See Figure 6.15.

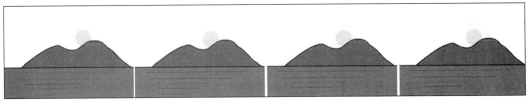

Figure 6.15
All the frames of the sunburst movie.

17. Save your movie. Then save your movie as a symbol, based on the instructions in the preceding exercise.

Flashing Lights

Flashing lights are, oh, so easy to make and, oh, so useful. A variation of the sunburst movie you just made, flashing lights can be the gleam in an eye, the blink of a headlight, or an idea about to be born. Actually, you would be smart to make a bunch of flashing lights and save them as a library of symbols. You could then use them all over a movie, plus they're very effective as buttons on a Web page.

Here's how to make flashing lights: Create several freeform splashes and fill them with a radial gradient. Then, eliminate the outlines and group each splash so that they can overlay one another. Then, select them all and use the Align command to stack them all at their centers. Copy them all to keyframes, and then move from frame to frame deleting the unneeded overlays. You can see a flashing light in Figure 6.16.

This exercise will show you how to make a flashing-light movie. Follow these steps:

1. Place the drawing of the object from which the flashing light will emanate on the canvas. For the purposes of this exercise, you will

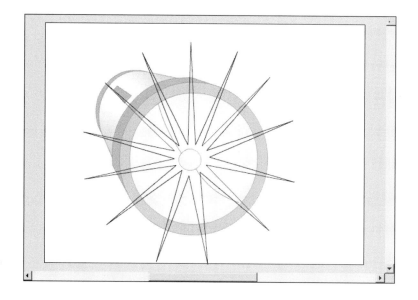

Figure 6.16
A flashing light.

find a single-frame movie called Flashlight.fla on the CD. Load the movie as a library by choosing File|Load As Library. Choose Window|Library and drag the flashlight symbol into the main frame. (You can scale it to any size you like with the Scale modifier.)

2. With nothing selected, press Cmd/Ctrl+G to create a new group. Now anything you do (until you choose Edit|Edit All) will be added to a new group.

3. Use the Line tool to draw a starburst shape.

4. Double-click on the starburst outline, or select it and choose Edit|Edit Selected. The lantern will fade to gray.

5. Now, we will make a radial gradient fill. Choose the Paint Bucket tool and then the Color modifier. A palette appears. See Figure 6.17.

6. Let's say you want to change one of the gradients in the row at the bottom of the Color palette. Click to choose the gradient you want to change. The palette disappears, and the chosen gradient appears as the Paint Bucket's Color modifier.

7. Click in the Color modifier box to reopen the palette; then click in the small palette icon (button) at the very top center of the palette. The Color dialog box opens. Click on the Gradient tab. See Figure 6.18.

8. On the left side of the Gradient tab is a slot with two sliders. These sliders indicate the stop and start colors of the gradient. To change any of the colors, click the color swatch inside the slider that's pointing at the color you want to change. Then, click and drag in the Color modifier on the right side of the dialog box to choose the color for that slider.

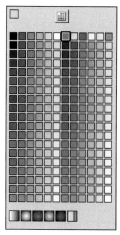

Figure 6.17
The color palette. Note the gradient in the row at the bottom of the palette.

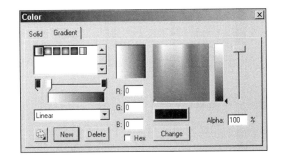

Figure 6.18

The Gradient tab of the Color dialog box lets you specify the colors and other characteristics of the gradient.

To the right of the color modifier, you will find another slider that indicates the intensity (brightness) of the color you have chosen. Use the Color modifier and the intensity slider to indicate a very light yellow (almost white).

9. Use the same procedure to pick a darker yellow for the other gradient slider. Leave the two sliders at opposite ends of the slot.

10. You'll want to be able to see through the "light," so drag the rightmost slider down until the Alpha box reads approximately 60%. (This setting makes the colors only 60 percent opaque so that you can see through the "light.")

    When the colors are set as you like them, click on the New button. A new gradient swatch appears at the bottom of the Swatches menu. You can find more about making gradients in Chapter 4.

11. Double-click on the starburst outline to edit its group. (If you've used the symbol I included instead of drawing the starburst, you'll need to choose Edit|Edit Symbols.) Choose the Paint Bucket tool, and click inside the starburst. It fills with the gradient.

    Select the outline and delete it, leaving only the gradient fill. Choose Edit|Edit All (or Edit|Edit Movie).

12. Choose the Arrow tool, and drag across frames 1 through 4 to select them. Place the cursor over the resultant black bar and Ctrl+click (Mac) or right-click (Windows) to display the Frame menu. Choose Insert Keyframes (or just press F6). You now have a copy of this first frame in each keyframe.

13. Select the first frame. Choose the Arrow tool and select the starburst. Because the starburst is grouped, a selection rectangle appears around it. Choose Modify|Transform|Scale And Rotate. In the Scale And Rotate dialog box, enter 75 (percent) as the Scale factor and 12 (degrees) as the Rotate factor.

14. Select the third frame. Choose the Arrow tool and select the starburst. Choose Modify|Transform|Scale And Rotate. The entries are those you previously set. Because you want the light to alternate size and position in every other frame, just press Return/Enter.

15. Press Return/Enter to play the movie. You will see a pulsating light. To make this movie loop, choose Control|Loop Playback. Now, if you press Return, the light will pulsate endlessly. Set the frame rate to 6 fps (frames per second). See Figure 6.19.

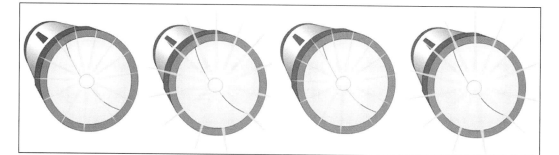

Figure 6.19

The four frames of the blinking-light movie.

Traveling

This is the easiest animation you can make and one that you'll use more often than almost any other. Traveling is just moving an object (such as a line of text or a speeding bullet) from one side of the frame to another. You can do traveling frame by frame—as you've done everything so far—or you can do it the smart and easy way: by letting the computer do it through a process called *tweening*.

You make a keyframe at the start of the movement. The item you are going to move must be an overlay: group, symbol, or text. Put the item to move at its start point in this first keyframe. Then choose Tweening from the Frame menu. Now add another keyframe several frames further along the Timeline. The content of the original keyframe appears. Select it and drag it to the location where you want its movement to end. If you like, you can also scale and rotate it. The computer automatically draws all the in-between frames. Figure 6.20 shows a simple traveling animation.

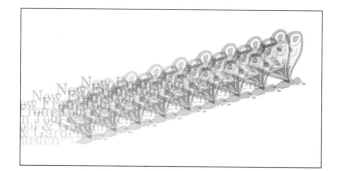

Figure 6.20

Onion-skin view of the automatically tweened traveling scene.

The exact steps for creating a traveling animation follow. Once again, we are using existing art because the point of this exercise is to teach you how to animate, not how to draw. Oh, we'll use some type, too. Follow these steps to create a traveling animation:

1. Open the file butterfly.fla as a Library (choose File|Open As Library). When the file is loaded, you will see a Library palette. Drag the butterfly symbol to the canvas. Select and drag the group to the right side of the frame. Then use the Scale modifier to make the group smaller.

2. Enter some type. Then scale and place it so that it is in position to be dragged by the butterfly.

3. Press Cmd/Ctrl+A to Select All (or choose Edit|Select All). Now, press Cmd/Ctrl+G to group everything. (Only groups and symbols can be tweened.)

4. Double-click on frame 1 in the Timeline. The Frame Properties dialog box opens. See Figure 6.21.

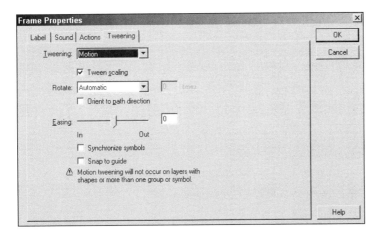

Figure 6.21
The Frame Properties dialog box, showing the Tweening tab.

5. Click on the Tweening tab. From the Tweening drop-down list box, choose Motion. Leave the rest of the settings at their defaults.

6. Choose the Arrow tool, and click in the Timeline at frame 25. Place the cursor on the highlighted frame, and click and hold (Mac) or right-click (Windows). Choose Insert Keyframe from the Frame menu.

7. With the last frame still selected, select and drag the butterfly and banner group clear off the canvas to the right.

8. Click in the Timeline slot for frame 1 to select it. The drawing group appears at its original position. Drag it to the left until it is off the canvas.

9. Press Return to play your movie. If it plays too fast, you can slow the frame rate. You can also insert more frames in place of any of the non-keyframe frames. Then the animation will play more smoothly, and the file size will remain the same. You can see the finished progression in Figure 6.22.

Figure 6.22
The flying banner.

Radiating Lines

Radiating lines can be used to imply that an object is outstanding, beating, bonging, or throbbing. The trick is to make the lines radiate in the right direction and along a specified path. I do this by first drawing a circle or oval with a dashed or dotted line, then scaling it at regular intervals with the Modify|Transform|Scale And Rotate command (Cmd/Ctrl+Shift+S). Then, I align the resulting images all on a center point, and make this a guide layer by choosing Guide from the Layer modifier pop-up menu (the button just to the right of the Layer Name bar in the Timeline). Then, I can copy my original drawing to a number of keyframes, turn on Snap, and drag the lines until they snap to the next concentric circle. When I no longer need the guide layer, I choose Delete Layer from the Layer modifier pop-up menu. See Figure 6.23.

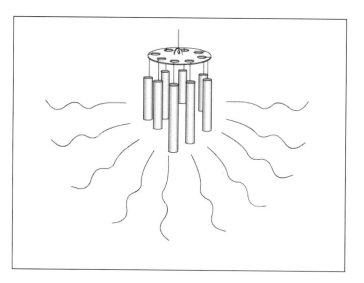

Figure 6.23
The wind chime and radiating lines.

Here's one possible scenario for ringing your wind chime. You'll think of several effective variations. Follow these steps:

1. Draw or import the wind chime (windchime.fla).

2. Now, you want to jiggle the chimes so that they bang into one another. Move the pointer to the first frame. Select the wind chime and then choose Edit Symbols. The radiating lines will disappear.

   Drag in the Timeline to indicate three new frames. Ctrl+click or right-click to display the Frame menu, and choose Insert Keyframe.

3. Move the pointer to the first frame, select every other chime, and then rotate and reposition them so that each chime just taps its neighbor.

4. Move the pointer to the third frame and repeat the previous step, except rotate the opposite set of chimes. When you've finished, choose Edit|Edit Movie.

5. Choose the Pencil tool and the Smooth modifier, and draw several squiggly lines until you find one or two you like. See Figure 6.24.

6. Erase all the lines you don't want to keep. I wanted all my radiating lines to be uniform, so I erased all but one. Drag the line into position alongside the wind chime and save it as a symbol.

7. Press Cmd/Ctrl+D to duplicate the squiggly line.

8. Choose the Arrow tool and then its Rotate modifier. Drag one of the corners of the squiggly line so that it rotates slightly, and then drag it into position. Repeat this step until the radiating lines surround half of the wind chime. See Figure 6.25.

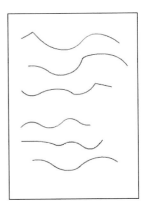

Figure 6.24
Making smoothed lines until you get one you like.

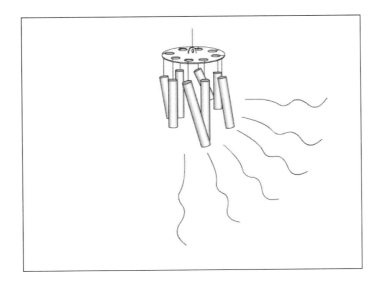

Figure 6.25
Lines radiating around half of the wind chime.

9. Select all of the radiating lines. Press Cmd/Ctrl+G to group the radiating lines. Be careful *not* to include any of the shapes that compose the wind chime. Press Cmd/Ctrl+D to duplicate the radiating-lines group.

10. Drag the second group of radiating lines to the opposite side of the wind chime. Choose Modify|Transform|Flip Horizontal. You now have the group of radiating lines that you need for the opposite side of the wind chime.

11. Copy the wind chime and radiating lines to three more frames by inserting four new keyframes. Drag across four frames in the Timeline, then choose Insert Keyframe from the Frame menu.

12. Place the pointer in the first frame. Select each radiating line in turn, choose the Scale modifier, and push one of the outside handles inward. Do this to the same degree for each of the radiating lines. When you've finished shrinking the squiggles, press Shift+click to select all of them, and then press Cmd/Ctrl+C to copy them to the Clipboard.

13. Drag the pointer to the third frame. Press Cmd/Ctrl+A to Select All, then Cmd/Ctrl+V to Paste the shortened squiggles into their place. Trouble is, they just land atop the original squiggles. Use the Arrow keys to position the pasted (still selected) squiggles so that their inside ends match (as closely as possible) the inside ends of the larger squiggles. When you have them in place, deselect them, and select and delete the larger squiggles. If you press Return/Enter, you will see that the lines expand in and out. So far, so good.

14. To make the movie loop (in the editor) so that the wind chime rings continually, choose Control|Loop Playback. See Figure 6.26.

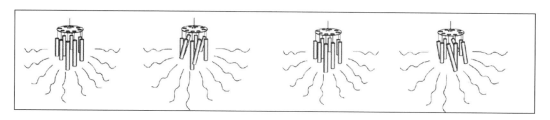

Figure 6.26
All four frames of the movie with the ringing wind chimes.

Spin And Zoom

This is another technique that can be done automatically (although it was done manually in the first exercise). You simply put the subject in the first frame, and insert a keyframe as many frames later as you want the spinning and zooming to end. Select the first keyframe, double-click on it to open the Frame Properties dialog box, and choose the Tweening tab. You can choose whether to tween Motion or Shape from the Tweening drop-down list box in the Properties dialog box, and then choose the type of rotation from the Rotation drop-down list box. Then click on OK. That's all there is to it.

In this exercise, we'll not only spin and zoom, but have tweening change the color and opacity of the text as well. Follow these steps to spin and zoom:

1. Start by entering the text you want to tween. If you want to tween an object that will move against a static background or that will move when there are other objects moving in other directions, create a new layer and place the tween on it. For now, we'll just keep it simple and tween in a new movie with a blank canvas.

2. Select the word(s) you just typed. Choose Insert|New Symbol to open the Symbol Properties dialog box. See Figure 6.28.

3. Type a descriptive name in the Name field. Leave the Graphic radio button selected. Click on OK.

4. Choose Window|Library. You should see your symbol in the Library. (This is just a check to make sure that you have saved your symbol. You don't need to do anything with the Library window at this time.)

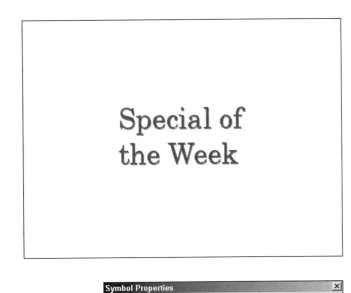

EDITING TWEENED FRAMES

Although you can't edit the tweened frames, you can change them into keyframes and then edit them. That way you get automatic positioning and re-scaling, but you also can make changes in individual frames. To do this, place the I-beam on the Timeline at the frame that you want to convert to a keyframe (click on a given frame in the Timeline). Then choose Insert Keyframe from the Frame menu. You will then be able to make any change or additions you like to this frame. You can also highlight all the frames and choose Insert Keyframe from the Frame menu to make all the tweened frames into keyframes. That's how I changed the color of the text in the spin-and-zoom example in Figure 6.27.

Figure 6.27
The text we'll spin and zoom.

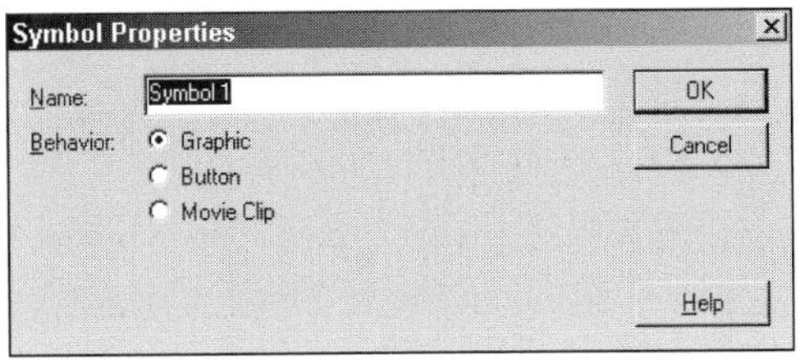

Figure 6.28
The Symbol Properties dialog box.

5. Select frame 10; then click and hold (Mac) or right-click (Windows) to display the Frame menu. Choose Insert Keyframe.

6. Choose the Arrow tool and select the symbol (if it's not already selected). Then choose the Scale modifier. Press Shift to enforce

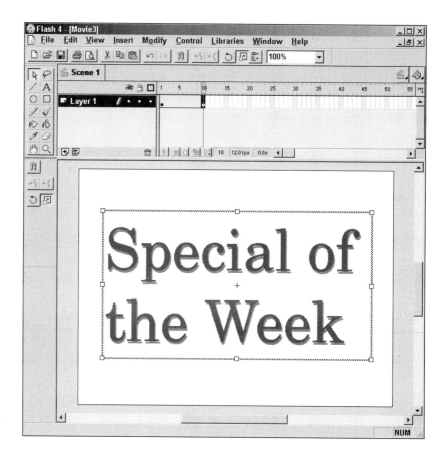

Figure 6.29
The scaled-up symbol in the last keyframe.

proportionate scaling, and drag one of the sizing boxes until the text fills about half the canvas. See Figure 6.29.

7. Double-click on frame 1 to open the Frame Properties dialog box. Choose Motion from the Tweening drop-down list box, and choose Clockwise from the Rotate drop-down list box. Also, type "1" in the Times field just to the right of the Rotate list box. Make sure that Tween Scaling is checked. (If it's not, just click in the box.) Click on OK.

You have just made a spinning and zooming animation. Press Return/Enter to watch the amazing effect. But wait, there's more.

8. Make sure the pointer is over frame 1. Choose Modify|Instance to open the Instance Properties dialog box. (This is why you made the text into a symbol; otherwise, you wouldn't be able to access the Instance Properties, so you couldn't tween between them.) Choose Color Effect, and drag the Alpha slider to approximately 10 percent. You can see the Instance Properties dialog box in Figure 6.30.

9. Move the frames pointer to frame 10, and choose Modify|Instance. When the Instance Properties dialog box reappears, click on the

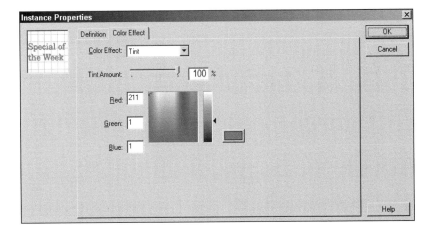

Color Effect tab. The choice of settings changes. (See Figure 6.31.)
Choose Tint for the Color Effect. Drag the Tint Amount slider to 100
percent. Use the Color modifier and the Intensity slider to choose a
bright red color. Click on OK.

Figure 6.31
Instance Properties settings
for Tint.

10. You have now made your movie tween a color change and a transparency change—in addition to the rotation. Figure 6.32 shows you
every other frame in the final sequence.

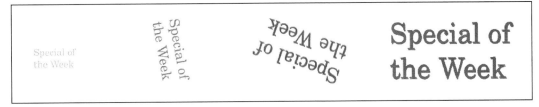

Figure 6.32
Four of the frames in the
tweened sequence.

Transition Effects

Transition effects are those that move us from one scene to another. Examples are wipes and dissolves. Flash has no built-in transition effects, but
you can animate them in several ways. One of my favorites is "fading in"

on a drawing. For the frame that you want to fade in (or out), you save it as a symbol, then use the Symbol Instance properties to modify the transparency of the start or stop frame.

This exercise fades in a photo of a flower. (The photo is shown in Figure 6.33.)

This one's really easy. Follow these steps:

1. Select the object you want to fade in (in this case, an imported PNG photo). Choose Insert|New Symbol. When the Symbol Properties dialog box opens, name the symbol, select the Graphic radio button, and then click on OK.

2. While the original imported photo is still selected, choose Edit|Clear or press Backspace/Delete to erase it. The canvas is now blank.

3. Choose Window|Library. Drag the flower symbol to the center of the canvas.

4. Choose Modify|Instance. In the Instance dialog box, click on the Color Effect tab. For the Color Effect, choose Alpha. Type "0" in the percentage box or drag the slider to the far left. Click on OK. The flower seems to disappear.

5. Select frame 10. Display the Frame menu—click and hold (Mac) or right-click (Windows) on the selected frame—and choose Insert Keyframe.

6. Select frame 1. Double-click on the selected frame to open the Frame Properties dialog box. Click on the Tweening tab. For the Tweening option, choose Motion. Leave the rest of the settings at their defaults, and click on OK.

7. Press Return/Enter to see your movie. The flower slowly fades into view, as shown in Figure 6.34.

Figure 6.34
The flower, fading in.

Animation Reference

The remainder of this chapter is a more thorough definition of the features in Flash that are used to create animations. Some of these features also contribute to Flash in other ways, of course.

You have now used the three fundamental types of Flash animation:

- Frame by frame

- Tweened

- Still-frame

You already have a good sense of the functions of frames and of where to find commands on the Timeline. In addition to discussing the three types of animation and how to implement each type, this section also shows you how to use layers to create complex animations, and how to use animated symbols to make animations even richer.

Frame By Frame

Frame-by-frame animations require that every (or nearly every) frame be a keyframe. In each keyframe, something changes, and you (not the computer) have to make the change. The walking stick figure in Figure 6.35 is an example of frame-by-frame animation.

Figure 6.35
Frame-by-frame animation of a walking stick figure.

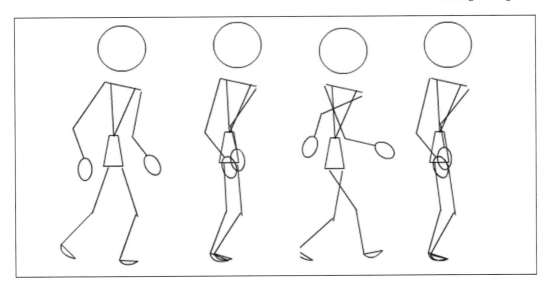

USING STICK FIGURES AS SKELETONS

Animating stick figures is a good way to make a "skeleton" for animating complex frame-by-frame movements. It's especially common for animating people and animals. You then can make that layer a guide layer, start a new layer, and draw (or move) your full-bodied figure according to the way the skeleton moves. That way, you can test your movement before you have to make painstaking changes to a full drawing in each and every frame.

When you're animating a skeleton stick figure, make all the lines for the left-side limbs red and all those for the right side blue. It will be much easier to keep track of what moved past what. When you finish the animation, you can change the color of the limbs.

Tweening

As we previously mentioned, tweening implies the drawing of two keyframes (to represent the starting and ending positions of a movement) with the in-between frames filled in by someone else. In the case of computer animation, the "someone else" is the computer software that automates the process. All of the following effects, except morphing, can be incorporated into the same tweening sequence:

- *Movement*—You can move a drawing from one position in the first keyframe to another position in the last keyframe. The drawing will appear to move in a straight line.

- *Movement along a path*—You can have the tweened movement follow a line or a curve in a guide layer.

- *Scaling*—You can stretch or change the size of the drawing (or part of it) from keyframe to keyframe. Flash can animate anything you can do with the Transform|Scale command or the Arrow tool's Scale modifier.

- *Rotating and skewing*—You can use either the Modify|Transform|Rotate command or the Scale And Rotate command if you prefer numeric entry.

- *Morphing*—You can cause the shape in the start keyframe to gradually become the shape in the end keyframe. Flash provides "shape hints" to let us control the order of points in shapes so that they can be made to blend smoothly. To create a morph, double-click on the first keyframe to open the Frame Properties dialog box, click on the Tweening tab, and select Shape as the Tweening option.

- *Color Shifting*—You can start with one color and end up with another. The in-between frames will be progressive mixes of the beginning and ending tints. Color shifting works only on symbols and is controlled by the Modify|Instance|Color Effect commands and is often referred to as color tweening.

- *Fading*—You can assign a symbol one level of transparency (alpha) in the start frame and another in the end frame. You can also fade by specifying different levels of brightness for the start and stop keyframes. In-between frames will graduate smoothly between the two. Fading can also be controlled by the Modify|Instance|Color Effect|Alpha command.

In Figure 6.36, you can see what happens to a zucchini when it's tweened by moving, scaling, rotating, and dimming (reducing in brightness) all at the same time. Because the zucchini is a symbol, you could animate the action of a whole field of zucchini.

Figure 6.36

Tweening a zucchini while moving, rotating, scaling, and dimming it.

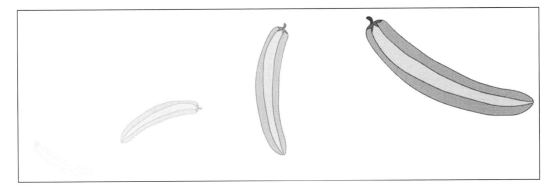

How To Tween

The rules to remember are:

- If you want to tween something, you have to turn it into a group or a symbol first. Tweening affects only overlays.

- If you want to tween more than one overlay in a scene, you have to place each overlay in a separate layer.

Here's the step-by-step procedure for setting up a tween. I'm going to use the zucchini I used in Figure 6.36, but you can substitute any overlay—that is, anything in the Library or anything that you first group.

1. Choose File|Open As Library, and open the Book Library from this book's companion CD-ROM. Choose Libraries|Graphics|Book to open this book's Library. In the Library window, choose Zucchini. When the zucchini appears in the preview window, drag it into your movie.

2. Choose the Arrow tool and click on the zucchini to select the symbol. Double-click in the Layer-1 Timeline at frame 1 (or whatever frame that you want to make the first keyframe). When the Frame Properties dialog box opens, choose the Tweening tab.

3. Choose Motion as the Tweening option. If you plan to scale, check the Scale box. If the tween is going to follow a path, also be sure to check the Orient To Path Direction box.

4. If you want the movement to accelerate as it begins, slide the easing slider to the left. If you want the movement to brake as it ends, move the slider to the right. (Sorry, you can't do both in this program.) Click on OK.

5. Click in the Timeline several frames later (depending on how long you want it to take for the tween to occur). From the Frame menu, choose Insert Keyframe. A red arrow appears in the Timeline between the first keyframe and the last. Move the frame pointer over the new keyframe.

6. Choose the Arrow tool (if it's not already active), and drag your overlay to its stopping point. If you want to scale or rotate, now is the time to do so.

7. Test your animation. All you have to do is press Return/Enter.

Tweening With A Path

It's really easy to make the tween follow any path you like, no matter how erratic (as long as you can draw it). The line that the overlay follows is called a *motion path,* and there's a special procedure for drawing one. The following steps assume that you've already followed the steps in the previous exercise and have created a tween.

1. Move the frame pointer to the first keyframe of your tween. From the menu for the layer in which you have created the tween, choose Add Motion Guide. A second layer appears. An icon of a curved blue path and tomato indicates that this is a motion-guide layer. Notice that this layer has become the current layer, so anything you draw will appear on it.

2. Choose the Pencil tool, and draw a zigzag path to the upper corner of the screen. Now all you have to do is attach your overlay to the path.

3. Choose View|Snap. Choose the Arrow tool, and drag your overlay (in this case, the zucchini) to the starting point of your motion path. A Snap circle will appear in the center of the circle when it is in the right position.

4. Move the frame pointer to the last keyframe, and drag the overlay to the endpoint of the motion path.

5. Choose Tweening from the Frame pop-up menu for the first keyframe, and then check the Orient To Path Direction box. Finally, because you don't want to see the motion path while previewing your movie, choose Hidden from the Layer pop-up menu.

6. Press Return/Enter to preview your movie.

Tweening Color Effects

Color-effects tweening lets you create all sorts of bizarre and wondrous illusions. You can make objects fade from view, flash and pulse, or just change colors. Tweening color effects works only with symbols—not with other types of overlays and not with anything you've drawn on the canvas (unless, of course, you first select it and choose the Insert|Convert To Symbol command).

The following exercise will take you through the not-so-painful process required to create a symbol.

1. Create a new layer by choosing Insert Layer from the Layer pop-up menu (unless, of course, you're doing this in an already-blank movie).

2. From any library, choose the symbol you want to tween and drag it into the current frame. This is called establishing a link to the symbol.

3. Follow the same procedure you would use to create any tween: Choose Tweening from the Frame menu for the first frame, choose Motion from the Tweening dialog box, check any desired boxes, and click on OK. Wrap things up by inserting an end keyframe. (Look at the previous exercise if you've forgotten how to do any of this.)

4. Move the frame pointer back to the first frame. Select the symbol. Choose Modify|Instance to open the Instance Properties dialog box. (See Figure 6.37.) Click on the Color Effect tab, and select the Color Effect that you want (None, Brightness, Tint, Alpha, or Special).

    If you want the first frame to be the same as it was when you linked the symbol, don't take this step.

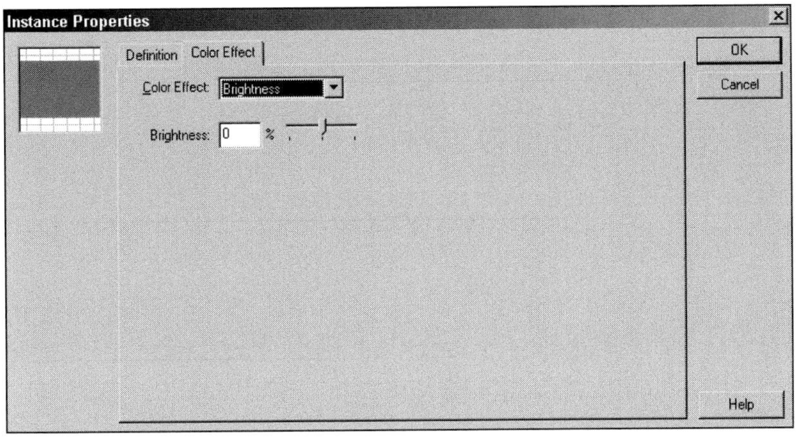

Figure 6.37
The Instance Properties dialog box.

5. Move the frame pointer to the end keyframe. Choose Instance|Modify again, and set the Instance Properties Color Effect as you want your effects to appear at the end of the tween.

6. Press Enter/Return to test your movie.

You can add other tweening effects to this symbol if you like. All you need to do is move the frame pointer to the first frame of the tween, choose Tweening from the Frame menu again, and this time check Tween Scaling and/or Tween Rotation. Move to the last frame of the tween, and scale, rotate, or both.

Tweening Shapes

You can't combine shape tweens (also known as morphs) with motion tweens, although the morph will move if the shapes to be tweened are in different positions on the layer. Otherwise, the steps are very similar to those described previously, except that you choose Shape as the Tweening option in the Frame Properties dialog box. The shape in the first frame will then metamorphose into the shape in the last keyframe.

The process of tweening shapes differs from motion tweening in two important ways:

- You can't shape-tween a group or a symbol. All the shapes must be basic drawn shapes.

- It's a good idea to tween shapes on a separate layer from the rest of the movie.

Step by step, here's how you tween shapes:

1. Unless you are starting with a blank movie, place the cursor over the icon just to the right of the active layer name. Click to pull down the Layers menu. From the Layers menu, choose Insert Layer.

2. Insert a keyframe where you want to introduce the original shape. Create or import a new shape. (I used the zucchini.) If you import the shape, or use a Library symbol, you will need to ungroup or break apart all the elements until the entire drawing is on the canvas for that frame.

3. Select a frame farther down the Timeline. From the Frame menu, choose Insert Blank Keyframe (or just press F7). Draw or import the shape that you want to use as the final shape. In this case, we used the tomato. It too must be composed of only drawn elements with no groups of shapes. Otherwise, break it apart until it is just drawn shapes.

4. Select the first keyframe and double-click it to open the Frame Properties dialog box. Click on the Tweening tab and choose Shape as the Tweening option. Click on the radio button that chooses between distributive and angular tweening, and drag the ease-in/out slider to the appropriate setting. Click on OK.

5. Play the movie. The resultant frames will look something like Figure 6.38.

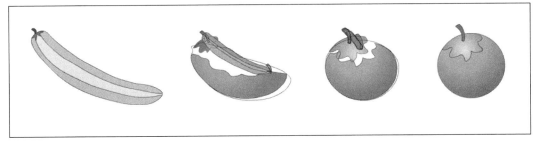

Figure 6.38
The zucchini becomes a tomato.

The Instance Properties Color Effects

You can also tween instance properties of symbols, as we mentioned previously. The properties that you're most likely to use this way are the color effects. Changes in color effects for a given symbol affect only that instance (the place where the symbol appears) and not the symbol itself.

To open the Instance Properties dialog box, either double-click on the instance in the movie or choose Modify|Instance. When you open the Instance Properties dialog box and click on the Color Effect tab, you are given a choice of settings:

- *None*—This one is self-explanatory.

- *Brightness*—Changes the overall brightness of the symbol from pure white to black. Use this control to fade an item without introducing transparency.

- *Tint*—Use this to change the overall color of the symbol. You can switch it to just about any other color. This is a good choice when you want to make a symbol fade into the background color. (This doesn't work on patterned and photographic backgrounds, of course.)

- *Alpha*—Lets you enter a value or drag a slider to indicate a percentage of opacity for the given instance. This is the way you make a see-through bubble or glass of water.

- *Special*—Lets you change the saturation and brightness of each primary color (red, green, and blue) individually.

Still-Frame Sequences

It may seem like an oxymoron to call a "still frame" a "sequence," but the only way you can extend the life of a single frame in Flash is to copy it to a number of subsequent frames. So, anytime you want an object or a scene to just sit there doing nothing, you want to create a *still-frame sequence*. The still-frame sequence has two components that will reflect the same image as in its parent keyframe: the keyframe that has the image in it and empty frames that follow it.

STROBING AN ANIMATION

Suppose that you want to create a strobe effect for your still-frame sequence. Insert blank keyframes at regular intervals along the way, and move the frame pointer to every other keyframe—in sequence. At each stop, tween a brightness effect. You can create similar effects for introducing wind or rain to your set by following this same technique.

One common use for still-frame sequences is as backgrounds. You can draw or import a "set" or "location," and then let your "actors" (drawings and overlays on other layers) perform in front of it.

Creating a still-frame sequence is so easy, you'll wonder why it has a special name. Insert a frame or an end-of-sequence marker after any keyframe, and the keyframe will be copied to all subsequent frames.

Step by step, here's the drill:

1. Click in the Timeline under the marker for where you want to start your still-frame sequence. From the Frame menu, choose Insert Frame and then Insert Keyframe.

2. Click under the marker for the last frame in which you want your still sequence to appear. If this is the end of the sequence and nothing is to follow, you're finished. On the other hand, if you want to start a new still-frame sequence or another type of animation, choose Insert Frame and then follow the proper procedure for a frame-by-frame, tween, or still-frame sequence.

By the way, any editing changes that you make in any frame of a still-frame sequence will automatically occur in all the frames in that sequence.

You can't interrupt a still-frame sequence, either. If you insert a new keyframe anywhere in the Timeline that is occupied by your sequence, the frames after it will take on all the characteristics of the contents of the new keyframe. You can work around this seeming limitation by inserting pairs of keyframes and making changes in between every other pair. You will find a good example of this in the next tip.

The Power Of Layers

So far, I've talked only about animating one sequence at a time. Truth is, Flash gives you tools that let you animate many things at once. This section is all about one of those tools: layers.

Theoretically (if you were really good at visualizing multiple-motion occurrences over time), you could hand-draw complex animations over a single span of frames. After all, Disney started out doing it that way. Imagine a scene in which six people are walking and running, all at different speeds and gaits. A flock of birds is flying overhead, moving from the opposite side of the screen. A helicopter is taking off, and the lights in the background cityscape are turning on and off. You can do all of this with Flash (maybe not quite as complicated if your project is expected to play on average computers on the Web). All you have to do is take one step—one layer—at a time.

With layers, you can run as many animations as you'd like, one atop the other. Because the canvas (background) for each of these layers is transparent, the activity on each of the layers seems to be taking place at the same time. You can change the stacking order of layers by dragging their name bars (just like layers in Photoshop, if you're familiar with that program).

Using The Layer Pop-Up Menu

There's a Layer menu button just to the right of the Layer Name box. The Layer pop-up menu contains 10 commands for showing, hiding, and changing the properties of the layer to which it's attached. Figure 6.39 shows the Layer pop-up menu.

Figure 6.39
The Layer pop-up menu.

The purpose of all the commands in the Layer menu is to make it easier for you to edit the contents of layers when your movie becomes crowded with them. Layers number themselves automatically whenever you create a new one, but it's a much better idea to name them in a way that will help you to remember their contents.

Let's look at the commands in the Layer menu:

- *Show All*—Shows all the layers. Saves you from having to individually unhide layers. Often used in conjunction with Hide Others to check which visible elements are on the current layer.

- *Lock Others*—Locks all but the currently selected layer. Make this one a habit.

- *Hide Others*—Hides all but the currently selected layer.

- *Insert Layer*—Opens the Layer Properties dialog box so you can name the new layer and then insert it below the currently selected layer.

- *Delete Layer*—Removes the current layer.

- *Properties*—Opens the Layer Properties dialog box so you can change the name of a layer.

- *Guide*—Turns this layer into a guide layer. Guide layers are not visible when printed or exported.

- *Add Motion Guide*—Attaches a new motion guide to the current layer.

- *Mask*—This feature turns the current layer into a mask. You'll find the process of masking detailed in Chapter 7.

- *Show Masking*—This new feature shows the masking layer.

There are also three icons that allow toggling of the properties of layers at one time:

- *The eye*—Toggles between show all layers and hide all layers.

- *The lock*—Toggles between all layers being locked and unlocked.

- *The square*—Toggles the multicolor outlines on and off.

Synchronizing Actions Among Layers

You can view a thumbnail of each frame's image in the Timeline. This can be a great help in synchronizing the action with one frame on one layer with the action in another frame on another layer. To view the Timeline in Preview mode, click on the Frame View pop-up button (just under the Edit Symbols pop-up button, with a downward-pointing arrowhead). Choose either Preview or Preview-In-Context. Preview shows the extent of the drawing in each frame (as large as will fit in the thumbnail). Preview-In-Context shows the drawings in all the frames at the same size that they will be in relationship to the entire movie. You can see what a preview looks like in Figure 6.40.

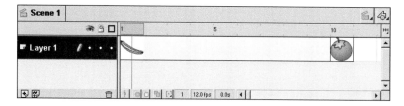

Figure 6.40
Viewing layers in the Timeline in the Preview mode.

Using Guide Layers And Motion Guide Layers

Guide layers are layers whose only purpose is to act as a snap-to placement guide for creating the art in frames on other layers. Using the same techniques as for any other type of layer, you can draw or animate anything in a guide layer. So, you can use anything that will help you to properly visualize the movement of animated objects on other layers. For instance, you might animate a skeleton on a guide layer, then create the full-featured animation of the same creature on another layer.

To create a guide layer, display the Layer pop-up menu for the layer that you want to turn into a guide, and choose Guide. In case you've forgotten, you display the Layer menu by clicking on the Layer icon (the little picture that tells you what type of layer it is, at the right of the Layer Name bar).

You can turn any layer into a guide and any guide back into a normal layer by repeating the same command. The fact that a layer is acting as a guide is signaled by a blue icon of a T-square to the right of the layer name.

Motion guides at first seem similar to guide layers, but motion guides can't be animated and can't be converted to regular layers. Also, motion guides have to be attached to their parent layer. The purpose of a motion guide is to create a path for the movement of a tweened symbol to follow over a series of frames.

To create a motion guide, display the Layer menu for the layer to which you want to add a motion guide, and choose Add Motion Guide. The name of the motion guide layer will be the same as its parent layer, but there will be a blue icon of an arcing path with a ball at the end of it.

To create a motion path, choose the Pencil tool and draw any path you like while the motion guide is the current layer. (See Figure 6.41.)

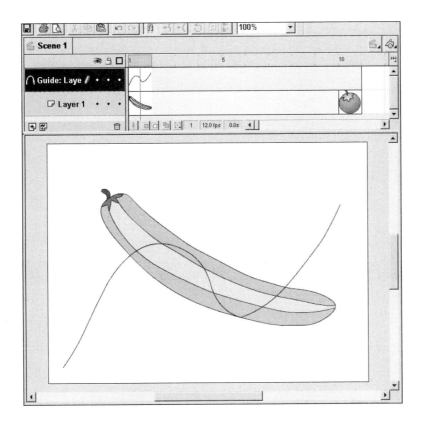

Figure 6.41
A motion path, drawn on a
motion path layer.

Only symbols can be made to follow a motion path. To attach a symbol to a
motion path, select it and then choose Tweening from the Frame menu. When
the dialog box appears, check the Orient To Path Direction box and click on
OK. Move the frame pointer to the first keyframe, then drag the symbol until
it snaps to the beginning of the path. Repeat for the end keyframe.

The Power Of Symbols

If you've gotten this far, you probably know that *symbols* are a kind of overlay and are closely related to groups. Symbols are another tool that Flash
provides to let you animate several things at once.

Symbols are one of the most powerful features of Flash. They significantly
reduce file size by making it possible to store all the data for a given shape
only once, no matter how many times that shape appears in the movie. In
other words, you can have a whole field of animated flowers—which appears
in the background of several scenes in the movie—stored as a single flower.

Symbols also contribute to online performance because they need to be
downloaded only once, no matter how many times they are used in a movie.

The chief differences between symbols and groups are as follows:

- Symbols can be stored in the Library and can be used in many different places in the same movie (different locations in the same frame,
  different frames in the same layer, different scenes). Symbols can

greatly reduce file sizes because the symbol's shape is stored only once. Its shape is stored in the Library and each symbol instance links to that same shape information.

• Symbols can be animated over any number of frames. In order to do this, you have to first choose Insert|New Symbol when nothing is selected. A single-field dialog box opens to let you name the symbol. Inserting a symbol when nothing is selected automatically creates a *symbol scene*. Symbol scenes have all the animation capabilities available in Flash but are created in their own space—so there's no chance of accidentally editing any other components of the movie. When you've finished animating your symbol, choose Edit|Movie. The symbol will instantly be stored in the Library under the name you gave it. It can then be used anywhere.

• The editing procedure is different for symbols. You select the symbol and choose Edit|Selected or Edit Symbol. Either command opens the symbol scene so that you can perform any editing operation possible in Flash, even adding frames and animating a static graphic symbol. You can also edit symbols by choosing Window|Library, choosing the symbol you want to edit, and then choosing Edit from the Options pull-down menu in the Library window. (See Figure 6.42.)

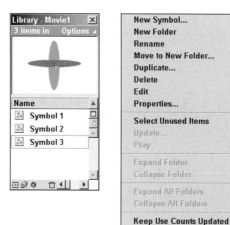

Figure 6.42
The Library window showing the
Library Options menu.

• Symbols can't be ungrouped. To drop the components in a symbol onto the canvas, you must select the symbol and then choose Modify|Break Apart. If the subject of the symbol is a single group, it will appear as though nothing has happened. Check the Modify menu. If Ungroup is not ghosted, choose it.

The number of frames you can see before and after the current frame depends on where you set the markers. (See the section called "Markers," later in this chapter.) For an example of what onion skin looks like with two previous frames showing, see Figure 6.46.

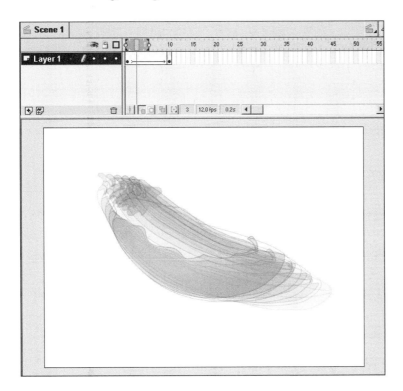

Figure 6.46
Onion skin with two previous frames.

Onion Skin Outlines

If you have to onion-skin very complex shapes as they move, you may really appreciate this feature. When you show Onion Skin Outlines, the onion-skin frames show only the vector outlines of their shapes, so it can be easier to distinguish the contents of the current frame from that of the onion-skinned frames. Take a look at Figure 6.47.

Edit Multiple Frames

This button lets you directly edit the frames within the current onion-skin range (whichever frames are between the markers). In Figure 6.48, notice that none of the frames is dimmed. If any of these frames were tweened, the tweened frames would be ghosted and would change in accordance with the edits made to keyframes.

Modify Onion Markers

Macromedia also calls this button the *Current Frame button*. (After all, consistency can be boring.) This is a pop-up button used to control the behavior

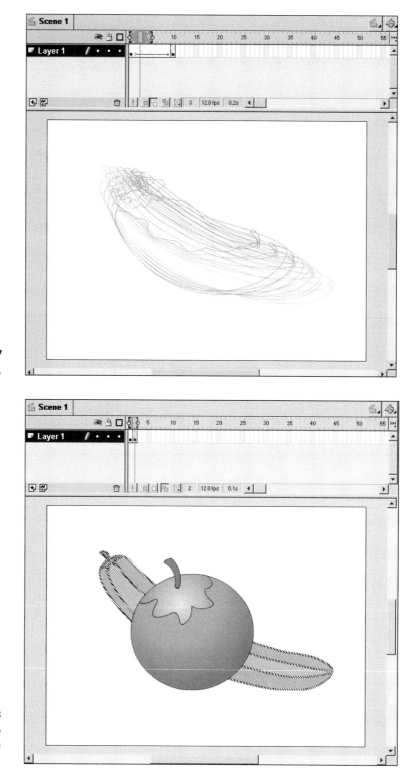

Figure 6.47

Onion Skin Outlines view.

Figure 6.48

The contents of multiple frames are visible when you edit multiple frames.

of the onion-skin markers. You can see the pop-up in Figure 6.49. Here are the functions of the items in the Modify Onion Markers menu:

Figure 6.49
The Modify Onion Markers pop-up menu.

- *Always Show Markers*—The markers are always visible, whether or not onion-skinning is active. This command is a toggle (switches on and off).

- *Anchor Onion*—Keeps the marker tabs in their current locations, regardless of where the frame pointer is located. The result is that onion skins of the same frames are always in view, but they are lighter or darker according to the location of the frame pointer.

- *Onion 2*—Shows two frames on either side of the frame pointer.

- *Onion 5*—Shows five frames on either side of the frame pointer. The markers move to reflect this, regardless of where you move the frame pointer.

- *Onion All*—Onion-skins every frame in the sequence. This can be useful for editing short scenes and sequences but could be very confusing if you applied it to a sequence of more than a few frames.

Markers

Markers bracket the frames that will be onion-skinned. You can manually change the number of frames that will be onion-skinned by dragging the markers. For instance, I often find it helpful to turn off onion-skinning for frames that follow the frame I am editing. All I have to do is drag the right-hand marker to the selected frame.

Moving On

This chapter has shown you how to make some simple animations and has given you basic training in using the various components of Flash's animation interface.

The next chapter will dive into symbols in depth. You'll learn all about the three symbol behaviors in Flash and how to maximize their power.

SYMBOLS AND LIBRARIES 7

KEN MILBURN

This chapter explains all three types of symbols: graphics, buttons, and movie clips. This chapter also explains how to work with bitmaps and sounds, which are also stored in the library.

Figure 7.1
The Library window.

Symbols are entities that can be repeated any number of times within a Flash movie and that can contain any and all elements of any Flash movie. Using symbols, rather than re-creating entities, has two main advantages: you create the symbol only once, and the data for the symbol is stored only once for the entire movie. This results in a smaller data file that takes less time to download. Symbols are one of the main reasons (in addition to the use of vector rather than bitmapped graphics) that Flash's Web performance can be so stunning.

All symbols are stored in the library of the current movie. You can drag and drop symbols into other libraries, so you can have a stockpile of symbol elements that you can use in all your movies, or in all the movies for a particular client or for a particular category. The Library window can be seen in Figure 7.1.

Flash has three distinct types of symbols: graphic, button, and movie clip. Two other categories of items are stored in the library: bitmaps and sounds. Each of these categories will be discussed in depth in this chapter. Then you'll learn how to edit *instances* (the individual occurrence of a symbol in a movie), how to tween instances, how to place sounds in a symbol, and how to edit symbols.

Graphic Symbols

This is the type of symbol that you'll use most often to store static graphics (such as picture icons) and geometric elements (such as rounded rectangles). However, graphic symbols can be animated, and they have their own Timeline.

So, what's the difference between a graphic symbol and a movie clip? Though a graphic symbol has its own timeline, its animation is actually dependent on the timeline it is placed in. A movie clip, on the other hand, runs on its own independent timeline. You could place a Movie Clip into a single-frame movie and it would play in its entirety. A graphic symbol is placed in a keyframe where its first frame will be displayed. Additional frames in that graphic symbol will be displayed in empty frames that follow the keyframe (or frames that contain the same graphic instance) based on the Behavior settings of the Graphic's instance. A graphic or animated graphic stops when there is a blank keyframe, which is a keyframe that does not include the graphic instance or when the Timeline of the containing movie stops. Also, neither sounds nor actions will work within a graphic symbol.

Creating A Graphic Symbol

You can create a graphic symbol (or any other type of symbol) either from scratch or from existing selected elements.

Creating a symbol from existing elements is simple: you just select the elements and press F8 (or choose Insert|Create Symbol). When the Symbol Properties dialog box opens, click on the Graphic radio button. Then click on OK. The symbol will automatically appear in the Library window. See Figure 7.2.

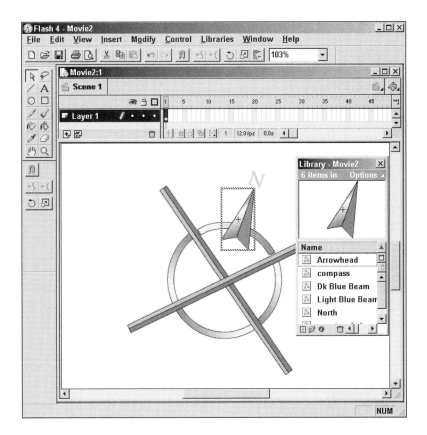

Figure 7.2
All the components of this compass are symbols.

When creating a symbol from scratch, first make sure that nothing is selected. (Choose Edit|Deselect All or press Cmd/Ctrl+Shift+A). Next, choose Insert|Create Symbol. You will find yourself in Symbol Editing mode, in which anything you create will then be stored as a symbol.

Buttons

Button symbols are four-frame movies in which the playing of each frame depends on the state of the mouse. Each frame is named after a mouse state: Up, Over, Down, and Hit:

- The Up frame describes the mouse button that has not been pressed and that the cursor hasn't passed over.

- The Over frame depicts the button when the cursor passes over it without pressing it.

- The Down frame depicts the button when you click on it (press it).

- The Hit frame is a graphic (which may as well be a solid color, because it will never be seen) that defines the shape of the area in which the other mouse events can occur.

Figure 7.3 shows the four-frame, four-state Timeline and the four "looks" that have been created for each state for a simple button. The figure is a composite screen shot; you won't normally see all four states of the same button on screen at once.

Figure 7.3
A button symbol and its Timeline.

You can insert movie clips and graphic symbols into button frames, but you cannot insert another button. You can also assign actions to any of the first three button frames (Up, Over, and Down).

Here's the skinny on how to create a button from scratch:

1. Press F8 or choose Insert|Create Symbol to open the Symbol Properties dialog box. See Figure 7.4.

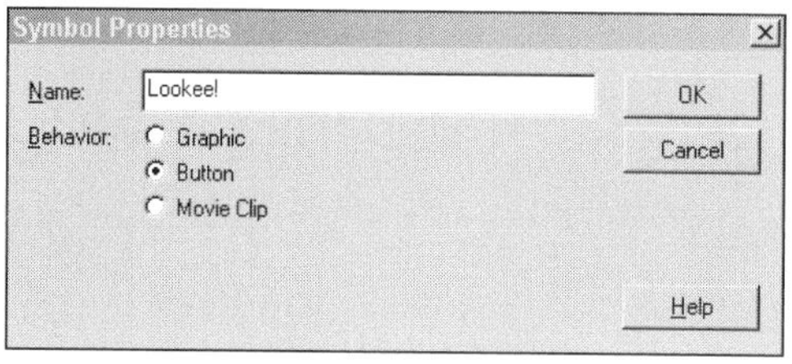

Figure 7.4
The Symbol Properties dialog box.

2. In the Symbol Properties dialog box, click on the radio button labeled Button. You may also want to give your button a more descriptive name than the default. If so, type the name in the Name field. Click on OK. The canvas clears.

3. You are in Symbol Editing mode. The Timeline shows four frames that are wider than movie frames and labeled Up, Over, Down, and Hit. Create the image for the Up-state frame by using any of Flash's drawing tools or by importing graphics or symbols (but not other buttons).

4. Click on the Over frame; then choose Insert|Insert Keyframe from either the main menu or the Frame pop-up menu. A copy of the first frame's image appears.

5. Select the copy of the first button and make any needed changes. (If you've previously used symbols to make up the parts of the button, choose Modify|Break Apart so that you can edit the individual components).

6. Repeat Steps 4 and 5 for the Down frame.

7. Select the Hit frame. Choose Insert|Insert Keyframe.

8. The movie might be a little smaller if you simplify the elements in the Hit frame. To do that, erase all the elements except the biggest shape in the button. Choose the Paint Bucket and make black the fill color. Fill the silhouette shape with black.

9. Choose Edit|Movie. The button is automatically saved in the library. The screen is blank. If you want to put the button in the movie, choose Window|Library. The Library window opens. Drag the name of the button you just created onto the canvas. See Figure 7.5.

> **Note:** In Flash 3, there was a bug that made the area between an outline and its fill to occasionally cause a flicker of the mouse at the internal border between an outline and its fill. To prevent this bug you can remove outlines from fills in the Hit frames of your buttons.

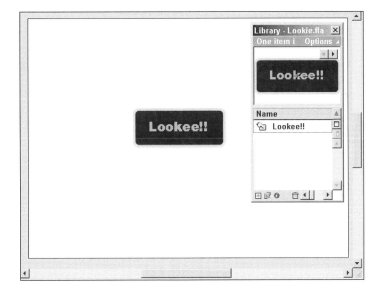

Figure 7.5
The finished button, shown on the canvas and in the Library window.

10. Test the button to make sure it does what you envisioned. Choose Control|Test Movie. A second window opens so you can test your button.

Adding Sound To A Button

You can add sound to any state of a button. Flash accepts only digitally sampled analog sounds, in the form of AIFF files on the Macintosh or WAV files in Windows. Because these aren't very efficient formats (analogous to bitmapped versus vector images), you should try to keep the sounds short. On the other hand, because sounds are stored as symbols, you can use the same sound several times in a movie without paying much of a penalty. Still, simple clicks and beeps are most appropriate. Use the following steps to add sounds to a button state:

1. Load a sound into the library. To do this, choose File|Import and use the Import dialog box to find and choose the sound file you want to use.

2. Sounds must always be on a separate layer and Macromedia recommends that each individual sound be given its own layer. Insert a new layer. To do that, place the cursor over the currently active Layer Name bar and Ctrl/Right+click to open the Layers menu. Choose Insert Layer.

3. Select the frame to which you want to add sound.

4. From the Frame menu (Ctrl/Right+click over the active frame), choose Insert Keyframe.

5. Choose Modify|Frame to open the Frame Properties dialog box. See Figure 7.6.

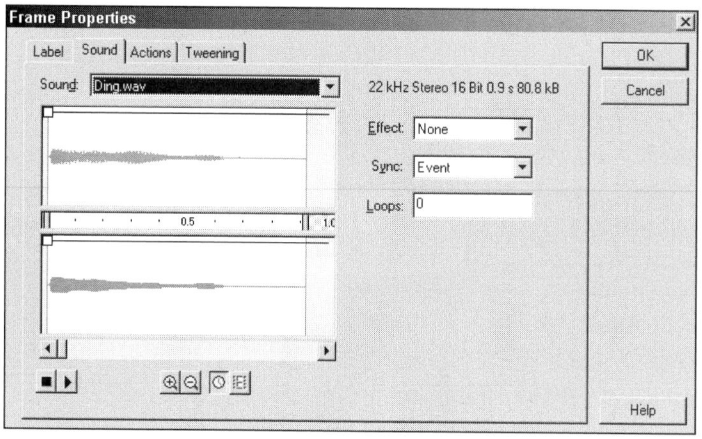

Figure 7.6
The Frame Properties dialog box.

6. Click on the Sound tab of the Frame Properties dialog box. Choose the sound file that you want from the Sound drop-down list box. For the Sync setting, choose Event. Leave Loops at zero and Effect at None. Click on OK.

7. Test the button. Choose Edit|Edit Movie. Then choose Control|Enable Buttons. Click on the button. When the mouse enters the state to which the sound has been attached, you should hear the sound.

You can associate a sound event with each of the following four states of a button by applying the sound to the button's Timeline:

-   *Up*—The sound event occurs on Mouse Out.

-   *Over*—The sound event occurs on Mouse Over.

-   *Down*—The sound event occurs on Mouse Down.

-   *Hit*—The sound event occurs on Mouse Release.

Creating Animated Buttons

This is very simple. Just place a movie-clip symbol in any (or all) of the button's first three frames. The Hit frame is always static.

More advanced animated button assemblies can be created with a movie clip that is external to the button or when a button is placed inside the movie clip. These movie clips would react as part of the button based on actions placed in the button's instance property.

Movie Clips

Movie clips differ from graphic symbols mainly in that they will play independently of the main movie's Timeline. Any feature that can be added to a regular Flash movie can be included in a movie clip. Also, both interactive controls and sounds function fully in a movie clip.

One of the primary uses for movie clips is animated buttons. You can place a movie clip in any or all of the first three button states.

To make a movie-clip symbol:

1. Press Ctrl+F8 to create a new symbol.

2. In the Symbol Properties dialog box, name your movie and choose the Movie Clip radio button.

3. Use the instructions elsewhere in this book to create an animation.

4. When you've finished the animation, choose Edit|Edit Movie. The Movie Clip will be stored in the library for the current movie.

Bitmaps

As soon as you import a JPEG, GIF, or PNG file, the data for that file is stored in the library. Without turning them into symbols you can reuse a bitmap as many times as you like in the same movie while only increasing the movie's file size slightly for each instance. Because even highly compressed bitmaps consume a lot of storage space, this is a very big deal.

Sounds

Although Flash 4's new default compression scheme uses MP3 compression, Flash does not allow importation of sound already compressed with MP3. Flash accepts only analog sound files for import, which, like bitmaps, are memory hogs. The fact that sounds are stored like symbols, however, means that you can make the doorbell ring as often as you like without greatly increasing the file size of your Flash movie. Flash can only import uncompressed versions of WAV (Windows) or AIFF (Macintosh) sound files.

If a WAV or AIFF sound does not import into Flash, it is probably compressed; you'll need to use an external sound program to convert it to a standard uncompressed sound.

Placing Sounds In A Movie

It's really easy to place sounds in a movie. Follow these steps:

1. Choose File|Import to open the Import dialog box. See Figure 7.7.

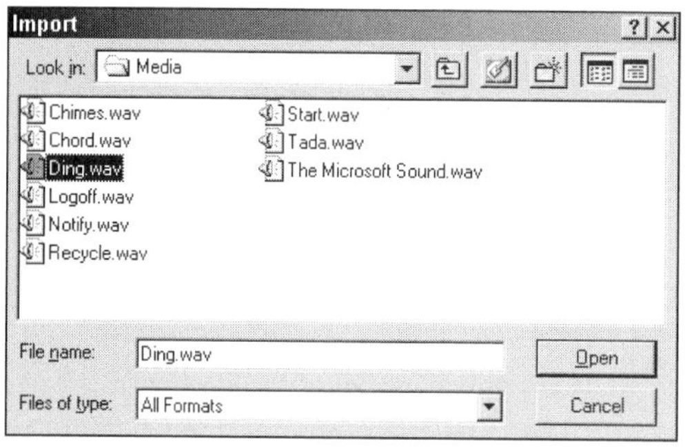

Figure 7.7
The Import dialog box.

2. In the Import dialog box, choose WAV (Windows) or AIFF (Macintosh) as the file type. Browse until you find the sound file you are looking for, and click on its name to enter it in the File Name field. Click on OK.

3. The sound appears in the Library window, with its file name immediately to the right of a speaker icon.

4. From the Layer pop-up menu, choose Insert Layer. Make sure that the new layer is the active layer.

5. Select the frame where you want the sound to start. From the Frame pop-up menu, choose Insert Frame.

6. With the new frame still selected, select the desired sound in the Library window. Its histogram appears in the Library preview; drag this preview onto the canvas. Nothing obvious happens, probably because the sound lasts longer than the single frame so far allocated to it.

7. You need to set the type of synchronization for the sound that you are entering. Click on the frame where you entered the sound, and choose Modify|Frame. When the Frame Properties dialog box opens (see Figure 7.6), choose a Sync setting. (The purpose of each of these is explained right after this exercise.)

8. Drag across a number of additional frames in the sound layer to highlight them. From the Frames pop-up menu, choose Insert Frame. A miniature version of the sound's histogram appears in the

Timeline. Figure 7.8 shows the Library window and the Timeline as it should look after the sound has been inserted.

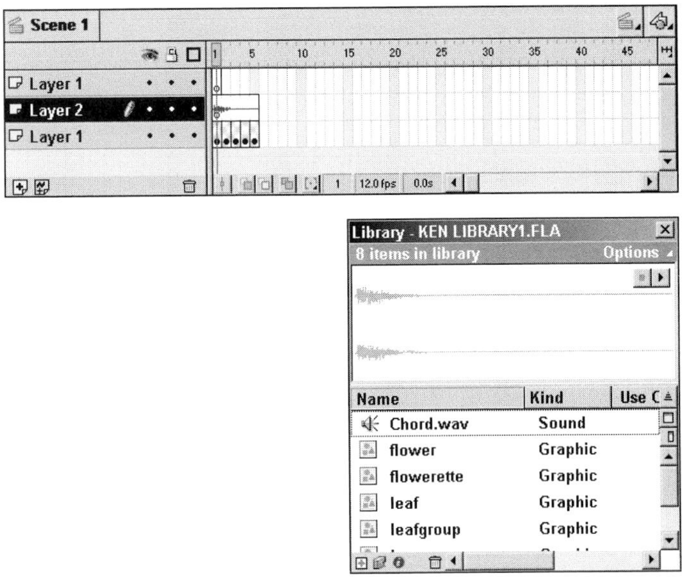

Figure 7.8

The Library Window and the Timeline after sound is inserted.

9. Select any unneeded frames and delete them. (Choose Delete Frames from the Frames pop-up menu.)

10. If you want the visual image to last as long as the sound, select the visual image's layer to activate it. Then, in the Timeline, drag across the frames that parallel the sound, and choose Insert Frame from the Frames pop-up menu.

11. Press Enter/Return to test your movie. If you don't hear anything, make sure your speakers are turned up. Also, choose Control and make sure that Mute Sounds isn't checked.

12. You may want the sound to play over and over. That can be a nice way to make a short sound do the duty of a longer sound. If you want to do this, select the frame where the sound starts, and choose Modify|Frame. In the Loop field, enter the number of times you want the sound to replay.

Synchronization Options

Here's what each of the synchronization options does:

- *Event*—The sound plays all the way through whenever its start frame plays in the animation. The sound isn't synchronized with the movie in any way. When you're placing the sound in a movie that loops (restarts as soon as it ends), you need to be careful not to designate sounds that will run longer than the animation.

- *Start*—This is the one to use in looping movies instead of Event. Otherwise, as with Event, the sound stops playing as soon as another sound starts.

- *Stop*—This option makes the target sound stop playing. To make a sound stop playing at a specified spot in the movie, select the frame where you want the sound to stop and then choose Modify|Frame. Choose the Sound tab and then choose Stop as the Sync setting.

- *Stream*—This option lets Flash synchronize the sound with each frame. In a browser, Flash is forced to stay in sync with sounds. Graphic frames will be dropped if needed to allow the sound to stay in sync.

Exporting Movies With Sound

When you export or publish your movie, you will want to ensure that the sound in your movie is stored in the most efficient way possible. You may want to edit the sound (and possibly recompress it to a lower setting) by using an external sound-editing program. Any sound-editing program will do, as long as it can save sounds in the format native to your operating system (AIFF for Mac OS, WAV for Windows). One of the big advantages of using an external sound editor is that you can trim the sound to exactly the length you need it to be before you turn it into a symbol in Flash. In so doing, you've ensured that you'll import no more data than is absolutely needed.

You can also control some qualities of the imported sound symbol by opening the Sound Properties dialog box and choosing some settings. To open the Sound Properties dialog box, select the sound's name bar in the Library window, then Ctrl/Right+click. The Sound Properties dialog box is shown in Figure 7.9.

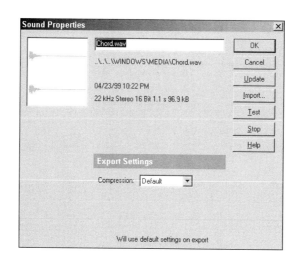

Figure 7.9
The Sound Properties dialog box.

Because you can use an external editor on the original sound file at any time, you'll want to click on the Update button if you've done external editing since you originally placed and specified the sound file.

If you want to substitute a different sound file for this symbol, click on the Import button.

After you've set all the other parameters that this dialog box allows, you may want to test the sound. To do this, just click on the Test button. To stop the test, click on the Stop button.

At the bottom center of the Sound Properties dialog box is an area labeled Export Settings and under that, a Compression drop-down list box. The Compression options are Default, ADPCM, MP3, and RAW.

- *ADPCM*—This option lets you determine the compression rate for ADPCM encoding. You can check a box to minimize your file size by converting stereo to monaural sound. The lowest setting, 2 bits, yields the smallest files and the worst quality; the highest setting is 5 bits. Sample rates range between 5 and 44 Khz. Once again, the setting with the smaller number means smaller files and lower sound fidelity.

- *Raw*—Exports the sound file exactly as imported. Eliminates sound compression. The only option is the Convert Stereo to Mono checkbox.

- *MP3*—This is the best format for longer soundtracks because it gives you the greatest compression with the highest quality. Bit rate is variable; can be set between 8 and 160 Kbps. The file size will be the same no matter which Quality setting (Fast, Medium, or Best) is selected.

In MP3 compression, if the sound for a particular bit is too complicated to be completely described at the current time, the compression program will look ahead to add the "extra" detail in future bits where the sound is less complicated. The Quality setting determines how much further ahead this extra data can be placed. The further ahead data can be placed, the higher the quality will be, because more sound data can actually be stored at a given data rate. It is important to choose the correct quality based on the connection speed and not your desire to get the "best" sound. Here are the options:

- *Fast*—This setting allows the shortest distance that sound extras can be stored. This is the setting you should use for normal Web use because the complete sound will be available sooner.

FLASH OFFLINE

You may be composing your Flash file (and its accompanying sound) for a medium other than the Web. If that's the case, you should do several things:

- Don't worry so much about compression. Go for quality. You've got the bandwidth.

- If you export sounds to video formats, such as QuickTime or AVI, all the sound layers will be compressed into one, so don't worry about how may sound layers you create.

- Make more use of stream synchronization. Once again, you have the bandwidth, and you might as well benefit from the dramatic effects you can gain from having synchronized sound.

- *Medium*—For CDs and other off-line productions.

- *Best*—Used for very fast connections or when all the sound is preloaded or already in memory or on a hard drive. This allows sound overages to be widely spaced from its original component for maximum utilization of all the bits that can be sent at the set bit rate speed.

Using The Library Window And Menu

The Library window has changed a bit since Flash 3, but the changes are mostly cosmetic and not nearly as far-ranging as was first planned. The really big change is that you can now view the window as a single column or in wide view. The wide view allows you to see the details of the symbol, such as its type, the number of times the symbol is used in the movie, and the date the symbol was last modified.

The Library menu has also been expanded to include commands pertinent to the fact that you can now have hierarchical folders of symbols, and makes it easier and neater to organize your symbols.

You've already used the Library window several times in this chapter, so you should already be familiar with most of it. This section explains it in a bit more detail so you can find most of what you will ever need to know about it under one index heading.

To open the Library window, choose Window|Library.

The Library window is the repository of all of a movie's symbols—regardless of type—and of symbol-like bitmaps and sounds. For a quick map of the functions of the Library window, note the labels in Figure 7.10.

Figure 7.10

Map of the Library window.

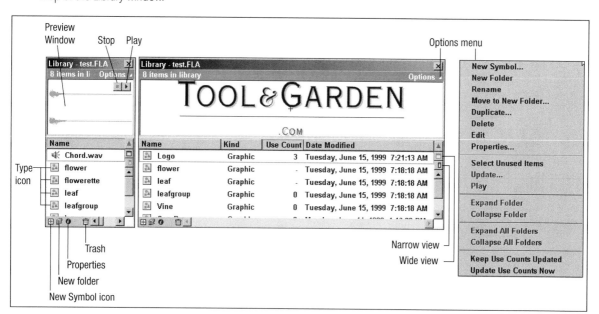

Here are the Library Options commands:

- *New Symbol*—Takes you onto an empty stage where you can create a new symbol. After using the Flash tools to create the symbol, choose Edit All to return to normal movie editing mode.

- *New Folder*—Creates a new folder. After a new folder has been created, any symbol can be dragged into it.

- *Rename*—Allows you to rename a symbol or folder.

- *Move To New Folder*—Creates a new folder inside the current folder and places the currently selected symbol inside it.

- *Duplicate*—Makes a duplicate of the currently selected symbol. Automatically adds "copy" to the current name, but the Symbol Properties dialog box lets you change the name and type of the copy.

- *Delete*—Deletes the currently selected symbol.

- *Edit*—Lets you edit the currently selected symbol without affecting any other entities within the movie.

- *Properties*—Brings up the Properties dialog box for this sound.

- *Select Unused Items*—Selects all Library symbols that have not been included in the movie. You can then choose Delete to remove their data from the movie file. This often-forgotten command is handy for optimizing file size.

- *Update*—Updates all instances of all symbols used in the current movie to reflect any edits.

- *Play*—Duplicates the function of the Play button at the top of the Library window. Plays the currently selected symbol in the preview window.

- *Expand Folder*—Shows any sub-folders that may exist inside the selected folder.

- *Collapse Folder*—Hides any sub-folders that may exist inside the selected folder.

- *Expand All Folders*—Shows all folders and sub-folders.

- *Collapse All Folders*—Shows only primary-level folders.

- *Keep Use Counts Updated*—Automatically updates use counts as symbols are dragged into the movie.

- *Update Use Counts Now*—Forces an update of the use counts.

By opening one movie as a movie and the other movies as libraries, you can use the method outlined in the preceding exercise to exchange symbols between movies and libraries.

Libraries Menu

The Libraries menu provides access to the five symbol libraries (FLAs) that ship with Flash 4. Each of these libraries contains elements that you can use in your own movies. You can also use them as templates that you can modify to suit your own purposes.

The new libraries are Buttons, Buttons-Advanced, Graphics, Movie Clips, and Sounds. On the CD, we have included additional FLA files that can be added to your Libraries folder if you wish.

To add an FLA to your libraries, simply drop it into the Libraries subdirectory of your Flash folder. For a Mac, if the FLA came from a PC, then open the file from inside Flash by selecting File|Open and choosing All Files rather than All Formats. Then save the file.

Adding Graphics From Another Movie

The following steps will take you through the process of opening the symbol library of a movie and adding graphics in it to the Library menu of the current movie:

1. Choose File|Open As Library to open the Open As Library dialog box. See Figure 7.11.

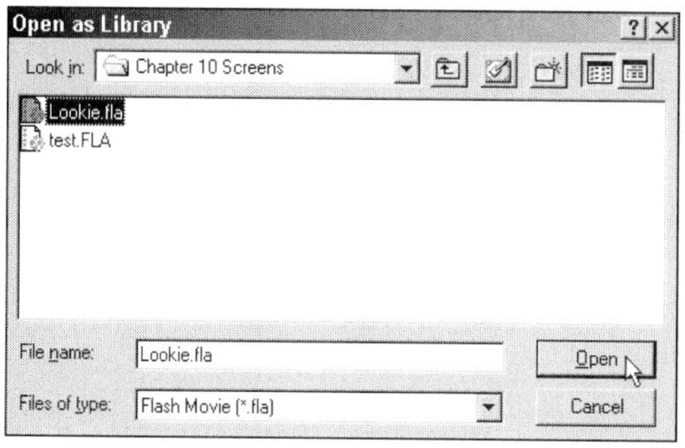

Figure 7.11
The Open As Library dialog box.

2. Navigate to the movie that you want to open as a library. Note that the Files Of Type field must read "Flash Movie (*.fla)." Double-click on the name of the movie that you want to load as a library.

3. Choose Library|Name Of New Library to open the Library window.

4. You can add any symbol in the Library to the current movie's Library window by dragging it onto the canvas. In this way, you can consolidate libraries from several movies. If you just want it in the library, delete it from the canvas and it will still be in the Library. Note, any symbol with the same name as a symbol in the current Library will not be imported and there will be no warning from Flash. You just won't have the newer symbol added.

Editing Symbols

Note: To break a symbol apart, all you have to do is select the symbol and choose Modify| Break Apart or press Cmd/ Ctrl+B.

Changing the shape and look of symbols is as easy as changing any other entity in any other Flash movie. The procedure is the same with one exception: You must change your symbols in Symbol Editing mode. There are several ways to enter Symbol Editing mode:

- Select the symbol. Choose Edit|Symbols or press Cmd/Ctrl+E.

- Select the symbol and choose Edit|Selected.

- In the Library window, scroll to and select a symbol. Then choose Edit from the Library menu.

- Open the Edit Symbol menu by dragging the pull-down menu for the Edit Symbol button just above and to the far right of the Timeline. The Edit Symbol menu lets you choose any symbol in the Library for the current movie.

Perhaps the ultimate edit of a symbol is breaking it apart while the symbol is on the canvas and when you're not in Edit Symbol mode. When you break apart a symbol, it stops being a symbol and becomes just another bunch of lines, fills, and geometric shapes on the canvas of a movie. Those lines, fills, and geometric shapes auto-edit one another as soon as the symbol is broken apart and deselected.

If the symbol contains other symbols, they will still be symbols. If the symbol contains groups, these will still be groups. You can, however, drop the contents of those groups and symbols onto the canvas by repeating the Break Apart command (Cmd/Ctrl+B).

Making Animated Symbols

Two symbol types or behaviors contain animations: graphic symbols and movie clips. The differences between these two types were explained previously, but the process of animating them is the same: Simply edit the symbol, and follow standard procedures for making a Flash movie or scene.

Until now, you may have had the impression that symbols were useful mainly for repeated static elements or for such interface components as buttons. Symbols can also be *sprites*. A sprite is a self-contained movie within a movie. Thus, you can animate the sprite as an entity in the movie while the sprite itself contains its own animation. A good example of this would be a running character. The animation contained within the sprite (or in Flash terminology, the animated symbol) would be the movement of the body and its limbs. The sprite (symbol) would then be animated as an entity to move it across the stage.

To animate a symbol, follow these steps:

1. Select the symbol.

2. Use any of the methods described previously to enter Symbol Editing mode.

3. Select a range of frames, and then choose Insert Keyframe from the Frames menu. A copy of the symbol will appear in each frame.

4. Use any of the Flash tools and commands to change the individual frames.

Instances And Instance Modifications

Any modification you make to a symbol in Symbol Editing mode is automatically applied to each instance of that symbol, regardless of where it appears in the movie—even if it's on other layers or in scenes other than the one in which you originally edited that symbol.

Making An Instance

Creating an instance of a symbol is simply a matter of dragging the symbol preview from the Library window onto the stage (also called the canvas). Here's the step-by-step process:

1. Select or create the layer or scene in which you want the instance to appear.

2. Select or insert the frame where you want the instance to appear.

3. Choose Window|Library (unless the Library window is already open).

4. If necessary, scroll through the Library window until you see the name of the symbol whose instance you want to create. Select the symbol name. The symbol appears in the preview window. See Figure 7.12.

Figure 7.12
The symbol in the Library's preview window.

5. Drag the thumbnail of the symbol from the preview window to the stage. Alternatively, you can drag the Symbol Name bar onto the canvas.

Changing An Instance's Properties

Although you can't Symbol Edit an instance without affecting all the other instances of the same symbol, you can change certain characteristics (which Flash calls *properties*) of an instance without affecting the other instances. You can change an instance in the following ways:

- Assigning actions

- Changing the behavior category

- Changing the color effects

- Changing the assigned symbol

The procedure for changing the properties of symbols is slightly different for each behavior type: graphic, button, and movie clip. All the possible changes, however, are accessed from the Instance Properties dialog box, shown in Figure 7.13.

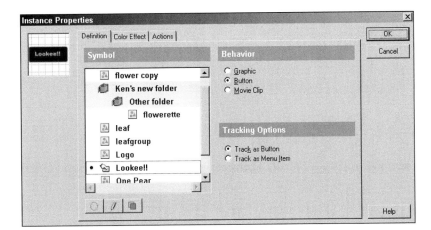

Figure 7.13
The Instance Properties dialog box for an instance of a button symbol.

Changing Properties Of A Graphic Symbol

Follow these steps to change the properties for a graphic symbol:

1. On the stage, select the instance of the symbol that you want to change.

2. Double-click on the selected instance (or you can double-click before you select it), or choose Modify|Instance. The Instance Properties dialog box opens, as shown in Figure 7.14.

3. If necessary, click on the Definition tab. Make sure that Graphic is the selected Behavior option. (You can change the behavior of an

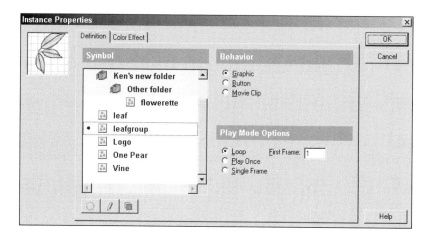

Figure 7.14

The Instance Properties dialog
box for an instance of a
graphic symbol.

instance by selecting a different Behavior option without changing
the behavior of the symbol itself.)

4. Choose the appropriate Play Mode option from the following:

   • Loop if you want the animation to play repeatedly.

   • Play Once if you want the animation to stop after the first play-
   through.

   • Single Frame if you want only the first frame of the symbol to
   appear.

5. In the First Frame field, enter the number of the frame that you want
   to be displayed first.

Changing Properties Of A Button

Follow these steps to change the properties for a button:

1. With the target instance selected, choose Modify|Instance, or double-
   click on the instance. The Instance Properties dialog box opens.

2. Click on the Definition tab. The dialog box now looks like Figure
   7.13.

3. To prevent other buttons from receiving mouse events while the
   mouse button is down, select the Track As Button option.

   Or, to let other buttons receive mouse events while the mouse button
   is down, select the Track As Menu Item option.

4. If you want to change the actions associated with the button, click
   on the Actions tab. (See Figure 7.15.)

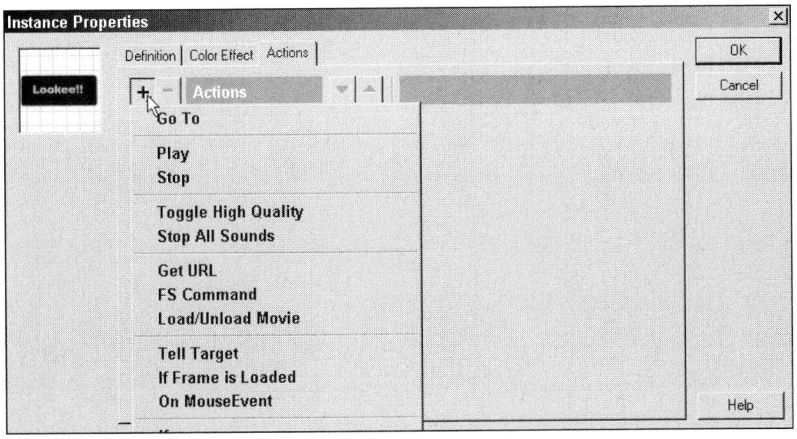

Figure 7.15

The Actions tab of the Instance Properties dialog box. This tab is available only when the selected symbol has the Button behavior.

Changing Properties Of A Movie Clip

Movie-clip behavior can be assigned to any instance of a symbol, whether or not it was originally created as a movie clip. You can alter movie-clip instances by changing color effects and by adding *tell target* Actions. Follow these steps to change the properties of a movie clip:

1. Select the target instance.

2. Double-click on the instance (or choose Modify|Instance if you insist on doing things the hard way). The Instance Properties dialog box opens. If necessary, click on the Definition tab. See Figure 7.16.

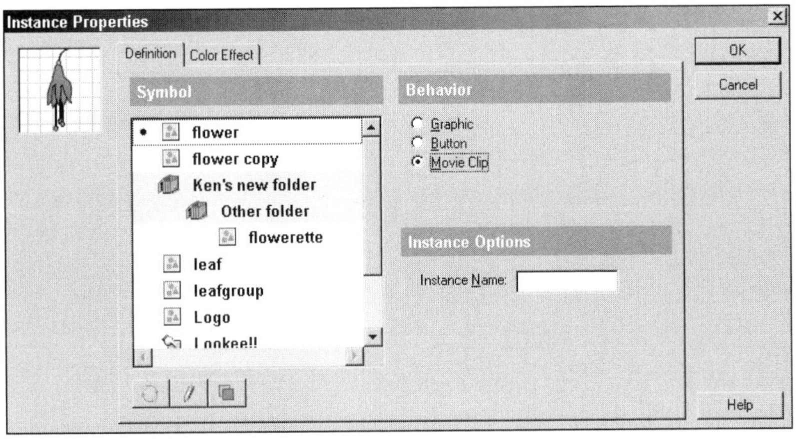

Figure 7.16

The Definition tab of the Instance Properties dialog box when a movie-clip symbol is selected.

3. This step is optional. Type a name in the Instance Name field. This allows you to refer to the instance by a name you can easily remember, rather than by searching for its occurrence in a complex movie. Also, when you're scripting or assigning actions, with Tell Target, it allows you to refer to this specific instance of the symbol.

4. To change the color effect, see the next section of this chapter.

Changing The Color Effect For An Instance

Color effects are used to change the color and transparency of an instance. Flash changes the color properties of the instance only in that frame (instance) in which the symbol appears, and not for the symbol in general. You can change the color settings for two instances that are a given number of frames apart and on the same layer, and then tween changes between the two frames.

To change color effects, follow these steps:

1. Select the target instance and double-click on it (or choose Modify| Instance). The Instance Properties dialog box opens.

2. Click on the Color Effect tab. See Figure 7.17.

Figure 7.17
The Color Effect tab of the Instance Properties dialog box.

Choose the appropriate color effect from the Color Effect drop-down list box. You will see the effect in the preview area in the upper-left corner of the dialog box. You'll be choosing from the following Color Effect controls:

- *Brightness*—Controls the overall lightness of the instance.

- *Tint*—Lets you either click on a color modifier or enter RGB values for influencing the overall color balance of the instance. The slider controls the amount of the tint mixed with the original color. A low percentage will affect color balance; at 100 percent (the extreme right end of the slider), all the elements in the symbol become the new color.

- *Alpha*—Controls the level of transparency of the instance. Use this effect when you want to be able to see other elements in the movie through the symbol. A slider controls the degree of opacity and transparency.

- *Special*—Allows you to control both tint and transparency for the same instance. Watch the preview area for the result of the adjustments you make. Click on OK only when you're satisfied with the effect.

Color Effect Tweening

You can achieve three results through the tweening of color effects:

- Gradual shifting of colors from one effect to another

- Fading in a symbol

- Fading out a symbol

Because the procedures for fading in and fading out are simply the reverse of one another, I'll detail just the procedure for a fade-in.

Creating A Fade-In Effect

To create a fade-in effect, follow these steps:

1. Make sure the frame where the color effect will first begin to appear is selected. If this isn't already a keyframe, choose Insert Keyframe from the Frames menu.

2. Double-click on the image of the instance on the stage. The Instance Properties dialog box opens. Click on the Color Effect tab. For the Color Effect option, choose Alpha. See Figure 7.18.

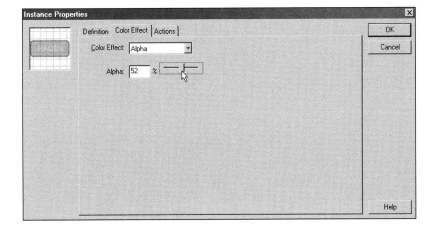

Figure 7.18
Using the Alpha slider to adjust the level of transparency.

3. Drag the Alpha slider to the far left. The preview will become either very faint or invisible. Alternatively, you can type a number between 1 and 100 (to indicate the percentage of transparency) in the Alpha field.

4. In the Timeline, drag to select the number of frames over which you would like the fade to occur.

5. With the cursor over the highlighted frames, right-click (Windows) or click and hold (Mac) to open the Frames menu. Choose Insert Frames.

6. Select the last of the newly inserted frames. From the Frames menu, choose Insert Keyframe.

7. Click in the area where the instance is located. (If you've set the Alpha slider to zero percent, you won't be able to see it.) A selection marquee appears.

8. Double-click on the selected instance to open the Instance Properties dialog box. Drag the Alpha slider to the extreme right. You will now see the instance on the stage.

9. Double-click on the newly created keyframe to open the Frame Properties dialog box. Click on the Tweening tab. See Figure 7.19.

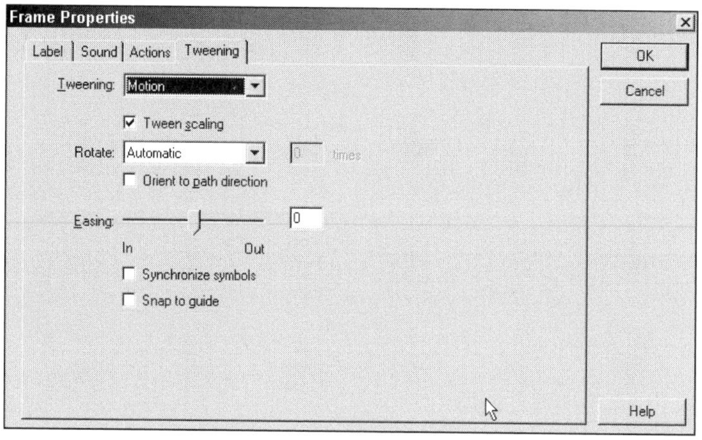

Figure 7.19
The Tweening tab of the Frame Properties dialog box.

10. For the Tweening option, choose Motion. Click on OK and press Return/Enter to preview the result.

Creating A Tint Effect Over Time

To create a tint effect over time, follow these steps:

1. Make sure the frame where the color effect will first begin to appear is selected. If this isn't already a keyframe, choose Insert Keyframe from the Frames menu.

2. Double-click on the image of the instance on the stage. The Instance Properties dialog box opens. Click on the Color Effect tab. For the Color Effect option, choose Tint. The appearance of the Color Effect tab changes to reflect the tint settings. See Figure 7.20.

3. From the color modifier in the dialog box, choose the color that you want to use in the effect. You can use the slider at right to change the brightness of the chosen color.

4. In the Timeline, drag to select the number of frames over which you want the fade to occur.

5. With the cursor over the highlighted frames, right-click (Windows) or click and hold (Mac) to open the Frames menu. Choose Insert Frames.

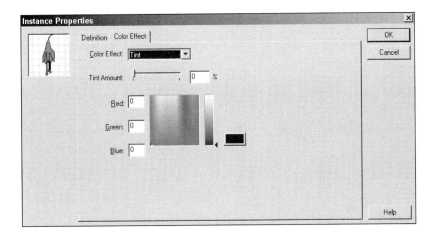

Figure 7.20
The Color Effect tab when Tint is selected.

6. Select the last of the newly inserted frames. From the Frames menu, choose Insert Keyframe.

7. Click on the instance. A selection marquee appears. Double-click on the instance to open the Instance Properties dialog box. Drag the Tint Amount slider to 100 percent.

8. Double-click on the newly created keyframe to open the Frame Properties dialog box. Click on the Tweening tab.

9. For the Tweening option, choose Motion. Click on OK and press Return/Enter to preview the result.

Moving On

This chapter has covered the use of Symbols and how to manage them in their Libraries. There has also been a discussion of how to edit symbols and how to assign different properties to their instances.

Chapter 8 will discuss advanced animation techniques.

PART III

TAKING IT LIVE

ADVANCED ANIMATION TECHNIQUES

8

KEN MILBURN
AND
JOHN CROTEAU

This chapter isn't so much about how to do animation as it is about the features in Flash (and Flash 4 in particular) that enhance animation. You'll also learn a few techniques to help you polish your animations.

This chapter is a collection of information, tips, and subtle tricks that you'll use to create and export advanced projects in Flash 4. We'll start with the basics, providing you more details about the Timeline and layers. Then we'll discuss animated graphics and show you how they compare with movie clips. We'll show you how the Tell Target action works and how you can use Tell Target to create advanced animations. Our examples will be simple, but once you understand these basics, you'll be able to create animations of amazing complexity.

We will also cover the Flash features of Get URL, Load Movie, and If Frame Is Loaded. We won't forget the new Flash 4 features of Drag Movie Clip, Duplicate Movie Clip, and Load Into Target. We will finish with how to use sound in Flash.

The Timeline

Understanding the Timeline is crucial to creating advanced animation in Flash. For those of you new to the Tell Target and Load Movie actions, not all of the following will make sense now, so remember to come back and reread this section after you finish this chapter.

This is what you need to know about the Timeline:

- Actions and images occur frame by frame, one after the other.

- The Play action moves horizontally along the Timeline (never vertically). There is also no reverse play in Flash.

- Images are displayed completely for each frame after all currently running actions have been initiated—except for frame one, where the image is displayed layer by layer (either Top Down or Bottom Up).

- Actions are executed layer by layer, starting at the top, and are executed in order within each frame Action window. It is best to put all actions in a single layer located at the top of the layer stack. If you do this, you won't have to hunt for stray actions, and you improve the ability to follow the action and stay organized.

- Actions are always started in order, but not all actions will be completed before the next action is initiated.

    Only the latest conflicting action in a frame will be executed. For example, if you have two competing actions:

    ```
    Go to and Play (20)
    Go to and Play (30)
    ```

    Then only the latest action—Go to and Play (30)—will be executed.

- Some commands will accumulate. For example, the following commands will advance the movie two frames on the main Timeline.

```
Begin Tell Target ("/")
    Go to Next Frame
End Tell Target
Begin Tell Target ("/")
    Go to Next Frame
End Tell Target
```

- Movie clips and the main Timelines of movies have active Timelines that support independent motion along their Timelines. They can be controlled from buttons or frame actions in other active Timelines.

- Graphics, buttons, and animated graphics have dependent Timelines and do *not* support actions on their own Timelines. Also, actions placed in the frames of the afore-mentioned symbol types do not function. Multiframe (animated) graphic symbols display their first frame image in the keyframe they are placed on. If there are empty frames following the keyframe, additional frames of the graphic are displayed based on the Behavior setting of the graphic.

- Flash is completely interactive. Action on a Timeline can be stopped, or it can be branched to another frame, where action can be paused or continue playing.

- Action can be directed either by actions initiated by button instances or by actions placed in an active Timeline frame (either a main Timeline or a movie clip). Actions will not work if they are placed in a graphic symbol's Timeline, nor will they work in any button frame (Up, Over, Down, or Hit).

- Flash allows multiple Timelines (including movie clip or other SWF movies loaded by the Load Movie action). Each of these Timelines can be in motion or stopped, independently of the other Timelines.

Combining Symbols

You know by now that you can use a symbol as many times as you like within a movie without significantly increasing the movie's file size. Symbols become even more powerful when you realize that you can make a symbol from a collection of other symbols, creating a whole new shape or animation sequence while adding very little new data. Be careful, though, not to overdo this nesting of symbols. There is a small penalty for multiple levels of movie clips that contain only actions, but there can be a heavy toll if you do multiple levels of nesting that include images on more than a couple of levels.

The process for combining symbols is so simple that it hardly seems worth making a fuss over. Here it is:

1. Place the symbols that you want to combine on the stage.

2. Arrange them in the positions that you want them to occupy in the new symbol.

3. Select all the symbols that you want to combine, and press F8 (or choose Insert|New Symbol).

Figure 8.1 shows you a symbol made by repeatedly combining the same symbol.

Figure 8.1

A symbol made by repeatedly combining the same symbol.

You can transform (scale, rotate, or skew) an instance of a symbol without affecting the symbol in the library.

You can also create combined symbols from scratch. As would be the case when you're creating a simple symbol, make sure nothing is selected; then press F8 or choose Insert|New Symbol. Import or draw your first symbol, select its parts, and choose Insert|New Symbol again. Keep doing this until your symbol contains all the symbols you want to combine.

Of course, it can get more complicated than that. You can combine symbols that are already combined symbols.

Now, all of this is easy as long as you're dealing with static graphics. Things get a bit more complicated when you combine symbols with different behaviors or different numbers of frames.

Combining A Static Symbol With An Animated Graphic Symbol

If you want part of an animated graphic symbol to move while the rest remains static, the static part of the symbol must have the same number of frames as the moving part. In Figure 8.2, I've placed an animated leaf symbol inside a static rounded-rectangle symbol.

When you combine these two types of symbols, the order in which you do it is critical to your success. Keeping the example simple should help you to see the process more clearly. The following exercise shows how you combine the symbols seen in Figure 8.2:

1. Open the movie leafrect.fla, located on this book's companion CD-ROM.

2. Choose Window|Library to display the movie's Library. See Figure 8.3.

3. Next, you need to know how many frames are in the animated symbol called "Animated Leaf." Select its name in the library list, and a faint leaf will appear in the preview. From the Library menu, choose Edit. The stage and the Timeline will now look as they do in Figure 8.3. Note that this symbol has ten frames.

4. You don't actually need to edit anything more in Edit Symbol mode, so choose Edit|Edit Movie. You are now back to a blank stage. Even if the stage weren't blank, that would be okay as long as you made sure that nothing was selected. Press Cmd/Ctrl+F8 to create a new symbol. You will see another blank stage.

5. Now you're going to create a new symbol that combines the two symbols. Again, make sure nothing is selected, and press Cmd/Ctrl+F8. When the Symbol Properties dialog box opens, name the symbol "Combo". You now have a blank movie in which to edit.

6. In the Library window, select the rectangle symbol, and drag it onto the stage. Click away from the symbol to deselect it.

7. Highlight the nine frames following the keyframe. Ctrl-click/Right-click on any of the highlighted frames; from the Frames menu, choose Insert Frame.

8. In the Library window, select the leaf symbol. Drag its thumbnail onto the stage and into the center of the rectangle. Press Return/Enter to play the symbol's movie. The rectangles will stay static while the leaf rotates and fades in.

9. To save the new symbol, choose Edit|Edit Movie. Then choose File|Save As, and give the movie a name of your choice.

If you want to use this symbol in another movie, open the other movie. Choose File|Open As Library. In the resulting dialog box, navigate to the movie you just saved, select it, and click on OK. A second Library window will appear. Drag your symbol preview onto the stage, and it will become a part of the current movie's library—even if you delete the instance from the stage.

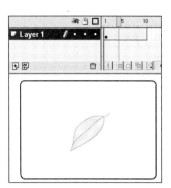

Figure 8.2
The leaf is animated, and the rectangle appears to be static.

Figure 8.3
The Library.

Using A Movie Clip Instead Of An Animated Graphic

In Flash, you will find that using an animated graphic is generally less desirable than using a movie clip for most purposes. The movie leaf-mc1.fla plays identically to the previous movie, leafrect.fla, but is made of a single frame. There is another, more important, reason why you will want to use a movie clip instead of an animated graphic: that is the Tell Target action and its ability to send commands to the movie clip externally. We will cover the Tell Target action later in this chapter.

Making Animated Buttons

A different kind of combined symbol is the animated button. In this type of symbol, movie-clip symbols are combined with button symbols because the animation needs to play inside a single frame representing a button state. Movie-clip symbols will play the entire animation, regardless of the number of frames in the host symbol, so they're ideal for animating buttons.

Why would you want to make an animated button? On the simplest level, animations are fun and they draw attention to the subject. What's more important, they can be instructional and can even make the user interface more intelligible. For example, you could have instructional text zoom out when the mouse cursor passes over the animated button. Or you could have a button transform into a directional arrow. By the way, the cursor moving over the button ("mouse over") is the event that's usually used for animating a button, although you can animate any of the button states.

When you make animated buttons, it's a good idea to start a new movie. Then you can import symbols (including your buttons) from that movie into any movie in which you want to make buttons. If you choose not to start a new movie, at least make sure that nothing is currently selected by pressing Cmd/Ctrl+Shift+A. Then follow these steps:

1. Press Cmd/Ctrl+F8 or choose Insert|New Symbol to open the Symbol Properties dialog box. Select the Movie Clip option. Type a name for your animation in the Name field. (See Figure 8.4.) Click on OK.

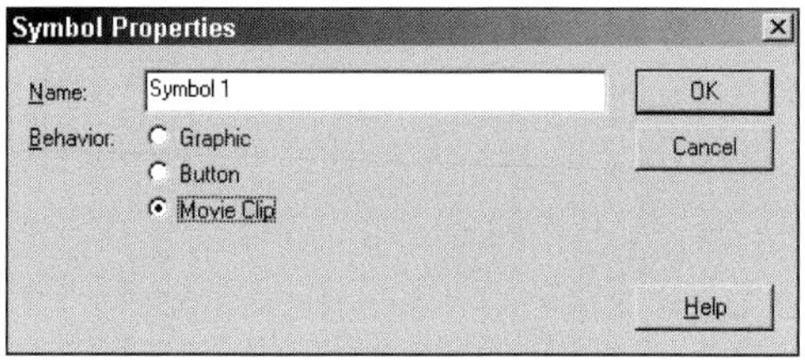

Figure 8.4
The Symbol Properties dialog box.

2. Create an animation for each of the button states (Up, Over, and Down) that you intend to animate. It's best to keep the animations

short and simple. Tweening is the technique likely to work best, although you can do anything that Flash 4 will create.

3. As you finish each animation, choose Edit|Edit Movie. This will store the animation in the library as a movie symbol. Then repeat the process for each of the other button states that you want to animate. When you've finished each one, remember to return to the main movie by choosing Edit|Edit Movie.

4. Now you're going to create a button symbol. Again, making sure that nothing is selected, choose Insert|New Symbol. This time, when the Symbol Properties dialog box opens, choose Button as the symbol type. Click on OK.

5. You get a new, blank stage. In the Timeline are four frames. The pointer will be over the first frame. If the Library window isn't already open, choose Window|Library. Select the symbol that you want to represent the Up state, and drag it into place on the stage. The placement of the first button isn't critical. Figure 8.5 shows you how this will look.

6. For the Over and Down frames, the procedure is the same. From the Frame menu, choose Insert Blank Keyframe. From the Library window, choose the movie clip or symbol that you want to use for that frame, and drag it into place. Be sure to place the center mark (the plus sign) in register with the existing center mark.

7. Insert a blank keyframe in the Hit frame. Draw a filled shape that covers the area that you want to be active when the mouse cursor passes over it.

8. Choose Edit|Edit Movie to go back to the main movie.

9. Repeat Steps 1 through 8 for as many animated buttons as you're likely to need.

10. Choose File|Save As and name your movie so that you'll recognize it as a button library, then click on OK.

11. Open the movie into which you want to place the animated buttons. Choose File|Open As Library. Locate the movie that contains the buttons (or any other symbols) that you want, and open it.

12. Choose Libraries|Your Button Movie (whatever its name may be). A Library window will appear. Select the buttons that you want, and drag the previews onto the stage of your target movie.

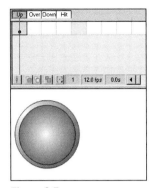

Figure 8.5
The first button in the Up state.

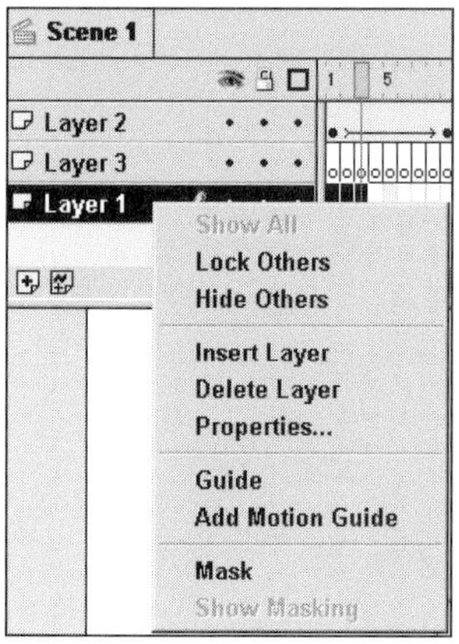

Figure 8.6
The Timeline's multiple layers.

An animated button is limited to playing only when the particular button state is activated. If you place a movie clip in the Over frame, that movie clip will start playing when you mouse over the button, and will stop immediately when you mouse away from the button. For more complicated effects, you will need to use Tell Target and button assemblies, which combine buttons inside of movie clips or combine buttons with the movie clips completely separate but acting and appearing as part of the button.

Creating Multilayer Animation

When you want to make different objects move with different timing and direction over the same background, layers make it easy. With layers, each object can be animated in its own movie. Since any part of a layer that isn't occupied by a shape is transparent, all you have to do is stack the movies atop one another. If one subject is supposed to move behind another, just make sure that its layer is below that on which the foreground subject resides.

To envision what layers can do, it helps if you first look at a Timeline with layers, shown in Figure 8.6.

Characteristics Of Layers

To understand layers and their purpose, you need to understand how their structure fits into the overall structure of a Flash movie. All of the other components of Flash movies—groups, symbols, and scenes—can contain multiple layers. Each of these layers has its own stage level and its own overlay (groups and symbols) levels. In any given scene of a Flash movie, each layer shares a common Timeline with the other layers.

Any portion of a layer that is not artwork (outlines and fills) is transparent. Thus, artwork that is displayed on other layers will be fully visible unless it is hidden by artwork on a higher level. You are not limited in the number of layers that can be placed into a given scene because there is no byte cost for layers. Let's repeat that—there is zero byte cost in the exported SWF for layers. If you are used to dealing with layers in bit-mapped editing programs such as Photoshop, this "layers are free" concept runs counter to your training, but believe me now or believe me later.

Creating Content On A New Layer

You'll find it best (or required) to create each new animated element on its own layer. To create content on a new layer, click the Modify Layers button on the Layer Name bar. The Layers menu will appear. Choose Insert Layer. The inserted layer will appear just above the current layer (unless you clicked on the tab for an empty layer). The new layer will always be selected by default.

Any new content created on an active layer will remain on that layer. If you want to copy an instance, group, or selection to another layer, first make the appropriate selection. Next, press Cmd/Ctrl+C (or choose Edit|Copy); then select the target layer to make it active. (A pencil icon will appear on the Layer Menu button.) Next, press Cmd/Ctrl+V (or choose Edit|Paste).

If you import a movie, it will always be imported on a layer of its own. This is true whether you import a Flash movie in SWF format or a series of still images in any of the still-image formats that Flash supports.

More Layer Controls

The Modify Layers menu has several commands that give you additional control over the behavior of layers. Included are commands for showing or hiding layers, locking layers, and specifying outline colors.

Showing And Hiding Layers

Because objects can hide one another and you can have as many layers as you like, editing can easily become confusing. It becomes much less so when you turn layers on and off. The following are options for showing and hiding layers:

- To show or hide individual layers, click on the dot under the eye icon in the Layer Name bar. If a red X appears under the eye, the layer is hidden. To show the layer again, click on the red X, and a black dot will appear in its place.

- To hide all but one layer, choose Hide Others from the Modify Layers menu of the layer you want to show.

- To show all the layers, choose Show All from the Modify Layers menu of any of the layers.

Locking Layers

Like hiding layers, locking a layer (or layers) will prevent accidental selection and editing of unseen objects. The difference is that you can still see the objects on locked layers. This is important if you want to check the relative position, shape, or color of the objects on the locked layers. The following are options for locking layers:

- To lock an individual layer, click on the dot under the padlock icon in the Layer Name bar.

- To lock all but one layer, choose Lock Others from the Layer menu of the layer you want to leave unlocked.

Changing The Colors Of Layer Outlines

One way to make it easy to see which objects are on which layers is to assign different colors to given layers and then use the Show Outlines command. The Show Outlines command will hide all the fills, making shapes transparent except for their outlines. Figure 8.7 shows what this looks like.

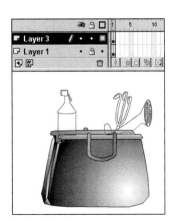

Figure 8.7
After using the Show Outlines command on Layer 3.

To edit your movie in outlined mode, with a different color assigned to the layer in each outline, follow these steps. (It is assumed that your multilay-ered movie is open.)

1. Choose View|Outlines. The fills will all disappear, and the outlines will all be black.

2. Now you want to assign the colors to each layer. Select a layer to change its outline.

3. From the Modify |Layers dialog box, choose Red, Green, Blue, Yellow, or Purple to assign that color to the outlines on that layer. (See Figure 8.8.) Repeat this step for each layer, choosing a different color each time.

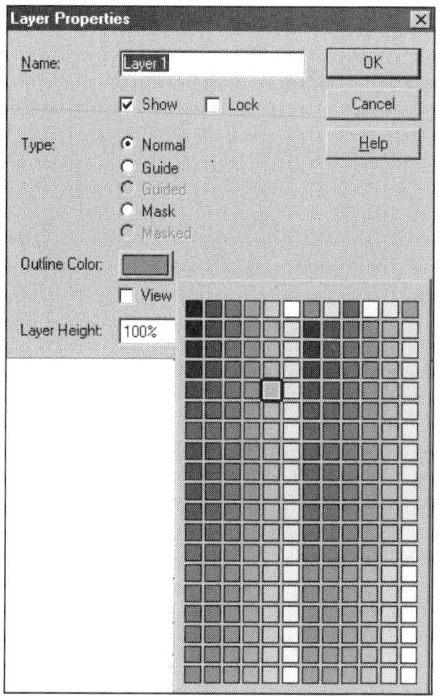

Figure 8.8
Assigning color to a layer's outlines.

The combination of showing outlines and using a different color outline on each layer is especially helpful when you have to do frame-by-frame ani-mation of natural movements. It gives you a chance to study each slight movement of a shape (or part of a shape) so that you can fine-tune the resulting illusion.

Specialized Layer Types

Three types of layers—guide, mask, and motion guide—don't appear when the movie plays, but they serve special functions, which are explained in the following sections. You can also dedicate a layer to sound (covered later in this chapter).

Guide Layers

Guide layers are simply layers that don't show when the movie is played or printed. Any shape that you place on a guide layer can be used to visually align objects on active layers.

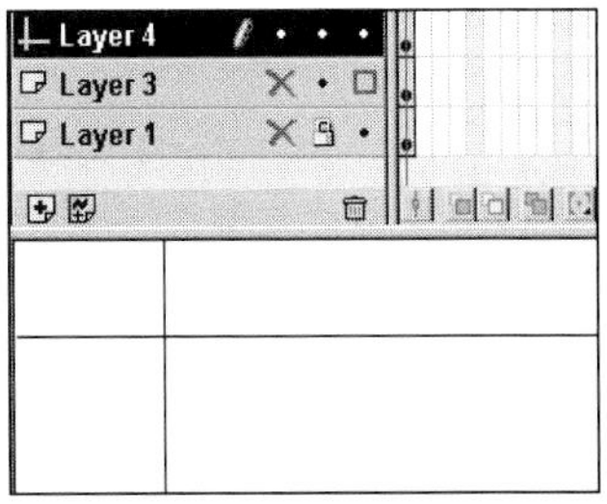

You can use any layer as a guide layer, but most of the time you'll want to create a special layer for that purpose. To create a guide layer, follow these steps:

1. From the Layers menu, choose Insert Layer to create a new layer that will serve as a dedicated guide.

2. Click on the Layers Menu tab, and drag to choose Guide. A checkmark will appear to the left of the command. You will know that your layer has become a guide layer because a blue T-square will appear to the left of the layer name. See Figure 8.9.

3. Make sure the guide layer is selected (active). Then use any of the Flash tools or commands to put lines, shapes, or grids on the guide layer.

Figure 8.9
A guide layer (Layer 4), identified with a T-square.

Motion Path Layers

A motion path layer is similar to a guide layer, but it is created with a different procedure to serve a different purpose. While guide layers provide only a visual placement and snap reference, motion paths are used to control the direction and position of tweened objects from frame to frame.

The process of creating a motion path is difficult to understand if you divorce it from the process of creating a motion tween. For that reason, the following exercise has you create a motion tween and then a motion path to which you'll attach the tween. Follow these steps:

1. Start with a new movie. (Choose File|New.)

2. Choose Libraries|Graphics to open the graphics Library window. Select Leaf Spinning from the list. You will see the maple leaf in the preview area. See Figure 8.10.

3. Drag the leaf icon onto the stage.

4. Choose Window|Library. The leaf is now in the symbols library of the current movie.

5. In the Timeline, highlight the first frame, which is a keyframe.

6. From the Frames menu, choose Motion Tween.

7. Click on a frame several frames after the first frame in the same layer in the Timeline. From the Frames menu, choose Insert Keyframe.

Figure 8.10
The animation in the preview area of the Library window.

8. On the stage, drag the leaf instance to its destination. Press Return/ Enter to watch the motion tween take place. The leaf will move in a straight line between its positions in the first and last keyframes of the tween.

9. Now it is time to create a motion path. Click the leaf's Layer button and choose Add Motion Guide from the Layers menu. A new layer will appear with the same layer name as the layer on which your tweened symbol resides.

10. Choose the Pencil from the Toolbox, and click on the Smooth modifier. Draw a path similar to the one in Figure 8.11.

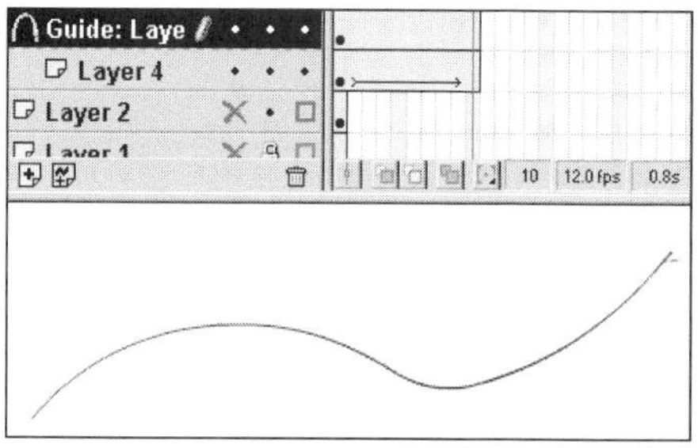

Figure 8.11
The path that will be used for the motion.

11. Click on the leaf's layer to activate it. Click on the Snap button in the Toolbar. Choose the Arrow tool. Drag the center of the leaf until it snaps to the lower end (beginning) of the motion path.

12. Drag the frame pointer to the second keyframe in the tween. You will see the tween happen, but it won't be following the motion path. Drag the center of the biplane until it snaps to the end of the motion path.

13. Press Return/Enter to play the movie. The leaf should follow the motion path.

Mask Layers

Mask layers are used to hide part of the underlying layers. The technique is often used to create a spotlight or keyhole effect. When you create a mask layer, anything you paint on that layer becomes transparent. If you animate or tween the shapes on that layer, the area that is revealed can be made to move.

When you paint on a mask layer, the normal 100-percent-opacity colors will hide what you're masking. This can be annoying and imprecise because what you are masking is actually what you want to have revealed in the final movie. Therefore, it's a good idea to change the Alpha channel opacity of the color you are going to paint or fill with. I've found that opacity of about 15 percent is clear enough to let me see what will be revealed and dark enough to let me see the area I've painted. This works because the opacity of the color used in the mask has no effect on the opacity of the actual mask. The flip side of this is that you can't create gradient masks or vignettes.

The following exercise demonstrates making a mask under an unmasked layer. Layer masks will reveal any shapes drawn on any layers under them.

1. Start a new movie by choosing File|New. Put some content on the top layer (perhaps some text and a graphic shape).

2. Choose Insert Layer from the Layers menu. Next, create a new layer so that you can import or create an image that will be selectively revealed by the masked layer you are about to make.

3. Revealing a bitmap with a mask can be very effective. To try this, choose File|Import. In the Import dialog box, navigate to a bitmapped image you would like to use and double-click on the file name. See Figure 8.12.

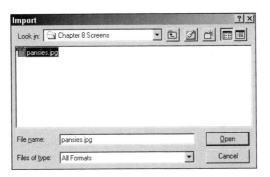

Figure 8.12
The Import dialog box.

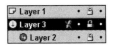

Figure 8.13
The icons left of the Layer name indicate that the outdented layer is a mask and the indented layer is a masked layer.

4. Next, between the top and bottom layers you need to insert a layer that will become the mask layer. While the image layer is still active, choose Insert Layer from the Modify Layer menu. A new layer will appear between Layer 1 and Layer 2.

5. From the Layer menu, choose Mask. Icons like those shown in Figure 8.13 will appear to the left of the layer names in Layers 3 and 2.

6. Draw a shape that you want to mask outside of. A circle makes a nice spotlight. Fill the circle with black (actually, any color will do).

7. From the Layer menu for the mask layer, choose Show Mask. You can see the result in Figure 8.14.

You can make the mask travel and expand by employing a motion tween in the mask layer to the mask shape. Unfortunately, there is no way to add a motion guide to a mask layer, so the motion tween will have to travel in a straight line. You can work around that by inserting keyframes instead of a motion tween and then moving and scaling the mask frame by frame.

Figure 8.14
The masked bitmap.

Figure 8.15
The stacking order of layers can
be changed.

Changing The Stacking Order Of Layers

You can change the stacking order of layers at any time. Drag the layer name (of the layer to be moved) to the layer name above which you'd like to move the original. For instance, in Figure 8.15, Layer 1 (originally the top layer) was automatically moved down to Level 3 as new layers were added. Layer 3 was then dragged down below Layer 2, so now the order is 2, 3, 1. For all but the smallest projects, it is important to name your layers. Use names that describe the purpose(s) of the layers to make the movie more understandable while you are editing it.

Moving The Content Of Multiple Frames To A Different Layer Or Movie

In Flash, the usual Cut, Copy, and Paste operations act on whatever object you select with the Arrow tool, regardless of the layer on which that object resides. However, if you want to move the contents of a specific frame or frames on a specific layer or layers, you have to go about it a little differently, as detailed in the following steps:

1. Select the frames that you want to copy. To select several sequential frames on the same layer, drag horizontally across the Timeline of the target layer. To select several frames on several layers, drag diagonally until the frames you've selected are highlighted. See Figure 8.16.

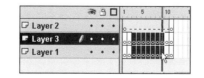

Figure 8.16
Selecting frames on several layers.

2. While the frames are still highlighted, choose Copy Frames (Cmd+Opt+C or Ctrl+Alt+C) from the Frames menu.

3. To place the copied frames into a different scene, select the target scene from the Edit Scenes menu (see Figure 8.17). Choose View|Tabs,

and then click on the tab of the target scene. (Skip this step if you want to place the frames elsewhere in the same scene's Timeline.)

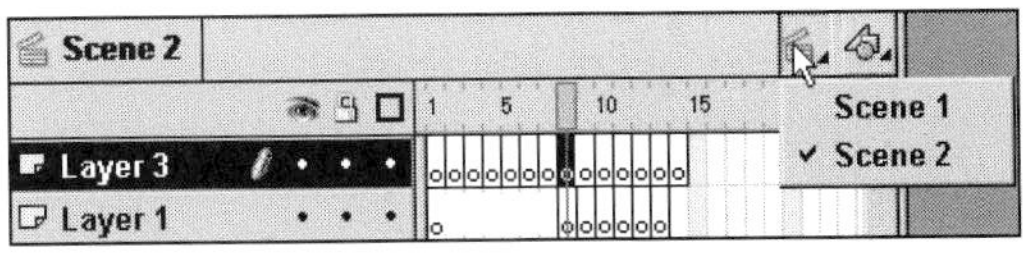

Figure 8.17
The Edit Scenes menu.

4. Select the frame where you want to paste the copied contents. From the Frames menu, choose Paste Frames (Cmd/Ctrl+Opt/Alt+V).

5. Of course, the frames you copy are still in their original locations. If you want to remove the originals, highlight them and choose Delete Frame from the Frames menu.

Combining Interactivity And Multiple Scenes

We have already discussed the basics of assigning actions to frames and buttons. Structurally, the only difference between a scene and a movie is that you can have several scenes within a single movie. Just as in regular movies, scenes can be a useful way to organize the specific events within a movie. Scenes also make it much easier to locate and change the order of events.

However, scenes are not exported to the Flash SWF file (that is, the Player movie that is embedded into a Web page), so no matter how many scenes are used, the final movie appears to be one long scene. Use scenes only to help you keep things organized while you are authoring.

Scenes can share any of the symbols stored in the parent movie's library. If you have objects appearing in more than one scene, be sure to convert them to symbols. Otherwise, the movie will store the same data for each scene in which those objects appear.

When you play a movie to test it while it's still in the workspace, only one scene will play at a time. When movies are played in the Flash player, all scenes are played without interruption unless you insert frame or button actions that tell them to do otherwise.

To test how all the scenes in a movie will play (with or without being influenced by actions), choose Control|Test Movie.

Creating And Naming Scenes

To create a new scene, choose Insert|Scene. Each scene is automatically named as it is created. The name assigned is Scene *n*, with *n* being the total number of scenes that have been created so far in the same movie. If you create four scenes, delete two scenes, and then create another, it will still be named Scene 5. If you create (insert) this new scene between Scenes 1 and 2, the automatically assigned name will still be Scene 5.

To rename a scene, choose Modify|Scene. The Scene Properties dialog box, shown in Figure 8.18, will open. Type any name you like in the Name field. Generally, you will want to use a name that describes the scene's purpose, contents, or category. Doing so makes it easier to organize the parts of a long movie.

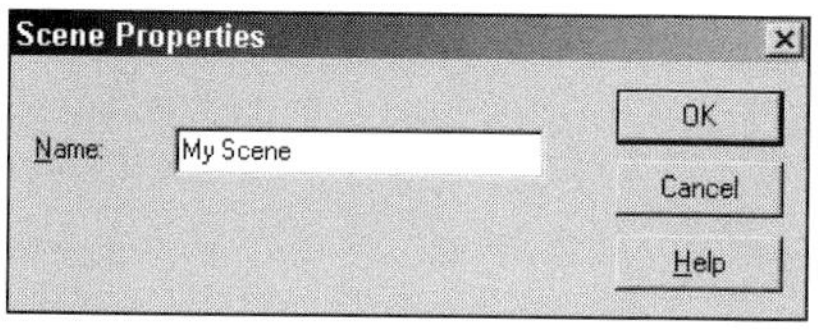

Figure 8.18
The Scene Properties dialog box.

Importing An SWF Movie

To import an existing SWF movie into a new scene, choose File|Import and then import the Flash movie or still-frame sequence of your choice. All imported movies will be interpreted as keyframes, so sounds and such data-saving devices as symbols, layers, and tweens will be lost. You can, however, move the frames from one scene to another by using the Copy Frames and Paste Frames commands in the Frames menu. Unless the movie is very small, though, this is a monumental task. The moral is to save your FLA working files and make regular backups because using an SWF file to reconstruct a movie is a nightmare.

Creating Transparency Effects

Alpha channels mask or partially mask artwork so that it becomes more or less transparent. Flash can apply transparency effects to imported bitmaps (GIF and PNG files), gradients, and solid colors. You can even set the level of transparency for an instance of a symbol. If that's not enough to suit you, you can tween the transparency of a color, gradient, or symbol instance over time. This section discusses the uses and methods for each of these applications of transparency.

Bitmaps And Alpha Channels

Flash 4 supports the transparent color assigned to GIF indexed-color files as well as that defined by the first Alpha channel (mask) stored in a true-color PNG file. In Flash 3, the GIF color that will be set as transparent has to be the zero index color (the upper left color in the color palette), but Flash 4 supports the GIF transparency no matter what index color it is set for.

This feature is a blessing because it allows photo cutouts and other irregularly shaped artwork to have a transparent background. Thus, you can "float" such art over other art, just as you always could with Flash's native vector artwork.

Symbol Instances And Bitmap Transparency

Flash can be made to control the overall level of any symbol's (including a bitmap's) transparency (or opacity, depending on whether you consider the glass half empty or half full). The following procedure will let you control the overall transparency of any symbol, regardless of how many shapes, colors, and other components that symbol may contain:

1. Select the bitmap that you want to make partially transparent.

2. Make it into an actual symbol by pressing F8. (Bitmaps are just treated as symbols when you put them in the library. If you want to apply Instance Properties, however, you have to make them into real symbols.)

3. While the new symbol is still selected, choose Modify|Instance to open the Instance Properties dialog box.

4. Click on the Color Effect tab. See Figure 8.19.

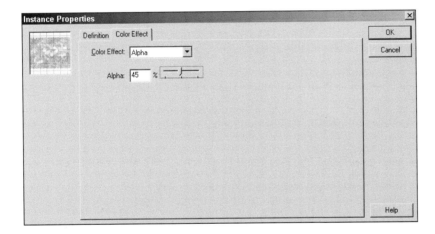

Figure 8.19
The Color Effect tab of the Instance Properties dialog box.

5. From the Color Effect list, choose Alpha. The dialog box will now show the Alpha field and slider seen in Figure 8.19.

6. Either type a percentage of transparency in the Alpha field or drag the slider to indicate a transparency level. When you think you've got it, click on OK. You can see the result in Figure 8.20.

Solid Colors

You can also control the transparency of a color that you use in a line or fill. The brush stroke in Figure 8.21 was made on the top layer of the movie, and its swatch color was designated as 60 percent transparent, so you can see all the shapes below it.

Read on for the steps needed to create a partially transparent color.

Figure 8.20
The partially transparent bitmap.

Figure 8.21
A brush stroke that's
60 percent transparent.

1. In the chosen tool's modifier section of the Toolbox, click on the Color Swatch. The Swatches menu appears. Click on one of the swatches to select a color.

2. Click on the Color Swatch again so the Swatches menu reappears. This time, click on the Edit Color button at the top of the swatches box. The Color dialog box opens. See Figure 8.22.

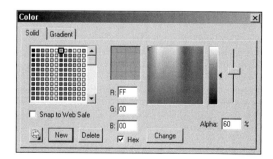

Figure 8.22
The Color dialog box.

3. Drag the slider at the far right. You will see the color in the sample swatch change slightly. The lower you drag the slider, the more the grid

underlying the color will be revealed. You will also see the percentage of transparency change in the Alpha field. If you want to change the current color, click on the Change button. If you want to add a new transparent color to the Swatch menu, click on the New button.

4. Paint as you wish, using the transparent color.

Gradients

A gradient is a smooth blend between adjacent colors. You can have many colors in a gradient (a rainbow is an example of a multicolor gradient) or only two. You can use the same kind of controls as previously demonstrated to determine the level of transparency of any or all of the principal colors in a gradient.

Making a gradient can be as easy as choosing one of the gradients that come with Flash 4. To fill a shape with a custom gradient, follow these steps:

1. Draw the outline of the shape that you want to fill with a gradient.

2. Choose the Paint Bucket tool. Click and drag on the Fill Color swatch to open the color palette, and click on the Color Edit button (it looks like a palette icon) at the top of the Swatches menu (or choose Window|Colors).

3. The Color dialog box opens. Click on the Gradient tab. See Figure 8.23.

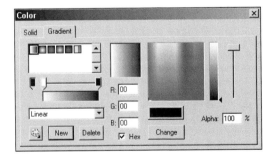

Figure 8.23
The Gradient tab of the Color dialog box.

4. From the Gradient Type list, choose a Linear or Radial (circular) gradient.

5. To change the colors in the gradient, click on the Color Pointer for the color you want to change. Next, click in the Color Space to indicate the color you want to choose for that pointer. Adjust the intensity of that color by dragging the Hue Bar slider. The color change will simultaneously appear in the pointer's swatch, in the Gradient Definition bar, and in the Gradient preview box.

Repeat this step to change the color assigned to any of the other pointers.

6. To change the center point of a color in the gradient, drag its pointer.

7. To add a new color to the gradient, drag the Pointer Well to the position over the Gradient Definition bar where you would like the new color to appear.

8. To fill with your new gradient, drag the Bucket Fill cursor in the direction of the fill. The first color will start where your drag line starts. Any space within the shape preceding the start of the drag line will be filled with the starting color. The last color will end where the drag line ends and will fill the rest of the shape.

The following steps are for changing the transparency of a color in a gradient:

1. Click in the Color Swatch to open the Swatches menu. Click on the Edit Color icon at the bottom to open the Color dialog box. Click on the Gradient tab.

2. Click on one of the gradient swatches at upper left to select the gradient you want to change. (I chose the one at far left.)

3. Choose Linear or Radial from the Gradient Type list (just under the Gradient Definition bar).

4. Click on the pointer for the principal gradient color that you want to change. This will make it the active color for editing.

5. Drag the Alpha slider at far right (or type a percentage of transparency in the Alpha field).

6. Click on the Change button to change the currently selected gradient, or click on the New button to create a new gradient. You can now paint with the partially transparent gradient.

In Figure 8.24, I have filled a rectangle with a black-to-clear gradient. Repeat this process for any additional colors whose transparency you would like to change.

Figure 8.24
The eggplant is overlaid with a black-to-clear gradient.

Tweening Transparency

It is possible to change the transparency of an area or item over time. One of the most frequent reasons for wanting to tween transparency is to simulate a fade-in, fade-out, or flashing effect. Flashing effects are made by fading in a symbol over a few frames, fading out the same symbol over a few frames, and then looping the effect. It is best done when an object is created as a new animated symbol.

You will often want to fade text in or out over time. In order to tween transparency, you must use a motion tween, which works only on symbols and doesn't include text. So, you must first enter the text and then save it as a symbol.

Here's a simple example of tweening transparency so that text fades in a motion tween. Follow these steps:

1. Paint a simple background so that you can see the transparency effect when you create it.

2. In the Timeline, highlight the next 15 frames. Then choose Insert Frames from the Modify Frames menu.

3. From the Modify Layer menu, choose Insert Layer. Make sure the new layer is above the background layer. (This will happen automatically if you have only two layers; otherwise, just drag the background layer's Name bar below the new layer's Name bar.)

4. Click the Layer Name bar of the new layer to make sure that it is active.

5. Choose the Text tool. From the text modifiers, choose a contrasting color for the text, and choose a sans serif font (such as Arial, Helvetica, or Trebuchet). Type "90" in the Font Size field. Click on the Bold button.

6. On the stage, click at lower left to indicate the start point for entering text. Type "Fade-Out".

7. Select the text by clicking it with the Arrow tool, then choose Insert|Convert to Symbol to open the Symbol Properties dialog box. You can enter a descriptive name for the text if you like. Leave Graphic as the chosen symbol type and click on OK. A selection marquee will appear around all of the text to show that it is now an overlay.

8. Select the first frame of the text layer. From the Modify Frames menu, choose Properties. The Properties dialog box opens.

9. Click on the Tweening tab. From the Tweening list, choose Motion. You may leave all other settings at their defaults. Click on OK.

10. Select a frame several frames farther along the text layer's Timeline. From the Modify Frames menu, choose Insert Keyframe.

11. This step isn't absolutely necessary, but it shows you that you can combine transparency tweening with motion, scaling, and transformation tweening. Drag the text symbol to the upper-right corner of the frame. While the text is still selected, choose the Scale modifier. Hold the Shift key to maintain the proportions while scaling, and then drag one of the corners inward so the text becomes much smaller.

12. Now, for the transparency tween, choose Modify|Instance. The Instance Properties dialog box opens.

13. Click on the Color Effect tab. From the Color Effect list, choose Alpha. Type "25" in the Alpha field, or drag the slider left until the Alpha field reads approximately 25 percent. Click on OK.

14. That's all there is to it. Press Return/Enter to play the scene. Figure 8.25 shows the scene after about three-fourths of the frames have been played.

Figure 8.25
The scene after about three-fourths of the frames have been played.

The Actions

Actions allow you to control certain aspects of your movie, including how it will play and how it will interact with the user and the outside world. Attaching an action to any frame on any layer in any scene is simply a matter of picking the needed action from the Actions list on the Actions tab of the Frame Properties dialog box, shown in Figure 8.26.

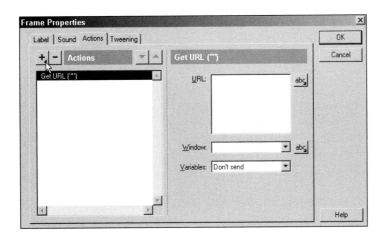

Figure 8.26
The Actions tab of the Frame Properties dialog box.

To open the Frame Properties dialog box, either double-click on the target frame or choose Properties from the Frames menu. Table 8.1 lists the names of all the frame actions and their purposes.

The Timeline Actions

The Play, Stop, and Go To actions are the actions that control action on the current Timeline. These actions give you control over the sequence of the current Timeline. With buttons, you can give the end user control over the movie (interactivity). A frame action can branch the action to any frame in the current Timeline in order to start, stop, move to, or play, starting in a new frame. Thus, you can reuse complete, multilayered, many-symbol sections of the movie (in whole or in part) as many times as you like within the overall movie. Frame actions don't require any participation on the part of the user; they simply execute when the frame that they are attached to plays.

Tell Target

Just as a Web server has a hierarchy of files and directories, Flash has a hierarchy of Timelines. To specify targets at different levels in the hierarchy, you add a path to the target name, using the same system as file paths or URLs. The Flash player that contains movies (SWF files) is at the top level of the hierarchy. Movie clips inside are children of the top-level movie.

The Tell Target action is used most often for navigation controls. Attach the Tell Target action to buttons that stop or start movie clips elsewhere on the stage. You can also make movie clips go to a particular frame. Normally, when a button or frame action is triggered, it sends a message to the Timeline that contains the button or the frame action. With a Tell Target action, however, you can send a message to any Timeline in your movie (a movie clip or a movie loaded by the Load Movie action).

Tell Target is the method needed to communicate between different timelines:

- Between the main Timeline and movie clips

Table 8.1   Frame actions and their purposes.

◇ indicates new feature

Action	Purpose
Go To	Jumps directly to the named scene and frame. The frame can be specified as a label number, or as the next or previous frame. The movie will freeze at the target frame unless you check the Go To and Play or Next box.
Play	Sets a frame to start playing any time an action jumps to it.
Stop	Sets a frame to stop playing any time an action jumps to it.
Toggle High Quality	Toggles anti-aliasing on and off.
Stop All Sounds	Turns off all current sounds.
Get URL	Loads an HTML document into a browser window. Options for target windows are Self (the current window), Blank (new window), and Parent (of the current window). You can also manually enter the name specified in HTML for that window.
FS Command	Sends strings to any host that the scripting environment (for example, JavaScript, VBScript, and Lingo) supports.
Load	Loads another Flash movie from the specified URL. You can also specify the stacking order of the movie with respect to the current movie.
Unload Movie	Turns off a movie being played by the Load Movie command.
Tell Target	Sends one of the other actions in this table to the specified instance of a movie clip, to the main Timeline, or to a movie loaded by the Load Movie action.
If Frame Is Loaded	Prevents an action from executing unless and until the player or browser has loaded the specified frame. The most frequent use for this action is to play an entertaining or informative short animation while the user is waiting for the main movie to download.
On Mouse Event	Allows you to add a mouse event before adding its action. This option is ghosted unless the action is being applied to a button.
◇If	Allows conditional scripting choices.
◇Loop	Allows limited script looping. Limited by 200,000 "Player Actions".
◇Call	Allows you to call an ActionScript located in another frame.
◇Set Property	Applies a property value to a movie clip or globally to the whole movie.
◇Set Variable	Sets the value of a variable.
◇Duplicate Movie Clip	Allows duplication of movie clips.
Remove Movie Clip	Allows removal of movie clips.
◇Drag Movie Clip	Allows you to drag-and-drop movie clips.
◇Trace	Provides text to be displayed for a particular frame in the Output window. The text can be derived from expressions.
◇Comment	Allows you to add a comment to the action window. Used for documenting the actions in the authoring environment.

- Between different movie clips

- Between the main Timeline and other movies loaded by the Load Movie action

- To movie clips in other movies that were loaded by the Load Movie action

- From JavaScript to a main Timeline or to a movie clip using FSCommand Flash Methods

To use Tell Target with a movie clip, the clip must have an Instance name. Because movie clips are symbols and we can have multiple instances of any movie clip, we can't use the Library name of the movie to identify a particular instance. To add or change an Instance name of a movie clip:

1. Select the movie-clip instance.

2. Choose Modify|Instance (or double-click on the instance) to open the Instance Properties dialog box.

3. Select the Definition tab.

4. Make sure the Behavior is set to Movie Clip.

5. Enter the name you wish to use for communicating with the movie clip.

For example, to tell a movie clip with the instance name of Leaf to play from frame 10, we would have:

```
Begin Tell Target ("/Leaf")
      Go to and Play (10)
End Tell Target
```

To use Tell Target with a movie loaded by the Load Movie action, we do not use names; rather, we refer to it by the level it was loaded on. Use _level$x$ where x is the level number of the movie loaded by Load Movie. For example, if we have a movie loaded into level 5 by Load Movie, and we want to have that movie play from frame 20, we would have:

```
Begin Tell Target ("_level5")
      Go to and Play (20)
End Tell Target
```

Tell Target Paths

There are three ways to communicate with movie clips:

- By referring to the main Timeline of the current movie. The / (slash) represents the main Timeline or root.

- By referring to the movie by its level position, in the form of _level$x$, where x is the level number. The original movie loads into level zero, which would be _level0.

- By the relative position between a movie clip and the main Timeline or another movie clip. In a movie clip that is on the main Timeline, you can use ../ to refer to the main Timeline, or you can use _level0 (if it is the original movie), but generally ../ is better.

Table 8.2 gives examples of Tell Target paths.

Using Tell Target is not difficult as long as you don't try to over-complicate the paths. Work from the root (/) of the main Timeline whenever possible.

Table 8.2   Tell Target paths.

Paths from the root (main Timeline) of the same movie:

Path	Relationship to root	Description
/	Root	Refers to the root directory (main Timeline).
/Fred	Child of the root	Refers to the movie clip "Fred" found on the main Timeline.
/Fred/Pebbles	Grandchild of the root	Refers to the movie clip "Pebbles," which is a child of the movie clip "Fred," which is on the main Timeline.

Relative paths:

Path	Relationship to root	Description
..	Parent	Refers to the movie clip (or the main Timeline) that is one level back toward the root. Note that .. and ../ are the same.
../../	Grandparent	Refers to the movie clip (or the main Timeline) that is two levels back toward the root.
Fred	Child	Refers to the movie clip "Fred," which is on the same Timeline as the Tell Target command.
Fred/Pebbles	Grandchild	Refers to the movie clip "Pebbles," which is a child of the movie clip "Fred." Fred is on the same Timeline as the Tell Target command.
../Fred	Sibling	Refers to a movie clip that has the same parent (movie clip or main Timeline).

Paths from the root of a movie specified by level number:

Path	Relationship to root	Description
_levelx	Root movie	Refers to the root movie by the level number "x" as loaded by Load Movie. The movie is referred to by its level number, which can be any number from 0 to 16,000. The original movie is always loaded into Level 0 (zero).
_level33/Fred	Child of root movie	Refers to the child of the root movie that was loaded into level 33 by Load Movie.
_level5/Fred/Pebbles	Grandchild of root movie	Refers to the grandchild of the root movie that was loaded into level 5 by Load Movie.

In leaf-mc2.fla, we show you how to use a button to control a movie clip from a different button. In leaf-mc3.fla, we show you how to use a button inside a movie clip to control itself (the same button).

Get URL (Opening Pages In HTML Frames)

The Get URL action is used to load a specific URL into a specific HTML window, or to pass variables via a URL so they can be acted upon in another program. If you're using this action to load another SWF file, you should load an HTML page containing the SWF file and not the SWF file itself.

Parameters of the Get URL action are as follows:

- URL specifies the URL of the file.

- Window specifies the target window where the page will be loaded. You can enter the name of a window (frame) as specified in the HTML frameset or JavaScript, or you can enter one of the four reserved target names:

- _self specifies the current HTML frame.

- _blank specifies a new window.

- _parent specifies the parent of the current HTML frame.

- _top specifies the topmost frame in the current window and will remove all HTML frames.

- Variables determine whether variables will be sent along with the URL and, if so, whether the GET or the POST method of sending them will be used. The GET method appends the variables to the URL; the POST method sends them in a header. POST generally allows longer strings to be sent.

Load Movie

Load movies—movies loaded with the Load Movie action—are completely separate Flash SWF files. They are organized into levels, with Level 0 being the level of the original movie loaded by Flash. Higher levels overlay content on lower levels. When you load a movie with the Load Movie action, you specify the level number. This level number—not a name—is how all load movies are identified. Only the original movie has a set level (zero). Any additional movies can have any level number between 1 and 16,000.

The Level 0 movie is special: its frame rate determines the frame rate for all other currently loaded movies. If you use the Load Movie action to load a new movie into Level 0, then the new movie will run at the speed (fps) that is set in the new movie, and all movies on all other levels will be unloaded.

Load movies are all loaded with the upper-left corners aligned, regardless of the size of the movies. So if you're going to stack movies with the Load Movie action, make them all the same stage size and frame rate for ease of manipulation. If one movie is smaller than the other is, put it into a new movie of the same size as the original, and then position it inside that larger movie to achieve your offset.

Load Movie And Tell Target

After you have loaded a movie, it can receive commands (Tell Target actions) from other movies, telling it what frames to go to, or targeting its movie clips to go to certain frames. For example, a movie might be parked in an empty frame until another movie tells it to go somewhere specific.

When you're targeting a movie loaded by the Load Movie action, you use the level that a movie is loaded into—rather than a name—to identify it. The form is _levelx where x is the number representing the level. (Note the

Note: You can use the new Load Into Target feature to load movies offset from the corner, but this is not recommended for normal stacking of load movies.

Note: The frame that is being called must already be loaded before you can send a working command to it. If a frame has not been loaded, a Tell Target request will be ignored.

underscore, which is required.) For example, if you want the movie loaded in level 5 to play starting at frame 5, use these commands:

```
Begin Tell Target ("_level5")
      Go to and Play ("Sunset")
End Tell Target
```

Parking

When you're working with load movies (and movie clips), all buttons remain active whether or not they are visible—except when they are covered by a button on a higher level. The solution is *parking*.

Parking moves a load movie (or a movie clip) to a frame that has no active components (buttons). There are two types of *park frames*:

- A frame that has no visible elements

- A frame that has visible components but either does not have buttons or has all the buttons' behaviors turned off (buttons were changed to graphics)

There are two basic parking setups. Which one you use depends on whether or not the movie is to start parked or start playing:

- *Start Parked*—The movie will begin with a stop action in frame #1, which contains no graphics. In other words, the movie is invisible, or "parked."

- *Park Later*—The movie will have a Go To and Play Frame 3 action in frame #1, which bypasses frame #2, which will be the park frame.

On The Web

Load movies are independent Web elements that load based on Web conditions. Any new movies loaded with the Load Movie action will start loading, and any previous Flash movies (or other Web elements) will continue to load. If you need a movie to load in an orderly process, then you should either load one movie at a time or use a movie clip in your original movie.

The Load Movie action is a very powerful feature in Flash, but when it's used on the Web, you should ensure that the various movies have loaded up to the point where you call them (using Tell Target). A back-and-forth communication in combination with the If Frame Is Loaded action is highly recommended for any movies that will require communication with each other.

Usually you can achieve similar effects to Load Movie by stacking movie clips on layers within one movie. But sometimes there's so much content, or navigation has become so complex, that you will want to break up the presentation into more than one movie. Large sounds, for example, are sometimes best loaded in a sound-only movie.

When should you use the Load Movie action?

- Any time you can't use movie clips, such as with scenes.

- When you have various large segments that will be called in an un-specified order. If segments are to be viewed in a standard order, one after the other, then you should probably include all the segments in the same movie. This allows random-access loading of content without the need to load content that may not be needed or is not needed yet.

- When problems with Internet Explorer 4.x for Macintosh can be overcome or are not important.

Internet Explorer 4.x for Macintosh browsers have problems with Load Movie. Usually, if you load only one movie at a time, these browsers will work fine, but version 4.5 of the Mac Internet Explorer browser fails to work properly with Load Movie.

Load Into Target

The new Load Into Target feature is found as an option of the Load Movie action. Rather than load a movie into a level, as a regular Load Movie does, the Load Into Target feature replaces a movie clip with an SWF movie.

The new movie will become a movie clip and inherit the position, rotation, and scale properties of the old movie clip. The position of the inserted movie (now a movie clip) will have its upper-left corner placed at the center of the current position of the movie clip it is replacing.

If Frame Is Loaded And Preloading

The If Frame Is Loaded action is a one-time check. It has two main purposes:

- When used as a preloader, it can be used to ensure proper streaming or to prevent buttons from being enabled before the frame they are going to has loaded.

- It allows you to bypass a beginning portion of your movie when it is replayed.

Preloaders

The most common preloaders usually involve creating a loop. The loop will constantly check to see if the target frame (LoadTest) is loaded; if it is not loaded, the loop will play the preload content that starts at LoopStart. When the preload content is finished, another If Frame Is Loaded check is made. The loop will continue until the target frame (LoadTest) has been loaded and tested, and then the Go To Frame Action To Start will be executed. To do this:

- Label as LoopStart the frame at the beginning of the preload animation.

- Label as Start the frame of the main animation.

- Label as LoadTest the frame that should allow streaming of your movie if it's loaded.

In the last frame of your preload animation, place the following actions:

```
If Frame Is Loaded ("LoadTest")
     Go to and Play ("Start")
End Frame Loaded
Go to and Play ("LoopStart")
```

The above preloader will always play at least once, even from your hard drive.

Preventing A Movie From Replaying An Introduction

The If Frame Is Loaded action can be used to prevent an introductory portion of your movie from replaying; it does this by testing to see if the last frame of the movie is loaded. If the movie is loaded, then a Go To action will take visitors to the frame you want them to see when returning to your Flash movie.

Label the last frame as Fini, and label your target frame as RePlay. Then place the following in the first frame of your movie:

```
If Frame Is Loaded ("Fini")
     Go to and Play ("RePlay")
End Frame Loaded
```

When you place an If Frame Is Loaded action—as described above—in your movie, the introductory portion will always be bypassed when it's played locally on your hard drive or with the Test Movie command. Therefore, you should disable this command when testing locally.

Drag Movie Clip

Drag Movie Clip allows a movie clip to be dragged so it follows the mouse. A movie clip remains in drag mode until it's stopped by a Stop Drag action, until another movie clip becomes draggable, or until the movie ceases to exist. Only one movie clip at a time can be dragged. Drag options are normally placed as a button action inside a button, which is placed inside the movie clip that is being controlled.

Two common start and stop button-event pairs are usually used with a drag-and-drop button. The most common pair is On(Press) for starting and On(Release) for stopping. The other common pair is On(RollOver) for starting and On(Press) for stopping. More complicated drag-and-drop animations can be created using the _droptarget property, which is discussed in the next chapter.

Parameters of the Drag Movie Clip action are as follows:

- Start Drag Operation starts the Drag Movie Clip action.

- Stop Drag Operation ends the drag operation.

- Target specifies the movie clip that is to be dragged. Targets are the standard movie-clip targets that we discussed earlier in the chapter. If you click on the "abc" button and choose the Target Editor, you can often select the movie clip with its complete path by clicking on it in the list. If the movie clip is controlled by a button that is on the movie clip's Timeline, leave this line blank to indicate that the path is to itself.

- Constrain To Rectangle allows you to specify a rectangular area beyond which the movie clip will not be allowed to move. The left, top, right, and bottom values set the limits of the constraint and are relative to the parent of the movie clip. If the mouse starts outside of the boundaries of the constraint, it will jump to the nearest point within the boundaries.

- Lock Mouse To Center centers the mouse to the movie clip. If it's not selected, the movie clip will maintain a constant position relative to the mouse and based on their initial positions when the drag operation began. If you have selected Lock Mouse To Center, the mouse will change to a hand (it has to go over the button). If Lock Mouse To Center is not selected, then the hand never goes over the mouse, and the cursor remains a pointer.

If your button resides in the movie clip, your actions might look like this.

```
On (Release)
      Start Drag ("", lockcenter)
End On
On (Release)
      Stop Drag
End On
```

Duplicate Movie Clip

Duplicate Movie Clip allows you to create a duplicate instance of a movie clip. The new, duplicated movie clip will always start in frame one of the movie clip, regardless of the frame that the parent movie clip was at when the duplicate was made. Variables are not copied to duplicate movie clips.

A duplicated movie clip can be removed only with the Duplicate/Remove Movie Clip action or if the Timeline it's on ceases to exist. If the duplicated movie clip is on the main Timeline and the original movie clip is deleted, the duplicates will continue to exist, even into another scene.

Parameters of the Duplicate Movie Clip action are as follows:

- Action allows you to duplicate or remove a movie clip.

- Target specifies the movie clip that is to be duplicated or removed. Targets are the standard movie-clip targets that we discussed earlier in the chapter. If you click on the "abc" button and choose the Target Editor, you can often select the movie clip with its complete path by clicking on it in the list.

- New Name is the instance name that will be used for the new, duplicate movie clip. Provide only the name without a path.

- Depth determines the stacking order of your duplicate movie clip. The initial Depth position is zero, which is the position of the original movie clip. If you duplicate a movie and use a depth position previously used, the new duplicate will replace the old one. Higher depths overlay lower ones. Duplicate movies are always above the original movie clip.

Sounds

In Flash 4, the new default compression technology used for exporting sound uses MP3 technology, which provides smaller and better sounds. Flash does not allow the import of any MP3 sound. The only sounds that can be imported into Flash are uncompressed versions of WAV (Windows) and AIFF (Mac) files.

Putting Sound In A Movie

Here are the basic steps for placing streaming sound on a Flash layer. Open any multiple-frame Flash movie that you've created. If you don't have one handy, make one (following the directions previously given for creating a shape tween).

1. Select a layer just above the layer to which you want to add a synchronized, streaming sound. From the Modify Layers menu, choose Insert Layer.

2. The layer will be placed just above the layer you've selected. Select the new layer, and drag it just below the layer from which you inserted it.

3. It is a good idea to name this layer after the sound you will place there. To do so, double-click on the Layer Name bar. The automatically assigned generic layer name (Layer N) will be highlighted, and you can simply type to enter a new name.

4. On the Modify Layers button of the new layer, you should see a pencil icon to indicate that the layer is active. If not, select the layer.

5. Choose File|Import to open the Import dialog box. From the Files Of Type list, choose either AIFF (Mac) or WAV (Windows). Now only the

specified type of files will show in the file selection windows. Navigate to the sound file that you want to import (anything will do for the moment), and double-click on the file name.

6. Choose Window|Library (unless the Library window is already open). The name of your chosen sound will appear in the list of symbols. A speaker icon will appear to the left of the name, indicating that this symbol is a sound. See Figure 8.27.

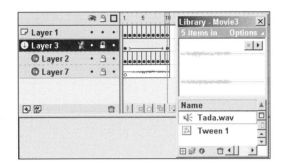

Figure 8.27
A speaker icon to the left of the name indicates that a symbol is a sound.

7. Drag the sound preview from the Library window to the stage. You will immediately see the sound's histogram in the Timeline. The histogram will occupy as many frames as it takes to play the entire sound. Later in this chapter, you'll learn how to edit sounds and animations so they stop and start at specific frames.

8. To test your movie, pull down the menu bar's Control menu and make sure that Mute Sounds is unchecked.Then press Return/Enter to play the movie.

Sound Events

Sounds in Flash can be triggered to start at any keyframe in the movie. The four triggers for sounds in the Timeline are Event, Start, Stream, and Stop.

-   *Event*—An Event sound starts playing as soon as the keyframe it's in is activated, and the sound plays in its entirety. The sound plays regardless of what sounds are already playing or what else is happening in the Timeline.

-   *Start*—Start sounds behave the same way as Event sounds, except that if the designated sound is already playing from a previous button or frame action, the sound is not triggered again.

If a sound is assigned to the Down state of a button with the Start sound trigger, and that button is pressed repeatedly, the sound is triggered only when the button is pushed and the sound has already stopped playing from a previous push of the button. If the Event trigger is assigned, then that sound starts playing over itself each time the button is pushed, and it becomes a jumbled audio mush.

- *Stream*—When Stream is assigned to a frame of a button or the Timeline, the designated sound starts playing as soon as the playback head enters the designated trigger frame. The differentiating characteristic of the Stream trigger is that it causes the sound to become the critical timing element for playback of the .swf file. If a sound is set to Stream, frames of the animation will be dropped (skipped, not rendered) in order for the animation of the movie to stay in time with the playback of the designated sound.

- *Stop*—Stop will stop the designated sound from playing. The Stop trigger is used to stop a particular sound. If you want to stop all sounds, choose the Stop All Sounds action from the Actions menu.

MP3 Sound Quality

MP3 sound is limited to a specific bit rate that you can set. But if the sound for a particular bit is too complicated to describe, the compression routine will look to add that overage detail later on, in future bits where the sound is less complicated.

You have three quality options for MP3 sound:

- *Fast*—Allows the shortest distance for which sound overages can be stored. This is the setting you should use for normal Web use because the complete sound will be available sooner.

- *Medium*—Best used for CDs.

- *Best*—Used for very fast connections or when all the sound is preloaded or already in memory or on a hard drive. This option allows a sound overage to be widely spaced from its original component for maximum utilization of all the bits that can be sent at the set bit rate.

A couple of warnings: First, when you're publishing MP3 for the Web, always use Fast (not Best) for Quality. You will not get best quality for the Web if you export sound as Best. Second, if this sound was originally compressed digitally, such as with MP3, you are going to have artifacts, and the sound will not recompress as well as the original tracks, which were never compressed with a lossy system such as MP3. If this sounds familiar, like the JPEG warning for Flash 3, it is because it is the same type of problem.

Flash 3, MP3, And Sound

The default sound setting for Flash 4 is MP3 compression, which will not be heard by visitors with Flash 3 plug-ins or ActiveX controls. The following are alternatives to get sound to visitors with the Flash 3 plug-in.

• If you don't use other Flash 4 features, you can export as Flash 3 only, but the file size will probably be substantially larger.

• You can set HTML to get (require) the Flash 4 plug-in or ActiveX control.

• You can make a selection or detection scheme to select either Flash 3 or Flash 4 depending on the version of Flash the user has. You would then export two versions of the SWF file: one as Flash 3, and one as Flash 4 (this is done in the Export Flash Player dialog box).

Sounds And Buttons

You can associate a sound event with each of the four states of a button by applying the sound to the button's frames. Because the sound is placed on the button's Timeline, the sound will be available for all instances of the button. These are the four button states:

• *Up*—The sound event occurs on Mouse Out.

• *Over*—The sound event occurs on Mouse Over.

• *Down*—The sound event occurs on Mouse Down.

• *Hit*—The sound event occurs on Mouse Release.

Moving On

Next up, the powerful and compact ActionScripts. We'll see how Flash's traditional actions are transformed, and explore Flash's new "language" that allows users more interactivity than ever before!

AUTOMATING FLASH WITH ACTIONSCRIPT

9

The new scripting options in Flash 4 have removed many of the limits to providing streaming interactive content on the Web.

JOHN CROTEAU

ActionScript is the name of Flash 4's new scripting language, which allows greater interactivity in Flash than ever before. The scripting interactivity, which has been added to Flash 3's traditional actions, is entered as a series of actions and merged together with Flash's traditional actions, such as Go To and Tell Target.

In Flash 3 the only way to internally keep track of data is by a method called Movie Clip Logic. This method uses movie clips to keep a tally by being incremented with Tell Target commands. An example of this is a Bingo game, as shown in Figure 9.1. A similar game with the same features was created with Tell Target logic, which took over 150K to implement using movie clips to store all the data and logic. A new version using ActionScript took less than 4K and can communicate with a database.

Figure 9.1

Bingo game created with ActionScript; a version of this game can be seen at **www.FlashCentral.com**.

Another example of using scripting and other advanced features of Flash 4 is the Virtual Blox game shown in Figure 9.2. In Flash 4, with the Drag Movie Clip drag and drop action and the Duplicate Movie Clip action now available, the number of block shapes is limited only by the available area of screen real estate and by design considerations. The example discussed here can be seen at **www.FlashCentral.com**.

ActionScript has a compact but powerful set of features. One of the main reasons Flash has become so popular is the small player size, and the addition of ActionScript to the Flash player has increased its size minimally. Despite its small size, ActionScript has most of the standard math, string, and logical operators, a few basic commands, a few built-in functions, and 21 special properties. The commands and functions were chosen to add maximum functionality, allowing you to build complex functions and routines, while still allowing a small and quick Flash player. The Plug and Play routines such as those at the site **www.FlashBible.com/members** allow easy addition of more advanced functionality and features to Flash when needed.

Figure 9.2
Virtual Blox.

ActionScript extends the functionality of Flash actions. Many new parameters are selectable from list boxes to make it easier to implement some commands. This makes learning and using many of ActionScript's features accessible even for the non-programmer. The experienced programmer may feel constrained by the small working areas and the inability to copy script into Flash from a text editor. Text can be copied to other programs from Flash, but not from other programs into Flash.

Script routines and actions can now be copied and moved within the Flash environment. You can click on a line of code, Shift-click to add further lines to the selection, copy the code, and paste it into another action window. In this way, you can easily build a library of actions and scripts and save them in FLA files for later use. Saving them in movie clips, as callable routines (using Call), is especially effective.

Variables

We will start with *variables*, which are simply storage places that hold information for later use. As your animation plays, you can save details stored as values in variables. This information can be evaluated and used to provide additional information to the user or guide him through the animation based on decisions he has made.

Types Of Information That Variables Store

Variables in Flash can store three types of data: numerical, string, and logical. *Numerical data* is simply numbers, which can be added, subtracted, multiplied, etc. *Strings* are collections of one or more alphabetic or numeric characters, which are stored one after the other like beads on a string. *Logical data* is one of two values: True or False. Flash can also use the numeric value of zero to be equivalent to False and any nonzero value would equate to True.

In the following expression, movie clip "OriginalMC" will be duplicated and the new movie clip will be assigned a name that will be stored in the string variable NewMC.

```
Duplicate Movie Clip ("OriginalMC", NewMC, Level)
```

Although both "OriginalMC" and NewMC are strings, the first is a string literal and the second is a string variable. A literal string is a string made up of a series of characters enclosed in quotes whose value is those exact characters and not that of a variable. The actual instance name of the original movie clip is OriginalMC; placing it in quotes shows this. Because NewMC does not have quotes, it is a variable and the name of the new movie clip is not NewMC but is the value that is stored in the variable NewMC. Level is a numeric variable that stores the number that will be used for the relative stacking order of the duplicated movie clip.

The following Set Property action, sets a logical value for an item called "Globe" to False: This will make it invisible.

```
Set Property ("/Globe", Visibility) = false
```

The following substitutes a variable Visible for the logical value; if the value of Visible evaluates numerically as zero, this will be the same as False and the movie clip will become invisible. Otherwise, the image will be set to be visible.

```
Set Property ("/Globe", Visibility) = Visible
```

Notice the equal signs in these examples. They are operators, and the presence of operators signifies that you're using an expression: a statement that's evaluated to yield a result. An expression is a combination of variables, values, and operators that yield a result upon evaluation. This resulting value may be assigned to a variable or used as part of another expression. Expressions and operators are covered in more detail later in this chapter.

Entering Variables

Many scripting languages require you to predefine what kind of data a specific variable will store (such as string or integer); each variable defined can store only one kind of information. In Flash, this isn't the case. Predefining a variable as a certain type is not only unnecessary in ActionScript; it's impossible. In Flash, the data type of a variable is determined by its context.

You can set a variable to a specific value using the Set Variable action from the actions list as shown in Figure 9.3. The actions list is available by clicking on the Actions tab and then the plus (+) button in the Frame Properties or the button Instance Properties dialog box. Figure 9.4 shows the Frame Properties dialog box.

Strings can be used as numbers, and numbers can be used as strings. The way a variable in an expression is evaluated—as a string, as a number, or as the logical value True or False—depends on whether the variable is operated on with a string operator, a numeric operator, or a logical operator, or whether the variable is enclosed in quotes.

When you're entering the names of variables, values, and expressions, many action dialog boxes have a Variable Type button that allows you to choose the String Literal (abc) option or the Expression (=) option, or allows you to access the Expression Editor. For some actions you may also have a choice of Numeric (123) or access to the Target Editor. Figure 9.4 shows the type selection options for a Set Variable action. When you choose the String Literal (abc) option, the value inserted into the script will be the series of characters that you specify, and quotes will be added automatically to identify this value as a string literal.

Figure 9.3
Frame Properties—the Action Selection pull-down menu.

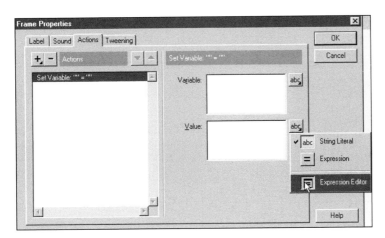

Figure 9.4
Select Variable type.

If you want to enter a numeric or logical value, or if you want your entry to be evaluated as a numeric or string expression, then you need to choose Expression (=). To enter a literal string in your expression then you must add the needed quotes manually.

The Expression Editor allows you to select most operators, functions, and properties from one of two lists to help prevent syntax errors (misspelling or punctuation). If Numeric (123) is an option, and you choose it, then whatever you enter will be evaluated as a number. The Target Editor allows you to point to and click on a currently available movie-clip path, instead of entering it by hand.

Variable Paths

When you use variables that are in the same Timeline, you can use just their names. You can refer to any variable in any Timeline (movie clip or main Timeline) by using the variable's full path. Variable paths use the same basic path structure as Tell Target does for movie clips and loaded

Note: Action and variable names in Flash are case insensitive, but the values of strings are case sensitive.

movies—with one addition. The path will be first, and a colon will separate it from the basic variable name. A variable path looks like this:

```
/movieClip1/movieClip2:variableName
```

Operators

An *operator* is a device used to combine or compare numbers or strings or to evaluate expressions. For instance, the plus sign (+) is used to add numbers, and the ampersand (&) is used to concatenate (combine) strings. The equal sign (=) compares two numeric expressions, but "eq" is used to compare two strings. Figure 9.5 shows an example of combining two strings.

Figure 9.5
Variable concatenation.

In the following examples, notice the different results obtained with different operators: + for adding, and & for combining.

```
3 + 12 = 15
3 & 12 = 312
```

The type of operator you use determines how a variable will be evaluated in Flash. These operators appear in the left-hand column of the Expression Editor which is shown in Figure 9.6. Table 9.1 lists the operators available in Flash.

Expressions

In Flash, there are three basic types of expressions: numerical, string, and logical. An expression can include other expressions, but the total expression must evaluate as one of the three types of data.

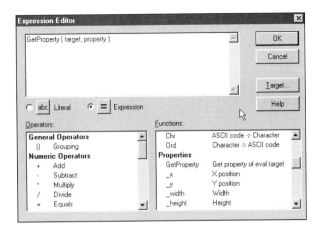

Figure 9.6
The Expression Editor.

Table 9.1   Types of operators.

General Operators

Operator	Meaning
( )	Grouping

Arithmetic Operators

Operator	Meaning
+	Add
-	Subtract
*	Multiply
/	Divide

Numeric Comparison Operators

Operator	Meaning
=	Equal to
<>	Not equal to
<	Less than
>	Greater than
<=	Less than or equal to
>=	Greater than or equal to

String Operators

Operator	Meaning
" "	String
&	Concatenate

String Comparison Operators

Operator	Meaning
eq	Equal to
ne	Not equal to
lt	Less than
gt	Greater than
le	Less than or equal to
ge	Greater than or equal to

(continued)

Table 9.1 Types of operators *(continued)*.

Logical Operators

Operator	Meaning
AND	And (as in: both this thing and that thing)
OR	Or (as in: either this thing or that thing)
NOT	Not (as in: not this thing; anything but this thing)

Numerical Expressions

The result of a numerical expression is a number. A numerical expression is composed of a numeric operator (+, -, *, or /), plus any of the following:

- A number

- A numeric variable

- A function that returns a numeric value

- Any combination of the three

Flash's arithmetic operators follow standard mathematics protocol, with items in parentheses being performed first, followed by multiplication and division, and then by addition and subtraction. You can create an animation that does dynamic calculation such as the Variables 1 tutorial shown in Figure 9.7.

Figure 9.7
Variable addition from
www.FlashBible.com/members/.

The following expression sets the sum of 1 plus 2 to the variable named Result:

```
Set Variable: "Result" = 1 + 2
```

See the example in Figure 9.8

The following expression sets the sum of the variable Subtotal plus 1 to the variable Result:

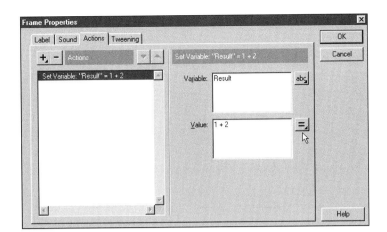

Figure 9.8
Set Variable—Expression.

```
Set Variable: "Result" = Subtotal + 1
```

If the Subtotal variable was not previously defined, it will be evaluated as zero.

If a string is composed only of numbers, it will be evaluated as the number it represents. If any of the characters in a string are not numeric, then the string will be evaluated as zero.

The following expression returns 24 to Result because + is a numeric operator:

```
Set Variable: "Result" = "23" + 1
```

The following expression returns 1 to Result because the numeric value of a string that has any non-numeric characters is zero:

```
Set Variable: "Result" = "23B" + 1
```

The following expression returns 7.5 to Result because if a string only contains numeric characters it will be evaluated as a number if the operator is numeric:

```
Set Variable: "Result" = 10 + "-2.5"
```

The following expression returns 10 to Result because the string "-2.5 " has a value of zero because it contains a space that is not a numeric character:

```
Set Variable: "Result" = 10 + "-2.5 "
```

If you divide by zero, the result will be the string #ERROR#.

String Expressions

The result of a string expression is a string. A string expression is composed of a string operator (such as &, eq, or gt), plus any of the following:

- A literal string (text surrounded by quotes)

- A string variable

- A function that returns a string value

- Any combination of the three

In the following script the variable Result is set to the literal string John.

```
Set Variable: "Result" = "John"
```

Figure 9.9 shows how the above script is entered in Flash.

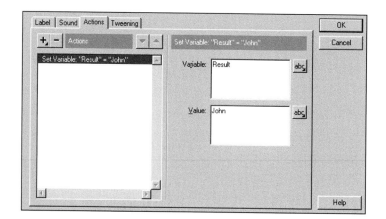

Figure 9.9
Set Variable—String Literal.

Logical Expressions

There are two logical (Boolean) values: True and False. A logical expression is composed of a logical operator (AND, OR, or NOT), plus any of the following:

- A string comparison

- A numeric comparison

- A statement or function that returns a logical value

- Any combination of the three

True and False are built-in functions that can be used to set a logical value to True or False. Logical expressions are usually used in If or Loop While statements.

In Flash, a logical expression or comparison expression returns either 1 for True or 0 for False. When evaluating a logical expression, Flash evaluates a zero as False and evaluates any non-zero numeric value as True. Any string that does not evaluate as a number will return a logical value of 0 (False).

Comparisons

In Flash you can compare two numeric expressions to each other or you can compare two string expressions. You can also use numeric and string comparisons in logical expressions.

Numeric Comparisons

Numeric comparisons compare two expressions to each other based on their numerical evaluations. The result of a numeric comparison is always either 1 for True or 0 for False. If the value of one of the numeric expressions being compared cannot be converted to a number, that expression will be evaluated as zero. Any string with any non-numeric character will not be evaluated as zero. The Drop Target tutorial shown in Figure 9.10 uses a numeric comparison of the vertical position of the falling ball to the bottom of the trash can to prevent the ball from falling through the trash can.

Figure 9.10
Drop Target, at
**www.FlashBible.com/members/
Drag/DropTarget.htm**.

In the following example, Result will be evaluated as 1 (True) because it is True that 8 is greater than 5.

```
Set Variable: "Result" = "8 > 5"
```

In the following example, Result will be evaluated as 0 (False) because 9 is not equal to 5.

```
Set Variable: "Result" = "9 = 5"
```

String Comparisons

String comparison expressions compare two expressions to each other based on a string evaluation of their characters. String comparisons, like numeric comparisons, always return either 1 (True) or 0 (False). They start by comparing the leftmost character of each expression. The numeric values of the characters—derived from each character's ASCII value—are used to compare one character at a time until the entire expression is evaluated.

These comparisons are case sensitive. Capital letters have lower ASCII values than do lowercase letters. Therefore, strings beginning with uppercase letters are always evaluated as less than those with lowercase letters.

In the following example, Result will be evaluated as 1 (True) because all the characters in both strings are the same except bats has an extra "s":

```
Set Variable: "Result" = "bats gt bat"
```

In the following example, Result will be evaluated as 0 (False) because all the characters in both strings are the same so neither is greater than the other:

```
Set Variable: "Result" = "bat  gt bat"
```

In the following example, Result will be evaluated as 1 (True) because the lowercase letters have higher ASCII values than uppercase letters. Thus the lowercase B is greater than the uppercase B.

```
Set Variable: "Result" = "bat  gt Bat"
```

In the following example, Result will be evaluated as 1 (True) because E is greater than A:

```
Set Variable: "Result" = "bet  gt bat"
```

Using Logical Expressions To Combine Comparisons

Numeric and string comparisons can be combined by using Boolean logic and the three logical operators (AND, OR, and NOT) included with Flash. When you use the AND operator in an expression, the result is True only if both statements are True. When you use the OR operator in an expression, the result is True if *either* statement is True.

Table 9.2 lists the results of various combinations of True and False statements combined with different logical operators.

The following expression, combines two numeric comparisons with the AND logical operator:

```
(Result >= 20) AND (Result <= 30)
```

Table 9.2 Results of various logical expressions.

Value 1	Operator	Value 2	Result
False	AND	False	False
True	AND	False	False
False	AND	True	False
True	AND	True	True
False	OR	False	False
True	OR	False	True
False	OR	True	True
True	OR	True	True

If Result is a number between 20 and 30, then the logical expression will return 1 for True. A number between 20 and 30 will return True for both parts of the expression: Result >= 20 and Result <= 30. If Result has another value, such as 100, then this logical expression will be False because only one part of the expression (Result >= 20) is True. Remember, when you use the AND operator, both parts of the logical expression must be True.

If you want to find out if Result contains either Red or Blue, you would use the following logical expression:

```
(Result eq "Red") OR (Result eq "Blue")
```

If Result is either Red or Blue, the expression will return True. When you use the OR operator, only one part of the logical expression has to be True for a True result.

Logical expressions are normally used in If and Loop While statements.

Conditional Statements

Conditional statements allow choices in the direction your animation can take. All conditional statements contain a condition, and the result of that condition must be either True or False.

An example of a conditional statement is "If it's going to rain, I'll wear my raincoat; if it's not going to rain, I'll leave the raincoat at home." This statement has three parts:

- The condition (if it's raining)

- The result if the condition is True (wear the coat)

- The result if the condition is False (leave the coat at home)

"If" is the basic conditional operator. Flash also provides two optional conditional operators: Else and Else If. "If" is one of the basic actions available in the Actions dialog box.

In our example, if Raining is True, then the Display variable will be set to "Wear the raincoat."

```
If (Raining)
      Set Variable: "Display" = "Wear the raincoat."
End If
```

To add a result if the condition is False, highlight the condition line If (Raining) and click on the Add Else/Else If Clause button, which will appear on the right. Go down to the Else clause, and use the plus (+) menu to choose Set Variable.

```
If (Raining)
      Set Variable: "Display" = "Wear the coat."
```

```
Else
     Set Variable: "Display" = "Leave the coat at home."
End If
```

The String Plug and Play routines (shown in Figure 9.11) make use of conditional statements by comparing characters in a string to the desired result.

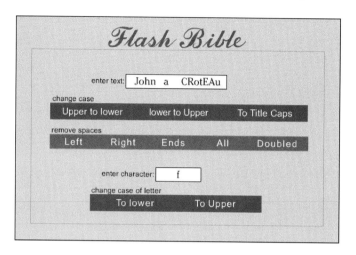

Figure 9.11
String Plug and Play at
www.FlashBible.com/members/
ActionScript/PlugNPlay/
Strings.htm.

What if the condition is more complicated? Suppose that, in an animation, you want to branch a movie based on the color selected by the user. If the user chooses red, your program will go to frame 10; if the user chooses blue, the program will go to frame 20; if the user chooses green, the program will go to frame 30; and if the user chooses another color, the program will go to frame 40. The first thing you should do is label your frames with the colors (10 as Red, 20 as Blue, etc.). If you label your frames, you'll be able to make changes in your animation that would change the frame numbers, and you won't have to change the numbers in the Go To actions that you are about to enter.

For a situation like this example, you set up an If condition and then set up as many Else clauses as you need. Here's how it works:

1. We start with an If action and add the condition Color eq "Red" in the Condition box on the right. See Figure 9.12.

   Notice that we are using eq instead of =. Remember that Flash provides different comparison operators for strings and for numbers. Use = when comparing numbers, and eq when comparing strings, as we are doing here.

2. After you enter the equation for the If condition, go to the Actions list and choose Go To. Then check the Go To And Play box on the bottom right. Now choose Label, and choose Red from the selection box to the right of Label. Your code should look like this:

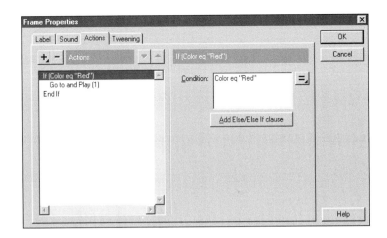

Figure 9.12
A conditional statement.

```
If (Color eq "Red")
      Go to and Play ("Red")
End If
```

3. Now highlight the If line. Click on the Add Else/Else If Clause option three times.

4. Go to the first Else. Highlight Else If, and add the condition Color eq "Blue". Do the same for the second Else, but change the condition to Color eq "Green".

5. Now we will add the results for the other conditions. Go to the line Go To And Play ("Red"), and copy it. Go to the line Else If (Color eq "Blue"), and paste; then change the label frame to Blue. Repeat for the other two conditions. The last condition should be just an Else and not an Else If. Your code should look like this:

```
If (Color eq "Red")
      Go to and Play ("Red")
Else If (Color eq "Blue")
      Go to and Play ("Blue")
Else If (Color eq "Green")
      Go to and Play ("Green")
Else
      Go to and Play ("Other Color")
End If
```

Loops

In Flash scripting, we use two basic types of loops: the Loop While action and the If Loop action.

The Loop While action sets up a loop that repeats a set of instructions until a conditional expression evaluates as True. The loop will continue as long as the condition remains False or until the total player actions in a frame exceed 200,000. (Flash does not allow infinite loops; it sets 200,000 as an arbitrary limit to prevent the Flash player or browser from appearing to be hung up.) To set up a Loop While action, display the Action list and choose Loop|Loop While.

A Loop While action is made up of two or three basic components: a condition, an incrementing action, and other actions that will be performed during the loop. The condition, which can be either a numeric or a string condition, will allow the actions within the loop to be executed until the condition becomes True. The basic setup looks like this:

```
Loop While (Condition)
      Action 1
      Action 2
 End Loop
```

To convert an angle that is over 360 degrees to its corresponding value under 360, we could use:

```
Loop While (Angle > 360)
      Set Variable: "Angle" = Angle - 360
End Loop
```

This example loop above will constantly loop subtracting 360 until the angle is less than 360. But this will fail if you enter a number greater than six million for the angle (see angle.fla). To prevent this failure, we can add a conditional statement. Below we have added a conditional statement that checks to see if the angle is less than 5 million and performs the Loop While as above if it is less than 5 million. If the angle is greater than or equal to 5 million, then we set the variable angle to That angle was ridiculously large. The limit might be smaller if you have other actions in the frame.

```
If (Angle < 5000000)
      Loop While (Angle > 360)
            Set Variable: "Angle" = Angle - 360
      End Loop
Else
      Set Variable: "Angle" = "That angle was ridiculously
large."
End If
```

Care must be taken in constructing Loop While actions. Endless loops as shown in Figure 9.13 and in the following script will continue to run until Flash hits its 200,000 player action limit, brings up an error dialog box and halts the operation of your animation:

```
Loop While (Angle)
      Set Variable: "Angle" = Angle + 20
End Loop
```

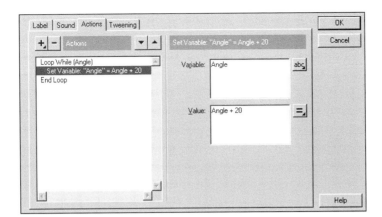

Figure 9.13
Loop While infinite loop.

Because Flash limits the number of actions used in a frame, if you need to have a longer conditional test it must be broken up in different frames on the Timeline. One way to do this is to use If loops.

A frame that contains an If action contains the same three basic elements (a condition, an incrementing action, and other actions) as a While loop, with one addition, and that is a loop back at the end of the actions:

- The condition is set in an If clause. As with a Loop While statement, you can use both numeric and string conditional expressions.

- The incrementing action and other actions can be in any of the frames in the loop, as long as they occur before the loop-back action.

- The loop-back action is normally a Go To And Play action implemented from the Timeline frame following the frame where the condition was set.

The loop can span many frames, but numeric accuracy will be best if the loop involves only two frames. The If-action frame can be in any frame of the loop, which can run indefinitely, as long as the loop spans more than one frame.

To test for a time delay, we can use an If loop. Though it is not as accurate as a Loop While action, there is no limit to the amount of time delay. (See the file timedelay.fla.)

In Frame 1, place a label of BeginLoop and no actions.

In Frame 2, place the following actions:

```
Set Variable: "/:Elapsed" = (GetTimer - Start)/1000
If (/:Elapsed < /:Delay)
      Go to and Play ("BeginUp")
Else
      Go to and Play (EndDelay)
End If
```

Properties

Flash provides three types of properties: movie clip, global, and text-field scrolling.

Movie-clip properties are variables that are available for use for every movie clip. You can set these values for movie clips with the Set Property command, and you can modify a property of a movie clip by changing the value of that property. Likewise, with the Get Property command, you can retrieve the value of a movie clip's property, and you can then evaluate and initiate actions based on that value. There are 16 movie-clip properties (see Table 9.3).

The Get Properties Demo (shown in Figure 9.14) demonstrates how a rotation property can be applied to a movie clip object.

Global properties are properties that are applied to an entire movie (not just to a clip). The three global properties are _highquality, _focus rectangle, and _soundbuftime.

Figure 9.14
Get Properties, illustrated by
Dorian Nisinson.

Two properties are used for text-field scrolling. These two properties—variable_name.scroll and variable_name.maxscroll—define how a text field's scrolling will work.

The names of movie-clip properties and global properties begin with an underscore character (_). Names of text-field scrolling properties do not. All properties except the two text-field scrolling properties are available in the Expression Editor.

When you set a property in Flash, you are giving the property a new value, not adding to an existing one. So, for example, if you set the rotation value of a movie clip to 45, and you set it again to 45, it will not change because it is already 45.

Table 9.3 Property variables.

Get Property Variables	Settable	Property #	Description
Movie-Clip Properties			
_x	*	0	Horizontal (X) position
_y	*	1	Vertical (Y) position
_width		8	Width
_height		9	Height
_rotation	*	10	Rotation
_target		11	Target path
_name	*	13	Instance name
_url		15	URL
_xscale	*	2	X scale factor
_yscale	*	3	Y scale factor
_currentframe		4	Current frame
_totalframes		5	Total frames
_framesloaded		12	Frames loaded
_alpha	*	6	Alpha transparency percentage
_visible	*	7	Visibility
_droptarget		14	Drag action's drop position
Global Properties			
_highquality	*	16	High quality
_focusrectangle	*	17	Show Focus Rectangle
_soundbuftime	*	18	Sound buffer time (default is 5 seconds)
Text-Field Scrolling Properties			
variable_name.scroll	*	n/a	Topmost scroll line
variable_name.maxscroll		n/a	Maximum scroll number (set by Flash)

Table 9.3 lists the property variables. The properties that are settable are Read (Get) and Write (Set). The property numbers are used with the new variable FSCommands, which are discussed in more detail in Chapter 12.

The Movie-Clip Universe

The movie-clip universe is not always what you might expect, so it is important to understand both the *registration point* (where 0.0 is) and how an inherited local coordinate system can turn the movie-clip world upside down. When you're trying to manipulate the x,y coordinates of a movie clip or a nested movie clip from another movie clip or the main Timeline, you can get unexpected results.

The registration point is either the center point or the upper-left corner of the movie clip. If Use Center Point is checked in the Properties dialog box, then the registration point is the center. Otherwise, it is the upper-left corner. The coordinate system for movie clips that reside inside other movie clips can be changed by their parent movie clip. It is important to understand this so you can get the results you are looking for. The _x and _y properties are measured in pixels, with the upper-left corner of the stage being (0,0). The _x and _y properties are specified in the local coordinate system of the parent of the movie clip. If a movie clip is on the main Timeline, then its coordinate system refers to the upper-left corner of the stage as 0, 0. If the movie clip is nested inside another movie clip, however, then the movie clip's coordinate system uses the center point of the symbol edit window as its center (0,0). (The center point is indicated by a plus sign.)

If you rotate a movie clip, then the local coordinate system of its children are also rotated. Up is no longer up, so to speak, for those child movie clips. This can get quite confusing, especially if you have no idea that this is possible. A movie clip inherits the local coordinate system of the movie clip it is in (its parent clip). For example, if a movie clip is rotated 90 degrees clockwise, it will give its children a coordinate system that is also rotated 90 degrees clockwise. Suppose that animated movie clip Earth sets the _x property to move a globe from the left to the right. Now suppose that you place the Earth movie clip into a movie clip Universe, which is rotated 90 degrees clockwise, and you apply the _x property to the globe in the movie clip Earth. The globe will travel from top to bottom instead of from left to right because the rotation of the parent movie clip (Universe) has rotated the coordinate system of its child movie clip (Earth).

Figure 9.15 shows the Flying Text Plug and Play routine which allows you to add your own text or other objects to the plug and play movie clip, which you can drop in your animation. Your text or objects will follow your mouse around the screen.

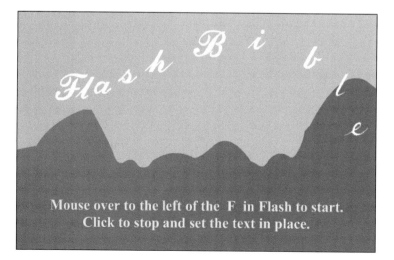

Figure 9.15
Flying text in Plug and Play.

Movie-Clip Properties

Every movie clip has movie-clip properties that can be defined by variables. These properties define how a movie clip will behave or allow retrieval of these property values so they can be evaluated and actions can be assigned to them.

Not all movie-clip properties are settable. The ones that you can set in your script are marked as settable in Table 9.3. The properties that are not settable are read only and you can only use the Get Property statement to retrieve their values. The Set Property action allows you to set all settable properties (except text-field scrolling). You can get the values of properties by using Get Property in an expression.

The following statement returns the horizontal (x) position of a movie clip whose instance name is TBall, and stores the position in the variable Xpos:

```
Set Variable: "Xpos" = GetProperty ("/TBall",_x )
```

Figure 9.16 shows how the script above is entered in the action windows. The left side of the equation is entered in the Variable (top) window and the right side is in the Value (lower) window. Flash automatically adds the equals sign.

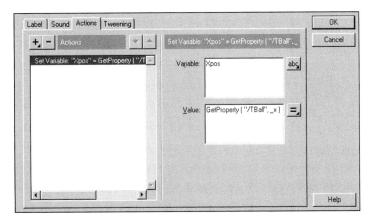

Figure 9.16
The Get Properties window.

The Movie-Clip properties are as follows:

- _alpha—The amount of transparency that is applied to a movie clip. The amount is specified in percentages from 0 to 100.

- _currentframe—The frame number of the current frame on the Timeline. Because buttons and movie clips can exist across multiple frames, this property can be very useful (read only).

- _droptarget—The name and path returned when a drag-and-drop movie clip is dropped.

  - If the clip is dropped over a named movie clip in level zero, then the path starts with the root, such as /TrashCan.

- If the clip is dropped over an unnamed movie clip in level zero, then _droptarget returns the name /instance1 for the first unnamed movie clip, and /instance2, /instance3, and so on, for additional unnamed movie clips, starting on level zero and continuing through the higher levels.

- If the clip is dropped over a movie clip on a level other than zero, then _droptarget returns a path and name starting with _level, such as _level5/leaf.

- If the clip is dropped over a movie clip on a level other than zero, then _droptarget returns a name in the form /instancex where x is the number of the unnamed movie clip. The numbering does not start over on each level.

- If the clip is dropped over a graphic symbol on another level (besides zero), then _droptarget returns _levelx where x is the level number. If the clip is dropped over a graphic symbol on level zero from a level other than zero, _droptarget returns /.

- If the clip is dropped over a button symbol on a lower level (besides zero), then _droptarget returns _levelx where x is the level number.

- If the clip is dropped over a button symbol on level zero from a level other than zero, _droptarget returns /. You cannot drop a clip on a button on a higher level.

- If the clip is dropped over an empty area, _droptarget returns an empty string.

- *_frameloaded*—The number of the frame currently loaded. This property provides the same function as an If Frame Is Loaded action but in ActionScript form.

- *_height* and *_width*—Provide the height and width of a movie clip in pixels. Because you can only get this property, you need to use _xscale and _yscale to change a movie clip's height or width (read only).

- *_name*—Provides the instance name of a movie clip (read only).

- *_rotation*—Set in degrees. This property is cumulative. (See _x.)

- *_target*—Provides the path of a movie clip (read only).

- *_url*—The SWF URL of the movie that the movie clip is in (read only).

- *_visible*—Can be set to True (default) or False. If this property is set to False, the movie-clip instance is invisible, and neither frame actions nor buttons in that clip will work. You can still Tell Target it, though, and sounds in it will play.

- *_x* and *_y*—The x and y coordinates of a movie clip in pixels. The _x, _y, _rotation, _xscale, and _yscale properties are all cumulative. This means they transform not only the movie clip but also any child movie clips that are nested in it. Transformation of the local coordinate system of a parent movie clip is transferred to its children (movie clips).

- *_xscale* and *_yscale*—Measured in percentages, with 100 as the default. Scaling is applied from the registration point of the movie clip. The scaling of the movie clip also scales the local coordinate system. There-fore, the effective values of the _x and _y properties are proportional to the scaling. This property is cumulative. (See _x.)

Flash provides a drop-down window to provide easy selection of the Set Property options as shown in Figure 9.17.

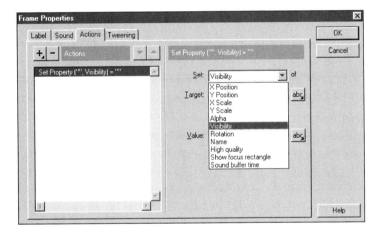

Figure 9.17
Set properties.

Global Properties

Three properties pertain to the whole movie instead of to movie clips. These properties are:

- *_focus rectangle*—Changes whether or not the yellow Show Focus Rect-angle property displays outlines when a user tabs, moving focus to the next button or text field in the Flash SWF player. False turns the de-fault to off. Remember to change to Expression (choose = from the variable type button) when you're entering False for a value.

- *_high quality*—Sets the quality of the movie. High is 1 and Low is 0. You can get or set this property to change the anti-aliasing of the movie.

- *_soundbuftime*—Sets the amount of time in seconds that sound is buff-ered ahead of time for streaming sound. The default is 5 seconds.

Text-Field Scrolling Properties

These variables are not available in the Expression Editor, and they work differently than the other properties. The variable (var_name) for a text field is used with either .scroll or .maxscroll appended to it. Unlike other property variables, variables for text-field scrolling do not begin with an underscore.

- *Var_name.scroll*—The number of the topmost line you will see in the text field. The default setting is 1 and is settable. When the text box is scrolled, Flash will update the value.

- *Var_name.maxscroll*—The maximum line-number value. It is set by Flash and is based on the height of the text field (read only).

Built-In Functions

Functions are routines that perform a set of instructions. Some functions require certain parameters (arguments) to function correctly. Functions built into Flash are described in Table 9.4.

Converting A Number To An Integer (Int)

The Int function in Flash works like the "floor" function in JavaScript and returns the greatest integer that is less than or equal to its argument. The syntax is Int(Num) where Num is the argument that is evaluated as a number. You can substitute any variable or value for Num as you like. The value is not rounded, but is truncated. Any string value is evaluated to zero (0).

Table 9.4 Functions built into Flash.

Name	Description	Result Type
Int	Converts a number to an integer	Integer
Random	Returns random number	Integer
Get Timer	Gets time	Numeric in milliseconds
True	Boolean True	1
False	Boolean False	0
Newline	Inserts a new line	Return string character.
Substring	Extracts substring	String
Length	Calculates string length	Integer
Chr	Gets character for an ASCII number	String character
Ord	Gets ASCII number for a character	Integer
Eval	Returns the value of a string expression	Could be string or numeric
MBSubstring	Extracts substring	String
MBLength	Calculates string length	Integer
MBChr	Gets character	String
MBOrd	Gets number for a character	Integer

In the following statement, the number Num is converted to an Integer placed in the variable Integer.

```
Set Variable: "Integer" = Int (Num)
```

Here are sample values to show how the Int function works with selected values.

```
If Num = 2.2        Integer = 2
If Num = 4.9        then Integer = 4
If Num = -7.2       then Integer = -7
If Num = -5.9       then Integer = -5
If Num = 22.4B      then Integer = 0
```

Getting A Random Number (Random)

The Random function returns a random integer from zero to one minus Num. The syntax is Random(Num) where Num is the argument that is evaluated as an integer. If Num is zero or a string, then Random (Num) will return zero.

Here's how to return a random value from 1 to 10:

```
Set Variable: "Result" = Random (10) + 1
```

Measuring Elapsed Time (Get Timer)

The Get Timer function returns, in milliseconds, the time elapsed since the movie began playing.

Set your starting time as:

```
Set Variable: "StartTime" = GetTimer
```

At a point later in the program, you can get your elapsed time, which will be stored in the variable named Elapsed.

```
Set Variable: "Elapsed" = (GetTimer - Start)/1000
```

Boolean Functions (True and False)

The two Boolean variables True and False are included as functions to allow you to insert True and False as values in logical expressions. True evaluates as 1, and False evaluates as 0.

Adding A New Line (Newline)

To add a new line in a string, you can use the ASCII function Chr (13) or the Newline function, as shown here:

```
Set Variable: "Result" = "Name" & Newline & "Numbe"
Set Variable: "Result" = "Name" & Chr (13) & "Number"
```

Both of the above display the same results, with Name followed by Number on a new line:

```
Name
Number
```

Extracting A Portion Of A String (Substring)

The Substring function allows you to extract a portion of a string. There are three parameters: the string (from which you are extracting a portion); the index (starting character number); and the count (the number of characters extracted). The syntax is:

```
Set Variable: "NewString" = Substring (string, index, count)
```

Let's look at an example. Say that we want to extract the five characters (count) that start with the sixth character (index) from "Four horses" (the string). We'll enter NewString in the Variable box, and enter Substring ("Four horses.", 6, 5) in the Value box. Remember to set the Variable Type button to Expression (=). Here's what the statement looks like:

```
Set Variable: "NewString" = Substring ( "Four horses.", 6, 5 )
```

To determine the substring in the above we start counting on the left. Our first character will be the sixth from the left; the h in horse. Then starting with the h, we count 5 characters to be included in the string. The result, horse, is stored in the variable NewString.

Getting The Length Of A String (Length)

To get the number of characters in a string, you use the Length function. The Length function returns the number of characters in a string, including spaces and punctuation. The syntax is:

```
Set Variable: "Result" = Length (string)
```

To find the number of characters in "The four horsemen.", we would use the following statement, which would return 18 in Result:

```
Set Variable: "Result" = Length ("The four horsemen.")
```

Getting A Character From Its ASCII Value (Chr)

The Chr function returns a character based on its ASCII value (see Appendix C). If the argument entered is greater than 255, then the character returned will be based on the value of the remainder of the argument when divided by 256. (This is the same value as would be returned by the mod function in VBScript using modulo arithmetic.) If 326 is entered, then 326/256 leaves a remainder of 70, and the character returned will be a capital F.

The syntax is:

```
Set Variable: "Character" = Chr ( asciiCode )

If asciiCode is   74      then Character is   J
If asciiCode is   115     then Character is   s
If asciiCode is   34      then Character is   #
If asciiCode is   323     then Character is   C
```

Getting The ASCII Value Of A Character (Ord)

The Ord function returns the ASCII value of a character or the first character in a string. If a space is at the beginning of the tested string, then Ord will return 32, the ASCII value of a space. An empty string returns zero as the value.

The syntax is:

```
Set Variable: "Result" = Ord (character)

If the character is   f     then ascii   is 102
If the character is   D     then ascii   is 68
If the character is   *     then ascii   is 42
If the character is   Dog   then ascii   is 68
```

MultiByte (MB) String Functions

There are four MultiByte functions. They work like the regular string functions except that arguments are based on the multibyte system, which combines the ASCII values of two characters into a single number. For values less than 256 only a single character will be returned, but for values between 256 and 65,535 two characters will be returned. Numbers above 66,535 are evaluated as in VBScript mode (multibyte). The formula for calculating a two-byte multibyte number is the multibyte number is equal to the sum of the ASCII value of the first character added to the product of the ASCII value of the second character multiplied by 256.

```
multibyte =   char1 + (256 * char2
```

The four MultiByte functions are as follows. They each work the same as the related string functions except they use the multibyte formula for their numbers.

```
MBSubstring
MBLength
MBChr
MBOrd

Set Variable: "Result" = MBChr (Num)

If Num = 19011, then Result is JC.
```

The ASCII value of J is 74, and the value of C is 67, so:

```
(74 x 256) + 67 = 19011
```

The Call Function

Call is used in a similar manner to functions in other languages. When a Call is made, the processing of actions in the action list is temporarily stopped and the actions in the called frame are then processed until they are completed, then the processing of actions continues until all the actions in that frame have been processed. All graphics in any called frame are ignored and only their actions are processed. At this point, actions such as the drawing to the screen, Tell Target commands, and Go To branching are all executed from the original frame regardless where the commands originated from (the original frame or one that was called).

A Call has one argument, which is the frame where it will process the additional action commands Call (frame). If the called frame is not on the same Timeline as the calling frame, you must include the path for the variable.

You can make calls from called frames (this is called nesting) and you can nest as many calls as you wish, but the 200,000 player actions limit per frame includes the actions in the original frame as well as all the frames called directly or indirectly from that frame.

The following sets up a Call to the Time Delay Plug and Play routine. The expression sets the value of the variable Delay to 10, which will be used in the time delay movie clip to set up a 10-second delay. The Call statement makes a call to the frame Labeled as Up in the movie clip Count, which is on the main Timeline of the movie.

```
Set Variable: "Delay" = 10
Call ("/Count:Up")
```

All Plug and Play routines use the Call action to initiate them. The Trigonometry Plug and Play (Figure 9.18) routine allows you to add sine and other trigonometric functions to your scripts. The demo of this plug and play routine at **www.FlashBible.com/members/ActionScript/PlugNPlay/Trig.htm** allows you to get the value of a sine, cosine, or other trig function when you enter the angle.

Creating A Simple Array

Flash does not allow you to create single-variable arrays, as you can with other programming languages. However, you can create an array that is a set of related variables. An array is simply a list or series of related lists normally visualized as a table. In Flash you might create one list of items with variable names item1 to item10. You might want to have a related list

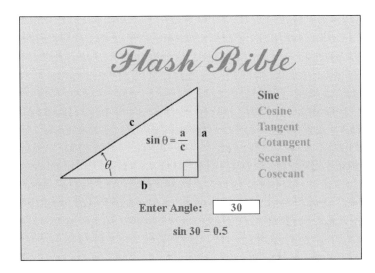

Figure 9.18
Trigonometry.

that has values for the color of these items. That list could be color1 to color 10 where color1 is the color of item 1, color2 is the color of item 2, and so on. Using the Eval function (which we describe next) we can compare these values or select items from one list based on the number in the list or the value in one of the other lists.

In our example, we will create a series of variables starting with Item1 and ending with Item10. In the file monkey.fla, we have created the array for you in Frame 1, but you could just as easily create the array by entering the values for each of the items one at a time.

```
Set Variable: "Item1" = "Bear"
Set Variable: "Item2" = "Cat"
Set Variable: "Item3" = "Monkey"
```

This list, or single column array, will be used in our sample use of the Eval function.

Evaluating A String Expression (Eval)

The Eval function allows you to determine the value of a string expression. The format for the Eval function is Eval(String) where String is a string expression. This function returns the value of the variable derived from the concatenations of the strings in the expression String. If String is a variable whose value is a string, then the expression Eval(String) is exactly the same as the variable String, but if String is not a variable or the value of String is not a string, then Eval(String) will be an empty (null) string.

Use the Eval function when you are evaluating a series of variables named consecutively, such as Item1, Item2, Item3, etc. In the following example, you have a series (an array) of variables named Item1 to Item10. This expression will determine whether one of those variables is set to the word

"Monkey". Then set the variable Display to "There is a monkey!", and you can display that on screen by setting a text field's variable name to the same variable (Display).

```
Set Variable: "count" = 1
Loop While (count <= 10)
  If (Eval ("Item" & count ) eq "Monkey")
    Set Variable: "Display" = "There is a Monkey!"
  End If
  Set Variable: "count" = count + 1
End Loop
```

Count is a temporary variable used to count from 1 to 10.

Each instance of **"Item" & count** is combined as strings (concatenation) to make Item1 through Item10, and then its value is compared to the string "Monkey". If any of the instances is equivalent, then Display will be set to "There is a Monkey!" and this will be displayed in the text field.

Moving On

Since we're talking Web, the next chapter addresses Macromedia's recent efforts to cater to Flash users. Find out how well Flash plays with others—other programs, that is.

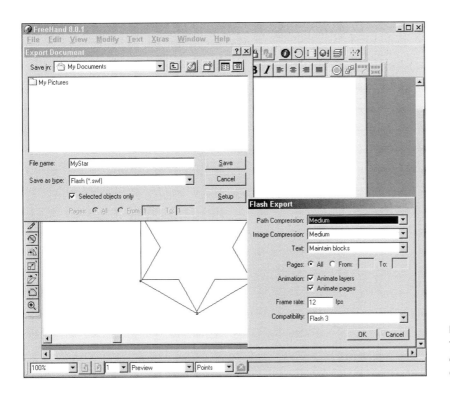

Figure 10.2

The FreeHand Export Document dialog box and the Flash Export dialog box.

Creating FreeHand Drawings As Flash Animations

A FreeHand drawing that has been created on multiple layers can be exported directly to Flash as an animation. You can then import that animation into an existing Flash movie, either as a new scene or as a continuing part of an existing scene.

This technique can be a very handy way to animate existing drawings done in FreeHand or other illustration programs. You can copy the drawing (or only those shapes that you want to animate) to new layers, edit each layer to suit the animation, choose File|Export from FreeHand's menu bar, select a couple of options, and then import the result into Flash 4.

To keep the basics of this procedure easy, in the following exercise you will create a simple three-layer drawing, export it as a Flash movie, and then import it into a Flash movie. Here's the dance:

1. Open FreeHand 8.01. (If you don't own the program, you'll find a demo version on this book's companion CD-ROM.) If a new file isn't already open, choose File|New.

2. You need to size your FreeHand document to match the size of the movie to which you want to export the files (or in which you want the movie to appear on a Web page). Choose Modify|Document to open the Document Inspector.

Note: If the drawing is on only one layer, then—no matter how many shapes are contained in it—the Flash movie will contain only one frame. Each of the shapes will be interpreted as a group, so when you select the entire drawing, you may see many framed selections. To break these down so that they autoedit one another, press Cmd/Ctrl+B as many times as it takes for all of the group frames to disappear.

Figure 10.3
Customizing within the
Document Inspector.

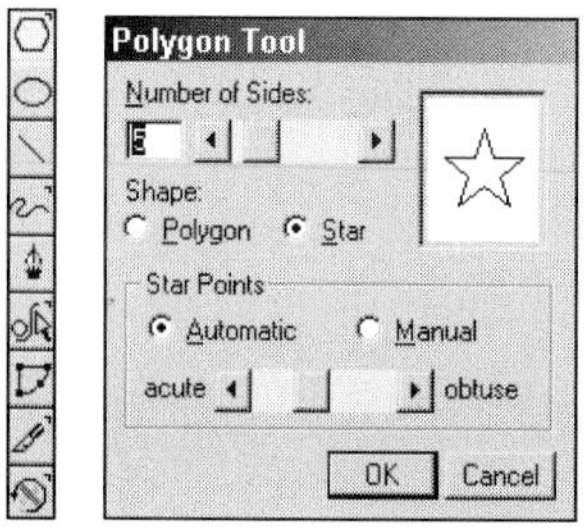

Figure 10.4
The FreeHand Polygon Tool
dialog box.

3. Click on the Page tab in the upper-right part of the Document Inspector. Choose Custom from the Page Size pull-down menu. Click on the Landscape button. Type "450" in the X field and "300" in the Y field. Press Return/Enter. Leave the rest of the entries at their defaults (shown in Figure 10.3). Press Return/Enter to make the new settings take effect.

4. Double-click on the Polygon tool in the Toolbar. A Polygon Tool dialog box will open. See Figure 10.4.

5. In the Polygon Tool dialog box, type "5" for the Number Of Sides. For the Shape, choose Star. For the Start Points option, choose Automatic. Click on OK.

6. Drag a star that fills the center of the page. If you want the star to stay upright, press Shift while dragging. If you need to rescale it, choose the Arrow tool and double-click on the outline. Scaling handles will appear. Drag them to scale the start. Double-click when you're done.

7. Choose Window|Panels|Layers to open the Layers panel. The screen will now look something like Figure 10.5.

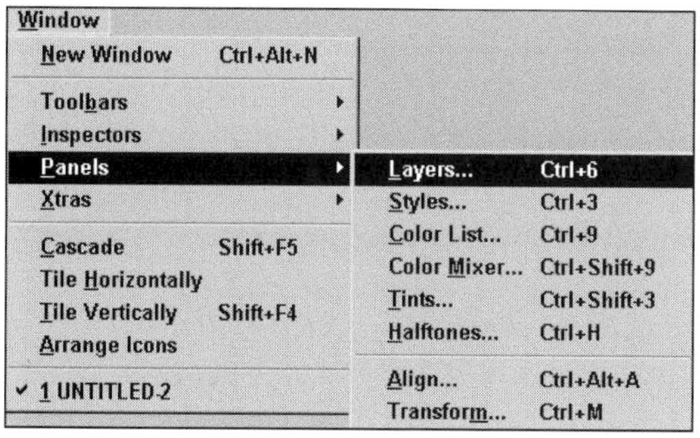

Figure 10.5
Opening the Layers panel.

8. Now you are going to copy the star twice and place each copy on a new layer. Choose the Arrow tool and click on the star to select it. Press Cmd/Ctrl+C to copy the selection to the clipboard. Now press Cmd/Ctrl+V twice. Drag the second copy slightly away from the first copy so that the copies are easier to select. You will now see three stars, all of which are currently placed on the foreground layer.

9. From the Layers panel's Options menu, choose New. Now do it again. You now have two new layers labeled Layer-1 and Layer-2.

10. Now you want to move one copy of the star to Layer-1 and another to Layer-2. It doesn't matter which copy is moved to which layer at this point. In the Layers panel, select the foreground layer by clicking on its name. A layer whose name is highlighted is the active layer.

11. Select one of the stars. Control points will appear at each intersection of a line. To move the selected shape to another layer, select Layer-2 in the Layers panel. Drag the copy of the star so that it registers directly on top of the original star. You can use the Arrow keys to nudge the selection one pixel at a time for perfect registration.

12. In the Layers panel, click on the Lock icon. This layer is now locked so that you won't accidentally move or edit the shape(s) on that layer. Now repeat Steps 8 through 11 to move another star from the foreground layer to Layer-1.

13. Lock all the layers except the foreground layer. Choose the Arrow tool, and drag each of the star's five inside points inward toward the center.

14. Lock all the layers except Layer-2. Drag each of the star's inward points outward. Your screen should now look similar to Figure 10.6.

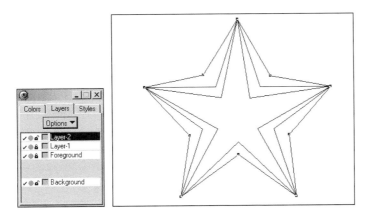

Figure 10.6
Dragging the star's points.

15. Now you have a pulsating star on three layers. When you export this file as a Flash movie in SWF format, each layer will become a keyframe in an animation. Choose File|Export to open the Export Document dialog box. See Figure 10.7.

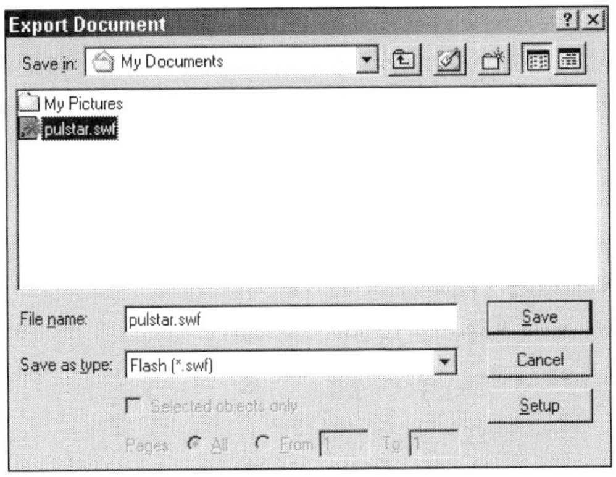

Figure 10.7
The FreeHand Export Document dialog box.

16. Click on the Setup button. In the Flash Export dialog box, make sure that Animate Layers is checked and that Animate Pages is unchecked. Leave other settings at their defaults, as shown in Figure 10.8. Click on OK. Then click on Save in the Export Document dialog box.

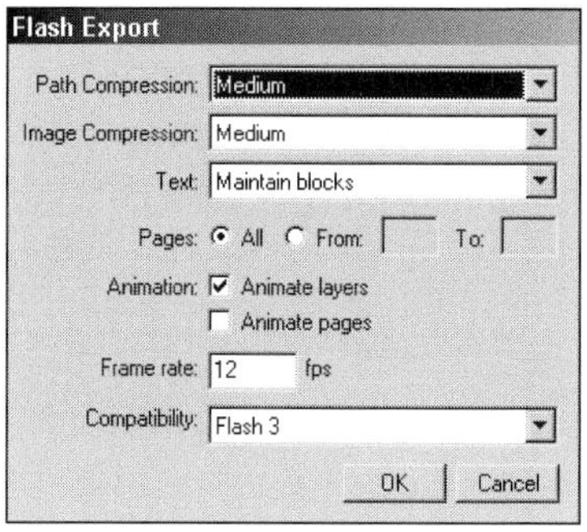

Figure 10.8
The Flash Export dialog box.

17. Now let's pretend that we're adding the Flash SWF file we just exported from FreeHand to an existing Flash 4 movie. Open Flash and start a new file.

18. Select the layer and frame to which you want to start importing new frames. (This step is not actually necessary when you're working with a new file with only one layer.)

19. Choose File|Import to open the Import dialog box. From the Files Of Type list, choose Shockwave Flash. Locate star.swf and double-click on the file name.

    You will see the image of the first frame on the stage, and you will find new keyframes appearing after the originally selected frame. See Figure 10.9.

20. Select Control|Loop. Play the movie by pressing Return/Enter.

Exporting FreeHand Files To Illustrator Format

You can also export a single-frame drawing as an Adobe Illustrator 88 file from FreeHand. If you plan to do this, it is best to draw your outlines in FreeHand and save them before you import them into Flash. Then do all your fills and gradients in Flash. For one thing, you may want to optimize the curves in Flash before you do the fills and gradients. For another, you won't have to worry about how well the fills and gradients translate.

Figure 10.10 shows a drawing that incorporates three properties that don't translate with predictable results to Flash 4 via drag-and-drop or cut-and-paste: blends, transparency, and gradient fills. (They translate perfectly if you import a Flash 3 movie exported from FreeHand.)

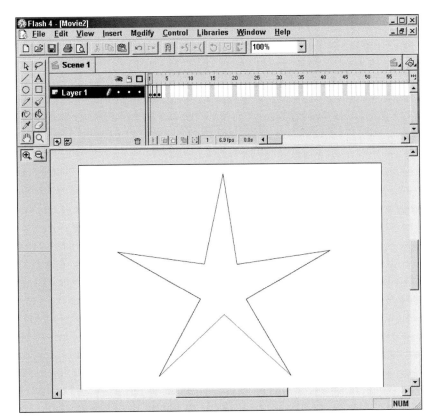

Figure 10.9
A FreeHand movie imported into Flash.

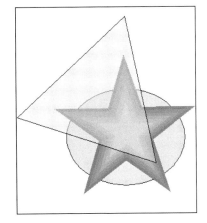

Figure 10.10
Some FreeHand properties that don't translate to Flash 4 via drag-and-drop.

Figure 10.11 shows the disparities in this particular drawing when it is imported as an Illustrator file.

To move all of these elements into a Flash 4 frame, follow these steps:

1. Create, import, or open the drawing in FreeHand. Choose File|Export to open the Export Document dialog box. From the Save As Type list, choose Adobe Illustrator 88.

Figure 10.11

The same drawing imported into
Flash 4 as an Illustrator 88 file.

2. Specify the folder/directory in which you want to save the file. Type the file name in the File Name field. Click on OK.

3. Switch to Flash 4 (or open a window in it). Choose File|Import to open the Import dialog box. From the Files Of Type list, choose Adobe Illustrator. Find the file you exported and double-click on it.

4. The imported file will open in Flash 4. In Figure 10.12, you can see that each entity is selected and has been automatically saved as a symbol.

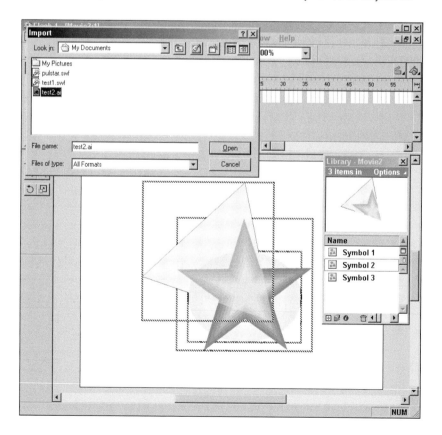

Figure 10.12

Importing into Flash an
Illustrator 88 file exported from
FreeHand 8.01.

Taking Advantage Of FreeHand's Advanced Drawing Capabilities

Illustration programs, such as Macromedia's FreeHand, are loaded with powerful vector-drawing capabilities. Using illustration programs, you can often create better-designed, more sophisticated graphics than you might have taken the time to create using only the tools afforded by Flash 4.

The most basic of these advanced capabilities is the one typical of illustration programs in general: Bezier control points. Control points determine whether the lines in shapes are straight or curved, exactly how curved and where, and how these lines meet. Lines can meet at sharp angles (cornerpoint), in a smooth curve (symmetrical point), or in a curve that is more severe on one side of the point than on the other (asymmetrical point). The degree of control inherent in Bezier curves makes it easier for you to draw shapes with fewer control points and, therefore, smaller data files. Figure 10.13 shows a curve being reshaped by moving one control-point handle.

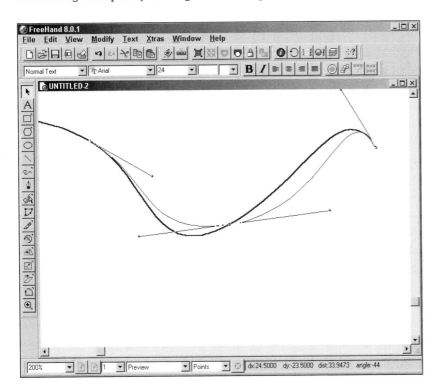

Figure 10.13

Reshaping a curve with a control-point handle.

FreeHand also has many more advanced time-saving drawing features. Some that you're most likely to use frequently are blends, text along a path, variable-point polygons and stars, embossing, envelope distortion, and automatic animations. Each of these is described and demonstrated below.

Blends

Blends are similar to Flash's shape tweens. The difference is that in FreeHand all of the in-between shape and fill transitions are drawn on the same layer. Figure 10.14 shows two blends between a star and a pentagon. The blend at the top occurs between shapes placed at different locations and outlined with a stroke. The blend at the bottom uses many more steps and occurs between superimposed shapes.

One thing that you can create with blends in FreeHand that you can't do at all in Flash 4 is a smooth gradient between shapes, as shown in the blend at the bottom of Figure 10.14.

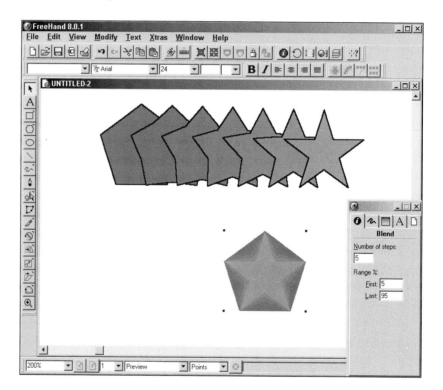

Figure 10.14

Two FreeHand blends created from the same two shapes. The only differences are the positions of the two shapes and their outline colors.

Creating a blend in FreeHand is amazingly quick and easy. FreeHand will blend any two shapes, regardless of whether they have the same number of control points or whether the control points were entered in the same sequence from top to bottom. The smoothest blends, however, are between shapes with the same number of control points, entered in the same sequence. Here's the basic procedure:

1. In FreeHand, double-click on the Rectangle tool. When the Rectangle Tool dialog box opens, drag the slider all the way to the left (no corner radius).

2. On the pasteboard, drag a rectangle.

3. Choose the Pen tool, and draw a four-point oval in the center of the rectangle. Be sure to place the first point at upper left and to move in a clockwise direction until the oval is completed. If the oval's a little eccentric, you can drag the control points and handles to make it more regular.

4. Select the rectangle. Choose Window|Inspectors|Fill to open the Fill Inspector. (See Figure 10.15.) From the Fill Type list, choose Basic. The rectangle will fill with black.

5. You're going to change the color of the fill. In the Object Inspector Fill tab, double-click on the color swatch to the left of the Colors menu. The Mixer panel will appear. (See Figure 10.16.)

   Click on the RGB button, and drag the three sliders to mix a blue color. Click on the Tints tab, and choose a light shade of the blue you mixed. Click on the Add To Colors button (the icon at the extreme right of the buttons above the sliders in the Mixer panel or at the top right of the Tints panel).

Figure 10.15
The FreeHand Fill Inspector.

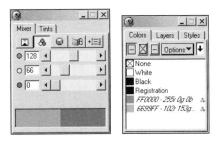

Figure 10.16
The FreeHand Mixer and Colors panels.

6. The Colors panel will appear. Select the rectangle, and then select the light-blue color in the color list. The fill color will change. Now fill the oval by repeating steps 4, 5, and 6— but this time choose a bright red.

7. Select both the rectangle and the oval shapes. (Their control points will appear so that you know they are selected.)

8. At the top of the Fill Inspector, you will see an icon of an S-shaped stroke, the Stroke icon. Click on it to open the Stroke Inspector. From the Stroke Type list, choose None.

9. Choose Xtras|Create|Blend. You will see a smooth color shift between the oval and the rectangle. You can see the result in Figure 10.17.

Note: If the rectangle covers the oval, select the rectangle. Choose Modify|Arrange|Send To Back. The rectangle will now be stacked below the oval so that the oval is visible.

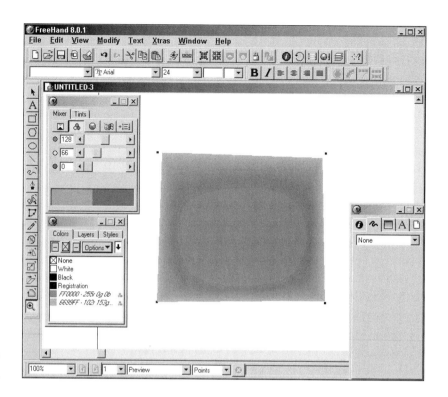

Figure 10.17
The result of the blend.

Text Along A Path

FreeHand allows you to place text along the curve of any vector path. Text arranged in this manner can be a very strong design element. The only way you could do this in Flash 4 would be to convert each letter to an outline, and then transform and position each letter individually. Figure 10.18 shows the effect of placing text around an oval.

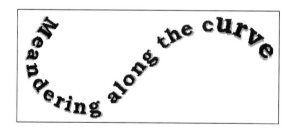

Figure 10.18
Text along a path.

Here's the routine:

1. In FreeHand, start a new document (File|New). Choose the Text tool.

2. Choose a font style to your liking from the Font Name menu, and select 36 point from the Font Size menu.

3. Click on the pasteboard location where you'd like your text to begin. (This isn't critical because you're probably going to move it later, anyway.) Type your text.

4. Choose Window|Inspectors|Text. Your screen should look similar to Figure 10.19. Make any needed adjustments in leading, kerning, and justification.

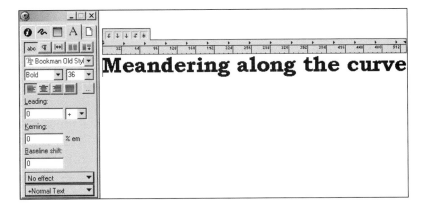

Figure 10.19
Entering text in FreeHand. The Text Inspector window is shown at left.

5. Choose the Arrow tool, and click on the text to select it. Just to see how powerful FreeHand can be when dealing with text, choose Zoom from the Text Effect menu in the Text Inspector window. The Zoom Effect dialog box will open. Choose the settings shown in Figure 10.20, and click on OK. The result should look something like that shown in Figure 10.20.

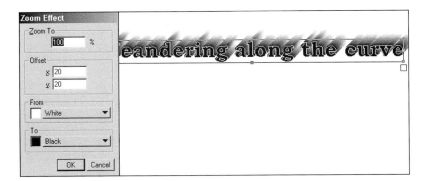

Figure 10.20
The Zoom Effect dialog box and its effect on your text.

6. From the Toolbox, choose the FreeHand tool. Draw a loose S-curve on the pasteboard.

   Choose the Arrow tool. Select the curve, and drag the control points and handles into the S-curve you'd like to see. You should have a curved line and the zoomed text, similar to Figure 10.21.

7. Choose Text|Attach To Path. The selected text will immediately flow along the path, starting at the first control point and continuing for as long as the text and its assigned spacing will allow. You'll notice in Figure 10.22 that the text doesn't extend the full length of the path.

8. To stretch the text to the end of the path, change the kerning (spacing between letters). Choose the Text tool, and drag it across the whole

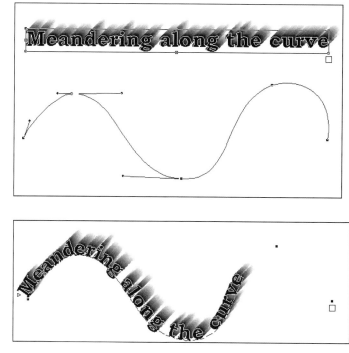

Figure 10.21
The text and the path, both selected.

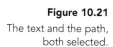

Figure 10.22
Text attached to the path.

text path so that all the letters are highlighted. In the Text Inspector window, type a larger number in the Range Kerning field and then press Return/Enter. The length of the text line will expand. Continue entering larger numbers until the curve and the text line are approximately the same length. You can see the result in Figure 10.23.

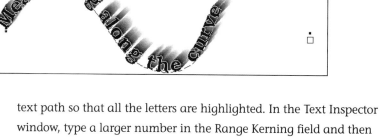

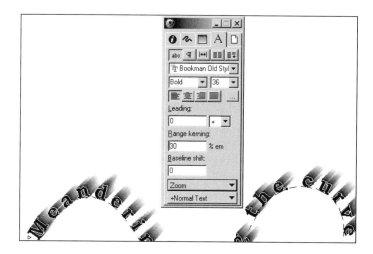

Figure 10.23
The final result: text stretched along the path.

Variable-Point Polygons And Stars

Making truly geometric shapes, such as regular-sided polygons and stars, is a painstaking process in Flash but a no-brainer in FreeHand. Figure 10.24 shows a number of shapes that can be made with absolute accuracy in FreeHand, using only two or three steps.

Figure 10.24
Polygons and stars made in FreeHand.

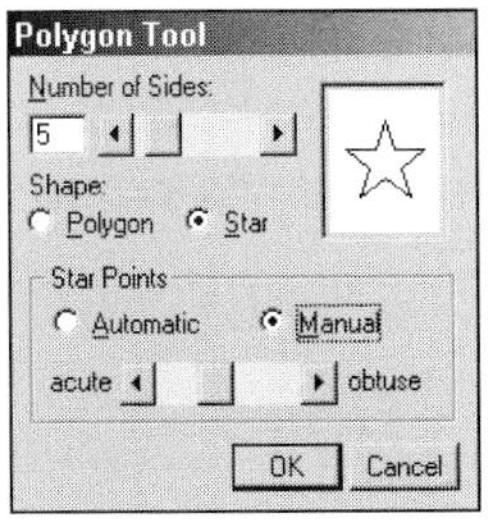

To make a star, follow these steps:

1. In FreeHand, double-click on the Polygon tool. In the Polygon Tool dialog box, select the Star option (unless it's already selected). The dialog box should now have all the settings shown in Figure 10.25.

2. Type "5" in the Number Of Sides field, or drag the slider until 5 is the value shown.

3. Just so you can see the power of this dialog box, select the Manual option and drag the Star Points slider from left to right. Notice the changes in the star shape in the preview box (upper-right corner of the dialog box).

4. To make this shape the standard five-point star, select the Automatic option and then click on OK. Press Shift to constrain the rotation of the star to 15-degree angles, and drag diagonally until the star is the size you want it to be. The star will look like Figure 10.26.

Figure 10.25
The Polygon Tool dialog box with the Star option selected.

If you don't want to make these shapes in FreeHand, you will find all of the above polygons on the CD-ROM in a file called polys.fla. Open this file as a Library in Flash, and you can drag, scale, rotate, and modify any of the shapes.

Embossing

Embossing in FreeHand can give your buttons and geometric shapes a three-dimensional appearance that can't be simulated in Flash without endless tedium. You can control the depth of the 3D effect and control whether it is rendered in colors or in shades of gray. Examples of an embossed star are shown in Figure 10.27.

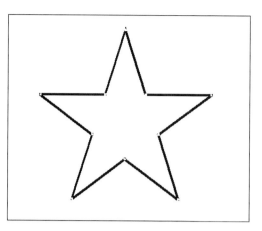

Figure 10.26
An automatically drawn star.

To emboss the star, follow these steps:

1. In FreeHand, draw a star or use the one you made in the previous exercise. Fill it with a solid color.

2. Select the star by clicking on it with the Arrow tool. All the points should be black.

Figure 10.27
Embossed star in FreeHand.

3. Choose Xtras|Create|Emboss to open the Emboss dialog box. See Figure 10.28.

4. Choose an embossing method from the icons in the top row of the dialog box. From the Vary list, choose Color. For the depth of the embossing, type a number of points in the Depth field (or drag the slider). Finally, type an angle for the embossing effect, and click on OK.

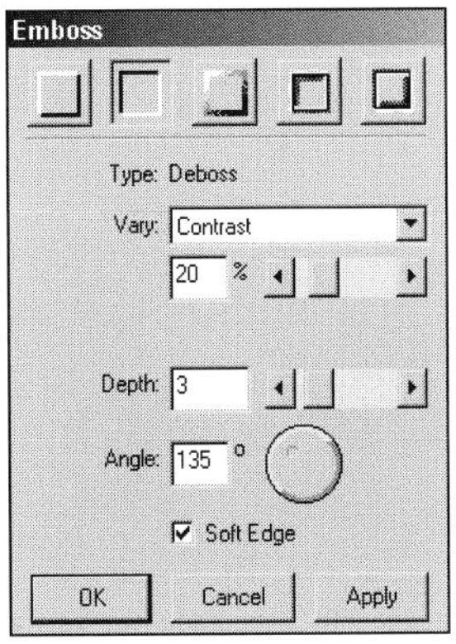

Envelope Distortion

Envelope distortions let you reshape all of the shapes in a drawing at the same time by making them fit within another shape. In Figure 10.29, you see three different shapes distorted by one of FreeHand's preset envelopes.

To make an envelope distortion in FreeHand, follow these steps:

1. Open or create a single-layer drawing that consists of several independent shapes.

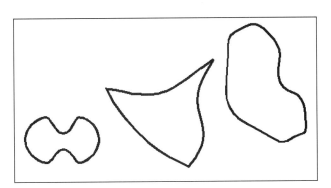

Figure 10.28
The FreeHand Emboss dialog box.

Figure 10.29
Left to right: Oval, triangle, and rounded rectangle distorted by envelope settings in FreeHand.

2. Choose Xtras|Distort|Envelope to open the Envelope dialog box. See Figure 10.30.

3. Drag any of the red points or handles so that the shape of the envelope is changed. The preview of the image will distort accordingly. You can also try picking a preset distortion from the Presets list. When you're satisfied, click on the Apply button.

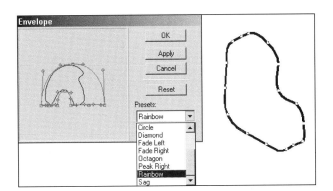

Figure 10.30
The Envelope dialog box.

Automatic Animations

FreeHand 8 lets you create a blend or attach text to a path, and then run an Xtra (a plug-in included with the program) called Animate that automatically places each shape on its own layer. Shapes are placed on layers in the order of their blend or path sequence. All that remains is for you to export the file as a Flash (SWF) movie. You can then either import the movie or play it with the standalone player in a Flash-ready browser.

Here are the steps for turning a blend into a Flash movie:

1. In FreeHand, draw two shapes and fill them with different colors. See Figure 10.31.

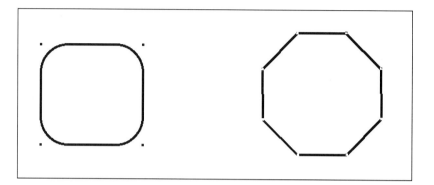

Figure 10.31
Two shapes that will be auto-animated.

2. Superimpose one shape over the other. This is an optional step. If done, the object will seem to change shape and color over time without moving in space.

3. Choose Edit|Select All, then Xtras|Create|Blend. A blend will occur, but you won't be able to see it because the larger star is superimposed over the smaller one.

4. Choose Xtras|Animate|Release To Layers. Choose Window|Panels| Layers. The Layers panel will open. (See Figure 10.32.) You will notice that there are now many layers in your document (one for each step in the blend).

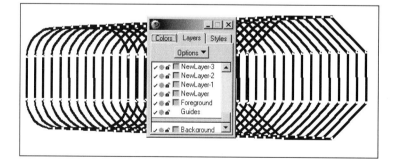

Figure 10.32
The Layers panel after you run the Animate Xtra on a blend.

5. Choose File|Export to open the Export dialog box. From the Save As Type list, choose Flash (SWF). Enter a file name for your exported file. Click on the Setup button, and make sure that Animate Pages is unchecked. Leave all other settings at their defaults. Click on OK to

close the Flash Export dialog box; then choose Save to close the Export Document dialog box.

6. Open Flash and choose File|Import. From the Files Of Type list, choose Flash. Choose the file you want to import and click on OK. Press Return/Enter to play the file.

Optimizing Bitmaps For Flash With Fireworks 2

For all that I've boasted about the speed, efficiency, and cleanliness of the vector-based graphics that Flash produces, there are occasions when bitmapped graphics simply work better:

- Some photographs need a full range of tonal values in order to be effective. (Think of photographers' or artists' portfolios.)

- Many Web designers like to create a standard HTML site that parallels the Flash site. When the first page opens, the viewer is given a choice of which version to tour. Or, at least, there's an HTML home (index) page that gives the viewer the opportunity to download and install Flash before proceeding. You can create the HTML site's graphics in Flash so they look the same, export them as bitmaps, and optimize them in Fireworks.

- Photos that need to be "floated" may need the partial transparency that Alpha channels provide. Some examples of this might be wispy hair in a portrait, soft edges on drop-shadowed text, or a fishbowl. Fireworks' native cross-platform PNG format is ideal for that.

- Graphics with gradient fills (smoothly blended transitions between colors) often have smaller file sizes as bitmaps than they do when created in an illustration program.

Another reason to use Fireworks is that it's brilliant at optimizing images (making the best compromise between file size and image quality). You can even see the results of your optimizing before you have to commit to saving them, and you can preview file-upload speed. This latter capability means that you will be able to judge whether the penalty you'd pay for better quality is worth the risk of making the viewer wait. You can see Fireworks' optimization interface in Figure 10.33. You can preview optimization settings in the Export Preview dialog box.

You probably already own image-processing software that is capable of producing Web-standard GIF, JPEG, and PNG graphics. Furthermore, the software you already own is probably capable of sophisticated darkroom and retouching operations.

COMPLEX AUTO-ANIMATIONS FROM FREEHAND

The example above may seem super-simple, but you can create fantastic effects by blending color and transparency over distance, exporting the movie, creating another blend of another set of shapes, blending and exporting them, and so forth. You can then import all of the resulting movies into Flash, each on a separate layer. Then you can edit and position frames individually because each movie has been imported as keyframes.

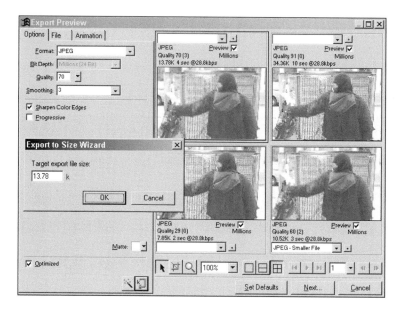

Figure 10.33
Optimizing a photo in Fireworks. Note the ability to preview up to four optimization settings at once.

So why use Fireworks? Here are a few good reasons:

- Fireworks is designed specifically for optimizing bitmapped Web graphics, and you can export to any of the Web-standard file formats. For every Web export format, you have extensive controls for transparency, Alpha channels, compression levels, palettes, dithering algorithms, and the number of colors. So you can "try before you buy," large preview windows let you compare the appearance of files exported to different formats or at different levels of compression—all before you actually export them. (You can have as few as one preview window or as many as four.) At the bottom of the preview window is a report on the file's size and on the file's download time over a typical modem. (You can even set the baud rate.) This means that you don't have to go through endless testing cycles in order to find the most effective formula for exporting a given image.

- Fireworks makes it very easy to do a brilliant job of creating vector-based shapes and then automatically converting them to bitmapped graphics. Instead of having to employ the usual route of creating logos, drawings, and buttons in a vector program (such as Flash or FreeHand) and then exporting them as bitmaps, Fireworks gives you the vector-drawing tools that let you control the precision of your shapes. Fireworks then automatically converts them to bitmapped graphics formats. In other words, you don't have to waste time switching from tool to tool. As soon as you create the shapes, you see the bitmap representation of the stroke, fill, and effect. You see exactly what you're getting. Even more important, you can change any of these characteristics at any time before you export the finished graphic. Figure 10.34 shows a pair of shapes that have been created with the Pen and Brush tools, filled or textured with a bitmapped pattern, and given bevel effects.

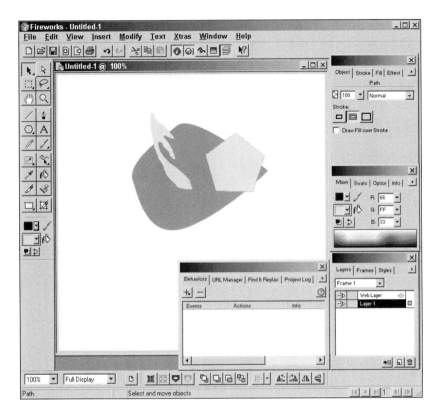

Figure 10.34

Shapes created with Fireworks Pen and Brush tools.

- Fireworks comes with a variety of fill textures, patterns, and gradients. Because you can change any of the characteristics of any shapes created in Fireworks at any time after their creation, you can create basic objects to which you can quickly give many looks. I've done just that with copies of the same shape in Figure 10.35.

- Fireworks automatically creates Web effects that have traditionally required a much higher level of programming expertise or the use of separate tools. These effects include sliced graphics and image maps. You can create JavaScript rollovers for both sliced graphics and image maps. (Arch-competitor Photoshop 5.5's ImageReady 2 can create events only for slices.) Fireworks 2 also features a redesigned and more feature-rich interface for creating JavaScript events. Lest the word "JavaScript" scare away non-programmers, you should know that absolutely no programming ability is required. You just choose events from a menu, and the program does the scripting for you.

Figure 10.35
Different stroke and fill patterns used on the same shape.

Enveloping Flash In Dreamweaver 2

Dreamweaver is a visual Web-design tool that automatically creates the needed HTML tags to incorporate Flash graphics and movies. Dreamweaver automatically does this in a form that is compatible with both major browsers. Dreamweaver also makes it just as easy to further enrich a Web site's design with cross-platform Dynamic HTML (DHTML) and cascading style sheets.

Dreamweaver is Macromedia's WYSIWYG HTML authoring tool. With it, you can visually and interactively create Web pages and sites with highly professional design and content without having to understand the complexities (or even anything at all) of the HTML language and its ever-changing permutations. However, unlike other products that allow you to do this, Dreamweaver creates professionally clean and accurate HTML code that any pro would find easy to tweak. It even comes with—and lets you automatically switch to—the most popular HTML code editor for the platform you're working with. (That would be BBEdit on the Macintosh or HomeSite in Windows.) At any time while composing your Web pages, you can switch to the HTML editor with a single command.

Placing a Flash (SWF) movie onto a Web page is easy with the new Publish feature in Flash 4. It's almost as easy in Dreamweaver. The process is the same whether the Flash content is only a graphic or animation on a page full of other Web media, or whether you've designed your entire site as a Flash movie.

Here are the steps to use Dreamweaver to place a Flash movie onto a Web page:

1. Open Dreamweaver. Next, open (or create) the document in which you want to place your Flash movie.

2. (Optional) If you're familiar with the use of tables as a means of forcing placement on a page, you may want to insert a table.

3. Click to place the cursor at the upper-left corner of the spot where you want the Flash movie to appear. Choose Insert|Flash to open the Select File dialog box. See Figure 10.36.

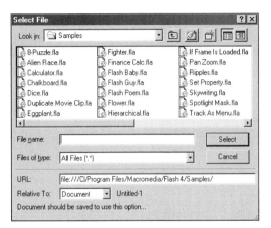

Figure 10.36
The Select File dialog box.

4. Find the file, and double-click on its name.

5. A Flash movie icon will appear on the page. To give the Flash movie the space you want it to occupy on the page, drag the scaling handles. (Remember? Flash movies are scalable; they look equally good at any size.)

6. At the same time that the Flash movie icon appears on the page, the Flash Properties Inspector, a floating window, appears. You can see both the Flash movie icon and the Flash Properties Inspector in Figure 10.37.

7. Enter all the properties that you want to assign to your Flash movie. Properties are the parameters that make the movie behave in respect to how you intended the movie to relate to the other contents on this page, such as what quality setting to use, how to align the movie, and whether the movie should be scalable to the browser size.

That's it. Now for a full explanation of all the properties and what they mean. These are the same properties discussed in Chapter 8, but they're explained there more in the context of how they relate to HTML code.

Dreamweaver's Flash Movie Properties

This section briefly explains the meaning of each of the fields and buttons in the Flash Properties Inspector (seen in Figure 10.38):

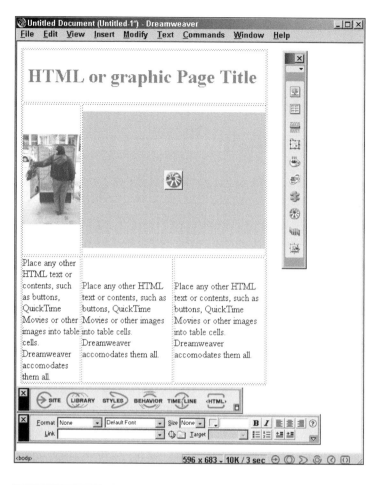

Figure 10.37

A Flash movie inserted into a Dreamweaver 2 HTML page.

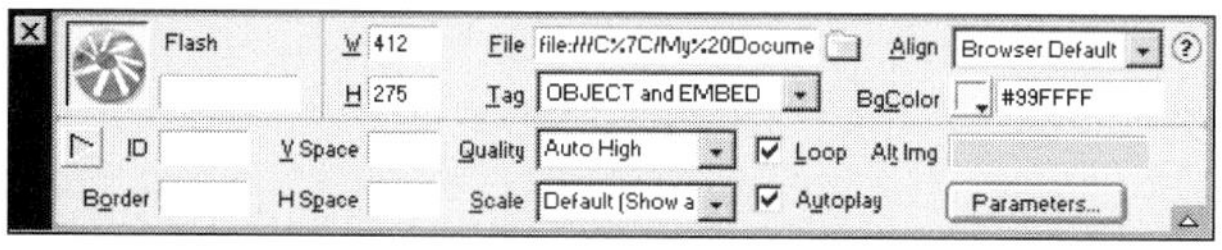

Figure 10.38

The Flash Properties Inspector.

- *Name*—What you enter (if anything) is entirely up to you, as long as it fits the field. The only purpose of entering a name is to identify this movie to any script that you might want to attach to this page.

- *W (Width)*—If you want to force a specific width for the movie, enter it here. The default unit is pixels, but by adding any of the following abbreviations immediately after the number, you can specify picas (pc), points (pt), inches (in), millimeters (mm), centimeters (cm), or percentage of the original file's value (%).

- *H (Height)*—The preceding explanation of width applies here, only now it's related to the forced height of the movie.

- *File*—The path and name of the movie file will be entered here automatically. Any time you want to change the movie that's playing in this spot, just enter a new path and file name.

- *Tag*—A list box that gives you three choices of HTML tags used to identify the Flash file to a browser: both **<OBJECT>** and **<EMBED>**; **<EMBED>**; or **<OBJECT>**. (Both is almost always the best choice.)

- *Align*—Defines how the movie will be aligned with other elements on the page.

- *BgColor (Background Color)*—The color of any transparent area assigned to the size of the Flash movie. Suppose you've assigned a width and height that are disproportionate to the size of the actual movie. On two sides of the movie, you'd see a border that was the background color.

- *ID*—The entry field for the ActiveX identifier.

- *Border*—Forces an open area around the file. The color of the border will be the page color, not the background color.

- *V Space*—The number of pixels above and below the height measurement.

- *H Space*—The number of pixels on either side of the width measurement.

- *Quality*—The manner in which anti-aliasing is applied to the movie when it's playing. Choose from four possible settings:

  - *Low*—No anti-aliasing. Fastest playback.

  - *High*—Forced anti-aliasing. Quality always takes precedence over speed.

  - *Autohigh*—Starts with anti-aliasing on, but turns it off whenever the frame rate drops below the rate you specified when building the movie.

  - *Autolow*—Turns anti-aliasing on only when the browser figures that download times and processor power will permit quality without forcing a slowdown in playback.

- *Scale*—You can choose to tell the browser to display the Flash movie at a specific pixel size or percentage of the screen. If you use the percentage parameter, the Flash movie will always use the same proportionate space in the window, regardless of what size you make the window. If you use the size parameter, the movie will stay the same size no matter what size the viewer makes the playback window. If you use percentage, you can apply any of the following three controls in order to avoid such problems as cropping or distorting:

- *Showall*—The movie's proportions will be maintained, but a border may appear.

IMPORTING 3D ANIMATIONS AS SYMBOLS

If you want to import a small 3D animation that will be used in more than one place in the movie, import it as a symbol. To do that, make sure everything is unselected (press Cmd/Ctrl+D). Then choose Insert|Convert To Symbol. A new symbol movie will open, and then you can import your 3D animation.

- *Noborder*—Same as above, but no border will appear.

- *Exactfit*—Proportions may be distorted to fit the specified size parameters.

- *Loop*—Checking this box forces the repeated playing of the movie. You cannot specify the number of loops.

- *Autoplay*—Checking this box forces the movie to play as soon as the page is loaded. Otherwise, the movie won't play until whatever conditions you've set in making the movie (such as the call from an action) have been met.

- *Alt Image*—The path and file for the location of a GIF or JPEG image that will automatically be substituted at this location if the visiting browser doesn't have Flash.

Creating 3D For Flash

A fair amount of interest exists for using 3D animations within Flash. Virtually any 3D modeling program that does animation is capable of exporting the animation as a series of sequential stills. You can use the animation power of the 3D program to create the animation, export it as sequential GIFs or JPEGs, import the series as frames in a Flash movie, and then use the Trace Bitmap command to convert each of the frames into a drawing. After you've done that, be sure to delete the imported bitmaps in order to optimize your file sizes and download times.

When you create your animations in the 3D program, try to keep the shapes, colors, and shading as simple and clean as possible. If you do, they will auto-trace into much cleaner vector files that you're much less likely to have to edit by hand. Of course, there's nothing (except for the fact that time is money) to stop you from enhancing the auto-traced drawings by changing the line weights, fills, gradients, and transparency.

Moving On

This chapter introduced the relatives of Flash that help to make your Web efforts well rounded: Freehand 8.01 for creating more sophisticated drawings and some automatic animations; Fireworks 2 for optimizing bitmapped images and making Web events; and Dreamweaver 2 for creating HTML Web pages that incorporate Flash.

The next chapter is a joint effort by me and John Croteau. It is all about using text in Flash. I cover understanding fonts, using the text tool, reshaping text, and editing text. John, of course, gets all the techie stuff: creating a form with editable text, understanding data field types, and interfacing with a database.

USING TEXT IN FLASH

11

KEN MILBURN
AND
JOHN CROTEAU

This chapter not only teaches you how to incorporate and animate text in your Flash 4 productions; it also teaches you about the two new text features: editable text fields and device-font designations.

Flash lets you do far more with type than you can (at least, easily) do with HTML. For offline productions targeted at systems with known font installations, Flash can use any PostScript 1, TrueType, or bitmap font. For Web productions, Flash provides three new typefaces (the device fonts), which are designed to appear faithfully in any browser. Also, although you pay a hefty speed and byte cost, you can use any font as long as you convert it to vector outlines by breaking it apart. However, you'd only want to break text apart on very rare occasions, otherwise you pay too large a byte cost.

As is the case with all desktop publishing and illustration software (and virtually no HTML editing software), you can accurately place text anywhere on the page and in precise relationship to other text on that page. There is no need to create tables or cells in order to keep text in its place. You can also scale, rotate, skew, or flip text without first having to convert it to an outline. Finally, you can change the color or style of text in the middle of a sentence or paragraph.

If Flash will let you do all that with text, you probably figure that you can also control the usual aspects of text: kerning and letter spacing, margins, justification, line spacing, alignment, and type size and style. Of course, you figured correctly.

You can also break down letters into drawing shapes and then use any of the editing tools in Flash to enhance the letters, fill them with gradients or photographs, or change their shapes. You can also turn these letter-drawings into symbols and then animate them with tweens.

Understanding Fonts

Despite the headline, this section isn't a dissertation on the virtues of PostScript versus TrueType or on the aesthetics of Helvetica versus Arial. What we want you to understand are the peculiarities of how Flash deals with fonts.

Flash can utilize virtually any font installed on your system. However, if your productions are going to be seen on the Web or played on other systems, they will be displayed accurately only if the viewer's system has the same fonts installed. If a system doesn't have the same fonts installed, it will look for the closest match. The problem is, that match may not be nearly close enough.

As an alternative, Flash 4 includes a special set of three fonts called *device fonts*. These device fonts are _serif, _sans, and _typewriter. These fonts cause the viewing computer to substitute the most commonly used typeface that matches the font used in your production. So _typewriter will always be some form of Courier, _serif will be either Times or Times New Roman, and _sans will be either Helvetica or Arial. Always use these fonts for body text unless you have a very good reason to do otherwise.

There's also one last complication you should be aware of: Not all the type you can set can be exported as a movie. There are no hard and fast rules for which typefaces will work and which will not, but there is a test: Choose View|Antialias Text. If the text displays jagged edges, its font isn't exportable.

When To Break Apart Text

If you need to set type for a large headline, you'll probably want it to appear exactly as you set it, regardless of the browser it's being viewed in. In that case, you can break the text apart into a drawing shape. Just be aware that, although drawing shapes are much smaller in data size than equivalent bitmaps are, they're still much larger than text that already resides on the viewer's computer. That's why you want to set most "wordy" text in one of the device fonts.

Break text apart only on rare occasions. For instance, a large headline or a logo won't be a large percentage of the type on your page, so in those cases, it's OK to break text apart. Otherwise, you shouldn't break apart text in Flash unless you are going to modify the text or use it in a Shape Tween.

In addition to increasing file size, breaking text apart makes the text hard to edit and eliminates the savings inherent in a font system that saves a font shape one time for each character. For instance, if you use 100 lowercase k's in the same font, the shape is saved only once.

One misconception that many animators have is that breaking apart text will increase the speed of text animation. This is not true. Broken-apart text will play faster than an intact-text animation—but only in the authoring environment. When these animations are exported to SWF files, there is no difference in playback speed, while there is an increase in file size for the animation using broken-apart text.

Using The Text Tool

The Text tool isn't hard to learn, despite its versatility. All you have to do to start entering type is choose the Text tool and then click on the spot on the canvas where you want the first letter to appear. How you click (just clicking, or clicking and dragging) will determine whether you've started a text block that will continue to widen as long as you type or a field that has a fixed width. A field with a fixed width forces the text to wrap to a new line as soon as the text reaches the field's border.

Fields that continue to widen as you type are convenient when you're not sure in advance how you want to size and lay out your type. As you will see in a moment, you can always do that later. To start a field that widens automatically, just click. The text field will show a small circle in the upper-right corner, as shown in Figure 11.1.

To start a fixed-width field, choose the Text tool, click at the start point, and drag to indicate the field's width. The text box will show a small square in the upper-right corner to indicate that this is a fixed-width field, also shown in Figure 11.1.

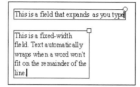

Figure 11.1

A text field that widens (top) and a fixed-width text field (bottom).

If you start with an ever-widening field, you can easily convert it to a fixed-width field whenever it looks like the type you entered is just (or near) the right length. Just drag that little circle to the desired field width, and you instantly have a fixed-width field. The little circle in the upper-right corner becomes a little square.

The Text Controls

Most of the text controls are found in the Text tool modifiers, shown in Figure 11.2. The Text tool modifiers, like all of Flash's modifiers, appear at the bottom of the Toolbox as soon as you choose the Text tool. Unlike some other tools, Text tool modifiers can be accessed only when the Text tool is chosen; there are no duplicate controls in the Toolbar.

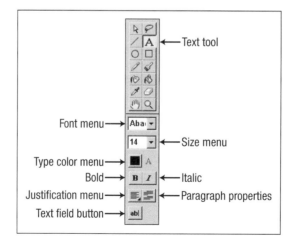

Figure 11.2

The Text tool modifiers.

Font Menu

To specify a font for an entire field, choose the font from the menu *before* you start typing. If you change your mind, or if you want to specify a different font for only some of the letters in the field, choose the Text tool and double-click on the text field. The edit box will reappear around the text. Drag the cursor across the text you want to change, and then choose a different font from the Font menu. In this way, you can change fonts as many times as you like within a given text field.

Size Menu

The Size menu works the same way as the Font menu. You can set the size of the font before you start typing, and you can change the size of any amount of selected text.

Text Color Menu

The Text Color menu works the same way as the Font and Size menus. (Click on the button to drop down the menu.) Choosing and editing color for text is similar to choosing and editing colors for fills, except that gradients are not available for text. To choose a color, click on the Text Color button. The Swatches menu will appear (see Figure 11.3). To edit colors, click on the Edit Color button at the top of the Swatches menu (it looks like a miniature swatches menu).

Bold

Click on this button any time you want to start typing in boldface. If you select text, clicking on this button will convert the selected text to boldface.

Italic

Click on this button any time you want to start typing in italics. If you select text, clicking on this button will convert the selected text to italics.

Justification Menu

Click on this button and drag to select a justification option: left, right, centered, or fully justified (each line of text is stretched to meet the borders on both sides).

If you select a text field (a checkered marquee surrounds it) and then choose a justification option, all of the text in that field will be justified in the same way. However, if you put the text in edit mode (click on it with the Text tool chosen), you can justify each paragraph separately. So the first paragraph can be left justified, the second centered, and so forth.

Paragraph Properties

By now, you've probably started wondering where the controls are for leading, kerning, and margins. Click on the Paragraph Properties button to open the Paragraph Properties dialog box, shown in Figure 11.4.

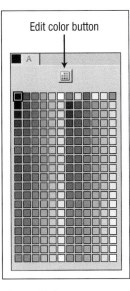

Figure 11.3
The Text Color menu and the Edit Color button.

Figure 11.4
The Paragraph Properties dialog box.

Editable Text Fields

Flash 4 provides a new type of text—the editable text field—which is used to enter or display data. See Figure 11.5 for an example. This data can be anything from entries in an online order form to answers in a quiz sheet that cause the viewer to see something that only that combination of answers could cause him to see. I wish Macromedia had called this "dynamic text" because text a viewer enters into a text field immediately changes the value of the variable associated with that text field. Text entry does not force frame actions to be redone, so don't expect dynamic action just because an entry has been made.

Options in the Text Field Properties dialog box are explained next.

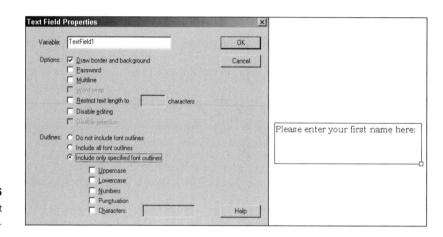

Figure 11.5

A text-entry field and the Text Field Properties dialog box.

Variable

All editable text requires a variable name that identifies it to an ActionScript and allows dynamic text replacement and entry.

Draw Border And Background

This option, the default, draws a border and a white background for the text. Deselect this option if you don't want the default border and outline.

Password

When this option is selected, the Password field displays only asterisks instead of the entered text. Use this option when you want a password to be hidden from view.

Multiline

This option allows line breaks for text entered or displayed in the published SWF movie. Note that this option has no effect in authoring mode.

Word Wrap

This option allows text to be wrapped to the next line when it reaches the right margin of a text field in the published Flash file.

Restrict Text Length To

This option limits the number of characters that can be entered in a text field.

Disable Editing

This option prevents users from changing the text in a text field, but still allows the text to be displayed dynamically.

Disable Selection

This option prevents text from being selected by viewers. This option is often used with the Disable Editing option selected and the Draw Border And Background option deselected so that text is displayed dynamically but does not look like a text field.

Do Not Include Font Outlines

This option is the default and should be used when the _sans, _serif, or _typewriter device font is chosen. If you select another font, you should be certain that the users' computers have the designated font.

Include All Font Outlines

This option will supply all 256 font-character outlines so your text will appear with its proper font shape in all computers. Use this option if you are not sure what characters will be used. Note that, because the whole character set will be exported, file size will be increased substantially.

Include Only Specified Font Outlines

Use this option when you want font shapes to be exported with the SWF file and you know or can control what type of characters will be entered or displayed in the text field.

You can limit the font outline shapes that will be exported with the SWF file to any combination of Uppercase, Lowercase, Numbers, Punctuation, or a list of characters that you select. This can save more bytes than the Include All Font Outlines option can.

Animating Text With A Tween

In order to animate text with a tween, you will often need to convert the text to a symbol. You can then employ any of the regular motion or color tween capabilities in Flash. One of the most useful motion tweens for text is a simultaneous zoom and spin. The procedure in Flash 4 is simpler than ever. Here it is:

1. Select the text.

2. On the first frame where the text will appear, Ctrl/Right-click to display the Frames menu. Choose Insert Keyframe. (If you're starting in the first frame of the movie, this step won't be necessary.)

ROTATING MORE THAN 180 DEGREES

The maximum you can rotate in a single tween is 180 degrees. If you want to spin more, start a new tween at the end of each 180-degree rotation.

3. Ctrl/Right-click on the same frame again, and choose Create Motion Tween.

4. Select a frame several frames further down the Timeline, and insert a keyframe again (see Step 2). As soon as you do this, the Timeline will display a straight line between the two keyframes, indicating that a tween will take place in this range of frames.

5. Select the first frame.

6. Select the Arrow tool, and select the text symbol you created.

7. Use the Arrow tool modifiers to scale the text to a different size and to rotate it 180 degrees.

8. Press Return/Enter to see the effect.

Reshaping Text

You might want to redesign the shape of some letters for a new logo design or make the letters seem to melt in an animation. To treat letters like any other Flash-drawn shape, all you have to do is turn them into a Flash drawing. To do that, just select the text and press Cmd/Ctrl+B. If you want to do it the hard way, select the text and choose Modify|Break Apart.

Broken-apart text looks just like the real thing (unless, of course, you edit it with the drawing tools). It will lose all of its text advantages, but there are occasions when this may be worth it. Broken-apart text does have some advantages of its own, though:

• The original font will look the same in any browser.

• You can fill the letters with a bitmap.

• You can fill the letters with a gradient.

• You can change the thickness and color of the outline, or add an outline.

• You can use any of Flash's editing controls to move curves or to transform any or all of the letters.

All of the above (except animation, of course) has been done to the text shown in Figure 11.6.

Editing Text As Curves

After you've broken text apart, you can do anything with it that you can do with any other drawing shape. If you skipped straight to this chapter because you need to know about text first, you might want to go back to Chapters 3 and 4 to find out more about what you can do in a drawing.

Figure 11.6
Text modified after being broken apart. This text was originally all one paragraph.

Following are a few edits that you'll find especially useful for dealing with text:

- Adding an outline

- Making beveled-edge text

- Expanding the shape

- Filling text with a bitmap

- Animating text with a tween

In case I was going too fast for you earlier in this chapter, before you can do any of these things, you have to break the text apart. To do that, select the text by clicking on it with the Arrow tool. Then press Cmd/Ctrl+B or choose Modify|Break Apart.

Adding An Outline

Adding an outline to text will let you put a different-color border around the text. You can also use the Modify|Curves|Lines To Fills command to fill the outline with a gradient or bitmap. Also, adding an outline is the first step in making a beveled edge around text.

Here's how to add an outline:

1. Choose the Ink Bottle tool.

2. In the Ink Bottle tool modifiers, choose the color for the outline, the thickness of the outline, and the Line Style. (Remember, any style other than Solid will use much more data.)

3. Click on each of the letters you want to outline. The outline will be added. You will also need to click one more time for each additional inside curve (for instance, you'd click an "O" twice, a "B" three times).

Figure 11.7 shows you the Toolbox and the text as it would look if you were adding outlines.

Filling Text With A Bitmap

This is a repeat, so I'm going to keep it short. Filling text is no different. The topic resurfaces here only because filling text with a bitmap is such a neat way to create the look of an old picture postcard. You can see it in Figure 11.8.

BEFORE YOU BREAK TEXT APART

Make sure the text isn't superimposed over a drawing. Otherwise, when you break the text apart, it will autoedit the drawing underneath as soon as you deselect it. You can avoid this by putting the text on its own layer. Put the cursor on the active Layer Name bar and Ctrl/right-click. The Layers menu will appear. Choose Insert Layer. A new layer will appear. Now create your text and break it apart. Because it's on its own layer, the text won't be a problem when it's edited. If you ever want to move the text to another layer, just select it and press Cmd/Ctrl+C to copy it to the clipboard; then activate the target layer and press Cmd/Ctrl+V to paste the text.

Figure 11.7
Placing an outline around text.

Figure 11.8
The letters have been filled with a photograph of leaves.

Note: If you add a thick outline around text, the text will grow by half the width of the line. You might want to keep the text the same size, however. In that case, shrink the text by half the line width; then add the outline. To shrink the text, choose Modify|Curves| Expand Shape. When the Expand Path dialog box appears, enter half the number of pixels in the Distance field, select the Inset option, and click on OK. Your text will shrink, and when you add the outline, the text will be exactly the same size as before.

To fill letters with a bitmap:

1. Insert a new layer, and make sure it's selected (active).

2. Choose File|Import. Navigate to your bitmap (there's one called garden.jpg on the CD) and open it.

3. As soon as the file opens, press Cmd/Ctrl+B to break apart the bitmap.

4. Choose the Eye Dropper tool, and click in the broken-apart bitmap. You will see that the color modifier has changed to a bitmap.

5. Delete the new layer.

6. Choose the Paint Bucket tool, and click inside each of the letters. That portion of the bitmap that would have been underneath (or above) the selected letter will appear there.

I find that it's also a good idea to outline letters that have been filled with a bitmap. It gives them better definition, and it's in keeping with the postcard effect.

The Documentation Booboos

On page 115 of the Flash 4 manual, under the heading "Using Type In Flash Movies," you will find somewhat misleading statements. The following list shows them (in italics), with our comments. These errors were probably due to planned improvements that didn't have time to materialize before the projected release of Flash 4.

- *You can use Type 1 Postscript fonts, TrueType [fonts], and bitmap fonts in your Flash movies.* You can use Type 1 PostScript fonts and TrueType fonts, but system bitmap fonts are not available for you to use in Flash.

- *Flash exports type to your final movie with all its system information intact.* Flash does export regular Flash text with its outlines (system information), but does not export PostScript or TrueType text with outlines.

- *Type you create while authoring on one platform may not appear properly on other platforms.* While you're authoring in Flash, the FLA working files do not include font shapes. Each viewing computer needs the same fonts installed. If these computers are on different platforms, even similar fonts may have different font names, and this can make authoring difficult.

- Moreover, your audience must have the type's font installed for it to display properly, even on the same platform. This is not true for regular Flash text. It is true only for field text and only if one of the three new device-font designations (_sans, _serif, _typewriter) is not chosen or if the default option Do Not Include Font Outlines is left selected.

Moving On

So now you know everything we know (almost) about how to use text in the Flash environment. You learned how to use the proprietary Flash fonts for most body text, how to create text fields, and how to "decorate" text by breaking it apart into lines. Next up, we'll take a look at using Flash dynamically with Generator and other programs. You'll also get a how-to for combining Flash content with QuickTime to create QuickTime files.

12

FLASH COMMUNICATIONS AND USING FORMS

JOHN CROTEAU

In this chapter, we will cover the ways that Flash can communicate with other programs, how it can be used dynamically with Generator and other similar programs, and what file formats Flash can create. We will also cover how Flash 4 is used to combine Flash content with QuickTime to create QuickTime files.

Flash 4 has added new features that make working with scripts and server-side programs much more dynamic. Using Flash as a front end for virtually any type of form or game is now possible with Flash 4. Whether you need to do a simple order form, a database retrieval system, or a multi-user game interface such as for Bingo, Flash 4 has the power and flexibility to accomplish these and more. Note that Flash itself may not do any more work for these applications than an HTML page, but the interface is more flexible and visually appealing and, with ActionScript, you can perform many functions in Flash that would normally require either JavaScript or server access, and Flash provides a better experience for your visitors with less of a load on your server.

Forms

In this section we will explore how forms can be used in Flash 4. Forms have two basic parts: a way to enter and display text and a way to send and receive this data. For the first part, we use Text Field text, which we have covered in Chapter 11. (See Figure 12.1.) Then, we'll cover how to send data from Flash (by using Send Variables) and how to bring in data (by using Load Variables). Next, we'll access data from a text file and explain how to connect to a server-side page. Finally, we'll put it all together with round-trip access to a database.

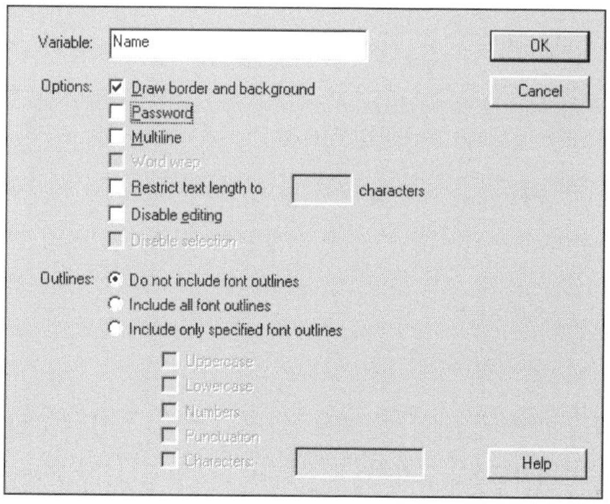

Figure 12.1
Text Field properties.

Text For Forms

Form fields in Flash are just Text Field text that is left in default mode so users can enter text. Every Text Field is identified with a variable whose value is displayed in the text field. The text displayed in a Text Field can also be changed by changing the variable associated with the Text Field. The Text Field display will be changed when Flash moves to another frame on the Timeline or if set in a button on the change of state (frame) in the button. Hidden text fields are simply set by setting a variable and not displaying it in a Text Field. For an example of a form, see Figure 12.2. For more information on Text Fields, see Chapter 11.

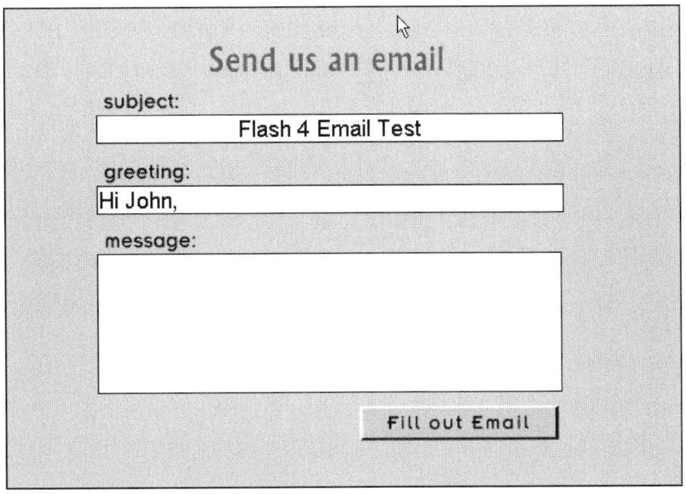

Figure 12.2
An email form.

Send Variables

In Flash 3, you could send query (search) data attached to Get URL and Load Movie actions. This data would follow a question mark (?), which would be placed immediately after the file name. For example:

```
Get URL ("picture.htm?data=13")
```

In Flash 4, you now have the Send Variables option for Get URL, Load Movie, and Load Variables (see Figure 12.3). This option allows you to send all the available variables automatically and has three settings:

• *Don't Send*—Variables are not sent with the URL.

• *GET*—Variables are appended to the end of the URL. Servers impose a limit on the size of the string that can be handled using this method.

• *POST*—Variables are sent in a separate header along with the URL. This method is capable of sending much longer strings.

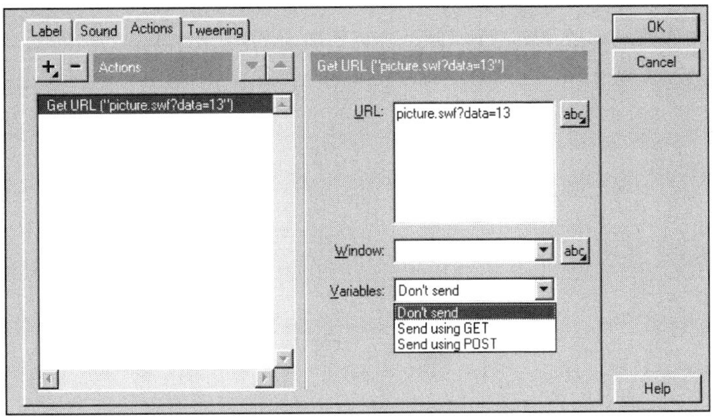

Figure 12.3
Send Variables options.

If you specify either GET or POST, Flash will send all the available variables on the current Timeline. Any variable that is associated with the sending Timeline (a movie-clip Timeline or a main Timeline) and that has a value (whether it is in a text field or not) will be sent. A variable name is assigned to all Text Field text. If text is entered into the Text field, that variable becomes active even if you have not referred to it in your script.

Variables that exist on other Timelines will not be sent. For instance, suppose that in a movie clip, you have a Get URL action with the Get parameter selected for Send Variables. In this case, only the variables in that movie clip will be sent. None of the variables set on the main Timeline or in other movie clips will be sent, even if they are visible in a text field.

Load Variables

The Load Variables action—which is available as an option of the Load Movie action—allows Flash to read properly formatted data from a text file or text generated by a server-side script such as a CGI script or an ASP server-side page. For example, if a user submits an order form, you might want a confirmation screen that displays an order number retrieved from a file on a remote server. See Figure 12.4.

With Load Variables, the text at the URL must be in the standard MIME format: **application/x-www-urlformencoded** (a standard format used by CGI scripts). Any number of variables can be specified. For example, the following statement defines several variables:

```
company=FlashCentral&name=John+Croteau&city=Rockville&state=MD
```

You will note that the variable and its value are connected with an equals sign (=), and that the variable pairs are separated by ampersands (&). Do not put returns after values in your file; if you do, they will be considered part of the values. The returns not only are displayed in text fields but also can cause nightmares for evaluating your variables.

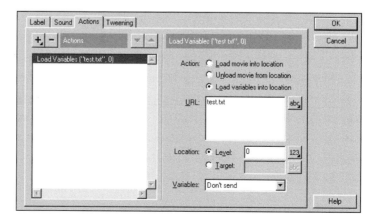

Figure 12.4

Load Variables from a text or ASCII file.

Accessing Data From A Text File

Accessing data from a text file requires three small steps:

1. Create a new Flash movie with two text fields named text1 and text2.

2. Place a button in frame one, and give it the following action:

```
On(Press)
     Load Variables("test.txt",0)
End On
```

3. Publish the movie. In the same directory in which you published the movie, create a text file named test.txt with the following content:

```
text1=John&text2=Flash+Central
```

Now open the page in a browser (you can use the Publish Preview option if you like). The text fields will be empty or will include the text that you typed in the text fields when you created them. Click on the button, and you will see that the text from the text file has been transferred to Flash and displayed in your text fields.

In order to send variables from Flash, you will need some kind of script to receive the output of the Load Variables action. This script can be almost any kind of server-side script.

Accessing Server-Side Pages

Flash 4 can read information from external data sources in two ways. One way is to have Flash statically read from an ASCII file. The other way is to have Flash read dynamically from an external data source via an intermediary that connects a Flash movie to the data source. This is done through a server-side script, which could be CGI, ASP, or virtually any other server-side page. This script could then manipulate your data or even connect to a database. Flash can then retrieve information using a Load Variables statement.

Round-Trip Access And Databases

With Flash 4, you can send and receive data from a dynamic server-side page by using a single Load Variables command with the Send Variables option, as shown in Figure 12.5. For example, this would send all the variables from the current timeline (movie clip or main timeline) using the POST method to a file called password.cgi. Flash would then retrieve the data that this file has or will have when the page is executed. Unlike a text file, a server-side page is written dynamically and can be based on the data that you sent to it.

```
Load Variables ("http://FlashBible.com/password.cgi", 0,
vars=POST)
```

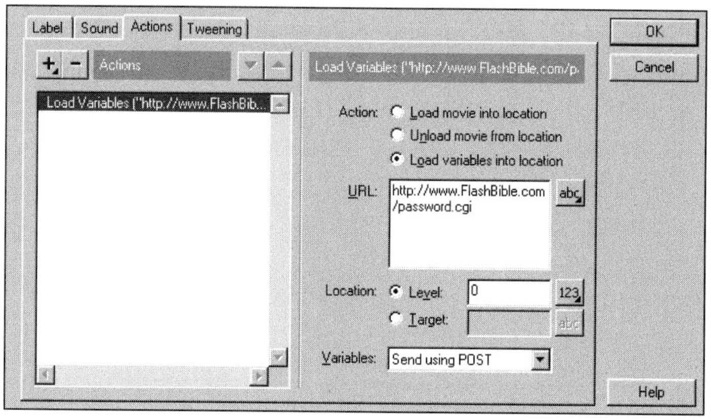

Figure 12.5

Round-Trip Access: Load and Send variables together.

Here are some things to keep in mind:

- Make sure you set the Send Variables option to either POST or GET, depending on the needs of your script.

- Make sure you provide the correct level or target where you want variables to be sent back to Flash. Flash's default of level one is rarely correct. If you want the variables to go the main Timeline of the original movie, you can enter a zero in the Level box of the dialog box.

- If you already have an application such as a CGI script, use the same URL address that you would use from an HTML page.

- Create a test variable to determine when data has been received from the server.

- In Flash, create a loop that checks the test variable to determine when data has been received from the server.

We won't get into the scripting of the server-side page because that will vary by language (Perl, ASP, PHP, Cold Fusion, etc.), by Web server software, by operating system, and by the actual application (database, mail server, etc.) to which the script will connect. Details on connecting Flash to these languages can be found in the members section of FlashBible.com (**www.FlashBible.com/members/Database/**).

Communicating With Scripts

There are three basic methods for sending commands to scripts from Flash:

- FSCommand

- JavaScript: Protocol

- Hidden frame or server-side page

Only FSCommand allows direct two-way communication between Flash and a script. The hidden-frame method is the only one that will work for all Flash-capable browsers. Table 12.1 shows which browsers work with which methods.

The JavaScript: Protocol

The JavaScript: Protocol method of communication is a simple method of sending commands from Flash to the scripting environment. It does not work with all Flash-compatible browsers, however, and it displays an error message with Internet Explorer 3 browsers.

The syntax is simple. It consists of placing "JavaScript" followed by a colon and the JavaScript function that you want to call, as shown in Figure 12.6. Place your statement in the URL window of a Get URL action. For example, this would call a JavaScript function OpenWindow, which might open a popup window:

```
JavasScript:OpenWindow()
```

Table 12.1   Browser capability to send commands from Flash.

Browser & Platform	HTML Get URL	JavaScript: Protocol	FSCommand/ Flash Methods
Netscape 3+			
Win 95/98/NT	Yes	Yes	Yes
Power Mac	Yes	Yes	Yes
Mac 68K	Yes	Yes	No
Win 3.1	Yes	Yes	No
Internet Explorer			
IE3 Win 95/NT	Yes	No and Errors	Yes
IE4 Win 95/98/NT	Yes	Yes	Yes
IE3+ Win 3.1	Yes	No	No
IE3 Mac	Yes	No	No
IE4.0x Mac	Yes	Yes	No
IE4.5 Mac	Yes	No	No

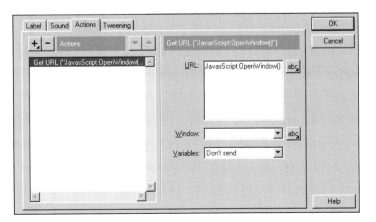

Figure 12.6
JavaScript protocol.

A JavaScript: Protocol statement can also be placed in the Command box in an FSCommand action, but doing this does not make the statement an FSCommand.

The Hidden-Frame Method

The hidden-frame method also uses a Get URL action but places a new HTML page in a hidden frame. This page can then execute any HTML or script placed on that page. My Christmas 1997 page used this technique to play and stop Midi music. This page can be found at **www.FlashCentral.com/Tech/xmas/**.

A variation of this method would be to call a server-side page and then have that page execute or call your script.

FSCommand And JavaScript

FSCommand is a mechanism that allows two-way communication between Flash and the scripting environment. FSCommand is actually made up of three basic methods:

- *Flash Methods*—Allows communication from scripts to Flash.

- *Flash Properties*—Returns the values of a condition of Flash to a script.

- *FSCommands*—Sends commands from Flash to the scripting environment. (Also lends its name to this group of methods.)

Browsers can communicate with Flash only by using a 32-bit implementation of either LiveConnect or ActiveX scripting. In Netscape browsers, JavaScript and Java must be enabled for FSCommands to work. In Internet Explorer, the ActiveX control for Flash must be installed (not the plug-in), and ActiveX scripts must be enabled. FS Commands do not work with Internet Explorer for the Macintosh or with Netscape browsers for Win 3.x and Mac 68K. No other brand or platform is known to work with FSCommands. (See Table 12.1 for more details on which browsers are compatible with FSCommand.)

FSCommands For The Standalone Flash Players And Projectors

Five special FS Commands are used to control Flash movies when they are playing in a standalone Flash player or projector. See Figure 12.7. These commands should not be used in a Flash file that will be used with a browser. The commands are:

- Quit

- FullScreen

- AllowScale

- ShowMenu

- Exec

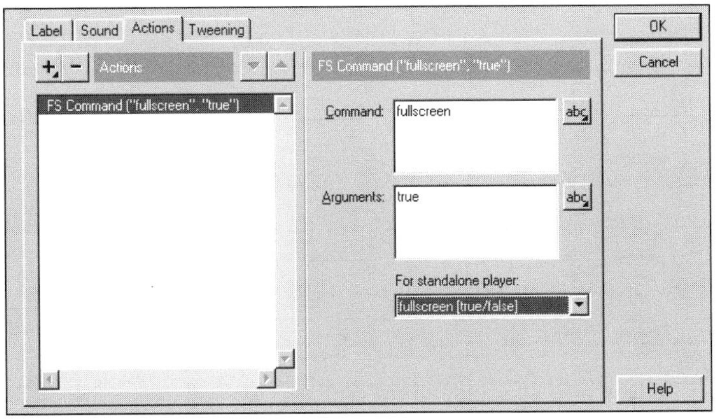

Figure 12.7
Standalone FSCommands.

For each FS Command, Tables 2.2 through 2.7 show the type of command (Flash property, method, or event), the versions of Flash they can be used with, and the values and types of parameters used with the command.

In Table 12.6, an asterisk in the Parameter (Value) column indicates that the property parameters are assigned numbers. See the Table 9.3 for values.

Table 12.2 Special FSCommands for standalone players and projectors.

Functions	Method	Property (Type)	Events	Flash Plug-in	Flash ActiveX	Parameter (Value)	Parameter (Type)
Quit			For standalone players and projectors			-	-
FullScreen				-	-	True/False	
AllowScale				-	-	True/False	
ShowMenu				-	-	True/False	
Exec				-	-	filePath	

Table 12.3 FSCommands for regular Flash Methods.

Functions	Method	Property (Type)	Events	Flash Plug-in	Flash ActiveX	Parameter (Value)	Parameter (Type)
Play	Yes			2,3,4	2,3,4		
StopPlay	Yes			2,3,4	2,3,4		
Stop	Yes			-	3 & 4		
GotoFrame	Yes			2,3,4	2,3,4	frameNum	Integer
Rewind	Yes			2,3,4	2,3,4		
SetZoomRect	Yes			2,3,4	2,3,4	left, top, right, bottom	Integers
Zoom	Yes			2,3,4	2,3,4	percent	Integer
Pan	Yes			2,3,4	2,3,4	x, y, mode	Integers
TotalFrames		Integer		2,3,4	2,3,4	totalFrames	
PercentLoaded		Integer		2,3,4	2,3,4	percent	
IsPlaying		True/False		2,3,4	2		
IsPlaying	Yes	True/False		-	3 & 4	True/False	
FlashVersion		Integer		3 & 4	3 & 4		

Table 12.4 FSCommands for events.

Functions	Method	Property (Type)	Events	Flash Plug-in	Flash ActiveX	Parameter (Value)	Parameter (Type)
OnProgress			Yes	2,3,4	2,3,4	percent	Integer
OnReady StateProgress			Yes	2,3,4	2,3,4	state	Integer
FSCommand			Yes	2,3,4	2,3,4	command, arguments	Strings

Table 12.5 FSCommands for the Tell Target action.

Functions	Method	Property (Type)	Events	Flash Plug-in	Flash ActiveX	Parameter (Value)	Parameter (Type)
LoadMovie	Yes			3 & 4	3 & 4	level, URL	Int, String
TGotoFrame	Yes			3 & 4	3 & 4	target, frameNum	String, Int
TGotoLabel	Yes			3 & 4	3 & 4	target, label	String
Tplay	Yes			3 & 4	3 & 4	target	String
TStopPlay	Yes			3 & 4	3 & 4	target	String
TCurrentFrame		Integer		3 & 4	3 & 4	target	String
TCurrentLabel		String		3 & 4	3 & 4	target	String

Table 12.6 FSCommands for variables, calls, and movie-clip properties in Flash 4.

Functions	Method	Property (Type)	Events	Flash Plug-in	Flash ActiveX	Parameter (Value)	Parameter (Type)
SetVariable	Yes			4	4	variable name, value	String, String
GetVariable	Yes			4	4	variable name	String
TGetProperty AsNumber	Yes			4	4	target, property# *	String, Int
TCallFrame	Yes			4	4	target, label	String, frame#
TCallLabel	Yes			4	4	target, label	String, String
TSetProperty	Yes			4	4	target, property#, Value *	String, Int, String
TGetProperty	Yes			4	4	target, property# *	String, Int

Table 12.7 FSCommands for ActiveX Control only.

Functions	Method	Property (Type)	Events	Flash Plug-in	Flash ActiveX	Parameter (Value)	Parameter (Type)
Forward	Yes			-	2,3,4		
Back	Yes			-	2,3,4		
ReadyState		Integer		-	2,3,4	0, 1, 2, 3, 4	
FrameNum	Yes	Integer		-	2,3,4	frameNum	String
Playing	Yes	True/False		-	2,3,4	True/False	
Quality	Yes	Integer		-	2,3,4	0, 1, 2, 3	Integer

(continued)

Table 12.7   FSCommands for ActiveX Control only *(continued)*.

Functions	Method	Property (Type)	Events	Flash Plug-in	Flash ActiveX	Parameter (Value)	Parameter (Type)
ScaleMode	Yes	Integer		-	2,3,4	0, 1, 2	Integer
AlignMode	Yes	Yes		-	2,3,4	+1, +2, +3, +4	Integer
Background Color	Yes	Integer		-	2,3,4	colorNum	Integer
Loop	Yes	True/False		-	2,3,4	True/False	
Movie	Yes	String		-	2,3,4	URL	String

The following list shows the undocumented FSCommands:

- FrameLoaded
- CurrentFrame
- getWindow
- isActive
- destroy
- init
- getPeer
- wait
- notifyAll
- notify
- toString
- equals
- hashCode
- getClass

Generator And Other Dynamic Servers

Generator is a Web server application that allows you to combine templates with content specified in a data source. This application lets you create dynamic Web-page animations and interactive content. With Generator, you can customize content for individual users and update content in a timely manner. Generator 2 is fully compatible with Flash 4.

As we have seen earlier, Flash 4 can read information from external data sources, as shown in Figure 12.8. This is done through an intermediary text file or a script that connects the Flash movie to the data source. With Generator, you gain direct access to the data sources. Generator provides all the necessary means, and you need no scripting to affect this dynamic relationship.

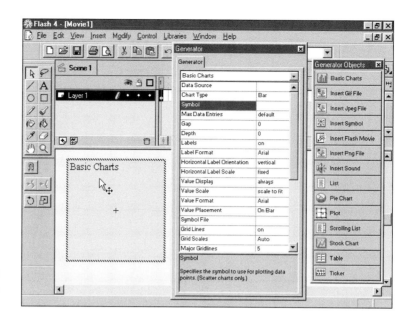

Figure 12.8

Flash 4 with Generator Objects and Inspector windows open.

You can use Generator to create content in a variety of ways:

- Create Generator objects include charts, tables, lists, and graphs. You can also apply Generator Symbol commands to symbol instances.

- Specify variables in a template when you create the content.

- Create data sources and assign them to a main Timeline or to specific objects.

- Choose Generator output. In addition to Flash, you can create JPEG, PNG, QuickTime 4, or GIF files using Generator templates.

- Specify parameters in the Generator section of Publish. This allows you to create content locally to check for errors and for modifications as needed.

After creating a Generator template with Flash 4, you can copy it to a Web server along with its associated data sources and associated external media content.

To add a Generator object, choose Window|Generator Objects from the Flash 4 program, and drag one of the 14 objects onto the stage. The Generator Inspector will open, giving you between 3 and 32 parameters that can be applied to that object. (You can also open the Generator Inspector for Generator objects and regular symbols by choosing Window|Inspectors|Generator.)

The following are the 14 Generator objects that you can add to a Flash 4 presentation.

- Basic Charts

- Insert GIF File

- Insert JPEG File

- Insert Symbol

- Insert Flash Movie

- Insert PNG File

- Insert Sound

- List

- Pie Chart

- Plot

- Scrolling List

- Stock Chart

- Table

- Ticker

We have gone briefly into the capabilities and features of Generator. For more information on Generator and other similar, dynamic content providers, go to Flash Central at **www.FlashCentral.com/Tech/And/Generator.htm**.

Exporting To Other File Formats

As was emphasized in the beginning of this book, Flash is quite good at exporting its movies to file formats that are more conventional. Now you can even export sound, animation, and actions to a QuickTime movie. Exporting to a QuickTime movie is covered later in this chapter.

To export a movie from Flash, follow these steps:

1. Choose File|Export Movie to open the Export Movie dialog box.

2. In the File Name field, type a name for the file.

3. From the Save As Type list, choose the destination file format. Then click on OK. Another export dialog box, specific to the format to which you are exporting, opens. See Figure 12.9.

4. Fill in the appropriate parameters in the dialog box and click on OK.

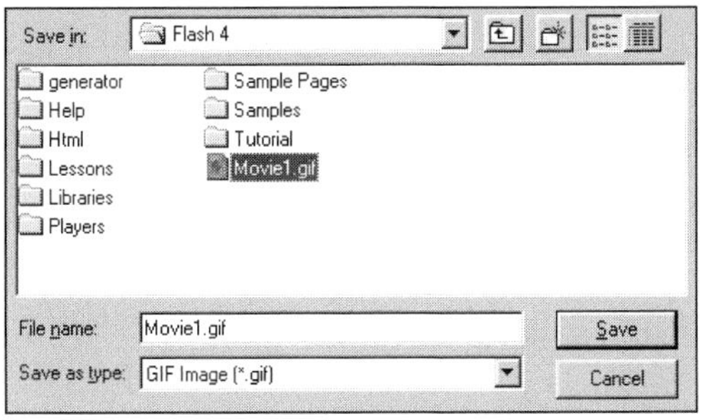

Figure 12.9
The Export Image dialog box.

To export a still image, follow these steps:

1. Choose File|Export Image to open the Export Image dialog box.

2. In the File Name field, type a name for the file.

3. From the Save As Type list, choose the destination file format. Then click on OK. Another export dialog box appears. See Figure 12.10.

4. Fill in the appropriate parameters in the dialog box and click on OK.

Figure 12.10
The Export GIF dialog box.

Exporting Movies

With the exception of Flash movies (including FutureSplash and Generator) and QuickTime 4, movies exported from Flash are incapable of interactivity. These non-interactive movies and sequences are not exported with functioning buttons, and only the first frame of movie clips is displayed. When Flash exports movies for a non-interactive format, Flash ignores branching (such as Go To actions), movie clips (except their first images), and all actions and ActionScripts. Flash converts the movie in a straight-line fashion, following the Timeline from beginning to end.

Of the non-interactive formats, only Windows AVI and the QuickTime 3 movie formats can include sound; the others will ignore the sound. RealFlash is another video format that can include Flash, but Flash does not export to this format, and you need to use special tools from Real to compose RealFlash movies.

Table 12.8 shows the formats (and their extensions) that can be exported or published from Flash and whether they are available for Windows and/or Macintosh computers.

Table 12.8 Movie export formats.

File Type	Extension	Publish	Windows	Macintosh
Adobe Illustrator sequence	.ai	No	Yes	Yes
Animated GIF	.gif	Yes	Yes	Yes
AVI	.avi	No	Yes	No
Bitmap sequence	.bmp	No	Yes	No
DXF sequence	.dxf	No	Yes	Yes
EMF sequence	.emf	No	Yes	No

(continued)

Table 12.8   Movie export formats *(continued)*.

File Type	Extension	Publish	Windows	Macintosh
EPS 3 sequence	.eps	No	Yes	Yes
Flash movie	.swf	Yes	Yes	Yes
Flash Windows projector	.exe	Yes	Yes	Yes
Flash Macintosh projector	.hqx	Yes	No	Yes
FutureSplash movie	.spl	No	Yes	Yes
Generator template	.swt	Yes	Yes	Yes
GIF sequence	.gif	No	Yes	Yes
PNG sequence	.png	No	Yes	Yes
QuickTime movie	.mov	Yes	Yes, 4.0	Yes

Exporting Images

Flash uses the first frame of a movie for an image export unless you have entered a label of #Static in the frame you want for your image. If you choose Export Image and select Flash, you will get a one-frame Flash movie image. See the formats used in Table 12.9.

Export For Use In High Resolution Printing

When a graphic created in Flash needs to be used for high resolution print output, it is important to find out whether the final output needs to be in vector or raster format.

Table 12.9   Image and sound export formats.

File Type	Extension	Publish	Windows	Macintosh
Adobe Illustrator	.ai	No	Yes	Yes
AutoCAD DXF	.dxf	No	Yes	Yes
Bitmap	.bmp	No	Yes	No
Enhanced Metafile	.emf	No	Yes	No
EPS 3	.eps	No	Yes	Yes
Flash Player image	.swf	No	Yes	Yes
FutureSplash image	.spl	No	Yes	Yes
Generator template image	.swt	No	Yes	Yes
GIF image	.gif	Yes	Yes	Yes
JPEG image	.jpg	Yes	Yes	Yes
PICT image	.pict	No	No	Yes
PNG	.png	Yes	Yes	Yes
WAV audio	.wav	No	Yes	No
Windows Metafile	.wmf	No	Yes	No

Vector

If vector is required, export in Adobe Illustrator (.ai) format. There is one area of concern: If your image contains fonts that you want to preserve, opening the .ai file in FreeHand is safer. Once the file containing fonts starts to open in FreeHand 8, FreeHand will report that the fonts used are missing and offer you a chance to replace them. It will do this even though the fonts are, in fact, installed on your system. Select Replace from the Missing Fonts dialog box and scroll down the list of installed fonts. Select the font you used. Now when FreeHand finishes opening the file, the fonts you used will be displayed and editable. In Illustrator, the fonts open with the correct font name with an asterisk next to the name, but they do not display as the correct font if they are not available.

Bitmap

If you need to output a bitmap (raster) file, it is important to find out the dpi (dots per inch) for the final artwork. A standard dpi setting for print work is 300. Assuming those are the dpi settings, the procedure is as follows:

1. Choose the frame you want for your image. (For this example, use frame 10.)

2. Insert a Label of #Static in the Label field of frame 10.

3. Select File|Export Image.

4. Select .bmp as the file type.

5. Enter the file name and click on Save. The Export Bitmap dialog box appears, as shown in Figure 12.11.

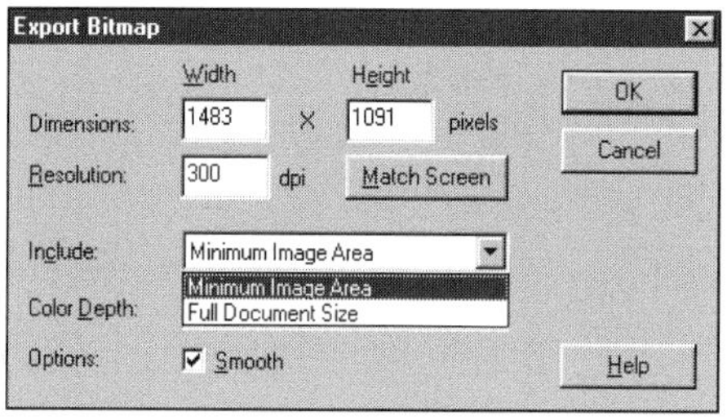

Figure 12.11
The Export Bitmap dialog box.

6. Leave Dimensions alone for the present and enter 300 in the Resolution box.

7. In the Include box you have two choices: Minimum Image Area and Full Document Size. If your Flash frame has artwork that is outside the stage canvas and you choose Minimum Image Area, the final bitmap image will include that artwork and the image size will be larger than the canvas. If the artwork takes up only a section of the

canvas, then the final bitmap image will be smaller than the canvas. If you choose Full Document Size, the final bitmap image will be the same as the canvas size and Flash will ignore artwork placed off the canvas.

You can see how these two choices affect your final output by looking at the Dimensions boxes as you change from Full Document Size to Minimum Image Area.

8. In almost all cases, Smoothing should be checked. If Smoothing is not checked, the edges of shapes will be jagged and gradients will exhibit serious banding.

9. For Color Depth, choose 24-bit color.

10. Click on OK and your bitmap image will be ready to export for high-resolution printing.

QuickTime 4 And Flash

QuickTime movies can be imported into Flash 4 for the purpose of adding a Flash layer to the QuickTime animation and exported back out in the QuickTime 4 movie format (mov). See Figure 12.12. You cannot export a QuickTime movie or any other movie format to the Flash SWF format. If you want a movie segment in Flash, it would have to be imported as a series of bitmap images and displayed frame by frame. Currently, only Flash 3 content can be incorporated in QuickTime 4.

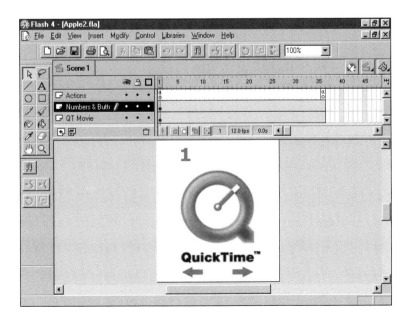

Figure 12.12
QuickTime in Flash.

We will be discussing QuickTime 4 in this section, but for those of you on Macintosh systems, there is another movie option—QuickTime Video—which is a non-interactive format. QuickTime Video exports your movie in QuickTime 3 format with all images converted to raster (bitmap) images.

When a QuickTime movie is imported into Flash, the movie file does not become part of the Flash file. When the QuickTime file is created, Flash puts the Flash movie on one track and puts any QuickTime movies on separate tracks. The Flash movie component in the QuickTime file will play as it does in the Flash Player, retaining all of its interactive features. You can scale, rotate, and animate a QuickTime movie in Flash, and the results will be seen in the exported QuickTime 4 file.

The QuickTime movie can be exported (File|Export Movie) or published (File|Publish) from Flash to the QuickTime MOV format. The Publish and Export QuickTime options are the same; they are discussed in Chapter 13.

Here are some important things to consider when you're adding Flash to QuickTime 4:

- You must have QuickTime 4 or later installed to import and Publish QuickTime 4 movies with Flash 4.

- QuickTime movies are not displayed in Test Movie mode, although you can see them work in the authoring environment by using the Play Movie command.

- QuickTime movies are not exported to Flash SWF files. A QuickTime movie is only in Flash 4 to add Flash content to the QuickTime movie and to be re-exported as a QuickTime-format movie (MOV) or to be used for timing in preparing Flash content to be used with QuickTime.

- Movies loaded by the Load Movie command will not work in the QuickTime movie.

- QuickTime 4 has strict time management, meaning that Flash frames will be dropped to keep the QuickTime movie on schedule. To prevent the dropping of frames, you can set the playback mode of the movie to Play Every Frame.

In the following exercise, we will import a QuickTime movie into Flash, add Play and Stop buttons, and then publish the file as a QuickTime 4 movie. Make sure you have QuickTime 4 installed on your computer before you start this exercise.

1. Create a new Flash file by choosing File|New.

2. Import sample.mov from the CD, or import another QuickTime movie if you prefer.

3. If QuickTime 4 is installed properly, you will see the first frame of the movie. Now add empty frames after the keyframe until you see an X'ed-out box instead of the movie image. Back up until you no longer see the X'ed-out box; then delete the X'ed-out frames. There will be 36 frames for sample.mov.

4. Add a new layer. Then add a button by choosing Libraries|Buttons| Arrow Buttons and dragging a Right Arrow button onto the stage. You can select a different button or create a new one if you like.

5. Copy the button. (Select the button and choose Edit|Copy.)

6. Move the new copy into place, and reverse it with Modify|Transform|Flip Horizontal.

7. Double-click on the button on the right side and select the Actions tab of the button's Instance Properties dialog box. (If double-clicking on the button does not bring up the dialog box, choose Control|Enable Buttons to deselect the button actions.)

8. Choose the plus (+) button in the upper-left corner of the dialog box, and select Play from the list. You should have:

```
On (Release)
        Play
    End On
```

9. Double-click on the left button, and select the Actions tab. Choose the plus (+) button in the upper-left corner of the dialog box, and select Stop from the list. You should have:

```
On (Release)
        Stop
    End On
```

10. Add another layer. Double-click on frame one, and select the Actions tab. Choose the plus (+) button, and select Stop from the list.

    You should have:

```
Stop
```

11. Go to the last frame (see Figure 12.13). Add a keyframe (or blank keyframe) by double-clicking on the frame and selecting the Actions tab. Choose the plus (+) button, and select Stop from the list. You should have:

```
Stop
```

Figure 12.13
Frame 17 in Flash authoring.

12. Now label your layers "Actions," "Buttons," and "QT Movie," or something similar.

13. Choose File|Publish Settings, and select the Formats tab.

14. Select QuickTime Movie.

15. Select the QuickTime tab, and look at some of your options. (You don't need to select any now.)

16. Choose Publish.

17. Choose Publish Preview to see your new movie in QuickTime (see Figure 12.14).

18. Save your movie.

You should now have a completed QuickTime movie with functioning (Flash) buttons to Play and Stop your movie.

Figure 12.14
Completed QuickTime 4 movie with Flash included.

Moving On

In the next chapter, we will be exploring the new Publish feature of Flash. Publish allows both multiple publishing of some file formats as well as the ability to create your HTML pages for your Flash movie.

13 PUBLISH AND HTML

Flash's Publish feature has two main purposes: exporting a complete set of files all at once; and using prepared templates to create your HTML pages. This chapter explains how to use Publish and how to customize or create your own templates. This chapter also describes the options for playing Flash in HTML and explains how to make sure that your server is ready for Flash.

JOHN CROTEAU

Publish allows you to export more than one file type at a time; if you need to create a single graphics file, Publish and Export will do the job equally well. But if you need to create more than one file format at a time, Publish is the obvious choice. And if you need to publish HTML pages for the Web, templates will make your life easier. With a little preparation and modification of existing templates, you will have your own customized HTML page (or pages) prepared and ready for you right from Flash. Anything you normally put in your HTML pages can be added to your templates. Use different page layouts and detection schemes simply by choosing different templates. Templates make publishing HTML pages fast, error free, and more complete—all straight from Flash.

Using The New Publish Feature

The Publish command creates an HTML document based on a template file that uses parameters that you have specified in the Publish Settings dialog box. If you are not familiar with HTML, you can use one of the prepared templates that comes with Flash or get other templates from Macromedia or other sites on the Web. A list of sites with Publish templates is available at the Flash Tech Resource site at **www.FlashCentral.com/Tech**.

What Happened To Aftershock?

Publish replaces Aftershock and is much more flexible and useful than Aftershock, which was a utility that came as an accessory with Flash 3. Aftershock made creating HTML pages for Flash easier. To adapt to new versions of browsers and Flash, you previously had to modify the code on each Aftershock page. Now you can change just your template(s), and all your subsequent Published pages will include those changes.

Flash 4 also uses a different method to identify which frames are used in static images, animated images, and image maps instead of the GIF-alternate image frame and the frame range for animated GIFs requested by Flash 3's Aftershock. To mark frames, you place special labels in the desired frames on Flash's Timeline. The labels are as follows:

- #Static marks frames for static images.

- #First and #Last mark the range of frames for an animated graphic.

- #Map marks the frame to be used with an image map.

Macromedia didn't supply a Java Publish template, but you can get it from other sources. The FlashBible.com member's area has a Java template as well as many others; you can download as many of them as you like at **www.FlashBible.com/members**.

Note: To place one of these special labels, follow the same procedure as with any Label addition. Go to the frame where you want to add the marker and bring up the Frame Properties dialog box (double-click on the frame) and select the Label tab, then enter the special code such as #Static to mark the frame to be used for a still image export to a graphics format such as GIF.

Publish Preview

Publish Preview is very useful for opening up a browser to preview your images, for launching the QuickTime movie player, and for playing your Projector—all without having to leave Flash or using the menu to open your file.

Using Publish Settings To Select File Formats

Before you publish any files from Flash, you first need to select the file formats in which you want to publish. You do this in the Publish Settings dialog box:

1. Choose File|Publish Settings to open the Publish Settings dialog box, as shown in Figure 13.1.

2. On the Formats tab, select the file formats that you'll need for the current project. When you select a format, a tab will appear and you will have a tab for each format you will publish. Each type of file has settings that may (or may not) need to be adjusted for your movie, so select those tabs and see if any changes are necessary.

3. When you're done adjusting settings, click on OK.

Now when you choose the File|Publish command, Flash will automatically produce all the files you have selected.

To update your published files, you just choose File|Publish again, and all your selected files will be updated with that single click. The Publish settings you specify are saved with the Flash FLA working file, so each file can have its own settings. When you use Publish again, you will export the same file formats using the same parameter settings set before.

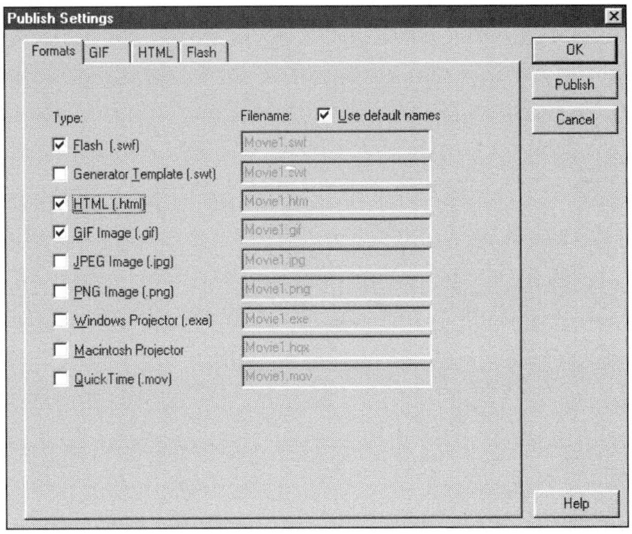

Figure 13.1
Selecting file formats for publishing output.

Flash Publish Settings

This section describes the various options used when publishing a Flash movie, as shown in Figure 13.2. They are a diverse set of parameters that make basic changes to the Flash SWF file itself.

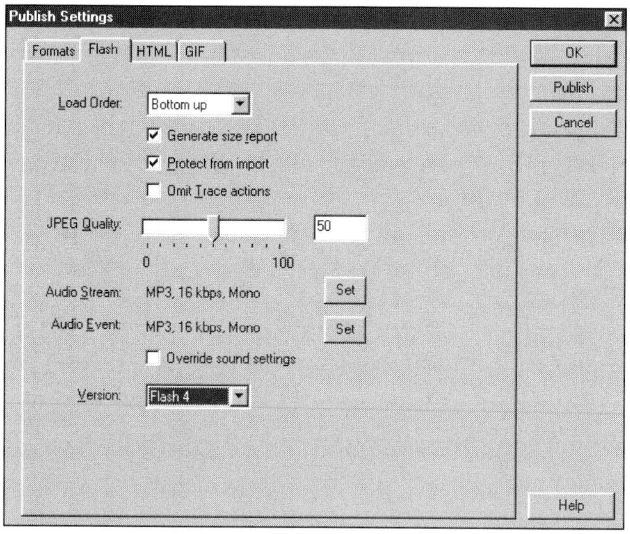

Figure 13.2
The Flash tab of the Publish Settings dialog box.

Load Order

The Load Order—either Bottom Up or Top Down—determines the visual loading order of a movie's first frame. Flash uses this option to determine what will appear first when the movie downloads. If you select Bottom Up, objects on the lowest layer of your Flash movie will appear first, then—layer by layer—additional layers will be displayed until the top layer is displayed. Load Order affects only the first frame of the movie. In all frames except frame one, the images appear together and are not layered in.

Generate Size Report

Check this option to create a text file that shows how many bytes are used by the various parts of your movie. The report has the same name as the exported SWF movie, but with a .txt extension.

Protect From Import

This option prevents your Flash SWF movie from being imported into your or anyone else's Flash editor.

Omit Trace Actions

This option turns off Trace Actions in the current movie. Trace is an option for tracing variables and troubleshooting scripting problems, discussed in depth in Chapter 9.

JPEG Quality

This option sets the amount of JPEG compression for bitmaps that use this default setting for Flash's internal JPEG compression. This setting is used for bitmap images only if Photo (JPEG) Compression and Use Document Default Quality are both selected. To get to these JPEG settings, select the Library and the bitmap image you desire, then select Options|Properties|Compression| Photo (JPEG). The JPEG Quality settings in Publish (or Export) are never used for images that were imported as JPEG files when the files are published in Flash 4 format. This is because the Library settings for individual images take precedence over the settings in Publish (and Export) and JPEG images are exported with their imported compression as default. If you turn off the defauld JPEG compression int the Library, this will open up the individual compression settings, which take precedence over the sttings in Publish and Export.

Higher quality produces larger files, while lower quality produces smaller files. The highest quality setting—100—provides the best JPEG picture quality with the lowest amount of compression applied, but the picture will not be lossless. To get a better picture, you must go to the Library and change the type of compression to lossless (PNG/GIF) for that particular image. This lossless compression will often result in a much larger file size.

Audio Stream And Audio Event

These options specify the default rate and compression for exported stream and event sounds. These settings are used only when you have not specified settings for the individual sounds in the Sound Properties dialog box, or when the Override Sound Settings option in the Publish Settings dialog box has been turned on.

Override Sound Settings

If you check this option, you will use the settings in this dialog box instead of those defined in the individual Sound Properties dialog boxes. Using this option can make it easy to create two versions of Flash SWF files: one with higher fidelity and a larger file size, and the other with lower audio quality and a smaller file size.

Version

This option specifies the version of Flash that will be used when the file is published in Flash format. New Flash 4 features will not work if the movie is published as an earlier version.

Generator Template Settings

Any Flash movie can be adapted for use as a Generator template (SWT) file. Generator is a server side application that can be used to supply Flash, text, and even other graphics based on easy to update templates. If you have purchased Generator and have the Flash authoring extensions for Generator installed, you will be able to create the SWT files needed for dynamic generation of files with Generator. The following options are the ones you will find with Generator 2. They are also shown in Figure 13.3.

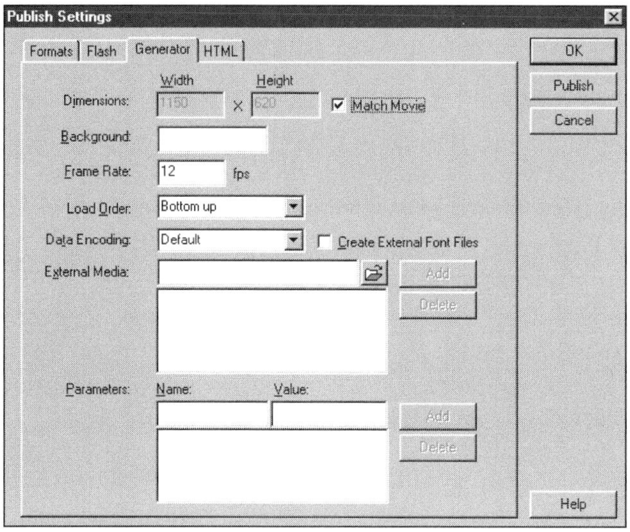

Figure 13.3
The Generator tab of the Publish Settings dialog box.

Dimensions

Here you set the Height and Width parameters for the movie. If Match Movie is selected, the size of the Flash movie will be used for the dimensions.

Background

Use this option to set a background color for Flash. This value overrides the background color set with the Modify|Movies command. Since Flash is normally not transparent, this setting will set the background color you will see in a Flash movie. You can set the value for this option in three ways:

- Use a Web-safe color name—for example, red, blue, green, or black.

- Use a Web hexadecimal value that starts with #—for example, #FFFF33.

- Use a regular hexadecimal value.

Frame Rate

This option sets the frame rate in frames per second (fps). It will override the setting chosen with the Modify|Movie command.

Load Order

The Load Order—either Bottom Up or Top Down—determines the visual loading order of a movie's first frame. Flash uses this option to determine what will appear first when the movie downloads. Load Order affects only the first frame of the movie.

Data Encoding

To communicate between Generator and an external source of data (such as a database), you must set Generator to the correct format so it can understand the data being delivered to it. This option provides the following choices for encoding of the data sources.

- Default

- ASCII

- UTF8

- SJIS

- EUC_JP

- MacRoman

Create External Font Files
If this option is selected, Generator will create font files, which will be cached and will improve performance when multiple fonts are used.

External Media
To use this option, you specify an external Generator SWT template that contains the symbols you want to use in this template. This will add the library from the specified file into the current file, allowing you to access symbols in that file as though they were in the current file. If the same symbol name is used in both the external template file and the current file, the external template's symbol will be used.

Parameters
Use parameters to manually define your variables. Generator displays content (graphics and text) based on templates if you do not supply values for your variables. Generator will be unable to display the results properly. Therefore, this option is especially useful when you're testing templates locally during development. Type the name of the variable in the Name box, and type its corresponding value in the Value box.

HTML Publish Settings
For a Flash movie to be played properly in a Web browser, it should be played from within an HTML document. Publish can generate this needed HTML document automatically.

Various settings affect the HTML parameters of your Flash movie, and you can change these settings on the HTML tab of the Publish Settings dialog box, as shown in Figure 13.4. These changes will be reflected in your published HTML page, depending on the HTML template that you select. You can use the templates supplied with Flash, but you'll probably want to modify or create templates that will be customized to suit your needs. See "Creating And Modifying HTML Templates" later in this chapter.

In the HTML page, two complete sets of parameters are usually needed to provide instructions for the different browsers. This creates two places for most parameters to be inserted in the HTML code. One set of parameters is contained in the OBJECT tag, for use with the ActiveX control and Windows

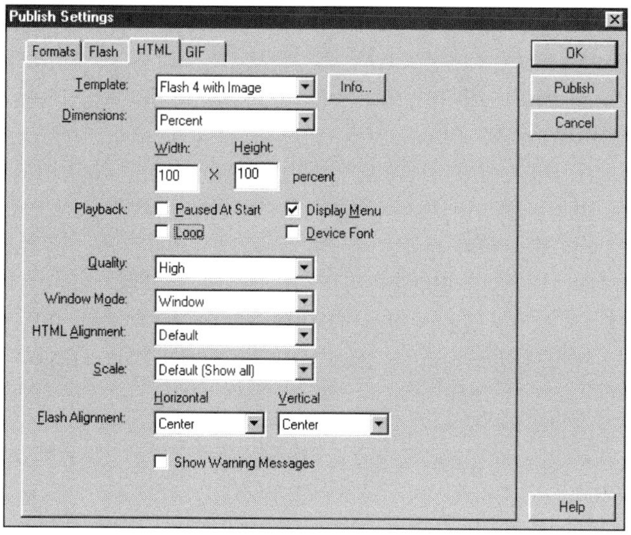

Figure 13.4

The HTML tab of the Publish Settings dialog box.

versions of Internet Explorer. Other browsers use the other set of parameters found in the EMBED tag. Publish can insert the chosen parameters in the OBJECT and EMBED sections of the template where applicable.

Template

Use this setting to specify which of the installed templates you want to use. All templates in the HTML folder will appear in the list, so be sure to remove backups from the folder to prevent duplicates and confusion. For a more complete description of the template, click on the Info button on the right. The original files supplied with Flash all have .html extensions. If you want your files to have different extensions, simply name or rename the template files with the appropriate extensions. For example, if your FLA file is Moses and you select BibleStandard, which is the name for the template file bible.asp, an ASP file named Moses.asp will be created instead of a file with an .html extension.

Dimensions

Here you set the dimension option to determine if the display will be a fixed size (Pixels or Match Movie) or scaled to fit the available browser window (Percent). If Pixels is selected, the Height and Width parameters for the movie can be set to a specific size. Here are the specifics:

- Pixels allows you to set the exact pixel size for the displayed height and width of the Flash movie in the browser. These settings will override the movie pixel dimension and do not need to be the same size as the stage in the authoring environment. Flash will scale the movie to fit the new dimensions you have set.

- Percent sets the movie dimensions relative to the browser window. Percentages of 100 for Height and Width are commonly used for scalable windows. If Percent is chosen, then only the resulting aspect ratio (proportion of height to width) matters in determining how Flash will fill a browser window.

- Match Movie sets the dimensions to the same stage size that was used while you were authoring your Flash movie.

Playback

There are four Playback options: Paused At Start; Loop; Display Menu; and Device Font.

- Paused At Start sets the PLAY parameters to FALSE, so the movie will start paused in frame 1 until play is initiated. Paused At Start is off by default.

- Loop sets the LOOP parameters to TRUE, so when the movie reaches the last frame, the movie begins playing again from frame 1. Loop is on by default.

- Display Menu sets the MENU parameters to TRUE, and makes a menu available to users when they right-click (Windows) or Command-click (Macintosh) on the movie. Display Menu is on by default.

    If you deselect the Display Menu option, then only the About Flash option will be available when the user right-clicks (Windows) or Cmd+clicks (Mac) in the Flash player. Flash provides no way to remove the About Flash option. However, a program named Projector Launcher (available at **www.mories.com/flashed.shtml**) can remove the About Flash option for Windows versions of Flash Projectors.

- Device Font (Windows only) sets the DEVICEFONT parameter to TRUE, so the user's computer will substitute (anti-aliased) system fonts only if the exact fonts are installed on the user's system. Device Font is off by default, and this feature's use is rarely recommended for use on the Internet. Some designers whose presentations are for a fixed community (such as those across an intranet) use devicefont because it allows for sharper font displays. This is not always the case; setting devicefont can give wide variations in display on various systems. In any case, only use devicefont if all the users have the same fonts (or font shapes are supplied) and you have your Flash file displayed at a fixed size rather than scaled to fit a window.

Quality

There are five Quality options: Low, AutoLow, AutoHigh, High, and Best.

- Low gives priority to playback speed over appearance. Anti-aliasing is not used.

- AutoLow gives speed priority at first, but switches to high quality whenever possible. Playback begins with anti-aliasing turned off; then when the processor can handle it, anti-aliasing is used.

- AutoHigh gives playback speed and appearance equal priority at first, but switches to low quality to maintain playback speed if necessary. Playback begins with anti-aliasing turned on, but if the actual frame rate drops below the specified frame rate, then anti-aliasing is turned off to improve playback speed.

- High gives priority to appearance over playback speed, and anti-aliasing is always used. If a movie does not contain animation, bitmaps will be smoothed; but if there is animation, bitmaps will not be smoothed. High is the most common setting and is now the default setting for Quality in Flash 4.

- Best provides the highest display quality. Everything is anti-aliased, and all bitmaps are smoothed. Best has been available for use in most versions of Flash, but was not properly documented before. You can use Best (if desired) in Flash 2, 3, or 4.

Window Mode

The Window Mode option is used only with Windows versions of Internet Explorer 4 and later (so far). In browsers that do not support the WMODE parameter, Flash plays in a WINDOW mode despite the setting. Window Mode has three options:

- Window sets the WMODE parameter value to WINDOW and plays a Flash Player movie in its own rectangular browser window. This setting generally provides the best animation performance.

- Opaque Windowless sets the WMODE parameter value to OPAQUE. With this setting, elements behind Flash movies do not show through.

- Transparent Windowless sets the WMODE parameter to TRANSPARENT. The background of the HTML page on which the movie is embedded will show through all of the transparent areas of the movie.

HTML Alignment (Align)

The Default option centers the movie in the browser window and crops the edges if the browser window is smaller than the movie.

The Left, Right, Top, and Bottom options align the movie along the specified edge of the browser window and crops the other three sides if necessary.

Scale

There are three Scale options: Default (Show All), No Border, and Exact Fit.

- Default (Show All) displays the entire movie in the specified area while maintaining the original aspect ratio of the movie. No aspect-ratio distortion occurs, but borders may appear on the movie. Where they occur depends on the aspect-ratio fit between the movie and the browser window it will fit into and on the Flash Alignment (SAlign) setting.

- No Border scales the movie to fill the browser window while maintaining the original aspect ratio of the movie. No aspect-ratio distortion will occur, but portions of the movie might be cropped.

- Exact Fit makes the entire movie visible in the specified area. No attempt is made to preserve the original aspect ratio. Unless there is a perfect aspect-ratio match between the window and the Flash movie, the movie will be stretched to fit either horizontally or vertically.

Flash Alignment

Here you set the SALIGN parameters. Two pop-up menus (Horizontal and Vertical) determine how a movie is placed within the movie window and how it will be cropped to fit that window if necessary.

- Choose Left, Center, or Right from the Horizontal pop-up menu.

- Choose Top, Center, or Bottom from the Vertical pop-up menu.

Show Warning Messages

If this option is selected, Flash will display error messages warning of probable conflicts in tag settings.

GIF Publish Settings

When you export an image, Flash exports the first frame in the movie unless you mark a different keyframe for export by entering the frame label #Static in a frame on the movie's Timeline.

When you create an image map, Flash uses the buttons in the last frame of the movie unless you place the frame label #Map in the keyframe that you want to use to create the image map.

When you create an animated GIF, Flash exports all the frames in the current movie unless you specify a range of frames for export by entering the frame labels #First and #Last in the appropriate keyframes. Flash can create animated GIFs (GIF89a), but optimizes them, storing only frame-to-frame changes.

See the GIF tab in the Publish Settings dialog box, in Figure 13.5.

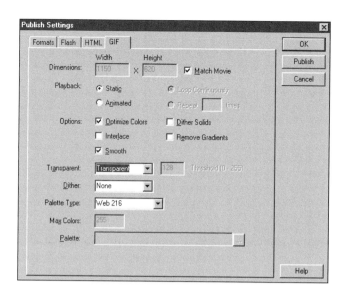

Figure 13.5
The GIF tab of the Publish Settings dialog box.

Dimensions

If Match Movie is not selected, you can use the Width and Height fields to enter a size—in pixels—for the exported bitmap image. The image will maintain its aspect ratio within the GIF canvas you define. If an empty canvas is created to maintain the aspect ratio, then the image will be centered (either horizontally or vertically) within that extra space.

If Match Movie is selected, the entries in the Width and Height fields cannot be edited, and Flash creates a GIF file the same size as the movie.

Playback

Either click on Static to export a still (single-frame) image, or click on Animated to export an animated GIF. If you choose Animated, then either select Loop Continuously or enter the number of times a loop should Repeat.

Options

The Options section of the GIF tab contains five choices:

• Optimize Colors removes unused colors from the GIF color table.

• Interlace makes the exported GIF appear in a browser incrementally as it downloads. An interlaced GIF allows the user to see a low-resolution version of the basic graphic content before the file has completely downloaded. An interlaced GIF might download faster over a slow network connection.

• Smooth enables anti-aliasing in the exported bitmap. Smoothing generally produces a higher-quality bitmapped image.

• Dither Solids dithers solid colors as well as gradients. Dithering is a technique that uses small dots of different colors in combination to approximate a color from a mixture of other colors when the required color is not available.

Note: Do not use Interlace with an animated GIF.

- Remove Gradients converts all gradient fills in the movie to solid colors, using the first color in that gradient. Gradients usually increase the size of a GIF and often are of poor quality. Choose the first color of your gradient carefully to prevent unexpected results when you're using this option. This setting is turned off by default.

Transparent

Choose one of these three settings:

- Opaque

- Transparent

- Alpha—Type an alpha threshold value between 0 and 255. In the GIF, values below that threshold value will be completely transparent (invisible). Colors above the threshold value will be left intact.

Dither

Dithering uses a mixture of pixels with similar colors to simulate colors not available in the current palette. Dithering can produce good pictures from smaller color tables, resulting in satisfactory pictures and smaller file sizes. With dithering off, Flash replaces a color not in the basic color table with the closest solid color from the color table; this method usually produces the smallest file sizes. When you're deciding whether or not to use dithering, compare the byte cost to the picture quality. Dithering settings are:

- None disables dithering.

- Ordered provides good image quality and the smallest increase in file size.

- Diffusion provides the best image quality but also increases file size and processing time more than Ordered dithering does. Diffusion also works with the 216-color Web-safe palette.

Palette Type

The Palette Type option provides four choices: Web 216, Adaptive, Web Snap Adaptive, and Custom.

- Web 216 uses the standard 216-color Web-safe palette. This palette provides good image quality and the fastest processing on the server.

- Adaptive creates a unique color table for the particular GIF. This palette type creates the most accurate color for the image, but the resulting file size is larger than one created with the Web 216 palette. To reduce the size of a GIF created with an adaptive palette, use the Max Colors options to decrease the number of colors in the palette.

- Web Snap Adaptive is the same as the Adaptive palette option except that it converts colors close to the Web 216 colors to those Web-safe colors. This setting produces better color for the image when it's viewed on a 256-color system.

- Custom lets you define your own palette that you have optimized for the current image. This setting provides the same processing speed as the Web 216 palette. Flash supports palettes saved in the ACT format used by Fireworks as well as its in own CLR format. You can also import a palette from a GIF file.

Max Colors

This option sets the maximum number of colors that can be used in the GIF image. Choosing a smaller number of colors may make a smaller file, but may also degrade or change the image because fewer colors are available to construct the image. This option is available only for Adaptive or Web Snap Adaptive palette types.

JPEG Publish Settings

JPEG images are highly compressed, lossy, and saved as 24-bit color bitmaps.

Flash exports the first frame of your movie as a JPEG file unless you have marked a different frame with the label #Static. See Figure 13.6.

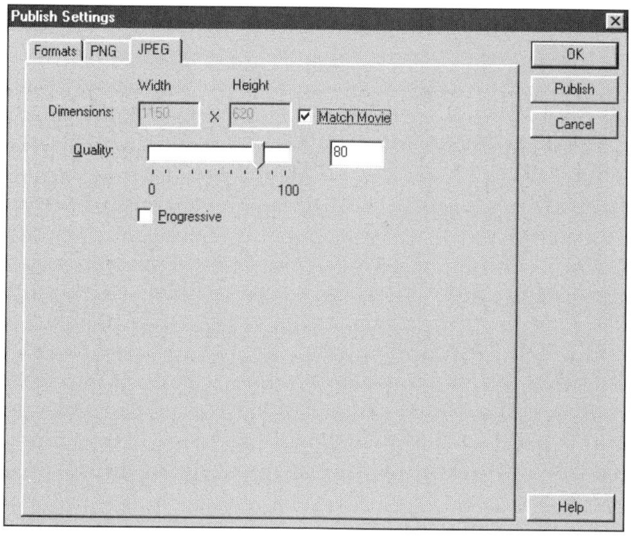

Figure 13.6
The JPEG tab of the Publish Settings dialog box.

Dimensions

If Match Movie is not selected, you can use the Width and Height fields to enter a size, in pixels, for the exported bitmap image. These entries don't seem to matter, however, because a JPEG file is created at the same size as the movie.

If Match Movie is selected, the entries in the Width and Height fields cannot be edited, and Flash creates a JPEG file the same size as the movie.

Quality

This option sets the amount of JPEG compression. The highest quality, 100, provides the best JPEG picture quality with the lowest amount of compression applied, but the picture will still not be lossless.

Progressive

If this option is selected, a progressive JPEG image will be created.

In both regular and progressive JPEG compression, the image is processed in 8×8 blocks of pixels, block by block from left to right, and from top to bottom. In a regular JPEG file, all of the data for each of the blocks is stored and displayed immediately. In a progressive JPEG file, only a portion of the data for each block is available on each pass (scan). Each additional pass adds more detail until the last pass, when the complete picture detail is available. Thus, the image goes from fuzzy to clear as each pass is decompressed and displayed.

PNG Publish Settings

PNG files can be created in three basic formats: 8-bit indexed color (similar to GIF), 24-bit true color (similar to BMP), and 32-bit (24-bit with an 8-bit alpha channel). See Figure 13.7.

Flash exports the first frame of your movie as a PNG file unless you mark a different frame with the label #Static.

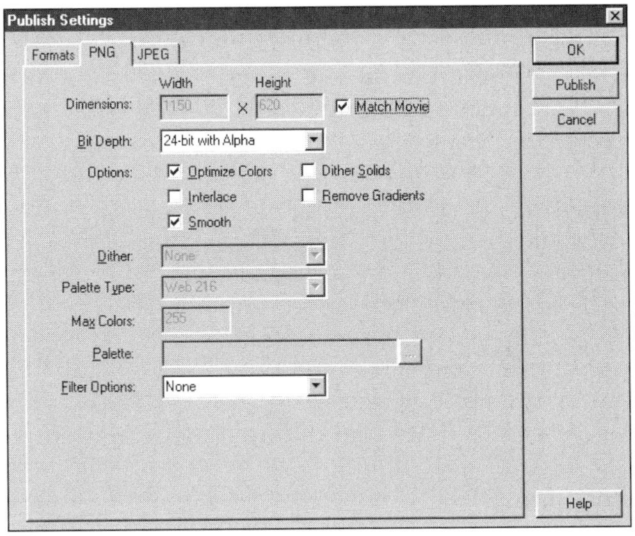

Figure 13.7
The PNG tab of the Publish Settings dialog box.

Dimensions

If Match Movie is not selected, you can use the Width and Height fields to enter a size, in pixels, for the exported bitmap image. The image will maintain its aspect ratio within the PNG canvas you define. If empty canvas borders are created to maintain the aspect ratio, then the image will be centered (either horizontally or vertically) within that extra space.

If Match Movie is selected, the entries in the Width and Height fields cannot be edited, and Flash creates a PNG file the same size as the movie.

Bit Depth

Your options here are:

- 8-bit indexed color (without transparency)

- 24-bit true color

- 24-bit with Alpha (true color with 8-bit alpha channel)

When you're selecting an option here, remember that higher bit-depth formats create larger files.

Options

Your choices here are:

- Optimize

- Interlace

- Smooth

- Dither Solids

- Remove Gradients

Contrary to the Flash documentation, there is no checkbox or other way to select the Transparent option for the 8-bit indexed mode of PNG. Therefore, if you need an indexed transparency for a PNG file, you will have to set it in another program, such as Fireworks or ImageReady.

For more details, see "Options" in the "GIF Publish Settings" section of this chapter.

Dither

Dithering settings are available only for 8-bit files:

- None disables dithering.

- Ordered provides good image quality and the smallest increase in file size.

- Diffusion provides the best image quality but also increases file size and processing time more than Ordered dithering does. Diffusion also works with the 216-color Web-safe palette.

For more details, see "Dither" in the "GIF Publish Settings" section of this chapter.

Palette Type

The Palette Type option, which is available only for 8-bit images, provides four choices:

- Web 216

- Adaptive

- Web Snap Adaptive

- Custom

For more details, see "Palette Type" in the "GIF Publish Settings" section of this chapter.

Max Colors

This option, available only for 8-bit images, sets the maximum number of colors that can be used in the PNG image. Choosing a smaller number of colors may make a smaller file, but may also degrade or change the image because fewer colors are available to construct the image. This option is available only for Adaptive or Web Snap Adaptive palette types.

Filter Options

This setting specifies the filtering method used in creating the PNG file. PNG filtering rearranges the bytes in an image before compression in order to optimize the compression. Filtering generally works best for true-color images and is not recommended for 256-color (8-bit) images. Filter options are:

- *None (Filter type 0)*—Provides no filtering.

- *Sub (Filter type 1)*—Transmits the difference between each byte and the value of the corresponding byte of the prior pixel.

- *Up (Filter type 2)*—Transmits the difference between each byte and the value of the corresponding byte of the pixel immediately above the current pixel.

- *Average (Filter type 3)*—Uses the average of the two neighboring pixels (left and above) to predict the value of a pixel.

- *Paeth (Filter type 4)*—Computes a simple linear function of the three neighboring pixels (left, above, upper left), and then chooses the closest of the three as a predictor.

- *Adaptive*—Undocumented option.

QuickTime Publish Settings

When you publish in the QuickTime file format in Flash, movies are created in the QuickTime 4 format and not in Flash SWF format. When Flash creates a QuickTime file, it puts the Flash movie on one track and puts any QuickTime movies on separate tracks. The Flash movie component in the QuickTime 4 file plays (Flash 3 content) as it does in the Flash Player, retaining all of its interactive features. Hopefully by the time the book comes out, Quicktime 4 will also support new Flash 4 content as well. See Figure 13.8.

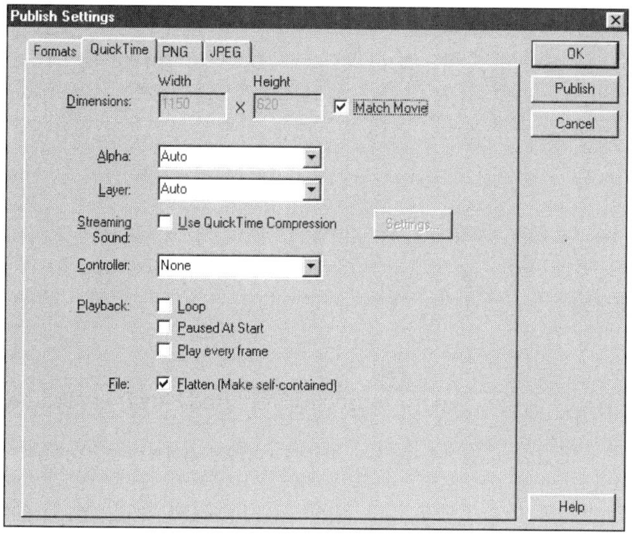

Figure 13.8
The QuickTime tab of the Publish Settings dialog box.

Dimensions

This option sets the size of the exported QuickTime movie to the number of pixels you enter in the Width and Height fields. If you select Match Movie, the entries in the Width and Height fields have no effect, and Flash makes the new QuickTime movie the same size as the Flash movie.

Alpha

This setting determines the alpha (transparency) mode of the Flash track in the QuickTime movie. Note that this setting does not affect any alpha settings within the Flash movie itself. The choices are as follows:

• Alpha Transparent makes the Flash track transparent. Any content in tracks behind the Flash track is visible.

• Copy makes the Flash track opaque. All content in tracks behind the Flash track is visible.

• Auto makes the Flash track transparent if it is on top of any other tracks, but makes it opaque if it is the bottom track or the only track in the movie.

Layer

This setting defines where the Flash track will be placed in the QuickTime movie. The choices are as follows:

• Top always places the Flash track on top of other tracks in the QuickTime movie.

• Bottom always places the Flash track behind other tracks.

• Auto places the Flash track in front of other tracks if there are Flash objects in front of video objects within the Flash movie. Otherwise, it places the Flash movie behind all other tracks.

Streaming Sound

Selecting this option makes Flash export all of the streaming audio in the Flash movie to a QuickTime soundtrack. It recompresses the audio using the standard QuickTime audio settings. Click on the Settings button to change these options. See the QuickTime documentation for a description.

Controller

This setting specifies the type of QuickTime controller used to play the exported movie. The choices are None, Standard, and QuickTime VR.

Playback

There are three Playback options: Loop, Paused At Start, and Play Every Frame.

- Loop determines whether or not the QuickTime movie loops continuously.

- Paused At Start determines whether or not the QuickTime movie starts automatically when it is opened.

- Play Every Frame makes QuickTime show every frame of the movie without skipping frames to maintain timing. When this option is set in a QuickTime movie, sound is not played.

Flatten (Make Self-Contained)

This option combines the Flash content and imported video content into the new QuickTime movie. When this option is not selected, the new QuickTime movie links to the imported files externally, so these files must be present for the movie to work properly. If the Flash file is external, the browser would have to have both the Flash and Quicktime plug-ins.

Creating Projectors

Use Publish to create projectors for both Window and Macintosh systems. There are no settings to specify for creating projectors. Just select Windows Projector or Macintosh Projector (or both) on the Formats tab of the Publish Settings dialog box as shown in Figure 13.9.

Although you can create a Macintosh projector using the Windows versions of Flash, you must convert the resulting file by using a file translator such as BinHex to make it appear as an application file in the Macintosh Finder. The Windows version of Flash names a Macintosh projector file with an .hqs extension.

Creating And Modifying HTML Templates

A Flash template is a text file that includes special variables. Each of these variables has three characters, including a beginning $ (dollar) sign. If you need to use a $ for another purpose in the document, you must use \$. For

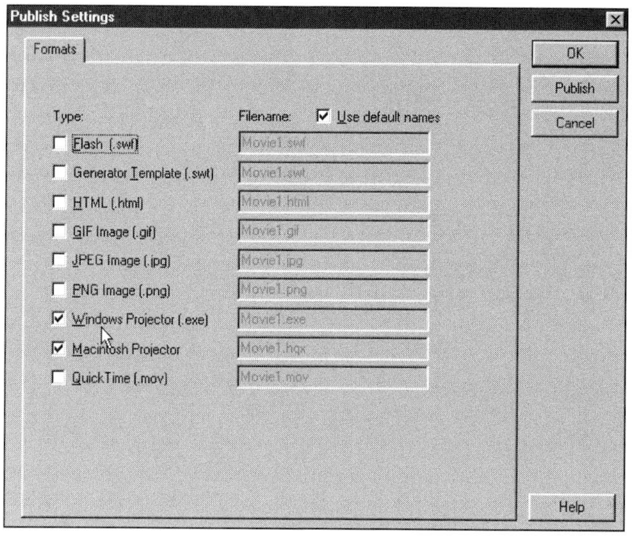

Figure 13.9

The Formats tab of the Publish Settings dialog box.

each variable in the template file, Flash substitutes the appropriate value from your Publish settings. Flash doesn't change anything in a template file except for the template variables, so a template file can include any desired HTML content, JavaScript, or even code for server-side applications such as ASP and Cold Fusion. A template does not have to include all of the template variables, and Flash won't insert values for any variables that are not used.

When you save a new file created from a template, Flash uses the file name of the Flash movie with the extension of the template. For example, if you selected a template named Viki (the template name for Viktoria.asp) for use with a Flash movie named light.swf, the resulting HTML file would be named light.asp.

When no template has been selected in the Publish Settings dialog box, Flash uses a template named default.html. If you choose not to use default.html as one of your templates, then select the file you want to use as default, and save the movie settings by using the Modify|Movie|Save Defaults command. Other current movie parameters will also be saved as default.

Flash template files have the following characteristics:

• A one-line title (following the tag $TT in the template file), which appears in the Template pop-up menu

• A description (enclosed between the $DS and $DF tags in the template file), which appears when you click on the Info button

• Additional template variables that have three characters (beginning with $), which specify where parameter values will be substituted when Flash generates the output file based on the template

- A file extension that is used for the extension of the new file generated from the template

In most cases, you will be able to use the shorthand template variables $PO (for OBJECT tags) and $PE (for EMBED tags) when creating your template movies. Up to 10 parameters will be automatically created for the EMBED and the OBJECT tags, making it pretty easy to create a template.

The following tags will always be generated with $PO and $PE:

```
MOVIE ($MO)
SRC   ($MO)
QUALITY ($QU)
BGCOLOR ($BG)
```

The following tags will be generated when non-default values have been selected in the Publish Settings dialog box:

```
PLAY ($PL)
LOOP ($LO)
MENU ($ME)
SCALE ($SC)
SALIGN ($SA)
WMODE ($WM)
DEVICEFONT ($DE)
```

Most template variables supply only the value of the variable and not the complete tag. The main exceptions are the shortcut template variables ($PE and $PO) and Image Map ($IM), which generate complete tags. The "variables" $TT, $DS, and $DF are not really variables but are markers that define where the Title ($TT) and Template Descriptions ($DS and $DF) are located. Two common template variables you may want to remove at times are Movie text ($MT) & ($MU). The usefulness of these tags that supply text (or URLs) from your Flash SWF files is limited by the fact that they can only retrieve text (or URLs) only from the main Timeline. Also, they can get text (or URLs) only from the main Timeline and not from Movie clips. This second limitation can be especially irritating if you use multiple copies of the same text (such as in tweens). I have seen cases in which the same short phrase was repeated in the HTML text more than 50 times though the actual text was on screen only once for a relatively short time.

Figure 13.10 shows a simple example of a template and the HTML page it will create.

Table 13.1 lists the template variables that are available in Flash. The parameters with a star in the $PE/$PO column are available when you're using the $PE and $PO shortcuts.

Template	HTML Page
$TTTest New	
$DS	
Use OBJECT and EMBED tags to display Flash.	
$DF	
<HTML>	<HTML>
<HEAD>	<HEAD>
<TITLE>Flash Bible - $TI</Title>	<TITLE>Flash Bible - Movie1</Title>
</HEAD>	</HEAD>
<BODY bgcolor="BG">	<BODY bgcolor="#FFFFFF">
<!--URLs used in the movie-->	<!--URLs used in the movie-->
$MU	<A HREF=www.FlashBible.com></A>
	<A HREF=www.FlashCentral.com></A>
<OBJECT WIDTH=$WI HEIGHT=$HE	<OBJECT WIDTH=100%l HEIGHT=100%
&PO>	<PARAM NAME=movieVALUE="Movei1.swf">
	<PARAM NAME=quality VALUE=best>
	<PARAM NAME=bgcolor VALUE=#FFFFFF>
<EMBED WIDTH=$WI HEIGHT=$HE	<EMBED WIDTH=100% HEIGHT=100%
$PE>	src="Movie1.swf" quality=best bgcolor=#FFFFFF>
</EMBED>	</EMBED>
</OBJECT>	</OBJECT>
</BODY>	</BODY>
</HTML>	</HTML>

Figure 13.10

Example of a template and the HTML page it will create.

Table 13.1   Template variables available in Flash.

Parameter	Template Variable$PE/$PO		Template Variable (Movie1)
Template Title	$TT		Name in Selection box.
Template description start	$DS		Description that appears in Info box.
Template description finish	$DF		Description that appears in Info box.
WIDTH	$WI		In pixels or percent (%).
HEIGHT	$HE		In pixels or percent (%).
SRC	$MO	*	Movie name for EMBED tag—"Movie1.swf".
MOVIE	$MO	*	Movie name for OBJECT tag—"Movie1.swf".
ALIGN	$HA		HTML alignment.
MENU	$ME	*	Default is True.
LOOP	$LO	*	Default is True.
Parameters for OBJECT tag	$PO		Includes complete tags for NAME, QUALITY, BGCOLOR, and many others when not default.
Parameters for EMBED tag	$PE		Includes complete tags for SRC, QUALITY, BGCOLOR, and many others when not default.
PLAY	$PL	*	Default is True.
QUALITY	$QU	*	Play default is AutoHigh.
SCALE	$SC	*	Default is Show All.
SALIGN	$SA	*	Flash file alignment. Default is both centered.
WMODE	$WM	*	Window Mode for Win IE4 and later only—Default window.
DEVICEFONT	$DE	*	Default is False.
BGCOLOR	$BG	*	Background color—overrides setting in movie.
Movie text	$MT		Text from movie.

(continued)

Table 13.1 Template variables available in Flash *(continued)*.

Parameter	Template Variable$PE/$PO	Template Variable (Movie1)
Movie URL	$MU	URLs from movie.
Image width	$IW	
Image height	$IH	
Image map	$IM	Complete image map container with tags.
Image file name	$IS	"Movie1.gif"
Image usemap name	$IU	"#Movie1"
Flash file ID	$TI	ID used with FSCommand—Movie1.
QuickTime height	$QH	
QuickTime file name	$QN	
GIF width	$GW	
GIF height	$GH	
GIF file name	$GS	
JPEG width	$JW	
JPEG height	$JH	
JPEG file name	$JN	
PNG width	$PW	
PNG height	$PH	
PNG file name	$PN	
Generator variables OBJECT tag	$GV	
Generator variables EMBED tag	$GE	

The HTML Page And Flash

To display Flash content properly in a Web browser, you need to use an HTML page with the proper tags and parameters. The OBJECT tag is used for the versions of Microsoft Internet Explorer that use a 32-bit version of Windows (95, 98, 2000, and NT). Other browsers use the EMBED tag.

For the EMBED tag, all settings (such as HEIGHT, WIDTH, QUALITY, and LOOP) are attributes that appear inside the angle brackets (< >) of the opening EMBED tag as follows.

```
<EMBED SRC="movie.swf" WIDTH="1150" HEIGHT="620"  QUALITY="high"
PLUGINSPAGE="http://www.macromedia.com/shockwave/download/
index.cgi?
  P1_Prod_Version=ShockwaveFlash">
</EMBED>
```

For the OBJECT tag, four settings (HEIGHT, WIDTH, CLASSID, and CODEBASE) appear within the OBJECT opening tag. Other parameters appear in separate PARAM tags that include a NAME and a VALUE.

```
<OBJECT CLASSID="clsid:D27CDB6E-AE6D-11cf-96B8-444553540000"
WIDTH="1150" HEIGHT="620" CODEBASE="http://active.macromedia.com/
flash4/cabs/swflash.cab#
  version=4,0,0,0">
```

```
<PARAM NAME="MOVIE" VALUE="movie.swf">
<PARAM NAME="QUALITY" VALUE="high">
</OBJECT>
```

If you want to place both tags together on the same page, the EMBED opening and closing tags should be contained within the OBJECT opening and closing tags:

```
<OBJECT .....>
  <EMBED ......>
  </EMBED>
</OBJECT>
```

If you combine the above OBJECT and EMBED tags, you get the following:

```
<OBJECT CLASSID="clsid:D27CDB6E-AE6D-11cf-96B8-444553540000"
WIDTH="1150"
HEIGHT="620" CODEBASE="http://active.macromedia.com/flash4/cabs/
swflash.cab#version
  =4,0,0,0">
<PARAM NAME="MOVIE" VALUE="movie.swf">
<PARAM NAME="QUALITY" VALUE="high">
<EMBED SRC="movie.swf" WIDTH="1150" HEIGHT="620" QUALITY="high"
PLUGINSPAGE="http://www.macromedia.com/shockwave/download/
index.cgi?
  P1_Prod_Version=ShockwaveFlash">
</EMBED>
</OBJECT>
```

It is perfectly acceptable to use two pages to display Flash content. One page can be used only for Internet Explorer browsers (Windows platform) using the OBJECT tag for the Flash ActiveX control player. The other page can be used for all other browsers using the EMBED tag and the plug-in. To implement this, you need a page that would direct the user to the correct page based on the browser type. This can be done in JavaScript or on a server-side page.

Using separate pages solves an alignment problem that leaves a border at the top of some pages in IE 4.x browsers on the Macintosh.

The HTML Tags For Flash

The following list of HTML tag attributes and parameters will help you understand the HTML that Flash needs. This will help you create Publish templates or write your own HTML for inserting Flash movies. All items apply to both OBJECT and EMBED tags unless otherwise noted in the description. The value or sample value of the HTML tag is shown in bold.

MOVIE (OBJECT Only)

This parameter sets the file name of the movie to be loaded.

Template variable: $MO

Sample value: NameOfMovie.swf

CLASSID (OBJECT only)

This parameter sets the ActiveX control number that identifies Flash.

Value:
```
classid="clsid:D27CDB6E-AE6D-11cf-96B8-444553540000"
```

CODEBASE (OBJECT only)

This parameter specifies the location of the Flash Player ActiveX control so that Internet Explorer will automatically download the latest ActiveX control if the user's current version is not equal to or later than the required version number (4,0,0,0 in the example below).

Value:
```
codebase="http://active.macromedia.com/flash4/cabs/swflash.cab
  #version=4,0,0,0"
```

WMODE (OBJECT only)

This parameter allows use of the advanced DHTML features of transparency, absolute positioning, and layering that are available in Internet Explorer 4 and later. These features are not supported in any version of Netscape 4 or earlier.

Template variable: $WM

Values:

- *Window*—The movie is alone in its own window on a Web page. (Default.)

- *Opaque*—Everything behind the Flash movie is hidden.

- *Transparent*—The background of the HTML page shows through all the transparent portions of the movie.

SRC (EMBED only)

This parameter sets the file name of the movie to be loaded.

Template variable: $MO

Sample value: NameOfMovie.swf

PLUGINSPAGE (EMBED only)

This parameter specifies the location of the Flash plug-in download page.

Value:

```
http://www.macromedia.com/shockwave/download/index.cgi?
  P1_Prod_Version=ShockwaveFlash
```

SWLIVECONNECT (EMBED only)

This parameter forces Java to start in Netscape 4 and later. Java is required for FSCommand interactivity, and this parameter should be set to True when you're using FSCommand.

Values: True or False (False is default)

HEIGHT

This parameter sets the height of the movie in pixels or as a percentage of the browser window.

Template variable: $HE

WIDTH

This parameter sets the width of the movie in pixels or as a percentage of the browser window.

Template variable: $WI

ALIGN

This parameter aligns the movie along the appropriate edge of the browser window and crops the other three sides if necessary. Default is used if none of the other four parameters is used.

Template variable: $HA

Values:

- *Default*—Centers Flash in the browser window and crops the edges if the browser window is smaller than the movie.

- *Left*—Aligns the movie to the left side of the browser window.

- *Right*—Aligns the movie to the right side of the browser window.

- *Top*—Aligns the movie to the top of the browser window.

- *Bottom*—Aligns the movie to the bottom of the browser window.

With the variable, use L, R, T, or B as the values, unless you want to use Default, in which case, do not use this variable.

BASE

This parameter sets the base URL that is used to resolve all relative path statements inside the Flash Player movie.

BGCOLOR

This parameter sets the background color of the movie, overriding the background color set with the Modify|Movie command. This parameter does not affect the background color of the HTML page.

Template variable: $BG

Sample value: #RRGGBB (Web-type hexadecimal RGB value)

LOOP

When True, this parameter sets the movie to repeat indefinitely (if the movie reaches its last frame). This command is overridden in Flash with a simple Stop action in the last frame. False sets the movie to stop at the end of the movie unless an action causes it to continue.

Template variable: $LO

Values: True or False (True is default)

MENU

This parameter sets the menu that the viewer will get when right-clicking (Windows) or Command-clicking (Macintosh) in Flash. If MENU is set to False, the user will get only the About Flash option in the menu. If True, the full menu will be displayed.

Template variable: $ME

Values: True or False (True is default)

PLAY

This parameter sets the movie to start playing automatically.

Template variable: $PL

Values: True or False (True is default)

QUALITY

This parameter sets the level of anti-aliasing and bitmap smoothing that will be used when the Flash movie is played.

Template variable: $QU

Values:

- Low gives priority to playback speed over appearance. Anti-aliasing is not used.

- AutoLow gives speed priority at first, but switches to high quality whenever possible. Playback begins with anti-aliasing turned off; then when the processor can handle it, anti-aliasing is used.

- AutoHigh gives playback speed and appearance equal priority at first, but switches to low quality to maintain playback speed if necessary. Playback begins with anti-aliasing turned on, but if the actual frame rate drops below the specified frame rate, then anti-aliasing is turned off to improve playback speed. (AutoHigh was the default setting for the Flash 3 Player; the Flash Player now defaults to High.)

- High gives priority to appearance over playback speed, and anti-aliasing is always used. If a movie does not contain animation, bitmaps are smoothed; if there is animation, bitmaps are not smoothed. High is the most common setting and is now the default Quality setting for Flash 4.

- Best provides the highest display quality. Everything is anti-aliased, and all bitmaps are smoothed.

SALIGN

This parameter sets the position of a Flash movie within the area defined by the WIDTH and HEIGHT settings. Flash crops the other three sides (or two in a corner) as needed. If no parameter is set, the default is centered in the window.

Template variable: $SA

Values:

- *L*—Aligns the movie to the left side.
- *R*—Aligns the movie to the right side.
- *T*—Aligns the movie to the top.
- *B*—Aligns the movie to the bottom.
- *TR*—Aligns the movie to the top right corner.
- *TL*—Aligns the movie to the top left corner.
- *BR*—Aligns the movie to the bottom right corner.
- *BL*—Aligns the movie to the bottom left corner.

SCALE

This parameter specifies how the movie is scaled and whether the aspect ratio is maintained.

Template variable: $SC

Values:

- Show All (default) displays the entire movie in the specified area while maintaining the original aspect ratio of the movie. No aspect-ratio distortion occurs, but borders may appear on the movie. Where they occur depends on the aspect-ratio fit between the movie and the browser window it will fit into and on the Flash Alignment (SAlign) setting.

- No Border scales the movie to fill the browser window while maintaining the original aspect ratio of the movie. No aspect-ratio distortion will occur, but portions of the movie might be cropped.

- Exact Fit makes the entire movie visible in the specified area. No attempt is made to preserve the original aspect ratio. Unless there is a perfect aspect-ratio match between the window and the Flash movie, the movie will be stretched to fit either horizontally or vertically.

Preparing Your Web Server For Flash (Setting Up The MIME)

To make a Web server Flash-ready, you need only one thing. That is to make sure that the MIME is properly set for Flash. Before you make your Web site public, make sure that MIME is set correctly. Just seeing a Flash picture is not sufficient to verify that the MIME is set correctly. You must do one of two specific tests to ensure that the MIME is set so you can be sure that your site is displayed properly.

When your files are accessed from a Web server, the server must properly identify them as Flash files in order to deliver them properly and for the browser to display them correctly. If the MIME type is not set correctly, the browser might display error messages or a blank image or might even crash the browser.

To ensure that all visitors can see your movies, make sure the MIME is set for Flash on your server. The MIME types and suffixes must be exact. For Flash and Splash, they are:

- *application/x-shockwave-flash—.swf*

- *application/futuresplash—.spl*

If the MIME is not set for Flash, contact your Website administrator, Internet service provider, Web master, or IT department, and ask that the MIME type information for Flash be added.

If your site uses a Macintosh server, the following must also be set:

- *Action*—Binary

- *Type*—SWFL

- *Creator*—SWF2

TIME FOR MIME

MIME, which stands for Multi-purpose Internet Mail Extensions, was originally designed (as its name indicates) for email. The MIME standard is now used universally by Web servers to identify the files they are sending to browsers and in what format they should transfer data. The browser then uses this information to decode the information and identify the application to use to view the file.

More information on checking and setting the MIME is available at the Flash Tech Resource (**www.FlashCentral.com/Tech/Server/Index.htm**). Information includes how to check the MIME, a special set of files for testing the MIME quickly, and specific details on setting the MIME for many Web servers.

APPENDIX A
A VISUAL GUIDE
TO FLASH 4

This appendix provides a quick reference to the
essential features in Flash 4. If you're in a hurry to
find out how to use a particular feature, this is a
good place to look. This is also a good place to
discover the new features in Flash 4.

KEN MILBURN

Flash calls everything it does a movie, even if there's only one frame in the shape of an 8.5×11-inch page. Actually, movies can be as large as 40×40 inches (or 2880×2880 pixels). You can have as many frames in a movie as you like, and you can vary the rate at which they play (within limits, which we'll get to later). Within a movie, you can also have as many *scenes* (movies within a movie) as you like. All these frames and scenes are placed in the proper sequence along a *Timeline*. The structure of a movie's frames can be complex, and an individual frame can have several components: *objects*, *groups*, *text*, *overlays*, *symbols*, and *backgrounds*.

This appendix will show you how all these pieces function together to help make your work in Flash more efficient and professional.

Flash's Interface Components

When you open Flash, you're confronted with a screen layout that seems fairly complex but this layout is simple compared to the interface for most animation programs (few of which have the range or functionality of Flash). Besides, once you know what each of the functional areas does, you'll start to feel right at home. Figure A.1 shows the Flash screen as you see it when you first start using the program.

The following sections describe the function of each of the main areas of the Flash 4 interface.

The Menu Bar

The menu bar is the row of menu titles that appears at the top of almost every window in programs for Windows or the Mac. Figure A.2 shows the Flash menu bar and a pull-down menu.

The menus and their functions are discussed next.

File Menu

The File menu appears on the menu bar of every Windows and Mac application. See Figure A.3. The Flash 4 File menu has some unique commands worth noting, as detailed in Table A.1.

Dialog Boxes For File Menu Commands

Here are the dialog boxes for commands in the File menu:

- *Open*—This is the standard File Open dialog box for the platform you are used to working on.

- *Open As Library*—Once again, the standard File Open dialog box. Opens only the movies Library (not the movie itself) and makes its window visible.

- *Save As*—The standard dialog box for saving files.

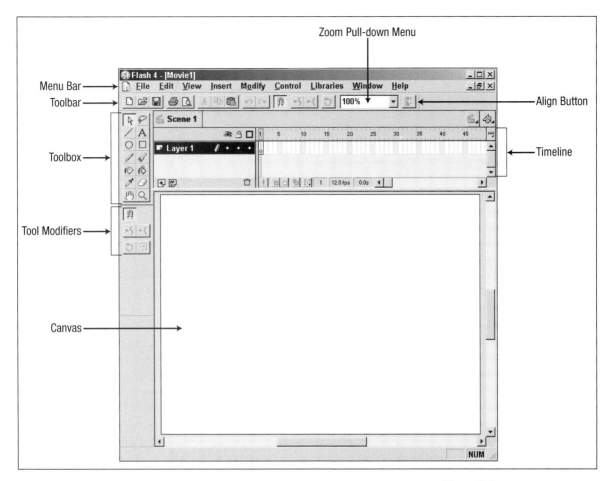

Figure A.1

The Flash 4 screen immediately after you open a new movie. Callouts indicate the nomenclature for each area of the screen.

Figure A.2

The Flash 4 menu bar and the Edit pull-down menu.

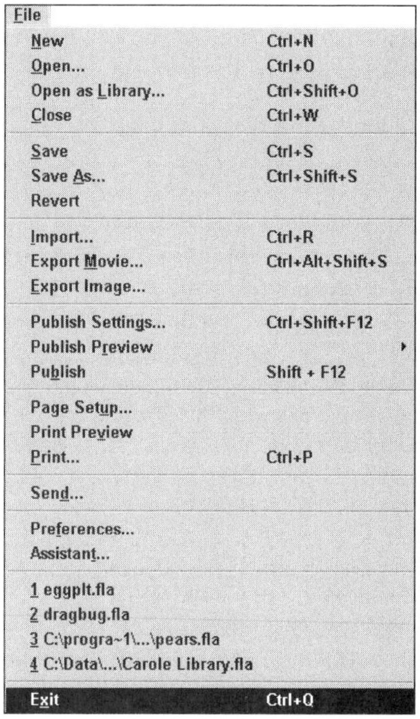

```
File
  New                 Ctrl+N
  Open...             Ctrl+O
  Open as Library...  Ctrl+Shift+O
  Close               Ctrl+W

  Save                Ctrl+S
  Save As...          Ctrl+Shift+S
  Revert

  Import...           Ctrl+R
  Export Movie...     Ctrl+Alt+Shift+S
  Export Image...

  Publish Settings... Ctrl+Shift+F12
  Publish Preview            ▶
  Publish             Shift + F12

  Page Setup...
  Print Preview
  Print...            Ctrl+P

  Send...

  Preferences...
  Assistant...

  1 eggplt.fla
  2 dragbug.fla
  3 C:\progra~1\...\pears.fla
  4 C:\Data\...\Carole Library.fla
  Exit                Ctrl+Q
```

Figure A.3
The Flash 4 File menu.

- *Import*—Looks like the standard File Open dialog box except that you get a long pull-down list of importable file types.

- *Export Movie*—Looks like the standard dialog box for saving files except that you get a long pull-down list of exportable file types.

- *Export Image*— Looks like the standard dialog box for saving files except that you get a long pull-down list of exportable file types.

- *Publish Settings*—Contains three tabs: Formats, Flash, and HTML.

- *Page Setup*—All the standard settings for printer page setup with a couple of notable additions: In the upper left corner there's a visual preview of how the page will look. At the bottom, there's a section called Layout that contains pull-down menus that give you the option of printing your movie as a storyboard in one of several styles. You can specify the number of rows and columns of frame shots and whether the frames will be labeled.

- *Print*—The standard Print dialog box for your operating system and your printer.

- *Preferences*—Lets you set the parameters for the size and resolution of clipboard bitmaps and gradients. You can also specify the number of Undo Levels and toggle the ability to use PostScript fonts, determine the method of adding selections and whether or not the Timeline will dock.

- *Assistant*—Options here are Off, Strict, Normal, or Tolerant.

Table A.1   File menu commands and keyboard shortcuts.

◇ indicates new feature; ❖ indicates updated feature

Command	Shortcut	Description
New	Cmd/Ctrl+N	Creates a new file. When you start a new file, you do not get a dialog box for setting page size, and so on. You do that by choosing Modify Movie.
Open	Cmd/Ctrl+O	Opens the standard dialog box for opening files.
Open As Library	Cmd/Ctrl+Shift+O	Places the library from any other Flash movie into the active movie. You can then place symbols from the imported library into your current movie.
Close	Cmd/Ctrl+W	Closes the active movie.
Save	Cmd/Ctrl+S	Saves the active movie with its current file name and disk location.
Save As	Cmd/Ctrl+Shift+S	Gives you the opportunity to save the active movie with a new file name and/or disk location. Use this command to create a new movie from elements of an old one without destroying the old one.
◇Revert	None	Replaces the current movie with the last version saved to disk. This is an excellent way to undo a whole series of commands at once.
❖Import	Cmd/Ctrl+R	Places content saved in other formats into your movie. File formats that can be imported are Enhanced Metafile (.emf), Windows Metafile (.wmf), Adobe Illustrator (.eps, .ai), Flash Player (.swf, .spf), AutoCAD (.dxf), Windows Bitmap (.bmp, .dib), JPEG (.jpg), GIF (.gif), PNG (.png), Windows WAV Sound (.wav), Mac AIFF sound (Mac), and QuickTime Movie (.mov).
Export Movie	Cmd+Opt+Shift+S or Ctrl+Alt+Shift+S	Allows you to save animations to other formats, including sequences of still images. Supported formats are Flash Player (.swf), Generator Template (.swt), FutureSplash Player (.spf), Windows AVI (.avi), QuickTime (.mov), Animated GIF (.gif), Windows WAV audio (.wav), EMF sequence, WMF sequence (.wmf), EPS 3.0 sequence (.eps), Adobe Illustrator sequence (.ai), DXF sequence (.dxf), Windows bitmap sequence (.dxf), Mac PICT sequence (Mac), JPEG sequence, GIF sequence, and PNG sequence.
Export Image	None	Exports a single-frame (still) image to any of the still-image formats listed above.
◇Publish Settings	Cmd/Ctrl+Shift+F12	Allows you to select files to be published and make settings for them.
◇Publish Preview	None	Exports the active file and opens it in the default browser.
◇Publish	Shift+F12	Allows you to create HTML pages together with Flash .swf files, GIF files, JPEG files, PNG files, Flash projectors, and QuickTime movies. You can create one, all at the same time, or any combination of formats.
Page Setup	None	Allows you to format storyboard output. Allows you to set up pages for printing (set page size, margins, and orientation).
Print Preview	None	Shows how your page will appear on paper. You can print directly from the preview window, change pages, see facing pages, and zoom to check detail and layout.
Print	Cmd/Ctrl+P	Opens the standard Print dialog box.
Preferences	None	Sets your preferences for current and all subsequent movies—until you reset them here.
Assistant	None	Displays the Drawing Assistant, where you specify how Flash's "drawing intelligence" will recognize shapes and will smooth or straighten lines.
Recently Loaded Files		Lists the last few files that were loaded so that you can open them quickly.
Exit	Cmd/Ctrl+Q	Closes the program, after asking if you want to save any unsaved work.

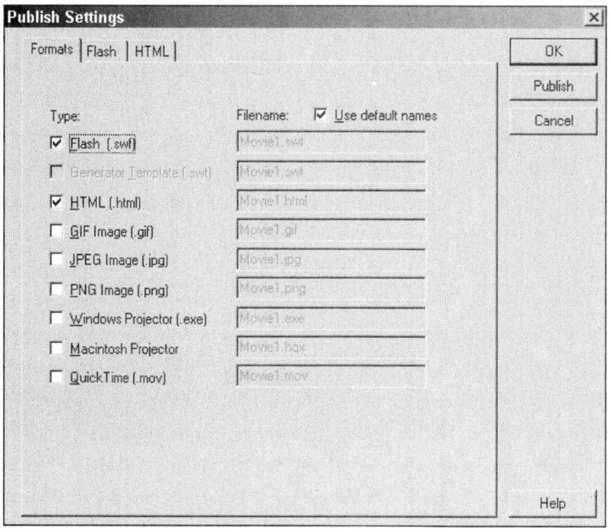

Figure A.4
The Formats tab of the Publish
Settings dialog box.

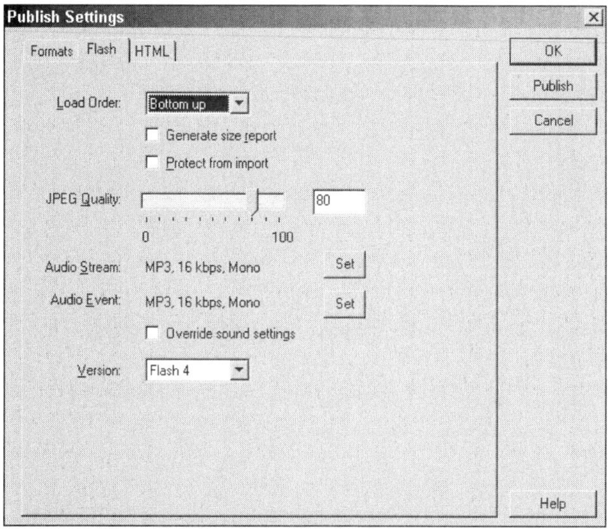

Figure A.5
The Flash tab of the Publish
Settings dialog box.

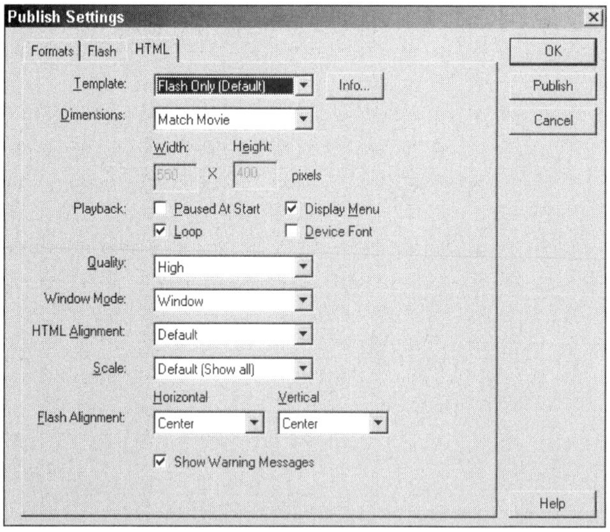

Figure A.6
The HTML tab of the Publish
Settings dialog box.

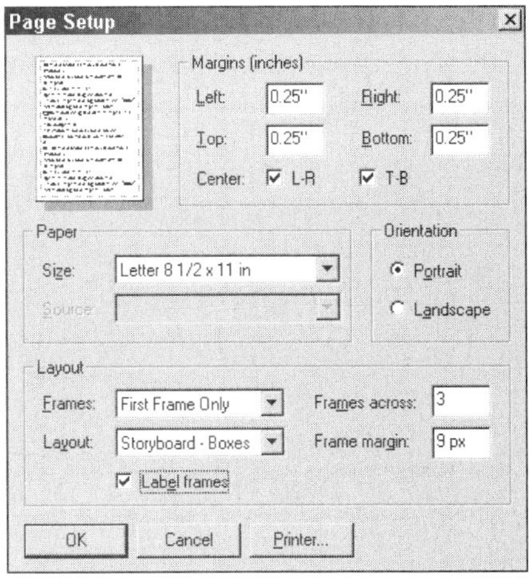

Figure A.7
The Page Setup dialog box.
Notice the Storyboard settings at
lower right.

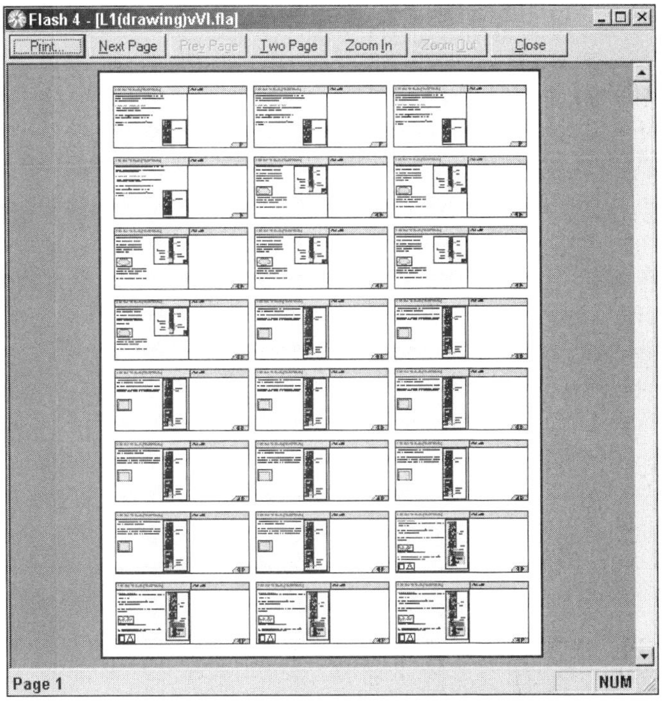

Figure A.8
The Print Preview window.

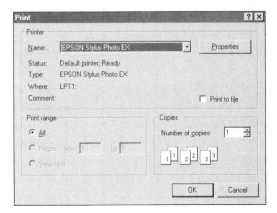

Figure A.9
The Print dialog box.

Edit Menu

This is the second menu that appears in nearly all Mac and Windows applications. See Figure A.10. You can use multiple (up to 200) Undo and Redo operations. The Edit menu also contains such commands as Paste In Place, Paste Special, Edit Symbols, Insert Object, and others. Table A.2 describes the options available in the Edit menu.

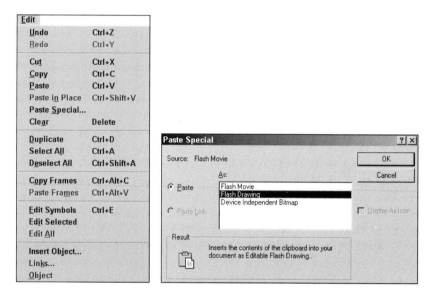

Figure A.10
(Left) The Flash 4 Edit menu.

Figure A.11
(Right) The Paste Special dialog box.

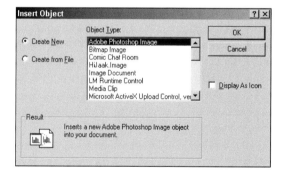

Figure A.12
The Insert Object dialog box when the Create New option is chosen. The Object Type list box shows some of the applications that can be used to create content within Flash 4. Clicking on OK opens the application inside Flash.

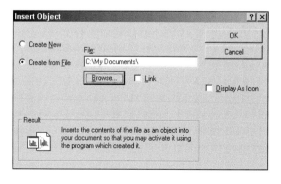

Figure A.13
The Insert Object dialog box when the Create From File option is chosen. Clicking on OK opens a second dialog box, which lets you browse for the desired file. The contents of the file are inserted, and you can click on the object to edit it in the original application.

Table A.2   Edit menu commands and keyboard shortcuts.

Command	Shortcut	Description
Undo	Cmd/Ctrl+Z	Reverses the last action you took. As many as 200 levels can be set in the Preferences dialog box.
Redo	Cmd/Ctrl+Y	Reinstates the last Undo, unless you have made a change in the meantime.
Cut	Cmd/Ctrl+X	Removes the current selection and places it on the clipboard.
Copy	Cmd/Ctrl+C	Places a copy of the current selection on the clipboard.
Paste	Cmd/Ctrl+V	Inserts the clipboard's contents. The pasted item will be the current selection and will be centered in the portion of the stage showing in the window. If you want to move the selection, take care not to deselect it first.
Paste In Place	Cmd/Ctrl+Shift+V	Inserts the clipboard's contents at the same location on the stage as the location from which it was copied.
Paste Special	None	Lets you insert the clipboard's contents as a Flash movie, a drawing, or a device-independent bitmap. Using the Display As Icon option, you can paste the item so that it appears as an icon, which, when clicked, reveals the contents.
Clear	Delete/Backspace	Erases the current selection without placing it on the clipboard.
Duplicate	Cmd/Ctrl+D	Copies the current selection to the current frame and layer.
Select All	Cmd/Ctrl+A	Selects everything in the active layers and frame.
Deselect All	Cmd/Ctrl+Shift+A	Drops any and all currently selected shapes.
Copy Frames	Cmd+Opt+C or Ctrl+Alt+C	Copies to the clipboard all frames selected in the Timeline.
Paste Frames	Cmd+Opt+V or Ctrl+Alt+V	Inserts all clipboard frames at the point of the selected Timeline frame. If several frames are selected, Paste Frames will replace them with the frames in the clipboard.
Edit Symbols	Cmd/Ctrl+E	This is a very cool and useful command. It lets you modify symbols without taking them apart, and it then automatically modifies all occurrences of that symbol throughout your movie. The symbol to be edited will appear in its own frame. (This is called switching into Edit Symbols mode.) You can switch to any symbol in the movie by clicking on its tab, which will appear on the right side of the workspace. This command is grayed out if there are no symbols in the current movie. To revert to Edit Movie mode, press Cmd/Ctrl+E or choose Edit|Edit Movie.
Edit Selected	None	Automatically switches modes to let you edit any selected group in an environment that's independent of other information in the movie, drawing, or layer. This feature is similar to Edit Symbols, but works only on grouped objects and doesn't have you editing on a clean screen. Instead, all other objects on the stage are dimmed.
Edit All	None	Takes you out of Edit Selected mode.
Insert Object	None	Opens another application so that you can create content that will be inserted automatically into the current Flash document, or lets you import the content created in another application and saved in a file.
Links	None	Lets you edit the properties of links between the current movie and other Flash movies, objects, or Web URLs. The command is grayed out if no links are embedded in the current movie.
Object	None	Lets you edit objects that have been created in other applications.

View Menu

The View menu controls how you see your workspace, the quality of the graphics display, and which interface elements are visible. See Figure A.14. Table A.3 details the View menu commands.

View	
Goto	▶
100%	Ctrl+1
Show Frame	Ctrl+2
Show All	Ctrl+3
Outlines	Ctrl+Alt+Shift+O
Fast	Ctrl+Alt+Shift+F
✓ Antialias	Ctrl+Alt+Shift+A
Antialias Text	Ctrl+Alt+Shift+T
✓ Timeline	Ctrl+Alt+T
Work Area	Ctrl+Shift+W
Rulers	Ctrl+Alt+Shift+R
Grid	Ctrl+Alt+Shift+G
✓ Snap	Ctrl+Alt+G
Show Shape Hints	Ctrl+Alt+H

Figure A.14

The Flash 4 View menu.

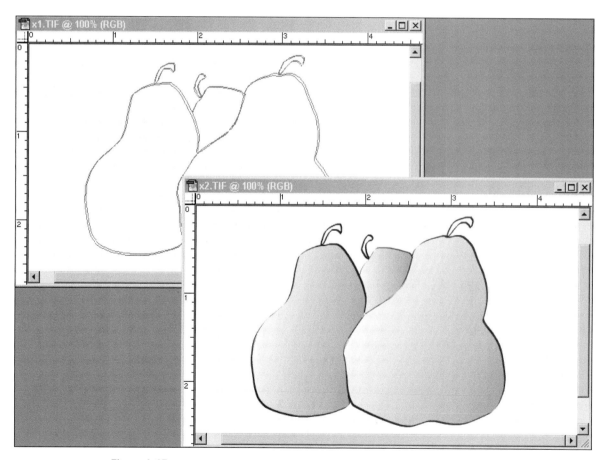

Figure A.15

The same Flash frame in Show Outlines (left) and Antialiased modes.

Table A.3   View menu commands and keyboard shortcuts.

✧ indicates new feature

Command	Shortcut	Description
Goto		Takes you to a specific part of the movie, which you specify.
100%	Cmd/Ctrl+1	Shows the image on screen at the exact size specified in the Movie Properties dialog box.
Show Frame	Cmd/Ctrl+2	Reduces the frame to fit inside the current window.
Show All	Cmd/Ctrl+3	Shows all objects on the stage, even if they've been pushed outside the boundaries of the stage.
Outlines	Cmd+Opt+Shift+O or Ctrl+Alt+Shift+O	Hides fills and line thickness, and shows the outline of objects in a color that can be chosen to stand out from the outlines on other layers. Each layer has its own outline color.
Fast	Cmd+Opt+Shift+F or Ctrl+Alt+Shift+F	Shows shapes without anti-aliasing (smoothed edges), which can slow Web performance.
Antialias	Cmd+Opt+Shift+A or Ctrl+Alt+Shift+A	Forces the edges of all shapes and lines to be smoothed by anti-aliasing. Text and bitmaps are not affected by this command.
Antialias Text	Cmd+Opt+Shift+T or Ctrl+Alt+Shift+T	Forces the edges of text to be smoothed by anti-aliasing. Shapes and bitmaps are not affected.
Timeline	Cmd+Opt+T or Ctrl+Alt+T	Shows the Timeline to make room for viewing more of the stage as you work. This command is a toggle; it also hides the Timeline.
Work Area	Cmd/Ctrl+Shift+W	When checked, forces the stage to fit inside the current window.
Rulers	Cmd+Opt+Shift+R or Ctrl+Alt+Shift+R	Places rulers around the borders of the work area. Ruler increments are specified in the Movie Properties dialog box.
Grid	Cmd+Opt+Shift+G or Ctrl+Alt+Shift+G	Shows a ruled grid with equidistant horizontal and vertical rules at the interval specified in the Movie Properties dialog box.
Snap	Cmd+Opt+G or Ctrl+Alt+G	Automatically aligns line ends, curves, or shapes to one another or to grid intersections. Grid intersections are active whether the grid is visible or not. Same as toggling the Magnet icon in the Arrow tool's modifiers.
✧Show Shape Hints	Cmd+Opt+H or Ctrl+Alt+H	Shape hints are placed in the tweening process to show the order in which shapes should be shifted to new shapes. This command is grayed out if no shape hints have been placed.

Insert Menu

The Insert menu (see Figure A.16) contains the commands that are used to insert new elements—such as symbols, layers, frames, and scenes—into a Flash movie. Table A.4 is provided for quick reference. If some of these terms are new to you, see the more complete discussions of them in Chapter 5.

Figure A.16
The Flash 4 Insert menu.

Table A.4 Insert menu commands and keyboard shortcuts.

❖ indicates updated feature

Command	Shortcut	Description
❖Convert To Symbol	F8	Creates a symbol from the active selection. If an empty symbol is created, a new symbol work area (clean drawing area) is displayed so you can draw the symbol without affecting other elements in the movie.
❖New Symbol	Cmd/Ctrl+F8	Opens a clean work area in which you can create a new symbol from scratch.
Layer		Adds a new layer to the scene and automatically makes it the current layer.
Motion Guide		Creates a motion-path layer so you can draw a path for a tweened overlay.
Frame	F5	Adds frames to one or more layers. To add a specific number of frames, highlight as many as you want to add following the frame currently selected in the Timeline.
Delete Frame	Shift+F5	Deletes any and all frames currently selected in the Timeline.
Keyframe	F6	Makes the currently highlighted frame (or frames) a keyframe (or keyframes). The contents of the first keyframe are automatically copied through all keyframes.
Blank Keyframe	F7	Same as Keyframe but does not copy the first keyframe into the new keyframes.
Clear Keyframe	Shift+F6	Deletes the keyframe characteristic from the frame, making it a regular frame.
Create Motion Tween		Starts the process for creating a motion or color tween.
Scene		Inserts a new scene (page) into the current movie. The workspace will be blank, so that you have essentially started a new movie within the current movie.
Remove Scene		Deletes the current scene (page) from the current movie.

Modify Menu

This is the menu to memorize. The Modify menu commands (see Figure A.17) help you tweak your creative efforts into a state of brilliance, or at least to look more like what you had in mind. See Table A.5 for descriptions of the Modify menu commands.

Figures A.19 through A.30 show the dialog boxes associated with the Modify commands.

Figure A.17
The Flash 4 Modify menu.

Table A.5 Modify menu commands and keyboard shortcuts.

✧ indicates new feature

Command	Shortcut	Description
Instance	Cmd/Ctrl+I	Opens the Instance Properties dialog box. Allows you to change the characteristics (such as alpha transparency and color) of a particular instance of a symbol. Also used to name an instance so that it can be used as the object of a Tell Target action.
Frame	Cmd/Ctrl+F	Opens the Frame Properties dialog box. Allows you to label a frame so that it can be used as the target of an action, and allows you to change the properties of an individual frame.
✧Layer		Open the Layer Properties dialog box so that you can change the properties for the currently selected layer, including the layer type (Normal, Guide, Guided, or Mask) and the Layer Height (in case you want a taller layer to better show a sound histogram).
Scene		Opens the Scene Properties dialog box so that you change the name of the current scene.
Movie	Cmd/Ctrl+M	Changes the parameters for the current movie. Any modifications you make here will affect the entire movie uniformly. The effects of most of the commands in the dialog box are obvious from their names, with the exception of the Match buttons. Match Printer sizes the movie to the page setup. Match Contents makes the entire movie as large as the largest drawing in the movie. (Use this to quickly adjust the movie to be the same size as something you just imported.)
Font	Cmd/Ctrl+T	Opens the Font dialog box. There's nothing mysterious or magical about this one. Style settings are limited to bold and italic.
Paragraph	Cmd/Ctrl+Shift+T	Opens a dialog box to let you set paragraph properties.
Style		Opens the Modify Style submenu. Allows you to change text to Plain, Bold, or Italic and to align text to the left, to the right, centered, or justified.
Plain	Cmd/Ctrl+Shift+P	
Bold	Cmd/Ctrl+Shift+B	
Italic	Cmd/Ctrl+Shift+I	
Align Left	Cmd/Ctrl+Shift+L	
Align Center	Cmd/Ctrl+Shift+C	
Align Right	Cmd/Ctrl+Shift+R	
Justify	Cmd/Ctrl+Shift+J	
Kerning		Opens up the Kerning submenu. Manually controls the spacing between letters.
Narrower	Cmd+Opt+Left Arrow or Ctrl+Alt+Left Arrow	Narrows the space between letters by a single pixel. Repeat this command to decrease the space between letters.
Wider	Cmd+Opt+Right Arrow or Ctrl+Alt+Right Arrow	Widens the space between letters by a single pixel. Repeat this command to increase the space between letters.
Reset	Cmd+Opt+Up Arrow or Ctrl+Alt+Up Arrow	Returns all selected text to the default spacing. Windows users can control kerning by pressing Ctrl+Alt and the arrow keys.
✧Text Field	Cmd+Opt+F or Ctrl+Alt+F	Allows you to specify or change the properties for the selected text field and to enter a variable name.
Transform		Opens a menu of possible transformations, shown below.
Scale		Changes the size of the selected object.
Rotate		Changes the orientation of the selected object.
Scale And Rotate	Cmd+Opt+S or Ctrl+Alt+S	Changes the size and orientation of the selected object.
Rotate Left		Turns the selected object 90 degrees counterclockwise.
Rotate Right		Turns the selected object 90 degrees clockwise.
Flip Vertical		Turns the selected object upside down.
Flip Horizontal		Reverses the selected object from right to left.

(continued)

Table A.5 Modify menu commands and keyboard shortcuts *(continued)*.

✧ indicates new feature

Command	Shortcut	Description
Remve Transf	Cmd/Ctrl+Shift+Z	Returns the selected object to the state it was in before it was transformed.
Edit Center		Lets you change the position of the center of a transformation.
Remove Clrs		Removes the colors.
Add Shape Hnt	Cmd/Ctrl+H	Allows you to insert a new shape hint.
Remove All Hnt		Removes all shape hints.
Arrange		Changes the stacking order of overlays in the overlay level.
Bring To Front	Cmd/Ctrl+Shift+Up	Brings the selected object to the top of the overlay stack.
Move Ahead	Cmd/Ctrl+Up	Raises the selected object by one level in the overlay stacking order.
Move Behind	Cmd/Ctrl+Down	Lowers the selected object by one level in the overlay stacking order.
Send To Back	Cmd/Ctrl+Shift+Down	Places the selected object at the bottom of the overlay stack.
Lock	Cmd+Opt+L or Ctrl+Alt+L	Keeps the selected object from being affected by other objects being transformed. Use this command when objects are stacked in such a way that you might mistakenly select the wrong object.
Unlock All	Cmd+Opt+Shift+L or Ctrl+Alt+Shift+L	Unlocks anything that has been locked.
Curves		Dictates how the Pencil tool or the selected line behaves. Options are Smooth, Straighten, and Optimize.
Smooth		Makes curves progressively smoother and joins brief segments; has no effect on straight lines.
Straighten		Makes line segments straighter and eventually will shorten them. Also turns shapes into geometric objects: circles, ovals, rectangles, squares, triangles, and arcs.
Optimize	Cmd+Opt+Shift+C or Ctrl+Alt+Shift+C	Works with the Optimize dialog box settings.
✧Lines To Fills		Changes lines to filled brush shapes.
✧Expand Shape		Increases the size of the selected shape(s) equidistantly from the edge by the number of specified units.
✧Soften Edges		Divides the edge shape by the specified number and redraws it so that each division's shading graduates to a lighter shade as it moves outward. See Figure A.18.
Frames		Allows you to do the functions described below.
Reverse		Reverse the order in which the selected frames appear.
Synchronize Symbols		Synchronize symbols with the number of frames available after the keyframe by inserting any needed additional frames.
Trace Bitmap		Traces a scanned image, digitized photo, or other bitmap into vector shapes according to changes in color in the original image and the settings you use.
Align	Cmd/Ctrl+K	Aligns the selected shapes either horizontally or vertically, along a side or center. You can also have shapes evenly spaced between the first and last objects you selected. You can also make the height and/or width of all the selected shapes match the first shape you selected in size by height, width, or both.
Group	Cmd/Ctrl+G	Combines all selected lines into a single selection and turns that selection into an overlay. If nothing is selected, anything you draw will be grouped into an overlay.
Ungroup	Cmd/Ctrl+Shift+G	Ungroups everything in the current selection. Also removes overlay characteristics.
Break Apart	Cmd/Ctrl+B	Breaks any selected overlays or symbols into their components. If you break apart a symbol, the components are actually copied to the stage, and the link to the symbol library is broken.

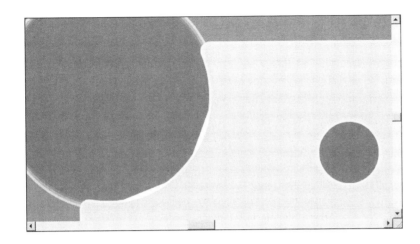

Figure A.18

The result of softening the edges of two overlapping shapes. Notice the gaps where the circle and the rectangle overlap.

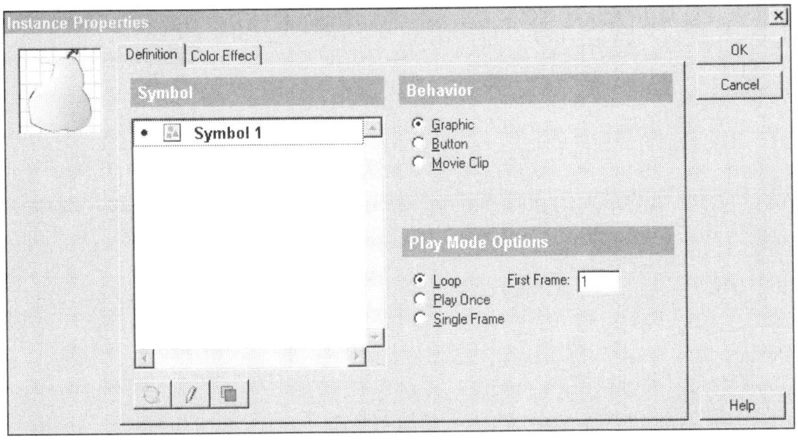

Figure A.19

The Definition tab of the Instance Properties dialog box.

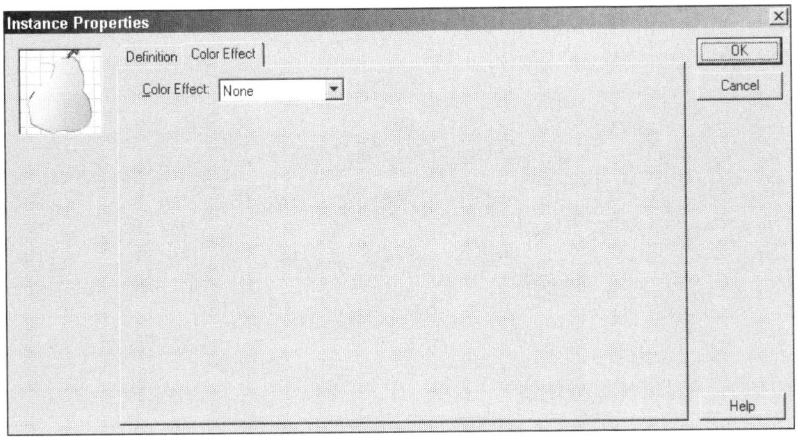

Figure A.20

The Color Effect tab of the Instance Properties dialog box.

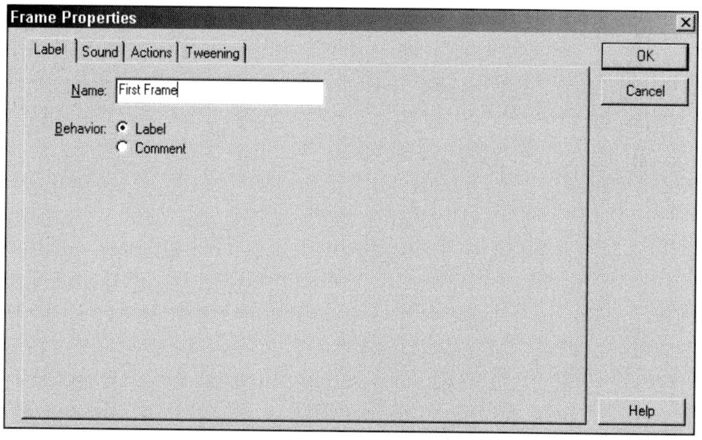

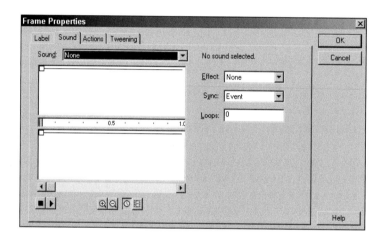

Figure A.21
The Label tab of the Frame
Properties dialog box.

Figure A.22
The Sound tab of the Frame
Properties dialog box.

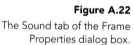

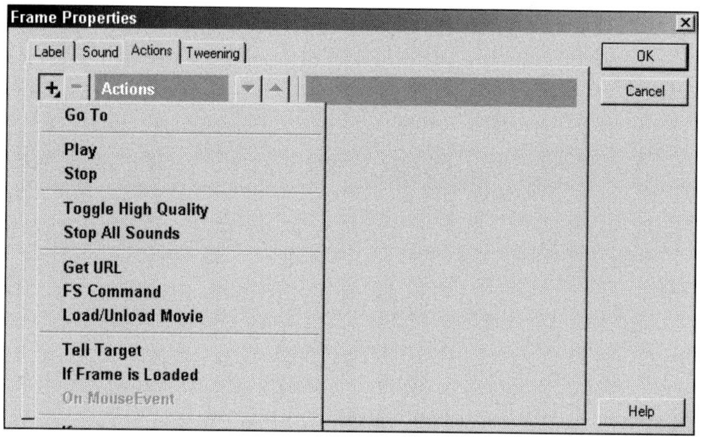

Figure A.23
The Actions tab of the Frame
Properties dialog box.

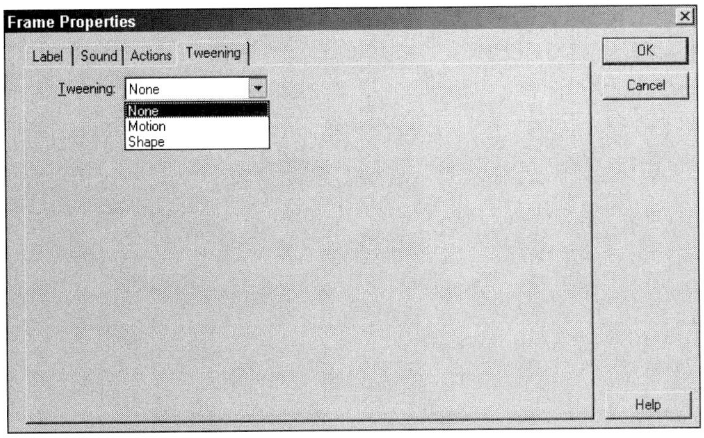

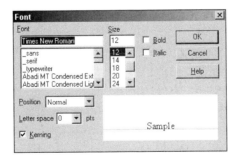

Figure A.24
The Tweening tab of the Frame Properties dialog box.

Figure A.25
The Scene Properties dialog box.

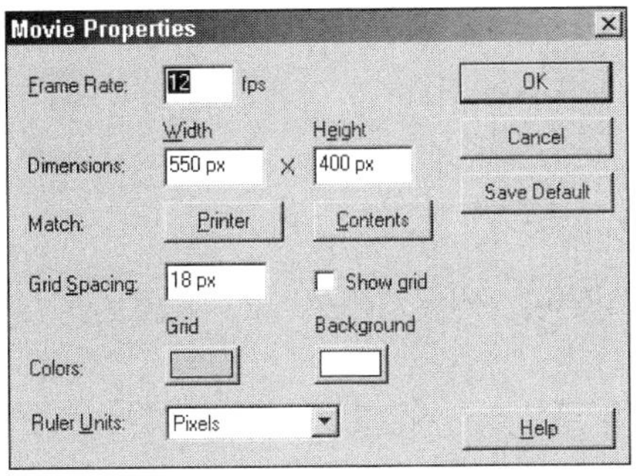

Figure A.26
The Movie Properties dialog box.

Figure A.27
The Font dialog box.

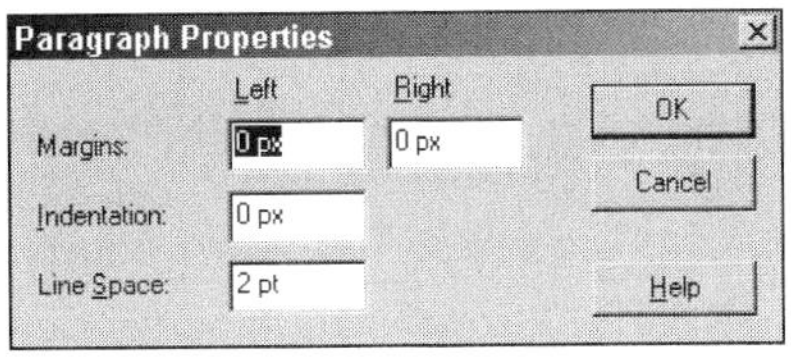

Figure A.28
The Paragraph Properties dialog box.

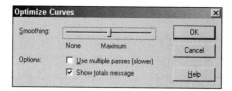

Figure A.29
The Optimize Curves dialog box.

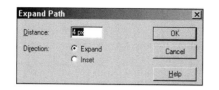

Figure A.30
The Expand Path dialog box.

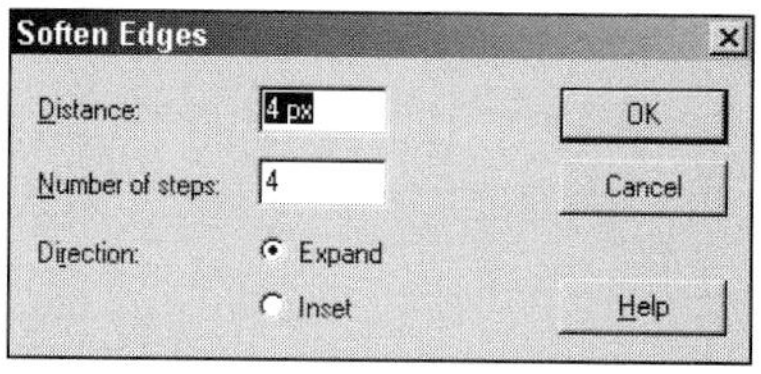

Figure A.31
The Soften Edges dialog box.

Control Menu

This menu doesn't control your work situation or the level of your temper. This is the menu (see Figure A.32) for controlling how animations play. Its commands are described in Table A.6.

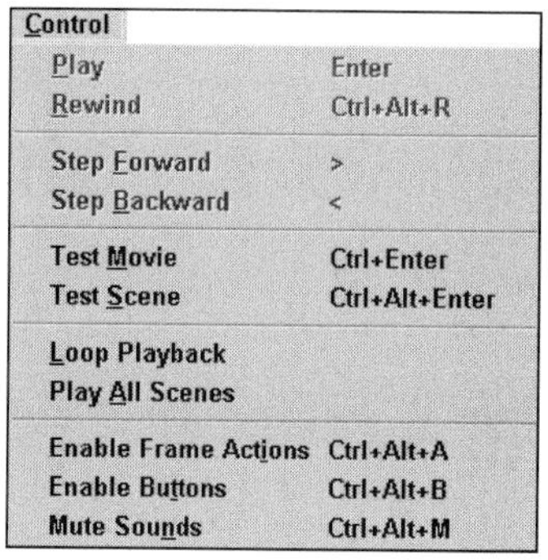

Figure A.32
The Flash 4 Control menu.

Table A.6 Control menu commands and keyboard shortcuts.

Command	Shortcut	Description
Play	Return/Enter	Toggles (turns on and off) the movie playing in the current work window.
Rewind	Cmd+Opt+R or Ctrl+Alt+R	Displays the first frame of the current scene.
Step Forward	> or . (period)	Moves forward one frame at a time.
Step Backward	< or , (comma)	Moves backward one frame at a time.
Test Movie	Cmd+Return or Ctrl+Enter	Exports the selected movies as an SWF file, which automatically opens in a new window, where it will appear exactly as it would on the Web. This command can be used to test all interactive functions and can be used instead of the Export Movie command.

(continued)

Table A.6 Control menu commands and keyboard shortcuts *(continued)*.

Command	Shortcut	Description
Test Scene	Cmd+Opt+Return or Ctrl+Alt+Enter	Exports the selected scene to an SWF file and then lets you test as above.
Loop Playback		When you're using the Control|Play command, the Loop Playback command causes the movie to automatically restart at the first frame after playing the last frame.
Play All Scenes		When you're using Control|Play command, the Play All Scenes command plays the whole movie, including all scenes, in sequence.
Enable Frame Actions	Cmd+Opt+A or Ctrl+Alt+A	When you're using the Control|Play command, the Enable Frame Actions command turns on any actions you've assigned to a frame. Actions are events that can occur at the instant a keyframe plays. For a complete list of Actions and their purpose, see Chapter 9.
Enable Buttons	Cmd+Opt+B or Ctrl+Alt+B	When you're using the Control|Play command, the Enable Buttons command allows buttons to be active or inactive. If buttons are active, you cannot double-click on a button to view its Instance Properties. All the buttons in the movie behave as buttons rather than as overlays.
Mute Sounds	Cmd+Opt+M or Ctrl+Alt+M	Lets you turn off sounds while you're editing. When you choose this command and then choose Control|Test Movie, the movie will play silently. This speeds editing, and you won't have to listen to constantly repeated sound snippets when you're tweaking transitions between short scenes.

Libraries Menu

The Libraries menu opens any Flash movies as libraries that have been placed in the Libraries folder inside the Flash applications folder. There is no command in Flash that places libraries on this menu. You just put any Flash movie in the Libraries folder using your operating system's normal methods for moving a folder. The contents of the Libraries menu consist of nothing more than the names of these movies. Macromedia has placed the following movies in this folder: Buttons, Buttons-advanced, Graphics, Movie Clips, and Sounds.

Figure A.33

The Flash 4 default Libraries windows: Controls, Counter, Forms-Windows Controls, Radio Button, and Reusable Components.

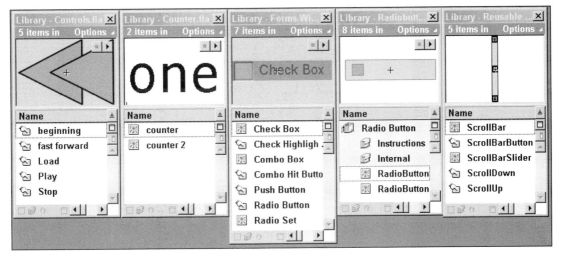

Window Menu

With Flash, you can open several movies at the same time, with each movie appearing in its own window. The Window menu (see Figure A.34) controls how these windows appear, in relationship both to one another and to individual user-interface content. Following Table A.7, three figures (Figures A.35, A.36, and A.37) illustrate the results of the Arrange All and Cascade commands and show Flash's Toolbars dialog box.

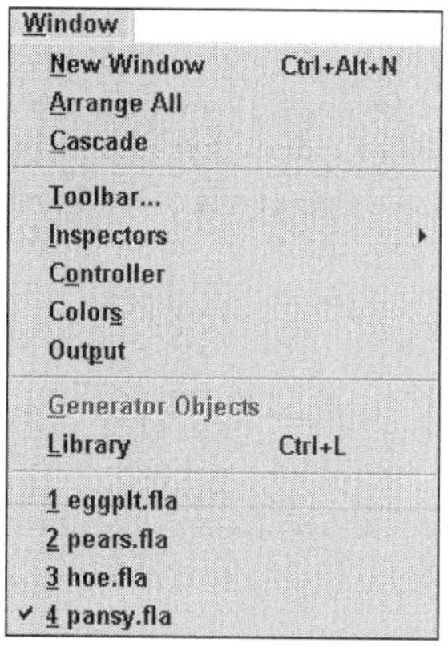

Figure A.34
The Flash 4 Window menu.

Table A.7 Window menu commands and keyboard shortcuts.

✧ indicates new feature

Command	Shortcut	Description
New Window	Cmd+Opt+N or Ctrl+Alt+N	Opens another window displaying the active movie. This allows you to view a different part of the movie or different sets of layers. This is particularly useful for editing different scenes or frames in the same movie. Any edits made in one window are automatically made in all other windows.
Arrange All		Puts all the open windows in columns and rows (tiles), so that they all become visible. You can see the result of the Arrange All command in Figure A.35.
Cascade		Arranges windows so you can see the title bar of each window.
Toolbar		Opens the Toolbars dialog box. Use this dialog box to show or hide various toolbars and to assign such properties as size and color to them.
✧Inspectors		Opens the Inspector window, for the type of object that is currently selected. The other types of inspectors are also shown on tabs: Object, Frame, Transform, Scene.
Object	Cmd+Opt+I or Ctrl+Alt+I	The Object inspector tells you the type of symbol, the location of the top-left corner of the symbol, the symbol's width and height, the symbol's name settings, and any applicable actions. You can change any of the dimensions by re-entering them and clicking on the Apply button.
Frame		Shows the frame's type, label, and sound attributes.
Transform		Shows the selected transformations scale percentage, whether scaling is uniform, degrees of rotation, and whether skewing is used. You can apply numeric transformations by entering numbers in the aforementioned fields and clicking on the Apply button.
Scene		Lists all the scenes in the movie and lets you move from one to the other by clicking on the scene name.
Generator		The Generator inspector lets you adjust the values for the currently selected Generator Object. You can also select a different Generator Object for the currently selected object.

(continued)

Table A.7   Window menu commands and keyboard shortcuts *(continued)*.

✧ indicates new feature

Command	Shortcut	Description
Controller		Remember this one. It lets you put a VCR control window on screen in order to play, stop, step, or rewind your movie at the click of a button.
Colors		It's in a strange place, but this is the command used to open the Color Picker dialog box so that you can choose colors for your graphics, text lines, and fills. You can choose either gradient or solid colors for both lines and fills. Text can use only solid colors (unless you ungroup it so that it becomes just shapes).
Output		Opens a window that shows any calls made to another device or browser window. Unless this window is open, there is no way to tell when action calls are being made because there is no Internet connection.
✧Generator Objects		Allows selection of one of the 14 different Generator Objects. Dragging the selected object on to the stage will also open the appropriate section of the Generator inspector for value entry.
Library	Cmd/Ctrl+L	Opens the Library window for the current movie. This library lists all symbols, bitmaps, and sounds currently used in the movie, whether they were opened from another library (such as one of those that ships with Flash) or created in the current movie.
Current Movies		Lists currently open movie windows.

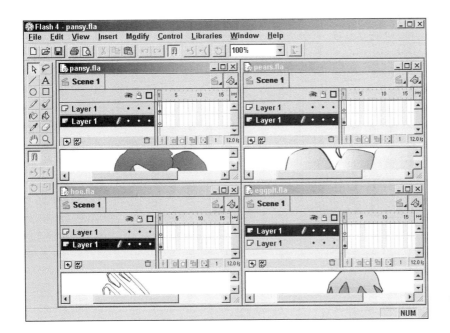

Figure A.35

The results of the Arrange All command.

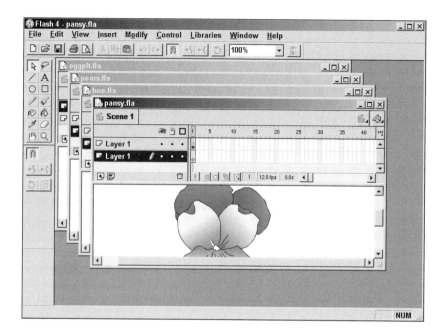

Figure A.36
The results of the
Cascade command.

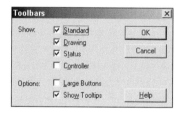

Figure A.37
The Flash 4 Toolbars dialog box.

Help Menu

Flash is one of the few cross-platform programs for which the online help is as complete on the Macintosh as it is in Windows. See Figure A.39. On the Macintosh, however, online help is accessed through the Help icon. Table A.8 details the Windows Help menu, but Mac users will find that their content is the same (although with slight differences in organization).

Figure A.38
The Flash 4 Help menu.

You can get additional, updated help online at the Macromedia Web site (**www.macromedia.com/support/flash**).

Table A.8 Help menu commands and keyboard shortcuts.

Command	Shortcut	Description
Flash Help Topics	F1	Presents the main contents page for Flash in your default browser. Clicking on any of the buttons takes you directly to the corresponding section.
Register Flash		Lets you register Flash online.
Flash Developers Center		Takes you to the Flash Support Overview page of the Macromedia Center site. You can click on a button to go to the Developers Center, What's New, Tech Notes, get Updates and Downloads, and access Support Programs.
Lessons		Takes you through an entirely new and more businesslike (some would say more practical) set of lessons that teach you the basics of Flash. These lessons happen within a Flash movie, not in a browser window.
Samples		Shows you several instructional samples within the Test Movie context.
About Flash		Displays the Flash splash screen. This is where you'll find your registration information (such as your serial number).

Figure A.39
The opening screen for
Flash 4 Help.

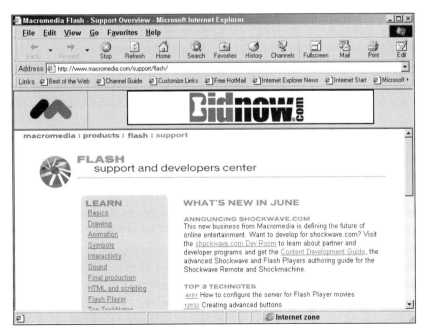

Figure A.40
The Flash 4 Developers Center
home page.

The Toolbar

The Flash Toolbar sits just below the menu bar and spans the window. This Toolbar is a shortcut to many of the functions and commands that are available—but perhaps not as readily visible—within other Flash interface components. You can see the Flash Toolbar in Figure A.41. It hasn't changed at all since Flash 2. Table A.9 describes the buttons on the Flash Toolbar.

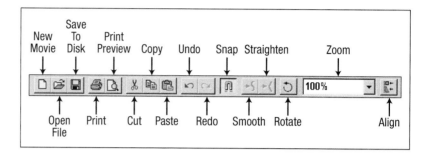

Figure A.41

The Flash 4 Toolbar.

Table A.9 The Flash Toolbar buttons.

Button	Description
New Movie	Creates a new, blank movie.
Open File	Opens a Flash movie previously stored on your computer. The standard File Open dialog box appears.
Save To Disk	Saves the current file. Opens the standard Save As dialog box.
Print	Opens the standard Print dialog box for the installed default printer.
Print Preview	Previews on screen the way the full page will look when the first frame of the movie is printed.
Cut	Deletes the current selection from the stage and places it on the clipboard.
Copy	Copies the current selection from the stage and places it on the clipboard.
Paste	Places the contents of the clipboard on the stage.
Undo	Returns the movie to its state previous to the last-issued command or the last-used tool. Repeated clicking on this button will move you back through commands issued, one step at a time, up to 200 levels.
Redo	Undoes the Undo. Also works at up to 200 levels.
Snap	Turns on Snap, which causes the mouse cursor to snap to the nearest grid point or drawing entity.
Smooth	Smoothes the currently selected line(s), regardless of which tool is in use.
Straighten	Straightens the currently selected line(s), regardless of which tool is in use.
Rotate	Rotates the currently selected line(s), regardless of which tool is in use.
Scale	Activates the Scale tool for currently selected object(s).
Align	The in-context Align button is at the right end of the Toolbar. Click on this button—and the Align dialog box will appear.
Zoom menu	The Zoom menu is the quick and easy way to change your view of the current frame to a specific percentage of magnification.

The Toolbox

The Toolbox contains the instruments for creating drawings. It's been re-drawn and rearranged in Flash 4, and several new modifiers have been added. The Toolbox can be seen in Figure A.42.

The functions of these tools are briefly described in Table A.10.

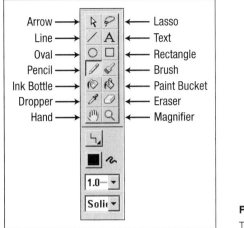

Figure A.42
The Flash 4 Toolbox.

Table A.10 Toolbox tools and keyboard shortcuts.

✧ indicates new feature

Tool	Shortcut	Description
Arrow	A	Selects individual graphic elements, such as lines and fills. Double-clicking on an object or symbol lets you edit it. The Arrow tool is also used for editing shapes.
Lasso	L	Selects irregularly shaped portions of the active layer(s). Moving or cutting the selection creates an entirely new shape.
✧Line	N	Draws a straight line as you click and drag.
Text	T	Lets you type and edit text directly on the stage. Text is entered as an overlay.
✧Oval	O	Draws ovals and circles (press Shift and drag).
✧Rectangle	R	Draws rectangles.
Pencil	P	Draws lines of any color, thickness, or style.
Brush	B	Paints solid colors that are shapes. In other words, you can change the shape of drawn elements.
Ink Bottle	I	Places a pencil line around any solid colors, or changes the color and style of existing pencil lines that have been selected.
Paint Bucket	U	Fills any area enclosed or semi-enclosed by shape outlines.
Dropper	D	Picks up the properties of a shape or line and imposes them on any other selected item of the same type.
Eraser	E	Alters any shape on the stage by removing any fill areas that are brushed with this tool. Will not erase bitmaps, symbols, or the contents of locked layers.
Hand	H	Pans and scrolls the contents of the currently active window.
Magnifier	M	Zooms in by 100 percent at each click or—if you drag a rectangle—to the area of the marquee. Zooms out in 50-percent increments if you select the Minus Zoom modifier.

Tool Modifiers

Tool modifiers are the group of icons that dictate the specific behavior of the chosen tool. The sets of modifiers are specific to each tool and will be described in detail in Chapter 3. Figure A.43 shows the modifiers for the Arrow tool.

Figure A.43
The Flash 4 Arrow tool modifiers.

The Timeline

The Timeline is the main repository of tools and commands for creating and editing animations. It is also the basic mechanism for controlling where various scenes start, stop, and overlap one another. The Timeline provides several in-context menus: the Onion Skin menu, the Frame View menu, the Layer menu, and the Frame menu. The functions of the Frame menu are the subject of Chapter 4, so I won't detail them here. In the meantime, you can see what the Timeline looks like in Figure A.44.

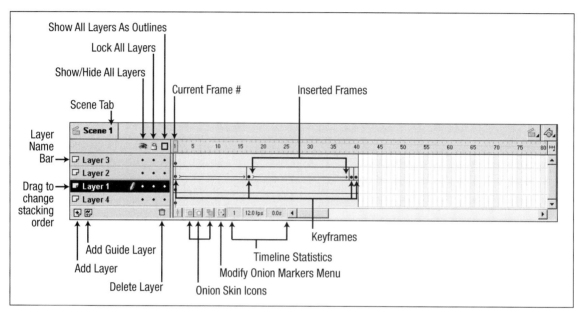

Figure A.44

The Flash 4 Timeline.

The Movie Area

This is the area that displays the visible contents of the active frame of your Flash movie. Drawing and editing are always done within the confines of this area.

Rulers And Grids

These are aids to help you organize and place elements in your movie. Figure A.46 shows rulers bordering the edges of the movie area, a grid superimposed over the scene.

Rulers can be set in increments of whatever unit you have specified in the Ruler Units box of the Movie Properties dialog box. Unit options are pixels, inches, decimal inches, points, centimeters, and millimeters.

Grid spacing is set by whatever unit number and type you specify in the Grid Spacing box in the Movie Properties dialog box. Grids are always evenly spaced horizontally and vertically. The snap points of objects will snap to grid intersections when they are within a three-pixel radius of one another.

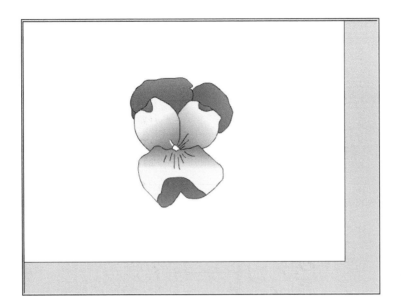

Figure A.45
The Flash 4 movie area, showing a flower.

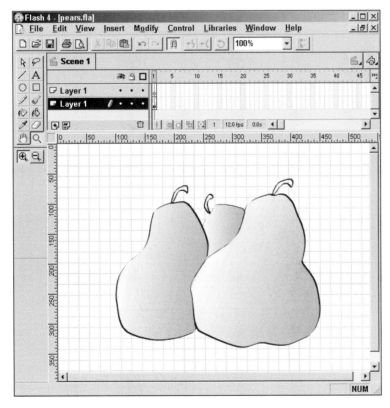

Figure A.46
The Flash 4 window, showing rulers, a grid, and a Scene tab.

The Stage (Formerly Called The Canvas)

The stage is Flash's basic creative environment. Each frame of each layer in a movie has a stage. Stages are always transparent except for what you paint, draw, or type on them. Painting or drawing on the canvas—although it results in vector-defined shapes—has more in common operationally with bitmap paint programs, such as Photoshop or Windows Paint, than with most other vector drawing programs, such as FreeHand, CorelDRAW, or Illustrator.

In Flash, anything you create on the stage sticks to it, and overlays and alters any previously drawn shapes that you've painted over. So if I first paint a blob, like this:

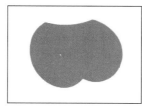

then I paint some areas and lines on top of it like so:

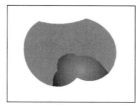

I can select, move, and fill any of the dissected parts because each has become a separate vector element, as shown here:

Notice that drawing new elements atop existing elements breaks all the elements into separate components. This makes it very easy to edit parts of shapes in Flash, but it has the disadvantage of breaking up shapes that you wanted to keep together. That's okay, though. If you want to make sure that a shape stays whole before you draw on top of it, select and group it (Cmd/ Ctrl+G). The group then becomes an overlay that floats in its own independent space. (For more information, see the "Overlays And Groups" section later in this chapter.)

To prevent a shape from combining with other drawn elements, you can do any of the following:

- Group the shape

- Convert the shape to a symbol

- Draw the elements on a different layer

Remember, each layer has its own stage. So if you draw something new on the stage of one layer, it's not going to affect anything you've already drawn on other layers. Layers are somewhat analogous to the cels used in traditional animation. You can see through any part of a layer that doesn't have something opaque drawn or placed on it. This feature gives you the ability to have one set of animating drawings playing atop another.

Organizational Features

Read on for how to use scenes, symbols, overlays, groups, and layers.

Scenes

Flash movies can contain any number of scenes, and a scene can contain any number of frames and layers. In other words, a scene is a movie within the movie.

> **Note:** Scenes are an authoring-environment device only. They are not exported to SWF player files.

To navigate directly to a scene, choose View|Goto. You'll get a menu of all the scenes in the current movie.

When you start a new movie file in Flash, you automatically open Scene 1. (In other words, all Flash movies have at least one scene.) Because a scene can be any length up to 65,536 frames, you can make very complex movies that consist of only one scene. You also can import Shockwave Flash movies into a new scene. Just remember that the imported frames will inherit the properties of the current movie, so you'll probably want to make sure that both movies have at least the same horizontal and vertical dimensions.

You can easily add and delete scenes and change their order. To add a scene, choose Insert|Scene. The new scene will have the same movie properties as the last scene because movie properties must be the same for an entire movie.

Symbols

Symbols is a strange name for what other programs call actors (in Director), characters, or sprites. The latter are all far more descriptive (although in Flash, symbols can be buttons as well as actors). A symbol is a self-contained drawing or movie with a transparent background that allows it to be "suspended" on the stage. You can have as many symbols within a scene (page) as you like (give or take the limitations of your computer's installed random access memory).

The real miracle of symbols is that they can be fully animated within themselves and can then be animated in a different way within your movie. For instance, you can animate a person's stride, save the animation as a symbol, and then animate the movement of the symbol along a path. The result is that arms, legs, and body make all the moves necessary to imitate the natural body movements that occur during walking, while the body itself (the symbol) moves across the frame. Remember, you can apply this technique to anything that moves: a bird, a plane, or a speeding bullet...even Superman himself.

Creating Symbols

It's usually easier to create symbols in a blank scene so that you don't have to worry about isolating the symbol from its surroundings. One way to do this is to create all the symbols first, save them all to a library, and then delete the scenes in which they occur. You then can reintroduce them into the movie as many times and in as many different frames or scenes as you like.

You certainly aren't limited to creating symbols as I've just suggested. Anything you've selected can be turned into a symbol. Just choose Insert|New Symbol. When you do this, a symbol work area (that can later be made to have multiple frames) is created automatically as soon as you name the symbol in the Symbol Properties dialog box. (See Figure A.47.) You have to name the symbol before it can become a symbol. If you click on the Button Behavior option, the symbol will automatically have the four frames required of a button.

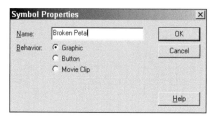

Figure A.47
The Symbol Properties dialog box.

The third approach to creating a symbol is to choose Insert|New Symbol when nothing has been selected previously. This method has the advantage of letting you create symbols in a blank symbol work area because the workspace automatically becomes a blank symbol stage. You then can draw and animate anything you like, over as many frames as you like—all independent of the rest of the movie. Anything you create—including text and other symbols—can use as many layers as you like, and can become a part of the new symbol.

To terminate the creation of a new symbol, either choose Edit|Movie or click on the Edit Scene button and choose the scene that you want to go to. (The Edit

Scene button is a clapboard icon above and on the right end of the Timeline.) The new symbol will automatically appear in the current movie's library.

Editing Symbols

You can change the elements, shapes, or behavior in a symbol by entering Edit Symbol mode. This mode lets you work on a symbol as if it were an independent movie, just as when you create a new symbol. There are three ways to enter Edit Symbol mode:

- Use the Arrow tool and, in the current scene, click on the symbol that you want to edit. Then choose Edit|Edit Symbols.

- Use the Arrow tool and double-click on the symbol in the scene. (This is actually called the symbol's *instance* because the symbol itself resides in the library.)

- Open the library (choose Window|Library), scroll to the symbol that you want to edit, and double-click in its image window. This method also lets you edit sounds and bitmaps.

Using Symbols

It's a good idea to create symbols and then use those symbols to create the graphic elements in scenes. Thus, symbols of only two or three people could be used to make a crowd, or a symbol of a flower could be used to plant a garden. Because the symbol is stored only once, repeated use of the same symbol saves huge amounts of file space and greatly speeds the playing of your movie. Use your imagination to find ways to maximize this technique. For instance, all the tiles on a roof could be the same symbol, as could all the chairs in a theater, not to mention all the navigational buttons in a Web site.

Overlays And Groups

Overlays are permanently combined elements that float above the stage. Groups, text, symbols, and (usually) bitmaps are all overlays as soon as they are created.

The most versatile type of overlay is a group because groups (like symbols) can contain any combination of other types of elements. You can draw and paint anything you like on the stage, and then select any or all of those elements and group them. You can make compound groups by selecting multiple groups, symbols, and text, and then combining them into a "supergroup." For example, suppose that you select the Pencil tool and sketch the following simple shape:

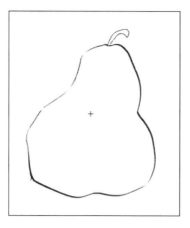

Several of the lines that make up this shape are separate elements. You can see in the next sketch that I have selected every other connected line in this profile and moved the lines individually, like so:

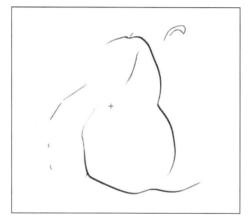

But if I select all the elements (line segments, in this case) and then group them, when I select anything in this group, the whole group is selected.

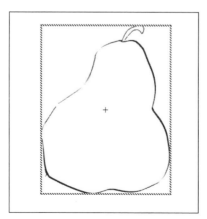

I can then add a symbol from the library, select both items, and group them. If I ungroup the resulting group, the original groups will still be intact, as shown in the next sketch:

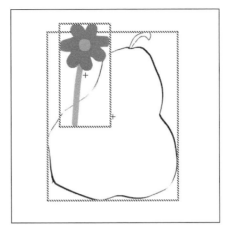

Creating A Group

Creating a group is easy. Select the elements that you want to group, and press Cmd/Ctrl+G. If you insist on making life harder than it is, you can create a group in these other ways:

- After selecting all the existing elements that you want to group, choose Modify|Group.

- Create an empty group by selecting nothing (you can ensure that this is the case by pressing Cmd/Ctrl+Shift+A) and then choosing Modify|Group. This method has the big advantage of letting you create your group in a clean, uncluttered, fresh workspace. When you terminate group creation, any elements that you have introduced are automatically placed in a single group that floats above the stage in which you were previously working.

Editing A Group

The procedure for editing a group is almost the same as for editing a symbol. Select the group, then either choose Edit|Select or use the Arrow tool to double-click on the selection. Everything in the current frame that is not part of the group will fade to about 50 percent of normal intensity. All the faded elements are now locked so there's no danger of affecting them when you edit the elements in your group.

Leaving Group Edit Mode

There are two ways to get back to normal Movie Edit mode: choose Edit|Movie, or double-click on any of the ghosted elements. When you see the ghosted elements return to normal intensity, you will know that you're back to normal.

Choosing Between Using Groups Or Symbols

Generally speaking, it is best to use groups for temporarily combining drawing elements. When you've got them all combined the way you want, convert the groups to symbols (unless there is simply no possibility that you'll ever use them again in this movie or any other movie).

Layers

In a sense, layers are another kind of overlay. Because layers can each hold any of the other types of overlays described earlier, we can think of them as supergroups. Each layer has its own transparent stage, so you can always create an independent drawing simply by creating a new layer and then drawing on it. Because layers are transparent (except, of course, for the drawings and overlays they contain), you can stack as many as you like. (You can also have transparency in the drawings and overlays.)

All elements (drawings, text, symbols, and so on) on a given layer are separate from the elements on any other layer. You can change the stacking order of layers anytime you like.

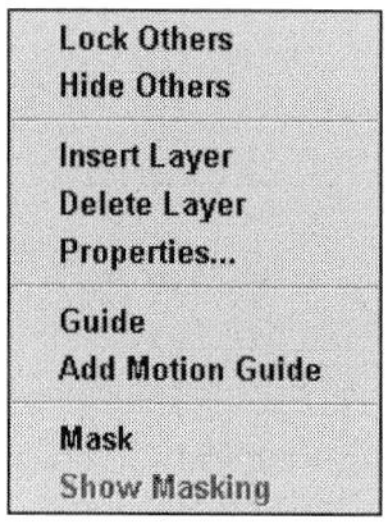

Layer Menu

The new in-context Layer menu makes certain Layer commands available by right-clicking (Windows) or by pressing Ctrl+Click (Mac). The Layer commands let you create, delete, show, hide, and otherwise control layers. The Layer menu is shown in Figure A.48, and its commands are described in Table A.11.

Layer Properties

You open the Layer Properties dialog box by choosing Properties from the Layer menu (see above). The Layer Properties dialog box is shown in Figure A.49. Table A.12 describes the options in the Layer Properties dialog box.

Figure A.48
The Layer menu.

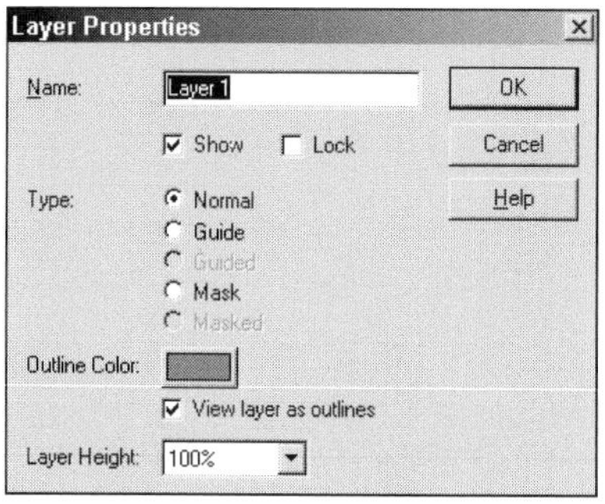

Figure A.49
The Layer Properties dialog box.

Table A.11   Layer menu commands.

Command	Description
Lock Others	Locks all but the current layer.
Hide Others	Hides all but the current layer.
Insert Layer	Adds a new layer just above the current layer.
Delete Layer	Deletes the current layer (and everything on it).
Properties	Opens a dialog box that lets you rename the layer and change its outline color, layer height, layer type, whether it is displayed as outlines, and whether it is shown or locked.
Guide	Designates the current layer as a guide layer.
Add Motion Guide	Creates a layer that is always attached to the layer that you used to create it. After you've added a motion-guide layer, draw the motion path with the Pencil tool.
Mask	Creates a new mask layer. Any filled shapes you make on this layer will appear as holes in the layer, making it possible to see the content of the layer immediately below.
Show Masking	Unless this command is chosen, the contents of a mask layer will appear in the authoring environment as the contents of a regular layer.

Table A.12   Options in the Layer Properties dialog box.

Dialog Box Component	Description
Name	Type a layer name in this field.
Show	If checked, the layer is visible.
Lock	If checked, edits will not affect this layer.
Normal	Makes the current layer a normal layer.
Guide	Makes the current layer a guide layer.
Guided	Indicates that the current layer has a Guide Layer attached.
Mask	Makes the current layer a mask layer.
Masked	Indicates that the current layer has a mask layer attached to it.
Outline Color	The color of this layer's outlines. Clicking on the Outline Color box opens the Color Picker dialog box so that you can change the color.
View Layer As Outlines	If checked, causes the layer's contents to be shown as one-pixel outlines in this layer's outline color, with no fill.
Layer Height	Expands the vertical height of the layer. This makes it easier to align sound histograms with frames.

APPENDIX B
FEATURES
INTRODUCED IN
FLASH 3

KEN MILBURN

Flash 3 didn't introduce as many new features as Flash 4 does, but those that were introduced were significant. These features included:

- Transparent graphics

- Shape morphing

- Multidirectional rotations tweened from only two keyframes (drawing the transitional frames between the first and last frames of a motion transition)

- Layer masks

- More-versatile symbols

- Expanded actions

- Ability to add labels and comments to frames

- Clearer and more informative interface (most frequently used commands are now on main menu)

- Inspector window that shows properties of objects

- Optional standard multiple selection

- Improved frame selection

- Improved cornerpoint creation

- Ability to create templates for interactive site content

- Automated creation of HTML code

- Instant performance reporting

- Support for PNG (portable network graphics)

- Improved support for and interfacing with FreeHand

- New standalone projector requiring no browser or ActiveX control

Transparent Graphics

Any color gradient can be as transparent or as opaque as you like. You can also apply transparency to symbols and groups. You can even make the transparency of a fill or outline fade over time. See Figure B.1.

It is also possible to import transparency in bitmaps, thanks to the support for the PNG format, which features Alpha channels.

Shape Morphing

Shape morphing makes it possible to make one shape change into another over time. You do this by defining start and stop keyframes in Flash's Timeline

Figure B.1

Flash can create transparent vector shapes and text.

and then placing the start and finish shapes in the appropriate frames. You then tell Flash to automatically tween the progression of shape-shifting frames. Because you need to download only two images instead of several, this process also can result in significantly smaller file sizes than was the case when each change needed to be drawn in an individual keyframe.

Multidirectional Rotations Tweened From Only Two Keyframes

This feature is amazing. You can place an element (object, symbol, or group) in a start keyframe and then in an end keyframe. You can transform that element in as many directions as you like by telling Flash to tween the transformations. In between, the object will rotate and transform in the same sequence you used in the end keyframe. It's powerful stuff.

Layer Masks

If you've worked in Photoshop, you know that you can use a layer mask to keep certain areas of a given layer from being visible to the other layers. You can do the same in Flash 3. You can, for instance, use a layer mask to simulate the point of view of someone who's trying to peek through a hole in a wall.

More-Versatile Symbols

In Flash 3, you can assign three types of behaviors to symbols: movie clip, button, and graphic. You can have animated buttons because movie clips can have all the interactive properties of a Flash 3 movie. Thus, you can have interactive movies within movies.

Movie-clip animations aren't dependent on the main Timeline, and they can play in a single frame (such as a button frame).

Graphics are the equivalent of the symbols in Flash 2 and are controlled by the Timeline.

Buttons are nearly the same as in Flash 2, except that (as already noted) they can include movie clips.

Expanded Actions

The actions in Flash 3 are much more powerful than in Flash 2. Actions cause Flash to do something when cued by the clicking of a button or the playing of a specific frame. In Flash 3, you can attach multiple actions to a single *event* (button or frame). You can also attach different actions to each *instance* (appearance) of any given symbol.

A dialog box has been added to help you assign actions to events.

Ability To Add Labels And Comments To Frames

You can add labels and comments to individual frames. These labels and comments stay with the frames even if their position is changed because you added or deleted frames from the movie.

Inspector Window That Shows Properties Of Shapes

This was the predecessor to the new Inspector Windows in Flash 4. When you want to know what the properties of an item are, you can choose Window|Inspector. A dialog box shows you the dimensions and type (such as shape, group, or symbol) of the item. The Flash 4 Inspector Window provides even more information and control.

Optional Standard Multiple Selection

Earlier versions of Flash kept selecting items as you clicked them. This made many users nuts because it was too easy to forget that you had already selected an item when you clicked to select another. After all, ingrained habits are hard to break. Every other Macintosh or Windows application drops any previously selected item when you select a new item (unless you press Shift as you click additional items to be selected).

Flash 3 uses the old maddening selection method as the default, but you can choose to use the standard Shift-Select method by checking it in the program's Preferences dialog box. Flash 4 makes the standard selection method the default.

Improved Frame Selection

This feature is another in the "why didn't they think of that sooner" category. In Flash 3, when you select (by clicking) a frame in the Timeline, it immediately appears on the stage, and the current frame pointer immediately moves to that frame.

Improved Cornerpoint Creation

In Flash 3, you can insert a cornerpoint into a curved section of a shape. You do this simply by pressing Opt/Alt (Option on the Mac and Alt in Windows) while dragging with the selection arrow to reshape the curve.

Ability To Create Templates For Interactive Site Content

A new Macromedia program, Flash Generator, was introduced to create server-based, interactive Web animations. In layperson's terms, this means that the animations change according to the data (which can be as simple as a yes/no button click) input by the viewer. Although authoring with Generator is a topic for advanced users, you can create templates to use with Generator directly in Flash.

Automated Creation Of HTML Code

Flash 3 shipped with a Macromedia utility called Aftershock. Aftershock automatically creates the **<EMBED>** and **<OBJECT>** tags needed to insert a Flash movie into an HTML document. This utility was a separate application, and has been supplanted by the new Publish features in Flash 4.

Instant Performance Reporting

You'll love this feature if you've spent time optimizing Flash files after discovering the hard way that some download times were unexpectedly long. You can test the movie, then call up the bandwidth profiler to see what the performance of the movie will be (given a specific modem speed). The default speed is 28.8Kbps for testing, but Flash reports a transfer speed of 2.3Kbps, which is more realistic and typical of actual Web performance over 28.8 modems.

PNG Graphics Support

Although GIF and JPEG have been the standard formats for bitmapped Web graphics, a new format has been incorporated into version 4 of the major browsers (Netscape Navigator and Microsoft Internet Explorer). This format, portable network graphics (PNG), supports Alpha channel transparency, both true-color (millions of colors) and indexed-color (256 or fewer colors), and compressed and uncompressed file formats.

The most significant aspect of Flash 3's support of the PNG format is that it allows you to specify transparent areas (such as the background) of true-color images.

Improved Support And Interfacing With FreeHand

FreeHand is Macromedia's professional-level, vector-based illustration tool, competing directly with Adobe Illustrator and CorelDRAW. FreeHand is arguably the most versatile of the three. Flash 3 made it possible to convert FreeHand CMYK (Cyan, Magenta, Yellow and blacK) files to RGB (Red, Green, Blue) for use in Flash. (The Web is an RGB medium.) What's more important, you can preserve layers when transferring files between FreeHand and Flash. You can cut a selected FreeHand graphic to the Clipboard and then paste it into a Flash 3 frame without losing any information regarding curves, gradients, or RGB color information.

It's worth noting that FreeHand 8 is capable of importing graphics from most of the popular vector-graphics formats (most notably Illustrator, CorelDRAW, and AutoCAD), thus providing a bridge for bringing all sorts of graphics into Flash, including maps and technical drawings.

Standalone Projector

The standalone player makes Flash 3 an excellent choice for creating offline (that is, disk-based) interactive content. If you double-click the file name or icon of a movie exported as a Shockwave Flash movie, it will automatically open in the standalone player application.

At that point you can choose File|Create Projector. The movie is then exported in a standalone version that can be distributed on anything from floppies to CD-ROMs. All it takes to play that movie is a double-click. No other software is required on the viewer's computer.

APPENDIX C
ASCII
CHARACTER
VALUES

Table C.1   ASCII standard keyboard values.

ASCII Value	Name	ASCII Value	Name	ASCII Value	Name
13	Carriage Return (CR)	76	L	121	y
32	Space	77	M	122	z
33	Exclamation	78	N	123	Left Brace
34	Double Quote	79	O	124	Bar
35	Number Sign	80	P	125	Right Brace
36	Dollar Sign	81	Q	126	ASCII Tilde
37	Percent	82	R	127	DELETE
38	Ampersand	83	S	128	(Unassigned)
39	Single Quote	84	T	129	(Unassigned)
40	Open Parenthesis (Left)	85	U	130	Quote Single at Base
41	Close Parenthesis (Right)	86	V	131	Florin
42	Asterisk	87	W	132	Quote Double at Base (Double Comma)
43	Plus	88	X	133	Ellipsis
44	Comma	89	Y	134	Dagger
45	Hyphen - Minus	90	Z	135	Double Dagger
46	Period	91	Left Bracket	136	Circumflex
47	Slash	92	Back Slash	137	Per Thousand
48	Zero	93	Right Bracket	138	S caron
49	One	94	ASCII Circumflex	139	Guil Single Left
50	Two	95	Underscore	140	OE
51	Three	96	Accent Grave	141	(Unassigned)
52	Four	97	a	142	(Unassigned)
53	Five	98	b	143	(Unassigned)
54	Six	99	c	144	(Unassigned)
55	Seven	100	d	145	Open Quote (Left)
56	Eight	101	e	146	Close Quote (Right)
57	Nine	102	f	147	Open Double Quote (Left)
58	Colon	103	g	148	Close Double Quote (Right)
59	Semi-colon	104	h	149	Bullet
60	Less Than	105	I	150	En Dash
61	Equals	106	j	151	Em Dash
62	Greater Than	107	k	152	Tilde
63	Question Mark	108	l	153	Trade Mark
64	At	109	m	154	s caron
65	A	110	n	155	Guilloche Right
66	B	111	o	156	oe
67	C	112	p	157	(Unused)
68	D	113	q	158	(Unused)
69	E	114	r	159	Y Dieresis
70	F	115	s	160	(Not Available) - NB SPACE
71	G	116	t	161	Exclamation Down
72	H	117	u	162	Cent
73	I	118	v	163	British Pound Sterling
74	J	119	w	164	Currency
75	K	120	x		

(continued)

Table C.1   ASCII standard keyboard values *(continued)*.

ASCII Value	Name	ASCII Value	Name	ASCII Value	Name
165	Yen	195	A Tilde	225	a acute
166	Broken Bar	196	A Dieresis	226	a circumflex
167	Section	197	A Ring	227	a tilde
168	Dieresis	198	AE	228	a dieresis
169	Copyright	199	C Cedilla	229	a ring
170	Ord Feminine	200	E Grave	230	ae
171	Guillemot Left	201	E Acute	231	c cedilla
172	Logical Not	202	E Circumflex	232	egrave
173	Minus	203	E Dieresis	233	e acute
174	Registered	204	I Grave	234	e circumflex
175	Macron	205	I Acute	235	e diersis
176	Degree	206	I Circumflex	236	i grave
177	Plus-Minus	207	I Diersis	237	i acute
178	Two Superior	208	Eth	238	i circumflex
179	Three Superior	209	N Tilde	239	i diersis
180	Accent Acute	210	O Grave	240	eth
181	Mu	211	O Acute	241	n tilde
182	Paragraph	212	O Circumflex	242	o grave
183	Period Centered	213	O Tilde	243	o acute
184	Cedilla	214	O Dieresis	244	o circumflex
185	One Superior	215	Multiplication	245	o tilde
186	Ord Masculine	216	O Slash	246	o diersis
187	Guillemot Right	217	U Grave	247	Division
188	One Quarter	218	U Acute	248	o slash
189	One Half	219	U Circumflex	249	u grave
190	Three Quarters	220	U Dieresis	250	u acute
191	Question Down	221	Y Acute	251	u circumflex
192	A grave	222	Thorn	252	u diersis
193	A Acute	223	German Double S	253	y acute
194	A Circumflex	224	a grave	254	thorn

COLOPHON

From start to finish, The Coriolis Group designed *Flash 4 Web Animation f/x and Design* with the creative professional in mind.

The cover was produced on a Power Macintosh using QuarkXPress 3.3 for layout compositing. Text imported from Microsoft Word was restyled using the Futura and Trajan font families from the Adobe font library. It was printed using four-color process and spot UV coating.

Select images from the color studio were combined with new figures to form the color montage art strip, unique for each Creative Professionals book. Adobe Photoshop was used in conjunction with filters to create the individual special effects.

The color studio was assembled using Adobe Pagemaker 6.5 on a G3 Macintosh system. Images in TIFF format were color corrected and sized in Adobe Photoshop 5. It was printed using four-color process.

The interior layout was built in Adobe Pagemaker 6.5 on a G3 Macintosh. Adobe fonts used include Stone Informal for body, Avenir Black for heads, and Copperplate 31ab for chapter titles. Adobe Photoshop 5 was used to process grayscale images, lightening from original files to accommodate for dot gain. Text originated in Microsoft Word.

Imagesetting and manufacturing were completed by Courier, Stoughton, Massachusetts.

If you like this book, you'll love...

What's On The CD-ROM

The *Flash 4 Web Animation f/x and Design*'s companion CD-ROM contains elements specifically selected to enhance the usefulness of this book, including:

- A 30-day full-version evaluation copy of Macromedia Flash 4
- Shockwave 7.0.2 and Flash 4 freely distributable players for Windows 95/98/NT and Macintosh
- Macromedia Dreamweaver 2.0 HTML editor 30-day full-version evaluation copy
- Macromedia Fireworks 2.0 Web graphics optimization 30-day full-version evaluation copy
- Macromedia FreeHand 8 Illustration program 30-day full-version evaluation copy
- Macromedia Generator 2 30-day full-version evaluation copy
- Plug and Play routines for advanced Flash functionality
- Tutorials by John Croteau
- VirtualBlox, a game that displays some of Flash's advanced features
- Flash files for all the book's tutorials

System Requirements

Software

- Windows 95/98/NT or Macintosh System 7.5 or later

Hardware

- Intel Penium 133 or equivalent or Power Macintosh processor
- RAM: Windows 32MB recommended, 16MB required; Macintosh 32MB required
- 20MB of disk space for Flash 4; you should have about 100MB free if all trial applications are to be installed at once
- A CD-ROM drive